THE NATURE OF
PUBLIC RELATIONS

THE NATURE OF
PUBLIC RELATIONS

JOHN E. MARSTON

Assistant Dean
College of Communication Arts
Michigan State University

McGraw-Hill Book Company, Inc.

New York   San Francisco   Toronto   London

THE NATURE OF PUBLIC RELATIONS

40618

5 6 7 8 9 – M P – 9 8 7

Preface

The occupation known today as "public relations" concerns itself basically with what groups of men think and why they think it. Isolationism in the world today no longer exists; the very idea has been rendered absurd by the sudden rise of vast industrial complexes, rapid communication, swift transportation, and startling new weapons. Since almost all men now know that they are dependent upon one another and must be concerned with what other men think, they realize that they must inevitably try to influence the thoughts of many groups of their contemporaries, wherever they may be.

The resulting effort, when practiced consciously and upon a large scale, is public relations, a relatively new profession or calling. It has long existed as a part of other activities but has only recently emerged as a separate discipline. In fact, public relations is so new that this book must approach its study not only or primarily through theory and historical description, but, more importantly, through numerous examples of public relations ideas in action. They are drawn from the files of many publications and companies and arranged so as to enable the reader to arrive at the fundamental principles of successful public relations by seeing how the most competent practitioners in the field handle its problems. Such an organized body of knowledge is one of the first hallmarks of an emergent profession.

Like many other persons, the writer *grew* into the practice of public relations, engaging in it for many years without being consciously aware of the real nature of the activity or of its importance. The evolution of a new field of work is often least observed by those participating in it; they are like Molière's hero, who discovered that he had been speaking prose all his life without knowing it.

The writer's thanks are due to all who have contributed generously to this book. They should go with deepest gratitude to many who could not have had any idea that the experience and study they offered the writer would lead to the composition of a book on public relations. Among them are the late Dean Frank L. Martin of the University of Missouri School of Journalism; E. B. Garnett, at one time Sunday editor of the *Kansas City Star,* who encouraged some early attempts to write feature stories; Joyce Swan, now executive vice-president of the *Minneapolis Star and Tribune,* who steered the writer into paths which led to the promotion managerships of the *Des Moines Register and Tribune* and the *St. Louis Star-Times*; those who were friendly when the writer served briefly as public relations director of Drake University; Q. J. Papineau, training director of Pet Milk Company, for his patient support when the writer served as managing editor of that

v

company; and finally, James R. Hansen, president of a St. Louis public relations counseling firm of that name, who first opened the writer's eyes to the true scope and nature of the work.

Others have contributed consciously through their encouragement and support. Among them are Dr. Gordon A. Sabine, vice-president of Michigan State University, Prof. John Crawford, head of the Division of Mass Communications, and Dr. Fred S. Siebert, dean of the College of Communication Arts. Credit would not be complete without acknowledgment of the assistance of the writer's wife, Jane, whose willingness to help explore new fields has been constant.

Inevitably, in thus acknowledging help, the writer will have omitted many persons who should have been included. Their consolation must be that they have contributed to a new field of knowledge and that their assistance is recognized and appreciated.

John E. Marston

Contents

PART II   PUBLIC RELATIONS AT WORK

PART III   THE WIDER DEVELOPMENT
OF PUBLIC RELATIONS

APPENDIX A. SOME ADDITIONAL EXAMPLES OF PUBLIC RELATIONS IN ACTION

APPENDIX B. FOURTEEN DO-IT-YOURSELF PUBLIC RELATIONS PROBLEMS

The Nature of Public Relations

PART I

What Is *Public Relations?*

Public relations is as hard to define as religion or education. Everyone
agrees that religion and education are important; yet no two people ever
define them in exactly the same way.

You probably have your own definition of public relations. So do your
friends and neighbors, if they have thought about the subject at all. Since
an increasing number of people are interested in the matter nowadays, we
shall all find it to our advantage to know what we are talking about. Making definitions acceptable to everyone is not easy. Perhaps, to avoid too
much preliminary hairsplitting, we might start with a very broad definition,
which we can sharpen later.

> Public relations is planned, persuasive communication designed to
> influence significant publics.

The key words here are "planned," "persuasive," "communication," and
"significant publics." Public relations is not accidental, but is planned carefully. It is persuasive because someone wants someone else to do something or to believe something. It must communicate to particular groups of
people rather than to scattered individuals.

The really important key word is "persuasive" because persuasion belongs to a very large and ancient family of human activity. The lawyer
presenting his case to the jury, the clergyman preaching a sermon, the
salesman selling machinery or shoes, the city school superintendent seeking
support for a new building bond issue, and the United States senator running for reelection are all members of the family of "persuaders." Each
of them tries to influence other human beings to believe as he does. The
men and women who practice public relations are persuaders, also.

Before trying to achieve a sharper definition of public relations, we may
find it more immediately worthwhile to consider what it is *not*. It is not
just being a pleasant fellow and glad-handing. Being friendly and making
people feel at ease may be an important part of public relations, but personal affability is too limited in the extent of its influence to reach many

3

people, unless, perhaps, it is projected to large groups by way of television, motion pictures, or the stage.

• Public relations is more than simple publicity—getting news or feature stories into newspapers and magazines or on the air. Spreading acquaintanceship and information in this way can effectively improve public relations; publicity is sometimes unfavorable or subject to various understandings, and frequently its very overabundance may cause bad reactions instead of good.

Public relations is not lobbying or legislative representation alone, although presenting a case well before the legislative or administrative branch of government is often an essential, persuasive communication to a very significant public.

Public relations is not advertising, although its relation to this other form of persuasive communication is very close. Advertising generally has more immediate sales objectives and appears in paid space or time. Public relations usually attempts to influence opinions over a longer period of time in many fields, such as community or employee relations, in which conventional advertising would be unsuitable. But the public relations and the advertising programs of a company are obviously closely connected. Why do you have a certain mental image of a particular company? Because you know its products? Because you have met some of its people? Yes, but also because you have seen its advertising. A company whose advertising is misleading, crude, or in poor taste can hardly enjoy good public relations. In these days of keen competition many similar products, all good and all selling at similar prices, may be on the market. In this situation the public relations of a company, the sort of institution the public imagines it to be, may be an important factor in its sales development. Product advertising sells not only products but an image of the company which makes those products.

Nor is public relations the same as "propaganda." This once-respected word, which originally meant simply the propagating, or spreading, of a belief, lost its neutral character during the two world wars; now propaganda has come to mean, for most people, false, exaggerated, or one-sided statements—often delivered under conditions of biased censorship. In a reaction against having been misled, some people now profess to believe nothing that they see, hear, or read; this alleged skepticism is a foolish attempt to escape the labor of decision and is as absurd as believing everything.

Toward a Sharper Definition

In an article in *Harper's Magazine* a few years ago, Robert Heilbroner referred to public relations men as "a brotherhood of some 100,000 whose common bond is its profession and whose common woe is that no two of them can ever quite agree on what that profession is."

This confusion of disagreement is not so much an indication that the practice is confused as that it is varied. Within the framework of planned, persuasive communications, public relations people work in many different ways for different causes. Since the resulting concepts of their work differ, we get definitions like these:

Public relations is any situation, act, or word that influences people.

Not much here will help us to decide how to go about practicing public relations. The definition only approaches a statement of the standard operating policy for any intelligent organization which seeks to be liked by the public it deals with.

Public relations is the art of making your company liked and respected by its employees, its customers, the people who buy from it, and the people to whom it sells.

This definition goes a bit farther and at least specifies some of the various publics that might be addressed. The word "company" in a definition should really be understood to mean any "organization," since a church, a school, or a governmental department often has public relations problems as pressing as those of a business firm.

Public relations is the skilled communication of ideas to the various publics with the object of producing a desired result.

Getting warmer, much warmer! But is a definition which covers only the verbal communication of ideas adequate? Aren't deeds a factor in public relations also?

Public relations is finding out what people like about you and doing more of it; finding out what they don't like about you and doing less of it.

Here a new thought appears—research; and the need of action is well expressed.

Public relations is the management function which evaluates public attitudes, identifies the policies and procedures of an organization with the public interest, and executes a program of action [and communication] to earn public understanding and acceptance.[1]

Now the definition is becoming adequate! The elements of *research, action,* and *communication* are all strong. Note also the words "management function." They indicate that good public relations is a fundamental part of the nature of a company—its people, its policies, its history, and its social enlightenment—and not just a bucket of whitewash to be splashed over an essentially ugly object. The words "with the public interest" are

[1] Definition from *Public Relations News.* The bracketed words "and communication" have been added by the author.

also significant, because the attempt to make actions counter to the public interest seem attractive to the public will not delude people long; a condition must not only be *said* to be right, it must *be* right!

The Growth of Public Relations

If you were to look under the heading "Public Relations" in the Manhattan classified telephone directory of 1935, you would find just ten names; today the listing runs over seven columns and 700 names. Among the top 300 companies in the United States in 1936 only one out of fifty had a fullfledged public relations department; today the proportion is three out of four. General Motors had no public relations department or counsel until 1931, and Standard Oil of New Jersey had none until 1942. Corporations are now starting new public relations departments at the rate of 100 a year. Today well over 5,000 corporations have departments or counsel.

This rapid development of public relations in business has been matched by its emphasis in welfare organizations, educational institutions, governmental bodies, labor unions, and trade associations, and by celebrities, political leaders, and assorted causes. An estimated 100,000 people work in public relations in the United States today in one way or another, and their annual earnings are about a billion dollars a year. How much more is spent on public relations activities beyond these wages can only be guessed.

This growth is not confined to the United States. The seeds of public relations are always lying in the ground, ready to sprout when the right circumstances of freedom, easy availability of communications media, rising living standards, and important issues invite public discussion. Since the end of World War II in 1945, groups of professional public relations men have sprung up in Great Britain, France, Holland, Belgium, West Germany, Norway, Sweden, Finland, Canada, Australia, Mexico, Brazil, and other developing areas of the world. In many of these nations public relations practices and principles resemble those in the United States, with differences depending on local circumstances.

Even more, the rapid spread of communications and travel has now exposed millions of people in Asia, Africa, and Latin America to a vast array of persuasive influences from which they were formerly insulated by distance, poverty, and illiteracy. The result is a great outpouring of persuasion by national governments, and varied ideologies not only to retain the support of their own people but also to reach out beyond their borders. The persuasive efforts of Communist China or the Soviet Union, Egypt's pan-Arabism, Israel's Zionism, and British and American government information agencies are all examples of a lively struggle to reach men's minds, now that new roads have been opened. At its best such persuasion may contain much useful information and new ideas; at its worst it may be false, inflammatory, and reckless. Some of the evaluation, of course, depends upon the person who is judging it, although real principles of truth and intent are involved. This new aspect of the struggle for men's minds will not soon disappear.

One thing is certain: The 1960s may well go down in history as the decade of the *communications revolution,* for never before have so many been so busy trying to say so much to so many. The prize for success is the right to shape the future organization of the world.

ADDITIONAL READING

The Bibliography of Public Relations

No attempt will be made in this book to give a complete list of all the' many books and articles which have been published on public relations and its related subjects. Only a few of the most pertinent are listed at the ends of chapters.

For a complete listing of almost 3,500 books and articles the reader is referred to *A Public Relations Bibliography,* compiled by Prof. Scott Cutlip of the University of Wisconsin and published in 1957 by the University of Wisconsin Press. This excellent work, partly made possible by a grant from the Public Relations Society of America, contains thirty-seven carefully classified major divisions of listings and was updated in 1963. Its use will provide detailed direction to sources of public relations information in almost any area in which the student may be interested.

Books in the General Field of Public Relations

Canfield, Bertrand: *Public Relations,* 3d ed., Richard D. Irwin, Inc., Homewood, Ill., 1960.
Cutlip, Scott, and Allen Center: *Effective Public Relations,* 2d ed., Prentice-Hall, Inc., Englewood Cliffs, N.J., 1958.
Harlan, Gene, and Alan Scott: *Contemporary Public Relations,* Prentice-Hall, Inc., Englewood Cliffs, N.J., 1955.
Stephenson, Howard (ed.): *Handbook of Public Relations,* McGraw-Hill Book Company, Inc., New York, 1960.

Periodicals in the Field of Public Relations

To keep up with the expanding and changing public relations field, a student will find it helpful to read magazines both within the area and also in closely related areas. Among them are the following:

Immediate Field

Public Relations Journal, the monthly publication of the Public Relations Society of America.

Public Relations News, a privately published weekly newsletter.

Related Fields

Advertising Age, a weekly magazine covering changes in advertising.

Broadcasting, a weekly covering radio and television.

Business Week, a weekly general business publication frequently bearing upon news related to public relations situations. A special section published on July 2, 1960, constitutes one of the most recent complete reviews of public relations in the United States.

Editor & Publisher, a weekly trade magazine of the newspaper field, covering public relations connections with the American press.

Journalism Quarterly, a publication of the Association for Education in Journalism, a university group, carrying occasional articles on public relations.

Public Opinion Quarterly, a scholarly publication which frequently carries articles of interest to public relations practitioners.

The Quill, the monthly publication of Sigma Delta Chi, a national professional journalism society, frequently containing articles of interest to public relations people.

Why Public Relations?

2

The rapid rise of public relations activity in the United States in the past generation is not an accident, nor is it a promotional bubble, destined to burst someday and leave us all in a simpler, quieter state. It is due to the great changes in our "living" and "communications" worlds that have made inevitable new ways for people to work together and understand one another. Wherever such changes occur elsewhere in the world today, public relations, unless prevented by other forces, can be expected to develop because it fills a modern social need.•

Changes in American Living Patterns

The United States census of 1910 reported that this nation had about 92 million people, or about one-half of today's population. The most striking fact in that census report, however, is that in 1910 more than 34 per cent of all Americans lived on farms and many more in small towns; today fewer than 12 per cent live in rural areas. This trend to the city has been apparent since the first Federal census in 1790, when by far the largest part of the less than 4 million population was rural.

Pioneers moving westward, though they inspired many exciting stories, were actually a minority; most Americans in the early days did not travel much. Farming demanded daily attention, cash was short, and transportation was limited. Of all the Union soldiers drafted in the Civil War, for example, only about 10 per cent had ever been more than about 25 miles away from home before they joined the army.

Even at the beginning of this century village and farm life was far different from life anywhere in the United States today. There were no automobiles, no paved roads outside the towns, no radios, no television sets, no motion pictures, practically no electric lights, few telephones, not much world news, and few travelers. People worked at their jobs long hours, six days a week, and much of the rest of their time was filled with farm or household chores such as stoking the coal furnaces, carrying out the ashes, washing, cooking, and baking.

Most Americans in 1900 weren't particularly unhappy, however. Times were much better than they had been; the country was growing; there were great opportunities (even if you personally didn't manage to seize them); and the United States was a big, happy, isolated land, securely resting behind its great white fleet and well insulated from the shocks of the rest of the world. For entertainment people went on picnic excursions now and then by boat or train or carriage, had home visitors on Sunday afternoons, took part in parties and plays, sang songs around the piano, and attended fairs. In this orderly and progressive world you might not know a great many people or travel far, but you knew your friends well; you had had school days together, had lived at home in the same town, and had gone on into the companionship of old age. Issues of debate were few and comfortably black and white; indeed, it was the kind of world in which a man might feel at home and be of some stature. When older people today remember the Gay 'Nineties fondly, they are recalling a time that really existed for many—a time when a visit to the Chicago World's Fair was more of a thrill than a jaunt to Calcutta or Rio today.

Now most Americans live in large cities or their suburbs. They live in a far better physical environment, work less, travel more, are healthier and better educated. Their children are bigger and live longer. Americans today have more leisure and less cause to worry about old age or illness. But along with these advantages come occasions for uneasiness and frustration.

Most of the units in American life today are large. In populous cities the citizens may be just numbers, voting for people they do not know, taking little part in governmental responsibility, and being ruled by people they have never even seen. In huge businesses employees often work for men whom they have never met and never expect to meet; many do not even know their employers. People are separated by their occupations, of which more than 30,000 are listed in one directory alone. Distances are great. Workers may be employed in a plant or office and live so many miles away that home and employment are in completely different realms. Schools and churches are large. Keeping a sense of proportion is a problem. The whole world seems both large and small—large in its newly realized complexity in which America is but one unit, and small as a dot in the exciting concept of space.

Modern Americans are likely to be rootless. Today few city dwellers live and die in the communities they grew up in. As neighborhoods change, people move; when a job opportunity beckons, they may shift half way across the country. When new types of work promise greater opportunity, people often change their trades or professions. Americans today meet far more people in the course of their lifetimes than their fathers or grandfathers would ever have dreamed possible, but they *know* far fewer of them.

Greater demands are made upon everyone. The swift march of science and human organization forces all of us to know and to decide many more things than our fathers had to consider. Today's citizen is expected to have intelligent, reasoned opinions on the merits of desegregation of races in schools, on halting the march of Red China toward southeastern Asia, on avoiding business recessions, on the proper roles of management, capital, labor, and government in the American economy, and on the right portion of the national budget to spend on interplanetary exploration!

One of the greatest changes since the 1930s has been the development of economic democracy in the United States. The old days when Commodore Vanderbilt, the railroad magnate, was reported to have said, "The public be damned," are now far past. The rise of powerful labor unions and widespread stockholding, among other factors, has caused many groups, including labor, management, stockholders, consumers, and government, to contend for the privilege of steering the nation's economic course and of sharing more of its benefits. Economic "laws" are no longer regarded with awe and felt to be fixed like the orbits of the sun and the moon. Whatever most people want badly enough and long enough they get; it thus becomes important to know what they want and why they want it. Whole new areas of economic discussion have been opened up to public argument that only a generation ago were largely reserved for experts.

In all this swiftly moving confusion, the ordinary American citizen tries to be informed and to make correct decisions on the many issues presented to him, difficult and distant though they may seem. It is to his credit that he has done as well as he has. Except on occasion, and then not for long, he has not given in to panic or thrown up his hands in despair. He has kept his temper and his wits, and although somewhat slow to act (for democracy is always slow), he has generally shown that he understands the problems presented and is prepared to tackle them.

The New Communications World

In coping with the depersonalization, bigness, and bewilderment of today's world, the ordinary American has been both aided and confused by the media of mass communications. The ways in which he gets his information and opinions are as different from those of the good old days as the physical world of the 1960s is from that of the early 1900s.

Today's communications world is huge, complex, and omnipresent. Modern men live in a sea of communications, deluged with a rain of words, sounds, and sights. Whereas a generation or two ago a few newspapers, magazines, books, public speakers, and friends provided the bulk of a rather limited communications system in which men largely had to make the effort to get information by their own reading or active investigation, today all sorts of communications thrust themselves at Americans continuously, free and unsought.

A man gets up in the morning and listens to chatter and song on the radio while he shaves and drives to work. Perhaps he reads a morning newspaper at breakfast or on the commuter train. His wife watches television as she does her housework. Numerous large well-illustrated magazines come into most homes. Paperback books are cheap and sold by the millions. The huge evening newspaper is crammed with literally hours of reading for anyone who wishes to spend that amount of time. Motion pictures are just around the corner or on the late-night television show. There are numberless meetings to attend, activities to participate in, and places to go to. The normal citizen can spend so many hours daily receiving communications that he can very seldom be alone or quiet.

Not only are these communications numerous; they also cover an extremely wide range of subjects, including the sciences, foreign events, and causes of worry ranging from the latest atomic missiles or the state of America's image abroad to the ups and downs of the stock market, new taxes, strikes, and riots. Occasionally, in the past, a newspaper was said to practice "Afghanistanism," meaning that it filled its columns with telegraphed reports of unimportant happenings in distant places while it neglected the harder and more expensive reporting of local news; today such an accusation would have little meaning because apparently almost anything in the world now has a bearing upon American daily life and is worthy of communication.

One effect of the pressure of modern communications has been to make it hard to gain people's *attention*. So much is presented daily that receivers have become adept at listening only to what they want to hear. This selectivity naturally concerns the commercial communicator (for example, the advertiser) because there are limits to how loud he can shout successfully for attention. At a certain point loudness collapses. Bigness and color in newspapers and magazines soon become quite expensive; shrillness and tricks and other devices to gain attention on radio and television, because they seem extravagant or domineering, are soon resented; yet the advertiser *must* be heard. For the public relations man the advertiser's problem becomes even more acute, because the public is ready to condone a degree of blatancy in advertising that it dislikes in public relations. It wants to be informed rather than manipulated.

The public relations man who wishes to be heard today has arrived at several solutions—a more careful selection of audiences with which to communicate, more skillfully prepared communications, and greater identification of communications with the existing interests of his audience. A man who wants to promote boats, for example, tries to select an interested audience, say the readers of a boating magazine or marine column or watchers of outdoor-sports television shows; he makes his message as pleasant and understandable as possible; and he tries to talk to boat-minded people about things close to their interests. If he does this well, he can scarcely say too much.

In addition, a public relations man who wants to promote some new scientific development by his company sends one type of story to *Scientific American* magazine and another type to a metropolitan Sunday newspaper, adapting his writing to each audience and relating his information to the degree of knowledge and interest of each group. Readers or listeners are usually willing to absorb a great deal about the things which concern them but easily ignore those not related to their lives.

Another problem is the present lack of *two-way* communication. People today are greatly talked *at* and get little opportunity to express themselves; a chance to ask questions or to challenge opinions would not only make them feel better, but would also clarify their thoughts. All mass media such as newspapers or television, no matter how excellent, are *one-way* means of communication; recipients listen, but unless they get sufficiently excited to write a letter or to telephone the newspaper or broadcasting station, they remain only receivers and are not participating senders. Very seldom does anyone talk back to a newspaper or to a television station. The recipient does not know the people who are writing or speaking, and realistically he expects little response; he usually prefers to mutter to himself or to his friends and family, or to say nothing at all.

The frustration of listening helplessly while being "told" is heightened when the recipients are city dwellers with few close friends. Many people move often and do not know their neighbors. Fellow workers often live in widely scattered areas and know each other only on their jobs. Even next-door neighbors are not often real friends in modern life because to-day location contributes less to friendship than do common interests; and one just doesn't talk much to stray people on the street or to chance acquaintances.

The knowledge that many people in America today live in this loneli-ness of the crowd and the realization of their need for self-expression and participation are keys that the intelligent public relations practitioner can use in obtaining their understanding and good will. To change the metaphor, one of the biggest problems of modern society is building bridges of communication between large groups of people who are emotionally iso-lated, lonely, and frustrated.

Three Ways of Securing Human Cooperation

Ever since men first began to crowd together, to communicate, and to establish complex social structures, their leaders have found three main ways of getting them to make concerted efforts—*power, purchase,* and *persuasion*—although in actual practice all three are usually mixed.

Power, typified by the strong man with the sword, the despot, says,

"Do this or I shall kill you, or beat you, or imprison you!" Power's chief limitations are the uncertainty of its duration, its difficulty of application, its wastefulness, its inability to progress, and its utter lack of moral principle, since the very essence of power is violation of the freedom of human will and choice.

Power has never ruled much of the world for long by itself; yet power, open or hidden, is found in almost all societies because some people cannot be governed otherwise. Between nations power remains dominant; yet we may wonder how long it will be so, since the value of power as a governing force varies with the nature of weapons. Between individuals, for example, the strong man with a sword was able to impose his will upon quite a number of lesser individuals until the invention of hand firearms. The rifle and revolver were great and deadly equalizers, and after their invention the tone of civil manners materially improved. Between nations the so-called "great powers" with large armies and navies were once able to dominate their lesser neighbors with impunity because in war they could inflict more hurt than they could receive. Perhaps the coming of the atomic-missile age has changed all that.

Purchase says, "Do this and you will receive an advantage in money, goods, position, or honor." People can be purchased, of course, only by that which they value. The offer of a knighthood in the British Empire would probably have little attractiveness to a Chinese Communist, and offering a barrel of whisky as a prize award to a temperance union would doubtless also be futile.

But purchase is widespread. Those who work for money or other gain, or those whose work we hire directly or indirectly, are all engaged in purchase. A boss purchases not only the physical working time of his employees, but also some of their interest and loyalty. The owner of stock in a corporation purchases the time and efforts of many people unknown to him.

Because purchase plays such a large and pervasive part in securing human cooperation in a money economy, people begin to think that they can buy anything, whereas in fact a great many things, like loyalty or love, are not for sale and can only be given. When Richard III, as Shakespeare tells the story, lost his horse in battle and dashed about the field vainly crying that he would give his kingdom for another mount, his plea was useless. Other fighters needed their own steeds too much at that moment either for battle or for flight, and Richard in that desperate time had no kingdom to give. Wealthy people, organizations, or even nations who think that they can buy good will and understanding are often mistaken. People are purchased by many things, but often seem to behave quite irrationally, "biting the hand that feeds them," preferring trouble and hardship to ease.

But purchase is more respectable than power, which always rests upon doubtful moral grounds. When purchase is a free transaction, the rights of human choice are not violated. Purchase may be obtuse and vain and it may degrade spiritual values, but it is not a negation of free will unless those who are purchased choose to let it become so.

Persuasion is the most complex method of obtaining human cooperation. Persuasion says in effect, "For these reasons which appeal to your mind or to your emotions, please believe and do these things." Religious or political beliefs have often been called "persuasions"; as St. Paul once put it, "I am persuaded [I believe] that neither death nor life . . . shall be able to separate us from the love of God. . . ."

Persuasion, in the sense of offering cogent reasons for belief, can be achieved only by communication. No words are necessary to explain the power argument of a gun or the purchasing power of a stack of coins, but people can be persuaded only by words, pictures, gestures, or other means of human communication. The world's great persuaders have been its teachers, preachers, prophets, writers, and artists. Through persuasion the religion of Jesus swept out of Judea and transformed the Roman Empire within a few generations; the writings of Marx, Engels, and Lenin animated the Communist third of the globe. Persuasion was the spark that ignited the Protestant Reformation, the American Revolution, the French Revolution, and the American Civil War.

There is an inescapable connection between persuasion, freedom, and democracy—because democracy is a system of government by persuasion. If enough people can be persuaded, rules may be changed in a democracy. For a democracy to exist, the right of free communication in order to persuade must be allowed, because otherwise nothing could ever change; gradual, orderly change is the essence and glory of a democracy.

In governmental systems depending upon power, whatever their disguise, the right of open persuasion is always carefully controlled or denied, and communication is a state monopoly. In a government depending largely upon purchase, economic weapons may be used to control persuasive communication; but the true test of democracy is its willingness to permit argument on many sides of issues. Obviously, public relations men can develop fully only in democratic societies.

A Brief History of Public Relations

In the past sometimes a combination of freedom and reasonably high living standards has allowed time for thought about important public issues, but widespread communications systems have been lacking until recent centuries.

Many of the small, ancient Greek city-states were political democracies in which the adult male population debated vigorously; yet the size of these democratic governments was limited by the persuasive range of the human voice. Since literacy rates were low, writing slow, and writing materials limited, public business had to be conducted in an arena in which a maximum of a few thousand participants might hear. These Greek cities produced some of the first hired persuaders and their teachers; they were the Sophists, or wise ones, who carefully studied the writing and delivery of speeches until their superior oratory could make their less sophisticated rivals sound tongue-tied and inept in swaying a voting assembly. Such capable Sophists were much admired, feared, denounced, and sought after by the would-be and actual political, military, and economic leaders of the day; they were hired to present causes before the assembly much as a lawyer or a public relations man would be employed today.

Republican Rome borrowed many Greek ideas, but the sterner ambitions of military power in Rome afforded less opportunity for the development of orators, although Cato, Cicero, Mark Antony, and others were noted for their eloquence. Writers could be persuaders. Julius Caesar's *Commentaries on the Gallic Wars* constitutes one of the most masterful propaganda tracts ever penned. But with the coming of the imperial power of the Caesars, the role of the orator and often of the writer declined to the dimensions of court lawyer, literary lion, and eulogist of the glories of the emperor. Roman despots, however, were not unmindful of the power of public opinion, whether in the well-financed ranks of the senate or in the roars of the street mobs. Simple forms of persuasion, such as triumphal parades, free grain, and free tickets to gladiatorial combats, replaced the soaring oratory or tight-clipped reasoning of Cicero or Brutus; banners, spoils, and pomp persuaded instead of words.

Rome's propaganda proved comparatively feeble a few years later in the face of the Christian saints and martyrs, who were among the world's greatest persuaders by letter, preaching, and example. The exciting words of the Christian evangelists, despite vigorous persecution, sent new blood coursing through the veins of a decaying empire which had lost its ability to inspire men and relied primarily upon power and purchase to govern; and they stole away the allegiance to the Roman ideal right from under the noses of the emperors. Romans simply would not believe any longer that the emperor was divine or that the imperial regime was worth fighting for. When he adopted Christianity, the Emperor Constantine shored up the situation for a few generations by removing the conflict between the church and the imperial power and substituting a new alliance of persuasions. Then, with the coming of massive barbarian invasions, the conditions of civilized living and free communications which had made possible any public persuasive activities disappeared. Yet in the monasteries and among the common people a body of scholarly and popular literature was being produced that was to emerge a few centuries later to belie the apparent stagnation of mind of Western Europe.

Almost a thousand years after the barbarian invasions a German named Gutenberg invented movable type and printed a Bible in Mainz in 1456, thus launching a new era of mass persuasion. New conditions of freedom and prosperity, within walled trading towns and, by sufferance, in the courts of some kings and princes, were ready to be united and strengthened by this new method of cheap communication. The world faced an upset, the first of many since.

The first outflow of printed persuasion was largely in the field of religion, which much concerned literate people in the fifteenth and sixteenth centuries. Since the books were widely distributed and eagerly read, their ideas proved inflammatory, and Europe was soon split by religious wars.

Not all printed persuasion was about religion, however; some was geographical, scientific, or economic; there were books on the new worlds in North and South America, arguments over the ownership of Brazil or the East Indies, journals of polar exploration, and trade reports. Newspapers and newsletters began to appear, and an increasing number of political arguments culminated in the writings of Voltaire, Rousseau, and Thomas Paine—and, in due course, in the American and French Revolutions.

But, exciting as was this ferment of ideas, it marked only the beginning of the change to be wrought by printing. When the communications revolution was wedded to the industrial revolution, society was really turned upside down. Setting type by hand, one character at a time, in the manner of Gutenberg or Benjamin Franklin and then impressing the paper upon a page of type one sheet at a time by screw press is, of course, infinitely faster than handwriting, but it is still slow, clumsy, and costly. When in about the 1830s the steam engine was commonly applied to printing presses, the cost of a newspaper fell from about 12 cents to 1 cent, and the size of newssheets was vastly increased. The result was that a whole new army of readers was informed, and popular democracy was greatly expanded.

With more and bigger newspapers came the rise of advertising and the spreading of many new ideas such as communism, nationalism, and other economic and political beliefs. Steam-powered railroads and steamships could take cheaply printed publications anywhere in a short time, and as a source of news the telegraph even outran them. Persuasive books and newspapers of the mid-nineteenth century look stuffy and dull in these modern times, but they burst like bombshells in their own world, which only a half century earlier had been more akin to the world of Julius Caesar than to that of today.

During the past two centuries as the means of communication have increased, the types of professional communicators have continued to increase also, and many of these might be considered precursors of public relations practitioners. First were the politicians, because, of necessity, politics in a democracy is the art of ascertaining and molding public opinion upon a large scale. During the American Revolution, for example, Samuel Adams relied upon letter-writing committees of correspondence and copies of the *Boston Gazette* to tell the independence faction's version of the Boston Tea Party or the Boston Massacre or other such events. And in the early skirmishes for power in the young republic between liberal and conservative thinkers, Alexander Hamilton scored heavily with the *Federalist* papers, setting forth viewpoints favoring the moneyed class and a strong government.

When, in the 1830s, Andrew Jackson achieved power, the United States already had more newspapers and readers than any other country in the world, and Jackson owed much of his success to his adroit use of them. His "press secretary," Amos Kendal, a former newspaperman from Kentucky, was a member of Jackson's unofficial Kitchen Cabinet. He ghosted the president's speeches, wrote pamphlets and news releases, arranged the president's press interviews, and made it his business to ascertain public opinion, both advising the strong-minded president as to what to say and then helping him to say it.

Political press-agentry had become a big-time operation by the time of the Bryan-McKinley presidential campaign of 1896. At the headquarters of both conventions in Chicago, newspaper coverage was elaborate.

Then, in the 1930s, Franklin D. Roosevelt showed that he was a master of a new communications medium, the radio; and later Dwight D. Eisenhower and, even more, John F. Kennedy both showed great skill in handling a newer medium, television. Expertness in persuasive communication is essential in any political battle, and as the news media grow more complex, the need of professional help in their use also grows.

But showmen, no less than politicians, need to seek public attention. In politics ballots mean winning an election; in show business admission fees mean a fortune. In the long years of his lifetime (1810–1891), the prince of showmen was Phineas T. Barnum, whose publicity was so successful that he implanted in our language a number of words which are still in common use but whose origins have been almost forgotten. Consider "jumbo," for example. Everyone knows that "jumbo" is a synonym for something large; yet few today know that Jumbo himself was a large African elephant which Barnum exhibited in the circuses. Barnum had to have a name for his curiosity, and "Jumbo" had a nice African jungle sound well-suited to short headlines. Jumbo was so well publicized that the term remains in the language long after its origin has been forgotten. Or consider "Tom Thumb." Most people today associate the words with something tiny, but not many know of the real midget, Charles Stratton, called "General Tom Thumb," whom Barnum exploited, and who presided over a troupe of tiny people, drove in a little coach drawn by ponies, and was even presented to Queen Victoria, making a very proper speech for the occasion. Mention might be made also of the Siamese twins, recognized by everyone today as twins fastened together by an accident of birth, named after a pair which the prince of showmen exhibited.

Barnum was not averse to buying advertising space, but he also knew the news interest of his attractions and reaped a harvest of free publicity. With Barnum, and after him, came a host of other press agents whose specialty was getting into free public print the names of actors and actresses like Lily Langtry or Anna Held, and later of a host of motion-picture, radio, and television stars. The agents' methods were not quite so important to them as the results. All manner of stunts, such as fake jewel robberies, marital spats, and love affairs were reported; and a mine of misinformation about marriages, divorces, clothes (or lack of them), opinions upon any subject, and travels was constantly explored. Unfortunately, the public, or at least a large part of it, loved it!

Some of the stories were true, and some weren't. Sometimes news editors let themselves be fooled and went along with the game for the sake of a lively story; sometimes they didn't know; and sometimes they were taken in. Being deceived hurt their egos; and newspapermen, derided by friends and readers, occasionally became vitriolic about press agents' morals. But none of this criticism stopped the press agents' output, or its use, and the lurid or sentimental stories ran through the papers in a great flowing stream. The racket reached an all-time climax in 1926, when, at the New York funeral of the movie idol Rudolph Valentino, some sixty to eighty thousand persons, mostly women, engaged in a near riot, which was finally contained by the vigor of almost two hundred policemen charging the crowds repeatedly on horseback.

There has always been a great difference, however, between the publicity efforts of American politicians and the press-agentry of showmen; politicians are interested only in creating favorable public opinion, because this brings its reward at the polls; showmen, on the other hand, are often interested in any kind of public notice, since the bad frequently pays off as well at the box office as the favorable (or perhaps better). The two motives—desire for understanding and approval by means of public relations and desire for notoriety through press-agentry—have been constantly confused. The misunderstanding has impeded the growth of responsible public relations, and for many years has needlessly embittered

the feelings of newspaper editors and other people involved in communications media toward public relations people. Today, fortunately, the differences are more widely understood.

In using public relations to reach people, American businessmen for
a number of reasons lagged behind politicians or showmen. Not until the
late nineteenth century did American business begin to, develop on a
really big scale. Before that the small merchant or manufacturer often
knew his customers, employees, suppliers, business friends, and fellow
townsmen by name. His public relations were personal relations conducted by word-of-mouth conversation, personal letters, and visits. The
business institution was then indeed the lengthened shadow of a man—and
the nineteenth-century capitalist whose lengthened shadow it might be was
not going to engage in any folderol about influencing public opinion unless
a cash return could be anticipated. Business barons of the 1800s tended
to be authoritarian, satisfied, and serenely confident of the goodness of
their work. Labor was voiceless; markets were constantly expanding; and
how the business was conducted or what it did was no outsider's concern.

But this freedom could not long endure, because as business firms
began to become nationwide mammoths, far more people were affected,
personal communications broke down under their own weight, and public
opinion formed and began to make itself felt through the actions of
government, which was sometimes more sensitive to votes than to dollars.

The first really big United States businesses were probably the railroads,
whose spectacular growth was accompanied by scandalous construction
frauds and government aid. Railroads, moreover, were monopolies in all
parts of the country where competing lines did not exist, since neither paved
cross-country highways nor the automobiles to run upon them had yet
even been dreamed of. The lordly independence of railroad personnel all
the way from conductors and country station agents to presidents was impressive to behold and quite indomitable, since if a man did not choose
to ride or to ship upon the railroad, his only alternatives were to drive a
horse and carriage or to walk. Perhaps one of the Vanderbilts did not
say, in 1882, "The public be damned" in reply to a newspaper reporter's
question about the public interest; but to many people the phrase seemed
so in keeping with railroad-magnate character that the words stuck and
have done harm to the railroads ever since. This in its way illustrates another fact about public opinion: Once established, it endures long after
the facts upon which it was based have been forgotten. Railroads today
may wallow in red ink and they may be strangers to an automobile-riding
public, but the bad image lingers on.

Following the railroads came the gigantic growth of great national corporations in oil, steel, coal, meat packing, banking, and public utilities,
whose proprietors, frequently lacking in humility, displayed an ostentation

in turreted mansions, fashionably gowned women, huge steam yachts, and stables of race horses which became the constant preoccupation of the readers of the cheaper press.

Public reaction was two-sided. On the one hand, many people admired all business success. Exuberant bigness seemed to befit a booming America. The big good deeds of Carnegie's libraries and the little good deeds of Rockefeller's dimes were extolled; the flowing champagne of Newport-mansion wedding feasts, mirrored in Sunday newspapers, was vicariously lapped up by moon-struck maids and matrons; the scandals of a Jim Fisk or a Diamond Jim Brady met with a tolerant "Just what I'd do if I had the money"; and the solemn pronouncements of only moderately educated millionaires upon the deepest matters of science, religion, law, politics, and social and international life tended to be regarded with quite unjustified awe.

On the other hand, however, large segments of the public were uneasy and hostile. Big business was feared because it seemed to have too much influence upon big government; slums and rural poverty were contrasted with the rich life of wealthy mansions pictured in the popular press; through drought, depression, and change farmers and laborers found their lives hard, their prices and wages low, and their independent futures obscure; moralists yearned for a return to a simpler life; and even smaller businessmen, pressed or absorbed by their larger competitors, became embittered. In a time of change, of improvement, yet of distress for many, there was too much one-way conversation by business to its employees, its customers, its communities, and the people in general. Somebody was about to talk back. The reply came from the "muckrakers" from 1900 to about 1914 and has continued, with interruptions, ever since.

During the first years of this century, big business was under almost constant fire from scores of magazines and newspapers intent upon exposing its sins. Ida Tarbell's *History of the Standard Oil Company* was advertised as "a fearless unmasking of moral criminality masquerading under the robes of Christianity and respectability." Upton Sinclair's novel, *The Jungle,* was intended to expose the mistreatment of meat-packing-plant workers, but along the way painted so foul a picture of slaughtering conditions that it resulted instead in a boost for the American Society for the Prevention of Cruelty to Animals and in a clamor for better Federal meat-inspection laws. In 1903 "Frenzied Finance" by Thomas Lawson in *McClure's Magazine* exposed Wall Street, and its success fired many imitators.

There is no doubt that the muckraking writers struck a rich vein of public response. Muckraking, considered both virtuous and profitable, resulted in great literary reputations and soaring magazine circulations. Nor were politicians, who knew a good thing when they saw it, tardy in capitalizing on the clamor. Both Teddy Roosevelt's Bull Moose Progressive Republicanism and Woodrow Wilson's Democracy owed much to the feelings expressed in the muckraking era.

Impartial assessment of the good and bad is difficult. One-sided as it was, muckraking was a necessary corrective in American progress. But affronted business barons, who sometimes seemed to consider *themselves* the embodiment of American progress, reacted with more violence and excitement than philosophy. A first impulse might be to sue, but company lawyers usually discouraged this response. Only a person who is lily white in all respects can afford to become involved in a libel suit; too much can be brought out in court and paraded over the whole nation for all to see. And anyway, the truth of a statement is generally a full defense against libel charges. Another reaction might be to threaten advertising cancellation as a club to bring the offending journal back into line; but often the newspapers might decide that exposure would be more profitable than silence. Newspapermen were an independent crew, as likely to fight back as to surrender. Bribery, another weapon, was likewise limited.

A final solution was whitewash. If you couldn't silence the opposition, you could try to paint a better picture of yourself! Large corporations began to hire former newsmen to set up news bureaus, which carefully fed the press "good" stories by various means and rigorously tried to conceal doubtful or bad reports. Gradually, through the influence of Ivy Lee and other publicists who laid the beginning of a foundation for modern public relations practice, this position was modified to the point where companies would not only issue good news but would refrain from impeding or would even facilitate the work of reporters covering controversial or unfortunate events such as railroad wrecks or strikes. The millennium had not yet arrived when a company public relations man would speak against his own cause, any more than a company lawyer would argue against his own case in court.

But the long war between many newspapermen and many corporate public relations spokesmen was nearing a truce. In an increasingly complex world the newsman now realized that he didn't have the time and knowledge to cover all the details and developments of great business organizations in which the public was seriously interested. He was now willing to give the company public relations man a chance to supply factual, newsworthy stories. The public relations man, on the other hand, knew that he had to meet a high standard of journalism, aid newsmen in covering the bad as well as the good, and beware of sheer puffery. During the boom years following World War I, in which adulation of business came back strongly, as was exemplified in the late *American Magazine;* in the dark years of the depressed 1930s, which resembled the era of the muckrakers; and after World War II, the understanding between newsman and public relations man matured. Each served a different master, each had his own code, and yet on the common meeting ground of supplying news, each could respect and cooperate with the other.

The public relations problems of the United States government (or any lesser American government) are quite different from the problems of a politician trying to get himself elected in order to control that government; yet the two are so inseparably intertwined that to this day their conflict has not been resolved nor does it seem likely ever to be.

Democratic government, if it is to be effective, needs citizen cooperation and understanding. The police ask you not to weave down the highways at 100 miles per hour, slaying yourself or innocent drivers in the process; the forest rangers object to your walking away from a smoldering campfire in the dry woods or littering a campsite; the internal revenue collectors want the right amount of income tax on time; if you are the right age, the Army, Navy, or Air Force may wish you to enlist; and the post office always pleads with you to mail Christmas packages early. Some of these goals may be attained by the *power* of government, but much greater success in matters of safety, conservation, tax paying, recruiting, and post office aid depends upon understanding cooperation. Cooperation, in turn, requires public relations, and without it democracy may break down.

In wartime such citizen cooperation becomes even more important, because during a war the government wants citizens to give money, save food, drive less, work at different jobs, go out to fight, and if need be even die. How is this heroic attitude to be inculcated? Only by the concerted persuasion of public relations effort.

In World War I (1917–1918) President Wilson, with the aid of journalist George Creel, made a gigantic successful effort to enlist support for this nation's war aims. After the war the propaganda backfired. Some of it had been false, strident, or overdone; naïve Americans were inclined to regard the whole conflict as an unfortunate accident and to wish to forget it as soon as possible. Wilson was defeated; isolationism returned; the League of Nations was rejected; World War II was made inevitable; and debunkers of idealism flourished in the material prosperity of the roaring twenties.

When America was catapulted into World War II on Pearl Harbor Sunday, 1941, government information programs were quickly organized, but on a more effective low-key basis under the direction of newscaster Elmer Davis. The American attitude now was much more mature than in 1917–1918. The absence of enthusiasm for the war caused some super patriots who insisted upon brass bands and cheers to worry lest the national spirit had decayed. Instead of excitement there was a grim determination to win as soon as possible at whatever cost. America knew what had to be done, and four-minute orators, parades, and yellow paint smeared on German farmers' barns were deemed travesties of patriotism. The direct impact of on-the-spot reporting of the Japanese surprise attack on the American fleet, followed by the powerful words of President Roosevelt, showed the contrast between the communications methods of the forties and those which had existed two decades before.

But although the government had no difficulty in mobilizing the support of its citizens during a war, the problems of day-by-day understanding and cooperation by citizens in a democracy are still acute; these problems will be discussed later in this book.

In the past thirty years two other major users of public relations have appeared. Beginning in the 1930s, large new labor unions began to seek support from the ranks of workingmen and wooed the general public through union publications, radio and television programs, speakers, and personal contact. Much development remains ahead. In these same years, welfare organizations, such as the Boy Scouts and the YMCA, and health agencies, such as the heart, cancer, and polio funds, as well as many local community united funds, became much more active in the public relations appeals upon which their success ultimately depended.

Other groups have also become much more active in public relations in recent years. Religious groups try to gain adherents, raise money, and support projects; associations represent activities as diverse as medicine, law, architecture, industries, trades, merchants, and tourism; and in education, city school systems try to obtain funds for new buildings, improved teacher salaries, and expanded programs, and universities ask for needed support in gifts and taxes. One of the biggest new fields is international public relations, the effort of groups within a nation to reach abroad or of nations themselves to influence others.

This is the "communications era." As more people have more to be concerned about in common and can communicate with one another more easily, it is inevitable that, for many reasons, attempts at widespread persuasion should increase. One cannot reasonably be "for" or "against" such a development, because changes cannot be turned back any more than the invention of television, the airplane, the steam engine, or even the printing press, or the discovery of a method of atomic fission can be done away with and forgotten. These things did happen, cannot be abolished, and will have their effects.

The important thing about modern public relations is not whether its development should be opposed or praised, but rather how well it is understood and used.

ADDITIONAL READING

**The History of Public Relations
and the Reasons for Its Development**

Bernays, Edward L.: *Public Relations,* University of Oklahoma Press, Norman, Okla., 1952.

Harlow, Ralph V.: *Samuel Adams: Promoter of the Revolution,* Henry Holt and Company, Inc., New York, 1923.

Mook, James O., and Cedric Larson: *Words That Won the War: The Story of the Committee on Public Information 1917–1919,* Princeton University Press, Princeton, N.J., 1939.

Pimlott, J. A. R.: *Public Relations and American Democracy,* Princeton University Press, Princeton, N.J., 1951.

Regier, Cornelius C.: *The Era of the Muckrakers,* The University of North Carolina Press, Chapel Hill, N.C., 1932.

The Nature of Communication and Public Opinion

3

Businessmen, industrialists, educators, and government leaders all talk about "communication." But are they departing from the essential meaning of the term? Haven't human beings always communicated with each other? In fact, isn't communication almost a definition of humanity's most characteristic activity? What's new? What is there to communication beyond the simple act of saying something to somebody?

There is something new, and that is the realization, within the past few decades at least, that in communication the *receiver* is at least as important as, and perhaps even more important than, the sender. Heretofore communication has been thought of primarily in terms of the sender and his message. The orator who made a speech, the author who wrote a book, the king who handed down an edict to his subjects, were all communicating. But were they? Who read or heard the edict? What did they understand from it? And in what ways were their actions altered? These are questions which might be asked about almost any communication.

Because of this preoccupation with the sender and his message, for a long time most of the study of communication centered upon the way the message was sent—whether the orator spoke loudly and distinctly, the printing was well spaced and legible, or the king's edict was worded in the best classical Latin and posted in all the important market places. These things are important, to be sure, and may alter the effectiveness of a communication materially; but they alone do not determine it. Much depends upon the receivers, since people usually cannot be made to listen or to understand or even to be interested in a communication except as it relates to their own concerns. When students of communication turned their attention to the receivers as well as to the senders of messages, they began to realize the unity of direction of all the different media and ways of communicating. Their discovery is of particular interest to public relations practitioners.

26

Different ways of reaching people, such as speaking, writing, and film making, though they require different technical skills, are all similar in that they may be addressed to the same persons. A public relations man may use any of these methods to communicate an idea to a receiver. He can do so with confidence only if he knows the nature of the receiver, and therefore the way in which his communication will be understood. A sender must realize that although receivers have various backgrounds of experience and various social contacts, they have much in common. On that common ground of shared life and thought the sender can meet them; and in the meeting he can go far toward solving the problem of conveying ideas.

We need to ask many questions about communication. Today, instead of defining the word very narrowly to mean only the means of communication, writers on the subject tend to call almost any act communication. Yet if a man talks to himself, is this communication? Are actions, such as buying a ticket to the zoo, communications of unspoken processes of decision making? Perhaps. It is true that gestures or actions do communicate; but we are concerned here primarily with purposeful, planned communication and not with introspection or actions designed to satisfy a man's personal desires, whose conveyance of a thought to others is largely incidental.

Why Do People Communicate?

It has been said that people communicate in order to *inform,* or to *persuade,* or to *entertain;* but seldom are these purposes clearly separated in the minds of the sender and the receiver.

Another school of thought holds that all communication is basically *persuasive,* that we always seek some response from others to even the most simple remarks, such as "Nice day, today" or "I think I'll get my hair cut." [1] Perhaps this is so; but often the connection between the remark or act and the response seems rather tenuous, especially among artists or writers who work primarily to satisfy some inner urge to express truth or beauty as they see it, and have little conscious thought about how others will respond. Is such communication persuasion, or is it simply an outflow of a personal thinking-through process?

Sometimes primarily self-expressive communication is referred to as "consummatory"; that is, it constitutes an end in itself. The communicator may hope that an audience will share his interest or he may not care greatly. When the chief purpose of a communication is to get an audience to do something, the message can be called "instrumental." To illustrate

[1] Aristotle seems to have held that communication was basically persuasive. For further discussion of the purposes of communication see Berlo, *The Process of Communication,* pp. 7–20, listed at the end of this chapter.

the two approaches, consider spring as the subject of a poem and of a soap advertisement. The consummatory purpose of the poem is to express the poet's joy in the season of the year; the instrumental purpose of the soap advertisement is to sell more soap by reminding people that hot weather brings forth body odors. Both are on the same subject; both are persuasive; both express truth. One is not necessarily superior to the other; they are simply addressed to different ends.[2]

How Do People Communicate?

People may be said to communicate by words, by means of speech, writing, pictures, gestures, and so forth, or by radio or newspaper or other media; but none of these statements express the full truth of the matter. They center upon the sender of a communication and the physical aspects of his message, such as sound vibrations or letters of the alphabet. They lead to our next question.

What Elements Are Necessary for Communication?

In his *Rhetoric* Aristotle discussed speech under three headings: "the speaker," "the speech," and "the audience." There have been many variations and expansions of his thought; one of the latest[3] adds two refinements to visualize the process of communication:

$$Source—Encoder—Signal—Decoder—Receiver$$

The process may be illustrated by such simple statements as "I (source) see a cat." "Encoding" here simply means transmitting English words by vocal air waves to a "decoding" receiver who listens, understands English, and is acquainted with the concepts of "seeing" and "cat."

This simple pattern may also be applied to something as complex as a great metropolitan newspaper, both a source in itself for some statements and a collector of others, putting them all into print and sending them out to millions of readers. In each instance, simple or complex, the patterns are the same. As far as each item in the newspaper is concerned, the transmission is to an individual reader. Though mass newspaper circulations, the diffusion of many identical signals, certainly exist, there is really no such thing as a mass reader. Each reader of the *New York Times,* for example,

[2] For further discussion see Leon Festinger, "Informal Social Communication," *Psychological Review,* vol. 57, pp. 271–292, 1950, and Wilbur Schramm, "The Nature of News," *Journalism Quarterly,* vol. 26, pp. 259–269, 1949.

[3] See Berlo, *op. cit.,* pp. 31–32. The idea is similar to Aristotle's. In 1947 a Bell Telephone Company mathematician and an engineer, Claude Shannon and Warren Weaver, conceived of communication mechanically involving source-transmitter-signal-receiver-destination. Other patterns have been developed by Schramm, Westley and MacLean, Fearing, and Johnson.

reads alone as an individual. He does not sit down with others and read in concert, affected by their presence. When something a newspaper columnist says makes him smile as he reads amid the noise of the New York Central or Long Island Rail Road commuter train, a personal communication reaches him from an unknown individual. The fact that there are hundreds of thousands of readers makes no difference. Knowing this, wise writers always write to individuals instead of to a nonexistent "mass."

The Source of a Communication

Although objects such as scenes can express meaning to a person, the basis of such meaning lies in the mind of the perceiver and not in anything the objects have intended. Our real concern is with the intentional transmission of ideas from person to person, from a human source to a human receiver. When people perceive things, they combine the percepts with other remembered concepts in their minds (some of them the result of communication); they react and then themselves become sources of communication. Here we are coming very close to questions about the fundamental nature of thought itself. Perception is not necessarily limited to personal observation; it also comes from communications, in which the transmission of ideas from other persons can be highly varied and complex.

Encoding a Communication

An idea remaining in the mind of its source and not yet cast into a form which can be transmitted to others is not part of a communication; it must be expressed in some way that others can understand. We may even ask if it actually exists unless so expressed. Does a person have an idea if he cannot verbalize it? Words are symbols of things; can we be said to have a thought if we cannot reduce chaotic mind pictures and feelings into words? Or are we just unable to communicate? [4]

Language is a major step in encoding; and although a gesture, hum, or motion may convey meaning almost as precisely, complex encoding usually depends upon language. If we do not know what to call things, we find difficulty in communicating to others about them.

The manner in which a source encodes a communication is a reflection of his own personal or vicarious experiences, including his entire social background. In talking about the ring, a prize fighter doesn't use the same terms that a painter uses. Unless we try hard to do otherwise and are gifted with an ability to imagine other people's lives, we tend to shape our encoding in terms of our own social background.

Encoding also involves selection of a medium of transmission. An in-

[4] S. I. Hayakawa, *Language in Thought and Action,* Harcourt, Brace & World, Inc., New York, 1949, will be found particularly interesting by those beginning to examine the relationship between words and thought.

formal chat with a friend, a talk before a supper club, and a formal article on a technical subject are all encoded in different ways.

Encoding is also the point at which "ghosts" (hired writers) usually first come into the picture. The man who knows what ideas he wishes to convey but who does not have the time or ability to encode them well, may hire another to do it for him; a politician may need a speech writer and a manufacturer may need an advertising writer.

Signal Breakdowns

The signal (message) may suffer mechanical breakdowns. A page of printed type may be too smudgy to read; a radio broadcast may squeal with interference; a poster may be located where few pass by it; or a play may be performed in an auditorium with muffling acoustics. Professional communicators spend great energy in correcting such deficiencies, and this is as it should be, since an inadequate signal ends the communication; but questions of who should want to read the type, hear the broadcast, note the poster, or attend the play, being less apparent than mechanical defects, often go unasked and unanswered. Perfection in the mechanics of delivering a communication is quite important, because in a world crowded with messages, listeners are not likely to struggle hard to receive one message when others are more easily available. But deciding *what* to communicate may be even more important.

Decoding the Communication

Once the success of transmission has been assured, the primary question is: "Can the receiver decode the message?" The answer depends largely on whether the receiver and the sender have overlapping experiences. The requirement of a common ground is implicit in the Latin *communicatus,* meaning "something shared."

A common language is itself a form of common experience and the first need in decoding a message. Similarity of language involves more, however, than a choice of English rather than French or Hindi; it is concerned especially with idiom and parallelism of expression within a given tongue.

The use of a common language breaks down for a number of reasons. Some well-educated people have as many as 30,000 words at their command, while many semiliterates have only a thousand or less. Even among people who have large total vocabularies, great areas of noncoincidence exist among the words that they do know. A Kansas farmer, for example, and a lifelong Manhattanite may each have a large store of English words, but those the farmer uses about weather, soils, crops, animals, and social institutions may not mean much to his fellow. The terms an atomic physicist commands differ from those of a jazz band leader; and a corporate treasurer's vocabulary (and hence his set of values) is not like that of a lathe operator in his plant.

The connotations of identical words constitute a problem, because meanings are understood in terms of differing experiences. Having a "good time" may mean one thing in Sauk Center, Minnesota, another in Las Vegas, and yet another in Harlem—and there will be considerable differences between individual good times within these places. A set of deerhorns means one thing to a hunter and another to a Frenchman; to an Eskimo rubbing noses has an affectionate social significance entirely lacking in the American wrestling ring; "reduction of the work force" gladdens the hearts of stockholders but darkens the skies of employees; and "Republican" means one thing to a Kalamazoo banker and another thing to a CIO leader. Even "peace" has widely different meanings for most Americans and for many Russians or Chinese, and the Russian understanding of the word may well be different from that of the Oriental.

Lack of common experience can seriously affect the ability to communicate. Consider, for example, the well-bred son of a steel-company president, who has grown up in a fine home in an exclusive suburb, has had plenty of spending money and his own car, attended the best schools, and associated with young men of similar wealth and position; he is given the job of editing a company publication which goes to hourly workers in the mill. How much will his experience enable him to communicate to his readers? Can he encode messages in terms they will decode? Or can he even select the right things to try to communicate to them?

Actions of the Receiver

Will the receiver try to decode the message? Much depends upon whether the receiver thinks his effort will be rewarded. The *reward* may be many things: satisfaction of sheer curiosity; a recognition of even deepening of previous experiences; strong motivational drives such as sex, fear, or pride; even hope of gain.

Effort involves the ease of decoding a message and the competition with other messages, other uses of time, and distractions. Decisions as to whether to expend such effort are often made quickly and almost unconsciously. A receiver leafing through the pages of a magazine decides in only a few seconds whether to flip on to the next page or to spend a measurable effort examining a particular message. To get more receiver attention, the reward for paying attention to the communication must be increased or the effort lowered—or both.

The Two-way Nature of Communication

It is doubtful whether communication ever takes place without being two-way. When the master shouts an order and the slave silently obeys, an unspoken reaction has taken place; and when the radio announcer speaks into an impersonal microphone, there is feedback from distant listeners, although it does not reach the announcer directly. Lack of easily ascertained, immediate response is one of the most serious problems of modern communication through the mass media because, without visible response, a sender cannot know whether he has communicated or what effect his words have had. When the slave nods, the master knows the order has been received and understood; a radio announcer has no way of knowing unless letters or telephone calls show response. Two-way communication is quite apparent when two people are talking face to face. Gestures, facial expressions, eye focusing and verbal response show the receiver's response, and the sender may, if need be, alter the message accordingly; but he is nonplused when the receiver simply looks blank and makes no response.

Two-way communication helps the sender to express himself, clarifies his thought, and bolsters his ego by the pleasant process of self-assertion. This is the pleasure of conversation. No matter how brilliant a lecturer may be, a time comes when hearers wish to reply. They answer directly or indulge in comments to their neighbors, or mutter, or perhaps go home and write letters to the newspaper. Listeners soon become bored in a one-way role; good conversations arise when the roles of sender and receiver are alternated, as most of us learn from experience. If you wish to be heard, you must listen at least part of the time!

Demonstrating Listening

Listening is apparent (although sometimes feigned) in personal conversations; but when senders are separated from receivers by distance or time, as they are when communicating by mass media, then they must devise ways of finding out who is listening and how well they are responding.

There are two reasons for listening. One is to gain information. This motive is often so strong in the sender that he resorts to tests, as in the scientific-opinion polling which has developed within the last few decades. Television advertisers want to know how many and what kinds of people listen to their messages, and therefore hire opinion surveyors to go out and ask people what they hear or install mechanical devices within television receivers' sets to keep a record of their listening. Magazine editors want to know what features are most popular in their publications; businessmen or labor leaders wish to discover public opinion upon current issues.

Such listening is not really two-way communication at all and should not be confused with it. The action is taken simply for information, and only a few people are aware that their opinions are sought; yet even under these circumstances, polltakers are frequently surprised at the gush of information which spouts out in response to "yes or no" questions.

Another reason for listening is to give the other fellow a chance to talk.

Public relations practitioners, politicians, educators, advertisers, clergymen, and others should realize that although the flow of communication today is mighty, *most of it is one-way!* Radio, television, newspapers, magazines, teachers, and preachers usually send out their messages with little opportunity for the receivers to respond. We are much talked at. Many messages are ignored, but those which are absorbed are still incomplete and frustrating because the recipients do not have a chance to express their opinions about them.

Perhaps this always being "told" may help to explain part of the extraordinary restlessness, frustration, and even violence of today's world. Everybody talks to young people, but few listen to them. The opinions of many other groups are little regarded. If we listened to them with understanding we might win their cooperation.

It is not enough, however, simply to say, "I am listening." Attentive listening must be demonstrated as well as proclaimed. Situations must be created in which receivers have the opportunity to return messages and to know that their replies have been received and understood. In mass media situations, such listening may be as complex and well organized as was the original effort to send out the messages.

For example, a company magazine editor runs an article expatiating upon the need for greater worker productivity within the plant because of foreign competition. He announces that readers' comments will be welcome (willingness to listen). Several letters come in. He replies by personal notes from top officers of the company (evidence of listening) which are also run in the magazine with appended editorial comment (widespread evidence of listening). Small group-discussion meetings are then held in which employees of various departments can discuss the subject (listening). At a company dinner special recognition is given to the most outstanding of these committee reports (listening), and some of the ideas are put into effect (final evidence of listening).

This kind of planned two-way communication causes company employees to say, "Our management really wants to know what we think," and makes them more receptive to all future company pronouncements of policy. In a small organization most of this interchange of opinion could be accomplished by a question from the boss: "Bill, Tom, and Joe, what do you think we should do about this problem?" But when there are thousands of men in scores of plants, the necessity for two-way communication is likely to be forgotten.

What Is Public Opinion?

Public opinion may be defined as the decisions of groups of people in connection with identifiable, stated issues. This differs from public *attitudes,* which are the predispositions, thoughts, or feelings of persons toward issues which have not yet materialized in a specific way. In New England, for example, prior to the Civil War, there were various public attitudes toward slavery, states' rights, the sanctity of the Union, and the Southern way of life, which were fused into public opinion upon the specific question of secession when Fort Sumter was fired upon. These attitudes had been long in the making and were molded by many communications, such as *Uncle Tom's Cabin,* the Lincoln-Douglas debates, reports on "bleeding Kansas," and the sermons of abolitionist ministers. Attitudes are opinions in the process of formation; once an opinion has been formed, such as that secession should be resisted by arms, it is not easily changed. Public relations efforts are usually most effective in dealing with attitudes which have not yet hardened into opinions, and the ability to foresee situations which may cause this solidification often leads to early and influential communication.

We often incorrectly assume that the opinions of a public are simply the sum total of the opinions of the individuals comprising that public. Public opinions may vary among groups because of the interaction of the individuals within each group. Conversations result in group communication and approval. The more the group becomes an interacting unit, the more the characteristics of cohesiveness, intolerance of dissent, and codification are magnified. The individuals within an interacting crowd differ in their behavior from isolated individuals, and the crowd itself differs from other groups of people that are casually thrown together without any reason for communicating or interacting with one another.

It has often been observed that in an interacting crowd individuals tend to shed their personal inhibitions, to respond to the crowd and to appeals which would scarcely move them or would even repel them if they were considered in solitude. The crowd itself tends to select lower common denominators of appeal and to respond with exaggeration or violence uncharacteristic of an individual. Such reactions account for the common experience of public relations personnel—that they may convince individuals of a viewpoint in private and then find that the same individuals will deny their previously expressed convictions when reacting with a crowd.[5] Within a crowd, communication is still made with the individuals comprising the crowd, but they are much altered individuals.

The term "public opinion" generally refers to individual opinions such as those which may be ascertained by questions or by secret ballot. Reasoned democracy depends upon solitary decisions by each citizen and is not to be confused with the aberrations sometimes apparent in crowds, parliaments, or legislatures.

A capable communicator knows the social backgrounds and pressures to which his receivers are subjected, and realizes the stake that each receiver has in being an accepted member of his group. The communicator does

[5] Herbert I. Abelson's *Persuasion* discusses this on pp. 20–40.

not often expect a man to set himself up alone against his fellows and habits, but instead tries to obtain a more permissive attitude from the group or to seek paths of action for its members which do not run entirely counter to group norms.

Communication and Persuasion

Whether or not all communication is persuasion, in public relations activities persuasion is almost always intended as a result of communication, and frequently the recipients are aware of the intent. Their awareness does not necessarily imply suspicion or hostility, but it means that the communicator should have some insight into the conditions which favor successful persuasion. The following sections discuss some of them.

Confidence in the Source of Persuasion

Emerson's line "What you are . . . thunders so that I cannot hear what you say" indicates how important it is to perceive the nature of a source if a listener is to evaluate a persuasive communication. Distrust of a source certainly makes persuasion more difficult, even though it is also true that listeners often remember *what* was said, even from a distrusted source, think about it, and then later accept it after they have forgotten where it came from.

The credibility of a source is enhanced if the communicator shares a common background or set of experiences with listeners. A political speaker who begins, "When I was a farm boy down in Carter County . . ." is demonstrating this principle (*a*) if talking to farmers, (*b*) if in or near Carter County, or (*c*) if speaking to former Carter County residents. Testimonials or recommendations are another cause of trust in a source. "I have known Congressman Smith for forty years and you can believe what he says . . ." carries weight with an audience which trusts the introducer. Introductions are important, because they can greatly affect the way in which a forthcoming communication will be received. Tests have shown that a group of laborers who were shown a rather indefinite editorial upon wage rates and were told that it came from the *Wall Street Journal* scorned it, whereas another similar group who were told that the same editorial had been published in a union newspaper, felt that it was most worthwhile. Groups of businessmen tested with the same material had opposite reactions.

Confidence in the Message Itself

What makes a message credible when its source is unknown or *neutral?* Corroboration by the receiver's own experience and by the known or imagined experience of others contributes to his willingness to believe; and social atmosphere and accepted stereotypes add their influence.

Few people today believe in witches, not so much because no one has seen a witch (none of the people at Salem in the 1600s had seen a witch either), but because a belief in witches is decidedly out of step with contemporary opinion. It was decidedly in step in the seventeenth century to claim acquaintance with them. On the other hand, believing in invaders from Mars in 1938 seemed quite reasonable to thousands of people when Orson Welles's simulated broadcast of a Martian attack created panic in New Jersey. Though Welles's listeners had never seen a Martian, society was ready to accept the existence of men from another planet.

Testimony, evidence, and proof do little to persuade hearers of a statement's validity unless they also believe in the worth of the testifier and understand the meaning of the evidence. Although logical argument is a clincher to those who are disposed to believe, it is seldom in itself a cause of belief.

The education of the receiver, both in general and in the specific field of the communication is important because it affects the range of the receiver's vicarious experience, creating a greater area in which common response can exist. Receivers are likely to believe things which match their information and are likely to doubt things which run contrary to it. Their belief or skepticism is produced not by actual information but also by the deep ego involvement of their expertise.

Broadly educated people are likely to take broad standards for their beliefs and to turn for validation to national, world, or other distant authorities with which they are acquainted even if only by hearsay. Less well-educated people depend more upon the opinions of their neighbors and friends for validation, and testimony from high, but distant, authority may even repel them.

Benefit to Hearer

Persuasion must serve a receiver's needs if communication is to occur. The benefits may be quite intangible, such as raising the social status of a receiver by making him an expert about a subject which his social group regards highly; or quite specific, like learning how to make money in the stock market. To a prisoner planning a jailbreak, any information about the hardness of steel bars or the time required to cut them with a hacksaw would be of sufficient benefit to justify careful reading.

Accordance with Value Systems

It is hard to persuade any person to believe in or to do anything which goes against the value systems accepted by his social group; and those most attached to the group and most prominent in it, who draw most of their ego support from it, are the least likely to be affected by such adverse persuasions. Those who "belong" have little tolerance for statements which upset them by contradicting beliefs which are socially acceptable.

Neither can someone be persuaded easily if accepting the persuasion will cause the receiver to lose face among his fellows because he has made a change. Perhaps the persuasion will have to be made to look like less of a change, or perhaps the norms of the group itself will have to be altered. Instead of persuading one person to change, it may be necessary to alter the whole group by means of discussion and the use of opinion leaders. If groups were always static, this would be a nearly impossible task, but in the flux of modern democratic society group change is common, and so individual beliefs can often be changed too.

To persuade someone who is very strongly attached to a group, it may be necessary to change his attachment to the group or else be content with a lesser degree of persuasion.

Other Facts about Persuasion

When listeners are already well informed the greatest amount of persuasion is usually accomplished by telling both sides of the story; but when they know little about the subject or when (for various reasons) they can give their attention to only one aspect of the case, then a one-sided presentation is more effective. When opposing views are presented together, the one heard last will probably stick longer.

Stating conclusions in persuasion is more effective than leaving the audience to guess at them or to make up their own. When left to their own devices, listeners sometimes arrive at conclusions entirely different from those the speaker intended!

The more extreme the change of opinion asked for by a communicator, the greater the change he is likely to produce. He can, of course, misjudge the temper of his audience; if the change conflicts too greatly with group norms, the speaker may be thrown out of the hall. But generally a weak request gets a weak response and a strong request, even if compromised, gets a stronger result.

But in persuasion, a mild threat seems often to be more effective than a more menacing statement. Hearers are repelled by a really strong threat and refuse to consider it or even to admit its possibility; but a little threat can be coped with and so is appraised. Americans, for example, can be sold to some extent on shallow atomic fallout shelters, because a minor fallout threat is within reason, but a program to build deep underground passages to avoid near hits envisages a danger too serious even to be faced.

Persuasion Everywhere

In confronting the fact of persuasion, we find it easy to be superior or cynical and to laugh at the peculiarly gullible group of people we have around us. But we must remember that *we* belong to that group all the time. All of us have been persuaded, in one way or another, about most of the things we are sure we know and hold most dear—the things which give most meaning and depth to life. Religion, education, patriotism, and all altruistic enthusiasms are "persuasions" which can generally be realized only by persuading others in turn. The man who says that he has received nothing from persuasion is either densely ignorant, a recluse, or self-deluded. Despite its abuses, persuasion is a gentle art in which wisdom, patience, love, and friendly enthusiasm are by far the greatest elements and it is much to be preferred to the more brutal, crass forms of forcing or buying human cooperation.

ADDITIONAL READING

Communication and Public Opinion

Abelson, Herbert I.: *Persuasion: How Opinions and Attitudes Are Changed,* Springer Publishing Co., Inc., New York, 1959.

Albig, William: *Modern Public Opinion,* McGraw-Hill Book Company, Inc., New York, 1956.

Berlo, David K.: *The Process of Communication,* Holt, Rinehart and Winston, Inc., New York, 1960.

Blankenship, A. B.: *How to Conduct Consumer and Opinion Research,* Harper & Row, Publishers, Incorporated, New York, 1946.

Doob, Leonard W.: *Public Opinion and Propaganda,* Holt, Rinehart and Winston, Inc., New York, 1948.

Harlow, Rex F.: *Public Relations and the Social Sciences,* Harper & Row, Publishers, Incorporated, New York, 1957.

Lippmann, Walter: *Public Opinion,* Harcourt, Brace and Company, Inc., New York, 1922.

MacDougall, Curtis: *Understanding Public Opinion,* The Macmillan Company, New York, 1952.

Schramm, Wilbur (ed.): *Mass Communication,* The University of Illinois Press, Urbana, Ill., 1949.

————: *The Process and Effects of Mass Communication,* The University of Illinois Press, Urbana, Ill., 1954.

Whyte, William H., Jr.: *Is Anybody Listening?* Simon and Schuster, Inc., New York, 1952.

Reaching Special Publics

4

What do you visualize when someone says "the public"? A cartoon character of timid little John Q. Public, perhaps, or a photo you recall of a crowd massed somewhere? Is it possible to communicate with such an abstraction?

It isn't, and for this reason people in public relations think almost always in terms of smaller, more specific *publics* drawn out of the general mass. Few people ever have occasion to communicate with the entire American public at one time anyway; only national political campaigns involve such an effort, and even these are largely confined to adult registered voters. The usual political campaign reaches toward many subdivisions of the general public, such as farmers, laborers, city dwellers, and old people. Even in such a local matter as a school bond vote, a public relations committee thinks in terms of groups of parents, teachers, real estate board members, civic clubs, retired people, religious groups, and other minor publics within the school district.

In fact, a public may be said to exist whenever a group of people is drawn together by definite interests in certain areas and has definite opinions upon matters within those areas. There are many publics, and individuals are frequently members of several of them which may sometimes have conflicting interests. In considering the school bond vote for example, a man might be torn between his feelings as a parent and as a member of a conservative economic group opposed to higher taxes; or an elderly couple, with no children now in school, might be the parents of a teacher. Conflicts of interest are common in America because we are great joiners; high economic status permits much varied individual activity; and the general high level of education creates wide interests. Americans, as compared to people in more static cultures, are hard to "type" into fixed social classes; they resent attempts at such typing and feel less ambiguity than most people of the world in belonging to numerous publics at one time.

Internal and External Publics

Internal publics are the people who are already connected with an organization and with whom the organization normally communicates in the ordinary routine of work. The question is not "Shall we communicate with them?" but rather "How shall we communicate, and to what extent?" Typical internal publics in an industry are the employees, stockholders, suppliers, dealers, customers, and plant neighbors. In a school system they would be the employees of various types, students, parents, suppliers, and the general public divided into various subgroups.

External publics, on the other hand, are composed of people who are not necessarily closely connected with a particular organization. For example, members of the press, educators, government officials, or the clergy may or may not have an interest in an industry. The leaders of the industry cannot assume any automatic interest and to some extent at least, can choose whether these groups shall be communicated with or not.

But it is not possible to be silent in dealing with the internal publics, for a number of reasons beyond the fact that communication with them is inevitable in the ordinary course of doing business.

1. The cooperation, or lack of it, of internal publics greatly affects immediate operating activities. Employees who don't want to give a fair day's work for their pay, dealers who would rather work with another company, or plant neighbors who would like to soak the company with higher property taxes, all affect profit-and-loss statements directly.

2. Outsiders form their opinions of organizations, to a large extent, by what those most closely connected with them seem to think. The university student home on a vacation who voices a low opinion of his instructors may not be well informed or even unbiased, but his parents and friends listen to him. The customer who has had bad relations with a company from which he bought an automobile shifts business to competitors by his public complaints. The employee who runs down his firm gets a ready audience: "He ought to know. He works there!"

3. Growth itself, of an industry and of organizations, as John W. Hill observes in his book, *Corporate Public Relations,* takes the leadership-communication function away from management and puts it into other hands. Unless planned efforts are made to remedy the situation, management becomes big, vague, and distant. Orders and information trickle down such a long chain of command that the internal public is often not much better informed than the external public. The worst situation exists when people outside the organization are actually better informed, through the press or personal acquaintanceship, than those who work inside; and this is not a rare occurrence!

In dealing with the various internal publics, a public relations man soon finds that his work runs into the domain of other departments of the organization, such as industrial relations or sales, which are charged with the main responsibility of maintaining employee efficiency or of the profitable disposal of the product to customers. Even with such overlapping, the public relations man can help if he remembers that his first means of aid to other departments is excellence in communication methods. The public relations head does not have the responsibility for policy or authority for personnel or sales. He can suggest, but he cannot order, because the public relations function is to give staff aid rather than to assume line command. If he feels that a personnel or sales policy is bad, he should not promise to "communicate" it into goodness by some hocus-pocus. Not every decision in an organization can be taken primarily in terms of its public relations consequences. There may be times when unpopular actions have to be taken or when policies that anger the public have to be pursued.

When this occurs the public relations man has the obligation to give useful advice, realizing full well that his understanding of the situation may be inadequate or that the condition may be inevitable. He can help straighten out public misconceptions arising from lack of information or false information; and he can explain motives and endeavor to instill trust in management decisions.

Such public relations activities are a delicate and difficult job, involving adjustment both to management and to the internal publics which receive the communications. They demand sober reflection, great patience, and confidence; and they must imply an enthusiasm in advancing the interests of the organization which will justify intrusion into what some persons may consider their own private operating spheres. Behind a tactful public relations director must also be a sympathetic and supporting management.

INTERNAL PUBLICS

The Employee Public

Large as this important internal public may be, it is usually divided into many subsections which differ greatly from one another and which often repay approaching in the ways best suited to their interests and reaction patterns.

For example, among employees there are hourly paid workers, salaried workers, and managerial staff—each group with its own special characteristics and outlook.

Production-line workers dress differently, spend their Saturday nights differently, and often have different goals for themselves and for their families than do their brethren who wear white collars and coats in the offices and are equally or sometimes less well paid—although the gulf between white collar and blue collar is not so deep as it once was.

The foreman, although called a member of management, is often spiritually closer to the shopmen than is the office worker; and foremen themselves are often quite removed from the higher echelons of management. In big industries the very nature of mass communication by bulletin boards, employee publications, and the public press often bypasses the foreman. Top management often speaks directly to assembly-line workers or negotiates directly with top labor chiefs without following a chain of command. Summit conferences occur, and the organization is like an army in which the noncoms know less of tomorrow's orders than do the privates with access to the scuttlebutt from the general's office.

Employees often have few interests in common. For example, unskilled diggers, skilled craftsmen, laboratory technicians, and scientists may all be engaged upon the same project for the same company, and yet have little mutual liking or friendliness.

New employees may be little attached to an organization, often coming from distant places and having few close friends; they contrast sharply with veterans who have grown old at their work. Men and women employees look at things differently. In multiplant companies there is a distinction between headquarters employees, who almost always feel superior, and branch-location employees, who may feel left out of the communications stream and deprived of opportunity. Even the size of departments makes a great difference, because in some companies everyone knows everyone else by name and in others numbers would be more appropriate than names. In fact, in any but the smallest, most simple organization, it is dangerous nonsense to consider employees as a homogeneous type.

What do employees most want from their companies and their unions? *Must* there always be antagonism between employees and the company? A number of years ago, after living for more than a year in the stockyards district of Chicago and interviewing scores of employees in the strife-torn meat-packing industry, Father Purcell of Loyola University in Chicago[1] came to a not very startling conclusion which yet was a novel concept to many old-line businessmen and to labor leaders: that employees want to have their cake and eat it too. Employee loyalties are divided; employees expect certain things from their unions, and they expect certain other things from their companies. They don't want to cleave entirely to one or to the other, and they dislike people or conditions which force them to make a choice.

Some of the things that employees of all sorts usually seem to want, although in differing degrees, are these:

Security. Is the job itself secure? Is the company making money, or are layoffs and shutdowns possible? Is the business progressing or declining? More particularly: How secure am I in *my* job? What about automation or changes in processes? Seniority? Arbitrary or unjust dismissal? Personnel

[1] Fr. Theodore Vincent Purcell, *The Worker Looks at Labor and Management,* Harvard University Press, Cambridge, Mass., 1953.

practices? And finally: What about retirement? What can I look forward to when age forces me to quit?

Respect. Am I recognized as a human being who knows something worth knowing? As personal skills increase, a worker's desire for recognition intensifies, and age also adds to his need for respect.

Participation. Am I just one cog in a big set of wheels, or do I know more of the process of which I am a part than just what happens in front of me? Not everyone has curiosity and ambition to the same extent—the need to be part of a bigger, more meaningful whole—but a surprising number of people do. It's the difference between the two medieval stone masons who were asked what they were doing. "Cutting stone," one man replied sharply. "Helping to build a cathedral," said the other.

Consideration. Am I informed and consulted about what's going on (or at least informed in advance of outsiders)? Is there an opportunity for me to express my ideas when I have them?

Recognition. What rewards are given for good and faithful service? Do people know about such rewards both inside and outside the plant?

Opportunity. Are promotion policies fair? Is there a chance to advance? Can I do what others have done? If the road is open and I do not take it, have I anyone to blame but myself? Does the merit of those at the top justify their eminence?

No organization can supply all these needs all the time to all its people; but the closer it comes to fulfilling them most of the time, the happier and more productive its work force can be if it is under efficient management.

Most employees expect management to manage. They understand that competent members of management should be reasonably rewarded for their services and risks. They recognize that investors deserve a return upon their capital and usually agree that the returns should be somewhat proportioned to the growth of the enterprise or the risks involved. The desirability of greater productivity is widely accepted. There is no great stampede in favor of government ownership, since most American employees have a distrust of government that makes them poor socialists and keeps them from being Communists. No one can impugn the intelligence or loyalty of the American employee public, but some major points of difference do exist between employees, ownership, and management.

Most employees, for example, think that business profits are much larger than they really are and tend to underestimate the risks of capital. They fear the effect upon themselves of automation and change. They sometimes do not have complete confidence in the wisdom or integrity of their managements. And, very often, they would like a bigger slice of the earnings pie distributed as wages.

In addition to these rather natural differences, almost all organizations have certain built-in friction points.

The
Kroger Co.
Reg. No. 7422

DEC. 31, 1958

$ 0.29 - Gr A
$ 0.29 - Gr A
$ 0.29 - Gr A
$ 0.29 - Gr A
$ 0.39 - Gr A
$ 0.39 - Gr A
$ 1.32 - Mt A
$ 0.58 - Mt A
$ 0.29 - Pr A
$ 0.30 - Gr A
$ 0.10 - Pr A

TALE OF THE TAPE

*$ 4.53 - TL A

Total Shown Above
THANK YOU

Kroger
TOTAL SALES 1958
$1,776,175,000

TALE OF THE TAPE

In 1958 Kroger cash register sales tapes told a tale of success — big success.

These tapes registered a record total of $1,776,175,000 in sales for 1958.

BUT...

Where did these dollars go?

Let's see what happened to one of them.

78⁷⁄₁₀¢
of that dollar went to processors, manufacturers, farmers, and other suppliers

This was our largest single expenditure. It paid for everything we sold in our stores, as well as various handling costs necessary to get merchandise to our stores.

The second largest part of our dollar

11⁴⁄₁₀¢
paid our wages and salaries

In total dollars our 1958 payroll amounted to $201,703,000 — an increase of more than $13,000,000 over 1957.

6⁶⁄₁₀¢
of our dollar went to pay all other costs of doing business

This included rent, heat, power, light, store supplies and repairs, as well as advertising, insurance premiums, transportation, telephone and telegraph costs, license fees, banking charges and various other operating expenses.

It also included $3,419,000 which the company contributed to our Profit Sharing Plan for 1958.

Taxes took
2¹⁄₁₀¢
of our dollar

Local, state and federal tax agencies collected a total of $36,572,000 from Kroger in 1958. The company's contribution of $5,109,000 to our Social Security tax payments is included in this figure.

After all these payments
1²⁄₁₀¢
of our dollar was left as net profit

From this amount we paid our 28,514 shareholders 5/10 of a cent for the use of their money. The remaining 7/10 of a cent was put back into the business to help pay for such things as the 100 new stores and 6 distribution centers to be opened in 1959 and to buy trucks and other equipment—all so necessary for continued progress and success.

PROFIT
is the most important part of our business

For all of us it means:

Better job opportunities—Kroger profits pay for the cost of expansion ... larger stores, improved transportation facilities and more modern plants. This makes our jobs even better and creates new opportunities for promotion and progress.

Better employee benefits—higher wages, sickness and accident benefits, life insurance, retirement ... all mean more financial security for us and for our families.

Profits make all of these things possible

And without profits, of course, there just couldn't be any Profit Sharing!

Kroger
LIVE BETTER FOR LESS

Kroger
LIVE BETTER FOR LESS

Figure 4-1. One of the world's smallest annual reports (each of the eight pages and both sides of each cover is shown approximately half original size), sent to Kroger Company employees, features profits as a basis for profit sharing.

There is a conflict in all types of work between the old-line employees and the younger men, between old craftsmen and younger. There are conflicts between skills; the highly skilled, brilliant scientist chafes at seeing the administrator better rewarded. There are conflicts between departments; sales, shipping, credit, and production departments are constantly passing blame back and forth. There are even conflicts between workers in clean and in dirty surroundings, or between those of different racial, religious, or geographic origins.

Some friction is inevitable, but good public relations organization and communication to the Number 1 public, the employees, can modify much of its roughness and can direct natural energies into greater development instead of wasteful cross fire.

Downward communications from management to employees are typified by employee magazines and newspapers, newsletters, bulletin boards, announcement posters, films, reading racks, letters, and ceremonies. Such downward communication is often well developed, although it is not always well conceived.

Upward communications from employees to management are much more feeble, consisting usually of surveys, suggestion programs, group meetings, and a vague "open-door policy." Because of management's neglect, much of the upward communication in a company has become a union prerogative, and this, according to Fr. Purcell, is one of the main reasons for union popularity among employees.[2] Business must not only *assert* that it listens to its employees; it must show that it does so in ways which they can see and believe. At this point the foremen and the lower echelons of management are the key persons.

The biggest challenge to understanding between employer and employee lies in mutual communication. In a 1961 talk in Florence, South Carolina, Donald F. Carpenter, General Manager of the Film Department of the du Pont Company, observed:

> We utterly reject the idea that there is any inescapable conflict between the employer and the employee. To the contrary, we are convinced that the interests of employer and employee are more closely parallel than those of almost any other groups in our society. Among the more important of their common objectives are:
> To make a good product.
> To maintain low costs.
> To give good service to customers.
> To maintain good working conditions.
> For the employer this means operation of a prosperous business; for the employee it means steady employment, good wages, good working conditions, and self-respect. When an employee likes his job and gives it

[2] *Ibid.*

his best effort, both he and his employer benefit. When an employer operates his business profitably, both he and his employees benefit. When employers and employees work in harmony, the entire community benefits. . . .

The "frame of reference" is ideal. How can it be established?

The Employee's Family Public

The wife, children, and relatives of an employee have interests in his organization similar to those of the employee himself but unlike his in scope and intensity. The world of the employee's family, though it impinges upon the plant or the office, is not a part of it, and the looser connection leads usually to a less intense interest and also to a greater opportunity for misunderstanding and distortion. The family may not know much about the employee's job, but they are seriously affected by it. Some of the keen interests of this special public, so vital to the happiness, productivity, sanity, and even the presence on the job of the employee himself, are:

Security. Often this is the first concern. How stable and growing is the worker's organization? Are its personnel policies fair? What does it offer in health benefits and retirement plans? How harmonious are the relations between management and labor? Are costly strikes a threat to family budget planning?

Opportunity. What are the breadwinner's chances for advancement? Can he hope for more pay or higher social status? Is educational help offered or study encouraged? Are there regular paid vacations?

Information. Just what does the wage earner do anyway? What does his organization produce and how does it do it? Who run the organization, and what sort of people are they?

There is a great lack of understanding of a man's job in a modern American family, largely because an urban worker's place of employment is usually far from his home. In earlier days, the village blacksmith's son had little doubt about what his father did for a living. He watched him work and as soon as he was able, he probably started helping him shoe the horses or hammer out the glowing plowshares from the hot iron. He knew his father's skill and brawn, his wisdom, and his weaknesses.

In modern industrial or office work, the father disappears in the morning and comes back in the evening to his well-fed, busy family, whose questions about his activities are largely for politeness' sake and are so understood. Many working men are poor communicators, and few families are good audiences; and the higher and more abstract a man's activities may be, the harder he finds it to explain them, and the worse is his family's misunderstanding. The mental pictures which the wife or son has of what the father does at his work are usually far from the truth. Sometimes this vagueness may be an advantage; more often it is a source of frustration and annoyance.

Employers can help to bridge this rift in the home, if they wish, by means of plant open houses, employee newspapers, letters, and other communication devices. But when they make the effort, they should be careful not to let the employee down, but to explain fully the importance of his work. In some highly automated industries, for example, an open house shows the wage earner fiddling with controls which seem unimportant unless their significance is made clear. We need some substitute for the image of the brawny, sweating, heroic laborer whom mural painters have loved to portray. In twentieth-century America, families need to know that the father's work often involves a high degree of intelligence. Employers can try to give them a lively sense of understanding.

Participation. The growing separation between the employee's family and the worker's job also poses some problems about the desirability of family participation in the social life of a plant or office. The job and the rest of life are usually rather closely connected in some small-town industries, among officers' wives on traditional military posts, and among faculty families on small college campuses. But increasingly in modern urban society, employee families have many other things to do than to hobnob with people at the office or plant. School and church affairs, voluntary groups of all sorts, gatherings of relatives, picnics, travel, and even television watching may all provide a more friendly and less caste-conscious social setting.

Some opportunities for employee family participation in social events may be welcomed, but if the company offers too many, they may seem an intrusion. Togetherness can be carried too far. Rare invitations are a treat, but frequent command performances become a worrisome chore. Almost unconsciously paternalism creeps in, even with management's best intent to avoid it. John Doe may be well acquainted with his various bosses, but their looks and mannerisms, which do not bother him because he knows them so well, may utterly devastate his wife, who reads all manner of dire intent into them concerning Doe's future with the organization; and the activities of the bosses' wives, whom Doe does not know, may also baffle and alarm him.

Perhaps semiformality on such occasions is the best answer. The top brass at an open house might well shake hands, make a speech, join in the refreshments briefly, and then—disappear. And when the pictures of the event are run in the employee magazine, one photo of the president at the event will be enough. Employee families desire participation and like to know the brass personally—but only to a degree.

The Stockholder Public

After the employees and their families, stockholders are probably next most closely connected to a company, and there are many obvious reasons for cultivating their interest and good will.

1. In theory at least, stockholders are the ultimate authority of a company, electing the board of directors, which in turn appoints the president and other major officers.
2. Stockholders are often an important source of additional funds for expansion or acquisitions. Their word also carries weight with interested non-stockholders who might wish to invest.
3. Stockholders are important for their "political" support also. Their influence is particularly evident among utility companies, whose rates are fixed by public bodies and who wisely try to get their stockholding as widespread as possible within their service areas. Many local companies associated with larger national concerns try to overcome the stigma of outside control by encouraging local stockownership in the parent organization.

The stockholder situation of companies, of course, varies greatly. Until recent times a few industrial giants have been family-held without sale of their stock to the general public. Others are still largely held by a few people, often an original family or two and the friends of an early inventor. Others, such as the public utilities or large national industrial concerns, have many thousands of stockholders. The classic concept, however, of a large company as an organization in which a relatively small group of stockholders keeps in close touch and exercises effective control through personal knowledge of people and policies is generally far from the fact.

Types of stockholders vary greatly; they include insurance and investment companies, wealthy people and those of moderate incomes, widows and orphans, church and educational institutions. Very seldom do these diverse types of people ever get together in an effective stockholder revolt unless conditions are very much disturbed and some leadership is offered. The usual recourse of unhappy stockholders is to sell out and to cease their connection with the company; yet such is the volume of trading on many stocks today, that to assume that all who sell are dissatisfied would be quite incorrect. They may be cashing in their gains or easing their losses.

Companies are obliged by law to render annual reports to their stockholders. At first these annual reports were just tables of figures and the necessary explanations, primarily of interest to financiers; but in recent years they have become increasingly elaborate, and now are often highly illustrated, beautifully printed, and well-written booklets, which are sent not only to stockholders but also to the press, community leaders, financial analysts, and frequently to employees also. Such annual-report booklets are often supplemented by films and stockholder meetings, depending upon the size of the company.

Many employees now own stock in the companies for which they work and thus have a divided interest. Frequently companies encourage employee stockownership; they may lend employees money to buy stock and promise to buy it back at the original selling price if the employee leaves the company. (Some companies require that employees sell such stock back to the company.) Often such stock "buys itself" because dividends are larger than the repayment rate on the loan.

The stockholding public usually wants to know certain things: Why are the dividends down? (They usually will not ask why they are up.) What is being done by the company about reinvesting in its future? What is the future of the business? Why are the company officers paid so well or offered attractive stock options? And why are relatives or friends of management or women on the board of directors or in key offices? When earnings are good, little may be said, but if they worsen, the questions may become numerous and insistent. Some other aspects of stockholder relations will be referred to under the discussion of external financial public relations later in this chapter.

The Community Public

Generalizations about plant communities are usually as fruitless as those about employees, since communities may differ from each other greatly in their sizes, interests, and in their relation with plants. In some instances, a large plant in a small town may be the lifeblood and main interest not only of that town but also of half a dozen others near by. Yet the identical plant in a city of a million people would be relatively unimportant, only one among many.

Some plants which produce consumer products may look toward their communities to absorb a large part of their output; others may ship all over the world, their sales success being made far from the production location. Some plants employ a large proportion of highly educated personnel, who naturally take a prominent place in the civic life of their communities; others employ only less skilled or even transient laborers. Even the differing social, religious, or racial attitudes of sections of the country have an effect upon community relations, and large multiplant organizations may find it difficult to install any single community relations program because of the variations in local conditions.

A community public is both internal and external; it includes the employees, their families, their friends, and relatives; yet it goes beyond these to include also people who are closely connected by interest with the organization and perhaps those who hardly know that it exists. Some people may benefit much from the activities of a business within a community and realize the advantage quite well; some will benefit and not know the source; and others will not benefit, or at least will not feel disposed to admit it. Yet, in all this variety, some natural contacts between community and plant occur frequently, although their importance depends upon conditions.

Plants need services from their communities; they need streets, sewers, water, lights, police and fire protection. Their employees need these services also, plus schools for their children, shopping centers, good homes, churches, and the other components of civilized life.

Plants get all or most of their employees from their communities, and they may draw many of their customers from this source also.

Industry pays taxes and may give gifts to community needs. Yet industry may also sometimes make noise, look ugly, smoke up the air, pollute the streams, dump unneeded workers on local relief rolls, and get involved in bitter strikes—all of which annoyances affect community relations.

What does a community expect of an industry?

Income. A community hopes that cash will flow in through wages to employees, perhaps from purchases from local suppliers and from tax payments.

Appearance. A community hopes that the plant appearance will not be a detriment to life in the town and, preferably, that it may be an attraction. Plants can often be good-looking, and some care spent on grass, flowers, and paint pays greatly in community appreciation. Many plants which emit odors, such as stockyards or oil refineries, or which belch smoke or make noises may be tolerated because they are a reason for the existence of the town, but if the town ever grows enough so that they lose preeminence, they may find themselves in trouble.

Participation. A plant is liked as an organization if it carries its load in necessary civic efforts such as school improvements, parks, welfare, and churches. Often this is done by individuals rather than by the company, and sometimes town fathers and company members may not agree as to how much is worthwhile, but willingness and interest are appreciated.

Stability. Fluctuating businesses sometimes bring more trouble than they are worth; the amount of trouble depends upon the size and nature of the town.

Pride. Many a city is on the map because it is the home of a nationally or even internationally known industry. Battle Creek means cereals; Rochester means Eastman Kodak; and so forth. Civic pride in the town's industry can be fostered and extended.

From its community an industry expects adequate services, fair taxation, good living conditions for its employees, a good source of labor supply, and a reasonable degree of support for the plant and its products if they deserve it.

Sometimes one party may expect too much from the other, but the important thing is that they should understand each other. Some communities, hungry for business, are willing to subsidize industry by cheap loans, low taxes, free or almost-free building sites and even buildings, low-cost utilities, and acceptance of low wage rates. But any industry involving substantial amounts of hard-to-move capital investment and locational advantages, would do well to consider such inducements carefully, since the advantages may turn to losses if ill feeling should later arise.

Good community relations cannot be established overnight, nor can bad opinions be altered easily. A sharp-dealing industry faces not only local political dangers but also the votes and voice of its own community people in state and national matters, over which it has no local control. The city fathers of Jonesville may be willing to put up with stream pollution, for example, but the other citizens of Jonesville and the towns downriver, through their voice in the state capital, may not be so compliant. A plant which pays substandard wages may find its workers pirated away by a new plant in an adjoining county a half-hour's drive away. As this nation grows into a greater metropolitan complex, local advantages tend to disappear, and community good citizenship and reputation affect an ever-widening area and pay off increasingly.

The Supplier Public

The people who sell to a company also form an important part of its internal public.

Many plants could not operate without suppliers of raw material: the dairy farmers who sell milk to evaporating, butter, or cheese plants; fruit-growers who sell to packing or canning plants; or farm wood growers and cutters who sell to paper or pulp-products plants. Such suppliers are as necessary to the plant as the employees who operate the machinery or keep its records, and the money paid to suppliers by the plant for sale of milk, fruit, or logs may be even more important to the area income than the plant's wage payroll.

Raw-material suppliers may also be very numerous. In some large milk-processing operations, for example, from several hundred to several thousand farmers may be selling milk to each plant—many times the number of employees.

Suppliers also may have numerous choices of where they will sell. In many areas a dairy farmer can easily sell milk to several markets, and plant competition for supplies is keen; or he may decide to go out of dairying altogether in favor of raising beef cattle, or even to take a city factory job. Both the large number of suppliers and the need for their interest and loyalty create a field for good public relations. The main responsibility for seeing that a plant receives a steady flow of raw material may belong to the production department, but public relations activities can assist greatly in obtaining valuable good will and understanding. Supplier publications, meetings, open houses, personal visits, and public relations advertising are the usual steps taken along with plant participation in city and regional events, to improve the community and its resources.

Another important class of suppliers is made up of those who sell component parts or materials to manufacturers who fabricate or assemble more complicated machines. The automobile industry, for example, draws upon hundreds of smaller manufacturers for items as diverse as glass, fabric, plywood, paint, chrome-plated parts, tires, rubber mountings, trim, springs, and screws. Frequently these subsidiary manufacturers will be scattered in dozens of smaller cities located near a large automobile plant. Since such suppliers do not sell to the public directly, their names often mean little to the public, and they are largely dependent for their orders upon one or two larger manufacturers who do sell completed products to the public.

In turn, however, the larger manufacturers are also somewhat dependent upon these subcontractors for the quality of their goods and certainty of delivery. A bad item in an otherwise good automobile causes customer complaints and hurts the reputation of the whole vehicle and its maker; and the inability of suppliers to meet demands may hold up an entire production program.

Since the number of such suppliers is relatively small, broad-scale public relations activities in this connection are not common. Many companies, however, such as General Motors Corporation, have long been aware of the public ignorance of how many smaller companies are sustained under the supplier system to the benefit of smaller industry and the widespread economic development of the nation. To combat such ignorance, they have used campaigns of public relations advertising showing the benefits of large-scale industry and sales and the manner of their diffusion through the entire country by means of a multitude of supplier contracts. The purpose is to effect public economic understanding as well as supplier good will.

There is yet a third class of suppliers, the local furnishers of office equipment, linen, food, building construction and repairs, and other services necessary to keep a large plant running. These people are such clear beneficiaries of their business connection and are so much a part of the community that usually no particular public relations activities are necessary with them except fair treatment, passing the business around somewhat evenly, courtesy, and information.

The Dealer and Distributor Public

The dealer and distributor public is primarily the responsibility of the sales department, but the special communications abilities of public relations men may frequently be called into play, especially if the number of dealers and distributors is large, if they are widely spread out, and if personal communications need to be supplemented by additional contacts.

Public relations staffs may be called upon, for example, to help produce dealer magazines containing news about new products and their uses, sales and contest ideas, personal items about dealer accomplishments, and changes in company policies. The arrangement for film production is a common task. Publicity help for dealers and manuals designed to enable dealers to get more favorable local publicity are frequently requested, as is also assistance in arranging sales-meetings programs and in supplying special exhibits.

Because of the public relations department's special knowledge of public opinion, it may be called upon to arrange or to advise upon surveys of dealer opinion about the company or its products.

The dealer-distributor public is often very close to the company's heart, and any real assistance that public relations can offer, working in close conjunction with the sales department's goals and desires, pays off at the cash register and may be much appreciated. Such assistance is one of the best ways to demonstrate the value of good public relations and to gain greater internal appreciation for the portions of public relations work which may be of less tangible or less immediate benefit.

The Consumer Public

The consumer public is also largely a responsibility of the sales department and of its right arm, the advertising department; but when consumers are numerous, or sometimes even when they are not, public relations methods of communication reaching beyond direct sales work or conventional means of advertising may become important. We might give some illustrations.

1. What creates the prevailing public attitude toward an organization? Though many companies in the United States today make similar products selling at similar prices, people often seem to prefer one of them to the others. What makes the difference? The product itself? Its advertising? The popularity of the manufacturing company—because of its good citizenship, enterprise, reliability, and the quality of its people? If public feeling is favorable, then how did people acquire their impressions?

2. How much does the public know about the product? Unless backed by giant introductory budgets (and often not even then), advertising usually does its best in selling a product with which the public is already familiar. Complete pioneering, creating a primary demand by advertising alone can be inordinately expensive, even futile. Yet since new products are *news,* they are well suited to public relations publicity, to films, exhibits, school contacts, and other unconventional ways of addressing audiences that usually result in a more active expression of interest than can be achieved in advertising by the mass

media. Reaching opinion leaders and making friends are also especially important in introducing new products.

3. Actual events such as contests, award programs, and visits to plants or laboratories may bring customers. With the permission of school authorities, programs and contests for students are increasingly used to awaken interest.

4. Employees can often exert a strong influence upon sales through their own public relations activities. The company can encourage them, in many instances, by informal training and by suggestions designed to obtain better cooperation.

5. Careful listening to what consumers have to say through surveys, panels, and less formal means is the joint concern of the sales, advertising, and public relations departments. Since customers do not differentiate among these departments, their feelings affect not only sales but also the labor, community, and political relations of a company.

It is growing increasingly hard to separate the external aspects of a company into neat compartments such as sales, advertising, and public relations, because outside observers get their impressions from all three plus the product itself. Consumer reactions are of political importance when they affect pricing, licensing, and government controls as well as sales. The face a company presents to the public is really a unity, although it may be a composite drawn by different departments; and the time may come (indeed has come in some industries) when there will be but two main divisions, (*a*) *communications* and *contacts* with various publics and (*b*) *production*. Under the first heading would come sales, advertising, public relations, and parts of employee relations; under the second would come production, personnel (in part), and maintenance of plants. Finance, the legal staff, and other service departments would assist both.

THE EXTERNAL PUBLICS

The publics mentioned so far in this chapter—employees, stockholders, the community, and customers—are all more or less intimately connected with a company and come into contact with it regularly through their normal activities. But there are in addition some much larger outside groups which affect a company's welfare materially and with which the degree of its contact and the nature of that contact is more or less voluntary. Such groups include the press and the other communications media, leaders of thought, political forces, financial experts, and others.

Probably the biggest difference between an *internal* and an *external* public is that people, like employees or stockholders, who are connected with an organization in some way will have a certain degree of interest in it, whereas to the outside world each company is just another organization, and unless some way can be found to relate its story to the interests of outsiders, they will probably not pay much attention to it.

There is, of course, interaction between internal and external publics. Yet it cannot be assumed that without effort good relations with insiders will ever be translated to outsiders. An employee who is quite happy in his work may be much more interested in bowling than in the fact that the firm has just opened a new branch in Australia. The firm must think of what interests the external public and not of what interests the firm. With employees and other internal publics there is a fair chance that all interests may coincide because all are connected with the same organization; with an external audience the assumption should be that the chance of such accidental coincidence of interest is slight.

The Press Public

"The press" includes newspapers of all sizes and types, television and radio stations, general magazines and trade papers. All of them serve as gatekeepers, opening the door to wider contact with a broad public through these media. The effective use of the media themselves will be discussed more fully in Chapter 8, "The Tools of Public Relations," but press staff men also constitute an important public in themselves, whose understanding and good will, regardless of their position, is well worth cultivating.

It is a mistake to think of newsmen as a peculiar group who demand special treatment. They are people like ourselves, who "live with bread" like us. They show a wide range of characteristics just as we do, from the conservatism of many publishers to the extreme liberalism of some young reporters.

Yet the nature of their profession does give them a few special traits or proclivities. In ordinary times the press exercises a tremendous influence over public opinion, and a newsman's words can affect the life of a project or organization. Bad reviews have meant the death of a play or book, and lack of publicity has prevented public interest in a good cause. Such power *can* corrupt in various ways. At the same time, newspapers and journals need the financial support of advertisers. This interdependence has tempted both advertisers and journalists to exercise pressure or to court favors from each other by questionable means. But such pressure is almost invariably a mistake and is resented by press and public alike. Most newspapers can well afford to be independent, and they value the traditional freedom of the press. The public, in the long run, recognizes a biased presentation of news or causes. Public relations men who want to get material into the press should avoid unwise pressure just as they avoid blackmail or bribery. Honesty in straightforward stories about good products is the best policy.

As a group, newsmen are intelligent—not only well educated but well informed through wide reading and experience. They appreciate direct, clear-cut explanations, since they themselves are experts in concise exposition and are usually hard pressed for time. Their contacts with many people and many political campaigns may make them mildly cynical about men's motives. Their anxiety to "get the news" leads sometimes to tactlessness and even callousness in its pursuit. But with that side of their work the public relations man has little to do. He will usually find newsmen extremely helpful, not only in getting stories into the papers but, more importantly, in interpreting public feeling. They know more about public relations than do people who get about less; they are trained observers; and they are often happy to give their impressions. In general, when treated with honesty and consideration, the press public is friendly, helpful, and stimulating.

The Educator Public

School people are another set of gatekeepers through whom messages may be relayed to other people; in addition, they also serve as "legitimizers," in that their approval of a proposition carries weight. This is particularly true in the college or university field, where competence in special subject matter is recognized. If a teacher of engineering, for example, speaks favorably of a machine to a class, his recommendation is important to them. The support of teachers (again, particularly of those in specialized fields) is important, also in connection with recruiting employees. Graduating students often consult with their teachers about the choice of firms who offer employment; and teachers can direct company recruiters to promising students, giving them detailed information about the qualities of the young people.

The key to successful contacts with the educator public is *service*. Teachers are willing to use commercially produced material in the classroom *if* it performs a real function which cannot be duplicated elsewhere or would perhaps be much more expensive. They are willing to read booklets or to attend meetings *if* they can get something of value out of them which they do not already know well.

Like members of the press, teachers are well educated and resent pressure, insults to their intelligence, or a waste of their time. They are independent-minded and perhaps equally suspicious of motives, but their pace is slower that that of journalists; they are less impatient and more willing to tolerate some dullness. Teachers are cautious about using material from an organization if they think it would expose them to charges of favoritism. They are pleased when others understand their educational ambitions, seek their advice, and offer to help make their work easier and more effective. Teachers are often willing to engage in joint efforts to improve education through award programs for outstanding students, summer in-

Figure 4-2. Factual educational material; a 12-page bulletin produced by the American Petroleum Institute.

ternships for teachers, and public events such as science fairs. They resent being herded into "business-in-industry days," being marched through plants, and being lectured about the merits of the free enterprise system. They particularly resent attempts to tell them what they should teach in the classroom, although from fear or politeness they will usually express their resentment only to one another.

The best way to serve the teacher public (and the press) is to find out what it wants and then satisfy the need.

The Clergy Public

Churchmen serve as legitimizers of ideas and activities rather than as gatekeepers, since little direct speaking from the pulpit or in meetings can be expected from them except on moral issues such as support of welfare or educational drives. Their understanding and their good will, however, may be reflected in their personal conversations, in their presence at events, and in the use of their names upon letterheads.

Clergymen are interested first in moral issues and then in civic and area development, in education, in world affairs, in sociological problems, and perhaps in science, medicine, or economics. Church leaders look at the world in terms of people rather than in terms of dollars or material production. In many churches they avoid becoming involved too deeply in material matters, both from a lack of personal interest and perhaps also from a concern lest they awaken controversy among their own church members. Clergymen, however, appreciate the opportunity of being informed about business activities and of being included in important plans or functions when their presence is appropriate.

Civic and Business Clubs

Groups like the Lions, Kiwanians, Engineers Club, or the South Side Improvement Association serve as platforms from which messages may be communicated to the attending members and perhaps also, by mail or by press reports, to those absent. Such groups act as gatekeepers in so far as their members relay their opinions to others; they act also, to some extent, as legitimizers from the simple fact that their acceptance or appreciation or formal endorsement of a speaker indicates approval in varying degrees. Such groups also furnish the occasion for a wider dissemination of information through the press. They may not be large in themselves, but they can be an important audience.

Business groups are usually inured to a reasonable amount of commercialism, at least within their own fields of interest, and do not resent it if it is presented as necessary information or without undue emphasis.

Professional clubs, which include doctors, lawyers, architects, and others, have a more precise focus of interest, and it does not matter greatly, in many instances, if talks presented to them are somewhat commercial as long as no disguise is attempted and the matter is genuinely germane to their professional interests. Indeed many talks must be commercial, because professional associations provide a formalized way of "talking shop." Skilled commercial presentations by experts, containing real information, well supplied with visual aids and demonstrations, are often welcomed because they improve the professional competence of each man present.

Membership within these groups, if it is possible for a member of a firm, helps public relations, since it usually indicates his willingness to be of personal service in advancing the interests of the profession, business, or area involved. Such personal generosity is particularly important in highly specialized fields or in small cities where group membership may be limited.

Women's Clubs

Women's clubs are similar to men's civic and business organizations, except that they tend to be in suburban locations and to be concerned about cultural subjects, children, gardens, welfare, and matters of particular interest to women.

Social Groups

Informal social organizations, such as city or country clubs or dance clubs, exist largely for the pleasure of the members, and admission to them almost always depends upon personal popularity. To a degree they are gatekeepers or legitimizers among the people who know of them. But since they are private groups, they are most valuable for the opportunities they afford for improvement of strictly personal relations. Often the leading social groups in a city together constitute a field which can be worked by the boss and his friends rather than by the public relations man.

Government as a Public

The government publics are primarily neither gatekeepers nor legitimizers, but rather groups of persons whose attitudes often have very concrete and direct effects upon the fortunes of many kinds of business and other activities. With the great expansion of government functions in this country within the past thirty years, the power of anyone associated with the government has tremendously increased. Government—city, state, or Federal—now affects big and little businessmen, farmers, laborers, teachers, transportation firms, merchants, scientists, and almost everyone else who can be named.

Work among such government publics differs somewhat from political activity as such, or from "economic education," or from the formation of pressure groups (although all are somewhat related), in that it involves the fundamental problem of fostering good relations with a large public associated with government—administrators, employees, and legislators.

Government administrative bodies—state highway departments, food and drug commissions, health authorities, and police forces, for example— often concern themselves directly with a business or organization; they may make regulations about such things as purchases of materials; may require statements about products; and may set standards of performance.

Government legislative bodies make the laws under which business and other activities operate. The process of legislation involves constant bickering about items as diverse as the size and weight of highway trucks, aid to dependent children, beer taxes, regulation of the practice of medicine, and the amount of money to be spent upon tourist promotion—all of which matters are of deep concern to certain business and professional groups and to the public relations people who represent them.

In a democratic government there is no question of the *right* of a business or interest group to present its case before a legislative body. It is part of the citizen's constitutional right of petition—the right to present facts before laws are made, hard-won hundreds of years ago from tyrannical kings. Nor is there any question about the *necessity* of such petitions. Government actions which may put a business out of operation or greatly reduce its earnings, which may beggar or enrich whole sections of the population, and which may pass the public's tax money around for better or for worse effect, are important. Anyone whose interests are strongly concerned, including those who fight for "causes," would be doing his organization an injustice if he did not do his best to present his case before government.

Lobbying isn't the sinister activity that it appears in the public eye, yet the word itself has become a smear term, suggesting all sorts of selfish people exerting undue influence, bribing and generally corrupting honest lawmakers and government administrators who would be paragons of wisdom and uprightness if only left alone. Actually, the activity of lobbying today springs out of the same big changes that have affected all communication and business in the United States within the past few decades. Lobbying, legislative representation, or whatever it may be called, is a natural outgrowth of bigness and great social interdependence. If it existed in the past only in the form of corrupting influence, that was because the dissemination of information was less needed.

Today a great many people are closely affected by many proposed laws and regulations about which they cannot pass a well-reasoned personal judgment. The doctor seeing his patients, the architect at his drawing board, the farmer plowing his fields, and the college teacher lecturing in his classroom are all so busy with their increasingly complex work that they do not have enough time to study and evaluate proposed new laws, and to decide to support or not to support them. Many scores of bills affecting business or professional activities are introduced at each session of a typical American state legislature. (For example, 1,200 bills are introduced at each legislative session in one typical large midwestern state, of which perhaps 100 will in some way affect the practice of medicine.) Someone must be the watchdog of these bills for each interested group—must read them, recommend positions, and present views—or otherwise no views will be heard, and the issue will be left to chance or to other pressures. This is lobbying.

In any matter of importance involving the continuing interest of government, someone has to be hired to watch changes, or to introduce them, and to make it his business to know the ropes—who legislators are, where they come from, what their beliefs and interests are, what the nature of their legislation is, and what they are responsive to. Such a representative also has to know what the group that he works for really wants, what the opposing interests are up to, and what the general public's reaction may be. This is obviously no job for a part-time amateur—although often people on the fringe of politics can help. The line between public relations and lobbying is a thin one; lobbying might be defined as the practice of public relations directed toward one very specific and important group.

There are, of course, crooked lobbyists, men who offer bribes, who pander in various ways, and who appeal to ignoble, narrow interests in a manner harmful to the general welfare. Corruptible people will be found also in many other human activities when the stakes are high and the temptations great. There are also honest, well-informed lobbyists who perform a valuable information service for legislators, their supporters, and the public. Many of the complaints about lobbying arise from groups of people who have no adequate representation for their own interests or who were defeated and seek a good excuse to explain their failure to their followers; some complaints come as a political smoke screen to explain legislative failure or inactivity; and still others come from genuinely concerned citizens who are afraid that underpaid, insecure, and sometimes naïve lawmakers may not continue to be honest and independent.

But the right of petitioning government is undeniable as long as democracy endures, and although the ground rules may be altered from time to time, the principle must be preserved. Government and political parties in the United States register the popular will and do not themselves decide it. Government cannot and should not insulate itself from listening to public opinion between election dates.

Lobbying, however, is an area of great sensitivity and subject to quick criticism. How, then, should the important government public be approached?

"Low pressure" is the key in dealing with government administrative people. For example, fact and study reports, truthful and with the sources well identified, are good material. No one can criticize a public relations man for making such reports available or an administrator for looking at them, since government is supposed to be well informed and to hear all sides before acting. Reprints of speeches by prominent or qualified people are also acceptable, although they may not be so well read as is desirable.

Bolder general publicity in a newspaper published in a state capital or upon radio or television might reach the persons at whom it is aimed along with the rest of the general public; but it might also reveal such pressures to public view and hence must be used with care if it is not to bring forth complaints from the opposition. Most big issues have several sides and several sets of lobbyists, acting sometimes in opposition to each other, sometimes in concert. The more apparent one effort is, the quicker and greater the opposition it may arouse and the greater the danger that government will be itself subject to attack if it supports a side that has been too well proclaimed.

Actually, nothing succeeds better with government people than personal contact. A man may establish contact with no immediate purpose beyond "You may want to know me. I represent so and so," and sometimes he may achieve it in the course of belonging to the same groups or of being helpful in other matters. In relations like these no one fools himself very much; the reason for the contact, like that of a salesman with a customer, is admittedly commercial. Yet, oddly enough, genuine liking between people often does spring up in these ways over the years and endures long after its original purpose has been lost. People would, of course, prefer to be liked for themselves alone rather than because of their positions, but motives are often hard to untangle and often it does not pay to examine them too deeply.

Public relations activities with legislative groups in government are more lively, difficult, and dangerous than dealings with administrative departments where tenure is secure, action slow, and the chief fear often that of offending someone important. When the chips are down in a legislative vote, issues will be either passed or scuttled, with resulting rewards or brickbats for the lobbyists who have won or failed. Like elections, these are what public relations people call "hard issues"; one either wins or loses, and there are no consolation prizes for second place. Legislative actions are so close to the limelight of publicity, that overzealous or effective lobbyists may be spotlighted by their competitors or by legislators upon the losing side who seek to explain their failure by shouting that they were swamped by undue influence. Success is never to be counted on; the tide of public opinion turns without warning; and all manner of extraneous issues and deals have a way of swimming into the scene suddenly, turning "sure things" into failures overnight.

The first problem of the legislative lobbyist is to know what's going on —to read, to understand, to be familiar with committee structure (the most important work is usually done in committees), to see the right people, and to present his case—usually not too formally. If a legislator is from a cotton-producing area, for example, a few accurate figures upon the effect of a proposed bill upon the cotton-crop income in his district might be pertinent and enough. These might be given at lunch or over a drink, neither of which is considered entertainment big enough to constitute bribery. In some cases the presentation might be more formal, as at a public hearing. Frequently the heads of schools or professional groups or other organizations will be called in by committees for information, often at their own petition. At the hearing the heads must do the talking, but very often a public relations man will have assembled the material and ideas which they present.

Some lobbyists come out of the ranks of capital-city newspapermen, whose acquaintanceships and observations are useful; others are former government officials or legislators; and others, like educators, come from the professions which maintain them. Some approach the public image of a lobbyist, being obviously well financed, effusive, and friendly; others, equally effective in their fields, may be quiet and conservative in their appearance.

Another way to influence legislative actions—one full of danger—is to take the case directly to the public in order to put pressure upon their elected representatives. Of course public relations activity makes this sort of appeal all the time anyway, but when it starts publicity in the heat of impending legislative action with the obvious intent of building a fire under a legislator right in his own home district, it sometimes amounts to a declaration of war. As Emerson once said, "If you strike at a king, you must kill him."

A legislator, however, has no right to expect immunity from phone calls, letters, or visitors; he is hired to listen. But if he rightly questions the integrity of those who exert such pressure, or if he doubts that it represents the sentiment of his home district, and if calls are critical or threatening, his fear may naturally turn to anger. Honest, calm pleas, truly representing the wishes of his constituency, raise no question about the right to petition, but excited pressures are upsetting. Legislators are just like other people, only perhaps a bit more sensitive, egotistical, and excitable, because it takes a certain hopeful, enthusiastic, warm temperament to enjoy and endure the perils of politics. A legislator may react too violently and illogically to the provocation of pressure, even to the point of endangering his own future. But we cannot expect him to be a cold logician: people act as they will, not as they should.

Public Relations with the Financial World

Dealings with the financial world skyrocket rapidly as more and more companies feel the necessity of telling their story to stockholders, banks, investment houses, security analysts, and other groups which might be of financial assistance at some time. Stockholder relations, discussed earlier, are only a part of financial relations, because cash may come from many other places. Companies need an active market for their securities to improve the corporation's position in mergers or in acquisitions, to create a market for future stock issues, and to broaden the base of stockownership. In 1959 a newsletter from the Public Relations Board, a Chicago counseling firm, put it well by telling this story:

This is a true story. Only the name of the company has been changed.

The Smith Company had been listed on the New York Stock Exchange for nearly thirty years. Two years ago its stock sold at $12 a share, a price which allowed the high yield of 6.6 per cent on the regular dividend. Interest in the stock was slight, despite the company's increasing sales volume and earnings, diversification of operations, and expansion into more profitable areas. Only about four hundred shares were traded each week.

Independent counsel conducted a survey among one hundred New York security brokers and analysts. Eighty-five men had never heard of the company. Twelve remembered the name but did not know one fact about the company. Three knew that the company was listed on the "big board"—and nothing more.

The Smith Company engaged . . . financial public relations counsel. The company's shares subsequently sold for more than $36 a share before a recent two-for-one split, a price that reflected a sharply higher capitalization of earnings. Volume rose to nearly four hundred shares a day.

A new survey of analysts showed one of the reasons why: 86 per cent were well informed of the company's performance and prospects, while the rest at least knew the company's name and where the shares were traded. . . .

Here are some surprising statistics behind the growth of financial public relations:

1. Nearly 50,000 publicly-owned corporations are bidding for the attention of investors through newspapers, financial publications, and security analysts.

2. Fewer than thirty daily newspapers carry more than one full page of financial news. Local corporations, of course, gain precedence for their news. That leaves nearly 50,000 other companies competing for space in perhaps a remaining half page.

3. The same 50,000 companies compete for the time of the security analyst, the backbone of the brokerage business. It is he who researches a company and reports on its value as an investment. His decision is passed along, verbally or by market letter, to his firm's customer men and to investors.

4. The average analyst covers a minimum of three hundred and fifty companies. As many as one hundred pieces of mail cross his desk daily. He is besieged with inquiries about individual securities. And he must still research, evaluate, and write up hundreds of companies annually.

5. Nearly 50,000 companies issue Securities Exchange Commission-required annual reports which they hope will attract the attention of investors and analysts.

The solution? Better news preparation and better cooperation with newsmen. Better liaison with security analysts. Better annual and interim reports. In short, financial public relations. . . .

The consensus of the sophisticated investment world is that (business)

managements will continue to broaden their use of financial public relations as an effective corporate tool. And much credit is given management now for the role it has played in bringing more investors into
"people's capitalism," as it has been called by the head of the New York
Stock Exchange.

When people buy stock in a company, of course, they also become
members of another of its publics (an internal one), but material aimed
at the outside financial community then serves them too.

The Trade Association Public

Every business or occupation in this country has its trade or professional
associations. Lawyers and engineers, rugmakers and hornblowers, railroad operators and plasterers, to mention only a few, band together, all
finding it worthwhile to be in association with each other, though they
may often be competitors within their own ranks. Sometimes an association's goals are to police its own activities or to present a united front
to government or to labor, but often there is also a very good public relations or sales reason.

Carpet or rug manufacturers do not compete with each other alone, or
perhaps even mainly with each other, but rather with alternate ways of
covering floors (or not covering them), such as plastic tile, wood, or
linoleum. When people choose these products, they do not buy woven
carpet material, except perhaps for throw rugs. Since no single carpet
manufacturer can afford to spend all his advertising effort in bucking a
problem which is common to all, the obvious procedure is to get together.
When all chip in, they can make a concerted effort to encourage the use
of carpeting instead of this or that substitute. Only by helping to increase
carpeting's total share of the floor-covering market can each carpet manufacturer acquire more business.

The same story lies behind programs like that of the American Institute
of Men's and Boys' wear, which the clothing manufacturers support in an
effort to make American men more conscious of the importance of dressing
well; of the American Music Conference, which encourages the buying
of horns or pianos to create homemade music; and of the National Highway Users Conference, which wants to increase the amount of highway
travel and shipping in the United States. The clothing-manufacturers group
bucks a trend toward informality in clothing; the musical-instrument
makers face the competition of listening to radio, television, and records;
and the highway users face the competition of other forms of transportation.

Group promotions like these are hard to organize because they demand
complete participation by all in an industry so that no single firm will
get a free ride upon the general promotional effort of all but must con-

tribute its just share. Getting a consensus of agreement from a group upon what shall be done once the money is available, is also often hard. Sales problems are sometimes baffling; there is no guarantee of success; and neither advertising, for which there is seldom an adequate amount of money, nor the most ingenious public relations can overcome a really deep-seated social trend. The most inspired advertising of the American Federation of Musicians couldn't halt the disappearance of costly pit orchestras when sound films arrived in motion-picture houses in the late 1920s; and in recent years the hatters have been having a hard time trying to stem a tendency to go hatless, first among men and then among women. But when public opinion is neutral and even more when it seems to be swinging toward the course advocated, group efforts can often have a marked effect.

In this way trade associations themselves constitute a special public for many businesses. Exerting influence within them is a means of reaching a larger public than any one company could manage to speak to without undue expense and too evident self-interest.

The Farmer Public

A generation ago, when hardly any public relations activity existed, there was a great gulf between city people and their rural neighbors. Farmers were isolated by mud roads, lack of communications, long, hard work, and a necessary absorption in their own interests. But beginning in the 1920s, this division largely disappeared as roads were improved, radio and then television became general, schools were consolidated and improved, and a revolution occurred in farming practices through the introduction of new machinery, new crops, fertilizers, and better agricultural methods. Today the farmers who produce the bulk of the nation's crops are in big business for themselves, often with capital investments worth hundreds of thousands of dollars, and with bookkeeping, tax, and farm-science problems far beyond the comprehension of the average city wage earner.

Yet old farm stereotypes still exist, and many urban people still regard farmers as country bumpkins, apple knockers rolling straws in their mouths and speaking a quaint dialect. In spite of the misapprehension, it is true that most farm people *do* differ from city people in the way they respond to attempts to influence them—recognizing, of course, that cotton farmers, corn-hog farmers, fruit farmers, and truck gardeners, for instance, are all quite different from one another. The alert public relations man will do well to take into account the differences between farmers and city people if he wishes to speak to the farmer most effectively. Various media, such as farm magazines, smaller newspapers, rural radio and television, and direct mail are available to reach farmers. The important thing is how to approach them.

Despite automobiles and more travel, farm people are more isolated in one sense than city people, less so in another. Farmers see fewer people in the course of a week, but they also see fewer strangers. The inhabitants of a very large city seldom look closely at the faces of the people they encounter upon the street, because they do not expect to know them. Farmers almost always look, because if they failed to recognize and to greet their friends, they would be considered high-hat.

Prosperous, well-established farm people move about less than city people and are more deeply rooted in their neighborhoods, although because of drifting renters, factory workers who live on farms, and suburbanization, there are a lot of newcomers in many farm areas today. Farm work hustles a man less than many city jobs, allows him to be more independent, but requires longer hours. Farmers have more time to think, and in these days of widespread communication their thoughts cover wide fields; they tend to think more deeply and to hold convictions more strongly than do city folk, although perhaps over a narrower range. Farming is usually a big personal business today, involving much careful calculation. It depends upon the weather, general prices, and political actions which are beyond any one individual's control. Farmers are classical capitalists who yet find it necessary to use government to unite and control their prices and production.

Because of these facts, farm people tend to be much attached to their own organizations—to farm groups, community-improvement clubs, youth groups such as the 4-H clubs, to schools, and churches. Such connections are often deep, and the opinions of fellow members of these groups and of other neighbors count for much in the attitudes taken by farm people. The higher the scale of living and education of the farmer, the more likely he is to draw his opinions from a wide range, including those presented nationally in the mass media; the smaller the farm operator and the less his education, the more likely he is to seek opinions from immediate neighbors and relatives.

Because they are property holders, farmers tend to be conservative unless driven into radicalism by force of circumstances, to distrust fast and flashy approaches, to count their dollars carefully, to say "no" the first few times that a new idea is presented, to resist pressure, and to move more slowly than city people, who often prize novelty for its own sake. Farmers also tend to be less affected by new ideas and to retain longer those which they have made their own. The better farmers are intelligent, have thought deeply, and often have broader national or world outlooks than city people who are immersed in municipal affairs.

Summary

A list of "publics" could be extended indefinitely. The public for a state conservation department, for example, consists primarily of sportsmen, farmers, foresters, and others; for a pet-food manufacturer it consists of dog and cat owners; and for another manufacturer the public might be just the broad group of men or women.

Almost all public relations practice is specific. It selects publics, analyzes them, plans its actions in relation to their needs and desires, and then aims its communications directly toward these specific publics by whatever means are most suitable and effective. Success depends largely upon how well each of these steps is planned and executed.

ADDITIONAL READING

Special Publics

Griswold, Glenn, and Denny Griswold (ed.): *Your Public Relations, The Standard Public Relations Handbook,* Funk & Wagnalls Company, New York, 1948. (Chapters on public relations with dealers, customers, educators, and the press.)

Hettinger, Herman S.: *Financial Public Relations for the Business Corporation,* Harper & Row, Publishers, Incorporated, New York, 1954.

Lesly, Philip (ed.): *Public Relations Handbook,* Prentice-Hall, Inc., Englewood Cliffs, N.J., 1950. (Chapters on public relations with government, customers, and dealers.)

Lundborg, Louis B.: *Public Relations in Your Local Community,* Harper & Row, Publishers, Incorporated, New York, 1950.

Newcomb, Robert, and Marg Sammons: *Employee Communications in Action,* Harper & Row, Publishers, Incorporated, New York, 1961.

Patterson, John C.: *Association Management,* Harper & Row, Publishers, Incorporated, New York, 1952.

Purcell, Fr. Theodore Vincent: *Blue Collar Man,* Harvard University Press, Cambridge, Mass., 1960.

Some Special Users of
Public Relations
and Their Needs

5

Public relations efforts sometimes fail because their originators are not adequately grounded in the fundamentals of research, action, communication, and evaluation; but they may also fail because the practitioners are ignorant of the particular characteristics of a given type of business or organization. Hence, it is instructive to examine the peculiarities of some of the special areas of public relations practice and to begin to develop skill in their analysis.

At the same time, it should not be forgotten that the practice of public relations is always a *unity*. While the circumstances of their application may vary, the fundamental principles of reaching and influencing people remain the same. A good public relations man can tackle the problems of a bank, an educational institution, or a retail store with equal success— *if* he learns enough about the nature of the organization whose problems he is attempting to solve. The advantage of specializing in public relations for particular types of accounts, is accompanied by the big disadvantage of so identifying oneself mentally with an organization or type of business that one becomes incapable of seeing how it looks to outsiders. Loyalty and concern are sometimes bought at the price of blindness.

There is no need to learn a different kind of public relations for each separate business, occupation, and cause. With diligent effort, the skilled practitioner can readily adapt his work from one area of practice to another, because the fundamentals are always the same. The successes of the great public relations counseling firms constantly demonstrate this unity of principle. Their comparative unfamiliarity with particular fields of action is generally quite offset by their understanding of basic processes

69

of communication and of the nature of the publics involved, and by a wealth of varied experience in many similar fields. Skill in analysis will dictate the application of principles to specific needs. Long exposure to new ideas is often a highly effective catalyst because it directs thinking toward the important receivers of communication rather than toward its self-conscious senders and results in greater ability to see both sides.

The Public Relations of Trade and Industry

Smaller retailers and service establishments. The size of a business is often a faulty basis upon which to generalize about its public relations activities. For example, the problems of a small grocery supermarket in Brooklyn, New York, are quite different from those of a store in Algona, Iowa (population 5,000) with the same yearly receipts; and a small hobby shop just off State Street in Chicago is obviously serving a public unlike the customers of a drugstore in Jackson, Mississippi, although both may have approximately the same annual total sales. These smaller stores have in common only a tendency toward more personal relations with their customers, smaller staffs, less opportunity for specialization of personnel within the business, and less money than larger establishments.

Much of what might be formalized public relations within a large institution becomes simple personal relations and standard operating procedure for everyone in a small organization. It goes without saying that clerks should be polite and interested, that the proprietor should try to remember the names and needs of good customers, and that the store should be clean and attractive; but these things should be done anyway. The real problem is to find ways to develop memorable, distinctive qualities in the business and to communicate them in some way to the people from whom trade may reasonably be expected to be drawn.

In a specialty shop, even in a large city, this kind of communication may not be impossible. A list of customers can be compiled and direct mail used to reach them. Small advertising can be placed in specialized parts of large publications, for example, in sports or garden sections of newspapers. The shop can participate in exhibits and special events. Despite intense news competition, it might hope for occasional publicity from the press, especially in suburban or neighborhood newspapers. Talks might be given to appropriate groups or award programs arranged. The main limitations are the operator's time and money, but the vehicles for public relations communication are often available if he has sufficient ingenuity and time to develop them.

In nonspecialty stores, such as the retail grocery in Algona, Iowa, the problem of reaching people can be mastered easily because of the small size of the market. Advertising space is readily available at a reasonable cost in the local newspaper which goes to everyone; publicity is easily achieved; time can be bought upon local radio stations with excellent coverage opportunities; and establishing personal connections with customers is easy. The main problems are to give the store a personality, to provide good products at competitive prices, and to sell ideas about good eating instead of concentrating on peddling staples. Such small, unspecialized businesses often do best in small communities where their size is commensurate with the size of the mass communications media available. The grocery store in Algona, for example, can perhaps buy a page in the local newspaper at a cost of less than $100; but in a large city the same $100 spent by a grocery store would buy only a very small ad, sandwiched in between more imposing neighbors like a minnow among whales.

The problems of the small supermarket in Brooklyn, part of a great metropolitan city, and of the ordinary drugstore in Jackson, Mississippi, are the most difficult and challenging. Perhaps the difficulty of communicating with people is the chief reason why this type of small proprietorship has almost disappeared in big cities within the past generation. The small store is at a disadvantage in prices, variety of merchandise, and advertising opportunities. If the owner cannot establish valid points of difference and distinction and communicate them to the proper publics, he may fail in business. His limited capital, credit, and supply sources, usually do not allow him to make economical use of the mass media of communication in a large city, such as the daily newspapers, radio, and television.

The problem of division of human abilities also enters in. A proprietor who has to run all aspects of a store usually has little time left for effective public relations and only rarely competes in this field with large organizations which can hire men who are skilled in planning communication and make it their sole business. Yet such skill in promotion, advertising, and public relations is vital to the small proprietor if he is to prosper in the face of competition. Otherwise his chief dependence is likely to be upon his employees' acceptance of longer hours and lower wages, or upon poorly paid self-employment, convenience goods, and area growth or fortunate location—all of which are likely to be transient advantages.

There are, of course, additional ways in which the small proprietor's problems can be eased, such as specializing within certain areas and engaging in cooperative effort, but they are not easy. They constitute a subject in themselves, which should be studied elsewhere by those interested.

Larger retailers and other businesses. Among larger retailers the competition is usually no less intense than among small businesses, but the available resources in time and money are more commensurate with the modern media of mass communications and the large concentrations of customers in modern urban centers.

In these large retail stores and service establishments, the employees properly become the first concern of the public relations department because the owners can no longer know all their employees well personally and supervise their activities. To the store's customers, the employees *are* the store.

Polite, capable employees contribute most importantly toward establishing a good image of this type of business in the minds of customers. But such men and women are hard to attract and keep. The selection, payment, and control of employees usually come directly under the responsibility of the personnel management department; but the workers' desire to enter the business, their willingness to accept training, their information, activities, and encouragement are closely related to public relations because they are basically communications problems. Employees are people of the community and do not magically adopt different minds and personalities when they walk into the store every morning. Many of their ideas have evolved before they became employees; many of their special concepts of the store are formed by their outside contacts.

People try to live up to whatever standard of conduct seems to be expected of them by whatever groups they value.

Large stores also advertise their merchandise extensively in local daily newspapers and by other means. Advertising is primarily the responsibility of top management and of the advertising department, which works closely with merchandise experts. Such advertising not only tells what the store has for sale but also expresses its personality. In recent tests, for instance, a group of Chicago housewives, shown advertisements from an Atlanta, Georgia, department store with which they were quite unfamiliar and from which the store name had been removed, were still able to describe the nature of the store quite accurately from the appearance of the ads alone. Readers associate certain types, layouts, and illustrational styles with certain kinds of merchandise and store patterns. Management must decide what image the store has or wishes to have, and then choose an appropriate physical advertising style. Projecting a proper and favorable public image of a store through its advertising demands the constant cooperation of artists, writers, and advertising-layout people, as well as those who select and price the merchandise to be advertised.

However, good advertising alone cannot create store identity, because any large city may have several stores which have nearly the same types of merchandise, price range, and advertising. Besides, in recent years store loyalties have weakened among customers because of their greater exposure to many communications media, their extreme personal mobility by automobile within an urban area, their change of residence from city to city—a tendency that brings large numbers of new, unattached customers—and a tremendous growth of population. The problems of downtown stores, in particular, have been rendered especially difficult by suburban movements of population which have placed customers at constantly increasing distances from the central stores.

The changes have led to the increased importance of at least three types of public relations activities in the retail field which are directed toward the establishment of store personality—institutional advertising, community services, and storewide promotions.

None of these are new, but in a time when it is hard to find any exclusive merchandise, lower prices, or favored locations, the feelings of customers about a particular firm because of its people, its record of reliability, or social responsibility, may be more important than ever before. Unless all department stores are to become discount houses, the background of a store, its projects in aid of young or old people, its interest in public education or health or recreation, its support of national goals or needs, its concern with the spiritual side of life as well as the material goods in which stores primarily deal are elements of more importance than ever before. None of these can overcome poor location, bad pricing, unattractive merchandise, or poor advertising. A good store image can assist success; it can make 100 into 120 but cannot stretch 40 into 80.

Among the public relations activities which become of increasing importance today are the storewide promotional events which give new reasons to go shopping at old places. Shopping should be an adventure, an education. If it isn't, what would attract people to one store rather than to another except convenience and price?

A good illustration of a storewide promotional campaign was the program staged a number of years ago by southern California manufacturers and tourist interests. They made up a complete California store promotion, including merchandise, window displays, menus for store restaurants, fashion shows, motion pictures, historic photos, paintings, maps, mission bells and reproductions, and well-known California personalities. This type of promotion elevates a store for a few days above and beyond being just "Scott's Department Store" and makes it exciting, glamorous, and interesting—a genteel combination of sideshow, boardwalk, museum, and travel-bureau window.

Such good storewide promotions are not easy to find; the danger of disappointing the buying public is worse than no event at all; and such attractions cannot be spaced too close together. The fact remains, however, that many big stores are commonplace, offering familiar merchandise at routine prices, in a competent but dull way; and if this is true, the customer is likely to buy where the prices are lowest (or at least where she thinks they are lowest) and where the parking is easiest. Most stores could do much more than they have in developing interesting special promotions.

In small stores the personality of the store is primarily the "lengthened shadow" of the proprietor; large businesses, with far more resources, can and should develop a planned image and project it to customers through the mass media by way of public relations techniques.

The Public Relations of Industry

The fundamental difference between an industry and a retailing or service establishment is that, in most instances, the problem of dealing with a mass of customers is one step removed from the manufacturer rather than his first, constant, and most immediate concern. Industries primarily make things, and retailers sell to the public what other people make.

Small industries usually sell to larger industries or to sales organizations, their goods moving perhaps to distant locations over a wide area. The close relations which small industries need with both their suppliers and their markets are brought about often by personal contact, salesmanship, and perhaps a limited amount of specialized trade-paper advertising. Small industries usually do not need the wide public patronage which is the lifeblood of a retail or service establishment.

There are hundreds of small industries in every large industrial city, specializing in all sorts of products. Each may have from a few dozen to a few hundred employees, and the disappearance or the doubling in size of any one of them would hardly be felt by the city as a whole—crucial as it would be to those directly involved. Their main problems are technical, financial, and personal; and the big currents of general business climate, major labor relations, government actions, and national public attitudes are beyond their control except, to some extent, through associational efforts. The boss in this type of industry succeeds because he knows the right people to buy his product, because the foremen get along well with the men, the engineers are ingenious in finding ways to pare costs, the bookkeeping office is diligent, everyone says "Good morning," and everyone can apparently be induced to turn out slightly more than a day's work for a day's pay. All these idyllic conditions contribute to success under conditions of sharp competition.

Small industries also have their important communications problems. Sometimes public relations and publicity can be applied to selling their products if they are at all noteworthy or unusual, and may catapult obscure little firms toward success or profitable mergers. Within themselves small industries seldom have the staff resources for specialized public relations development, but they offer a fruitful field for the work of small public relations counseling firms or for the public relations arms of advertising agencies which may also handle their limited trade-paper business. In fact, public relations counseling firms tend, on the one hand, to serve these small organizations which cannot afford to support internal public relations staffs, and on the other hand, tend to give high-level, objective counsel to larger firms whose main need is for new thought and good advice.

What we have called a small industry, however, when located in a small-town environment, gains both in stature and responsibility. In a town of 3,000 people it is probably the leading employer, "the plant," usually eagerly welcomed with offers of land, low taxes, and low wage rates. Its small payroll makes the difference between profits and stagnation for local merchants, supports school systems, and upholds town income.

With this prestige, however, a small industry in a small town finds that certain things are expected of it, such as reasonable cleanliness, modest participation in civic affairs, local purchasing when possible, some employee information and activities, and a certain amount of social contact with the townspeople. Laborers may be cheaper in smaller places, but they are also limited in numbers and in skill; and since they have the great automobile-based mobility of all American people, they may always be lured away to distant places by greater opportunities. A firm's cultivation of good will and its reputation as a good place to work may be much more important than it seems. Such public relations functions in small-city industries are usually the responsibility of the general manager, his assistant, and the superintendents, and often involve employee committees and other participation.

Small chain industries in small towns have the additional problems of transient management and of the habit of local personnel to pass the buck to distant headquarters whenever anything is wrong or unpleasant —sometimes to forestall the wrath of unconsulted managers, sometimes to avoid responsibility for unpleasant actions at home. Such chain industry may be respected and feared because of its national connections and financial power, but it may also be less liked than a local plant and so may need additional promotion if it is to become a part of the community.

Large industries, employing thousands of people, since they constantly face a breakdown of personal communications, find planned communication programs with many publics a matter of great importance. The old days when the boss could know and talk to everybody are long gone. Employees need to be informed, encouraged, and listened to; the support of stockholders and financial sources becomes vital; the good will of the community is involved in such matters as the recruiting of new employees, fair treatment in regard to local taxes, costs of utilities and services, police and fire protection, and even sales of merchandise. Large industries have much more to give to their communities; but they also have much more at stake, since their capital investments are greater and often not easily moved, and their labor problems may also be more acute.

Large industries are a part of the national or even the world scene. National public opinion, as reflected in Washington, may determine their profit-or-loss statements, and competition spreads, not only with other similar industries within the nation but also overseas. Big industries are not necessarily helpless in the face of national and world trends; sometimes alone, and often in association, they have the power to help direct and channel them. Large industries were among the first to recognize the importance of public relations to their growth and prosperity, and they are now the major employers of public relations specialists in the United States.

The Public Relations of Banks

Imagine being in a business in which all the merchants operate in about the same way and have the same goods to sell at almost identical prices! Bankers are in just such a business. All banks look much alike, offer much the same customer services in the same way, lend money at the same interest rates, and then pay depositors the same returns upon their savings. This being the case, why should customers prefer one bank to another? Yet they do!

Banks are in competition, not only with each other, but also with building and loan associations, cooperative credit unions, consumer small loan companies, and the credit departments of all sorts of businesses from automobile dealers to department stores. There are many ways in which to save or to borrow money besides using banks. Investing in stocks and bonds helps corporations—and even the government—to compete with banks for the public's funds; and other uses of money, such as simply spending it, which is attractive in inflationary times, offer a kind of competition.

In addition, the public has a bad image of banks, which is a legacy from a previous generation, compounded out of folk tales of flinthearted bankers and unhappy memories of the great crash of 1929–1933 in which many American bank depositors lost a great deal of money despite the solidity implied by heavy bronze name plates, granite pillars, marble halls, and impeccably dressed bank officials.

To many people money is a strange and corrupting influence, understandable only in small amounts and to be spent for immediate benefits. The ancient stigma against moneylenders clings to "filthy lucre"; its power and use as a measure of success is resented; and the very Greek-temple architectural glory of the typical old-style bank, intended to reassure and impress the small citizen, also frightens and depresses him. Such an awesome temple is obviously intended only for doing business with the demi-gods and not for such trivial human wants as borrowing money for a new car, refinancing an elderly mortgage, or saving for travel or for a Christmas fund. And in talking about money matters, most people are somewhat abnormal anyway.

Another problem of banks arises from their relations with government. Thanks to the Federal Deposit Insurance Corporation and to closer regulation, bank depositors no longer fear for their savings, but they are often inclined to favor yet more regulation and control. If this amount has worked well, more would work better. Today there seems to be little popular drive toward government banking, as it exists either in the postal savings plan or in the systems now favored in some other countries, but there might be sometime. And in addition, banks are also involved in many places in the consideration of projected laws about branch banking, taxes upon bank deposits, regulation of hours, interest rates, and limitations upon their fields of lending. Regulation of bank mergers is also often a major issue.

What steps do banks usually take to improve their public relations?

1. The place of business is more important to the image of a bank than it is to many other institutions. Since banks deal in a service, the location must be convenient, primarily to business people. Downtown, this means a prime corner in a good block location; in the rapidly expanding suburbs, it means drive-in facilities and parking.

Since, to uninformed customers, the manifestation of the bank itself is found in the bank building rather than its balance sheets or the integrity or ability of its staff, bank atmosphere presents a nice problem in public impressions. On the one hand, a bank has to seem substantial and efficient. It can be modern in its architecture or colonial (to suggest sturdy early American virtues of thrift), but in no case can a bank afford to look jerry-built, temporary, or insecure. On the other hand, a bank's atmosphere should be warm, somewhat intimate, and homelike. It should have a floor space large enough for traffic movement, necessary safety features, and private consultation facilities. All these requirements present a problem to the architect which is still only partly solved.

Because the bank buildings are so much a personification of the bank itself, they frequently appear in advertisements and upon letterheads. The modern symbolism for banks is yet to be fully developed; the devices recently adopted by Chase Manhattan and others are of interest. Meanings come to be attached to symbols quite apart from the nature of the symbols themselves, if indeed they have any meaning alone.

2. Employees are particularly important in service institutions such as banks because their attitudes, competence, and appearance do much to determine public reactions. Unfortunately, the public stereotype of a bank clerk tends to run to an underpaid, meticulous slave who occasionally breaks into the headlines by embezzling a million dollars and running off to Brazil with the wife of the teller in the next cage or perhaps with a church choir singer. Examining

the employees of any modern bank or keeping a statistical check upon the frequency of embezzlement will quickly show that these beliefs have little foundation; but the persistent image shows that public means of communication, such as institutional advertising, news, and feature publicity, as well as actions, might be used more than they are to contradict the impression.

3. As substantial institutions, holding the keys to financial undertakings, banks are expected to lead in community progress. Bank people are expected to work on Community Chest drives, to be active in Rotary and Kiwanis, and to lead in city-planning commissions. Unpaid as it is, this service has its own reward by bringing bankers into contact with many important people with whom they may also do business, and it results in much good publicity.

4. Since thrift is still preached as a virtue in America, banks have a ready entry into the schools with savings plans, personal-budget advice, and economic information.

5. Bank advertising has increased steadily in volume and in quality in recent years. Its tone is particularly important since a bank deals in an intangible service.

6. Minor stunts and activities (always properly dignified) can be of service in establishing the personality of a bank, such as returning all change on a given day in freshly washed and polished coins and newly printed bills, holiday music in a bank lobby, or special tours and receptions.

7. But, above all, since a bank depends upon service, the greatest asset a public relations man can have is a lively, sympathetic, imagination that will enable him to put himself constantly into a customer's place and to think: "How would I feel about that treatment of an overdraft?" "Would it be embarrassing to ask for a loan?" "Why were my check charges last month $2.50 and only $1.80 the month before?" The imperatives in bank public relations are to anticipate questions before they arise and to provide a reservoir of good will against inevitable moments of misunderstanding and dispute.

Public Relations Problems of the Utilities

The public relations staffs of the telephone companies, the electricity companies, the gas companies, and a smaller number of privately owned city water companies, are usually among the best in the nation, with the longest experience and the most carefully planned courses of action looking far ahead.

Their excellence is not an accident. Public utilities sell a largely intangible but vital service, and the whole functioning of civilized urban life depends upon their constant watchfulness. No one notices the gas or the electricity or the water until it stops coming, and then everything goes to pieces—homes grow cold, babies cry, hospitals are plunged into blackness, thieves prowl the streets, fires rage unchecked, and even bridge-club arrangements may be seriously interrupted. Public utilities are monopolies regulated by the government, and they hold their monopolistic position by virtue of their promise to give good service efficiently and courteously. If they fail to do so, a clamor for government ownership is always ready to burst forth.

In arguing for a system of private ownership, the utilities contend that because they are business-managed, they operate more efficiently and are more interested in progress, that they pay taxes, give low rates which have been relatively reduced over the years, are good employers and good citizens, and earn only a reasonable profit. Their continued existence is evidence that most Americans believe these things to be true.

They are attacked by those who would like to see more government ownership of public services. They are charged with too high profits and sometimes with refusal to extend their service into unprofitable areas. Critics remember that some private power companies were slow in supplying remote rural areas and that their recalcitrance encouraged the development of the federally financed Rural Electrification Administration. Water-power developments, also, have usually fallen into Federal hands, since the multiplicity of river uses—flood control, irrigation, navigation, and the like—often seem to justify the cost of high dams which would be uneconomical for power production alone. Water power, however, is often seasonal, depending upon varying river flow; when the need arises, as it did in the case of the Tennessee Valley Authority electrical system, to add steam-power generating plants to help balance the load, private power companies complain bitterly that their domain is being invaded by subsidized competition.

The big, unsolved struggle of the 1960s and the future may be precipitated by the atomic generation of electric power. The wartime birth of atomic energy and the related government control of fissionable matter gave a running start to the advocates of public power in this field, and the challenge was not refused by the private power companies. Various atomic reactors and associated electric generating plants, both private and public and of several designs, have been built over the country, most of them at a much greater cost than could be offset by any present savings in generating electricity by conventional coal plants. Construction costs have also often proved higher than anticipated. In the early 1960s extensive tests were being conducted by private power companies to see if the expense of generating electricity from atomic sources could be materially reduced. If it could be, they intended to be ready to supply the service to their customers.

The extent of public ownership of utilities varies. Water plants are usually owned by the city or by a water district, perhaps because water is the oldest utility, most common in its supply and need, and is thought of, along with air, as a general good. Although predominantly in private hands, the electric power industry is often city-owned, or is federally owned in connection with most major water power production, or is cooperatively owned in rural REA areas; in one state, Nebraska, it is entirely publicly owned. Gas, because of its distant sources of supply, is usually privately owned. Telephone systems, with the exception of a few small-town or rural systems, are almost entirely privately owned, largely through the American Telephone and Telegraph Company and its many Bell Telephone Company subsidiaries. (In England, the telephone service is operated by the Post Office.)

The private utility business has had its historic problems, also. During the 1920s Samuel Insull and others pyramided holding company upon holding company, only to see their unreal empires collapse with the ruin of many small investors in the 1929 crash and give the whole utility business a bad name. The conspicuous expenditures of some utility heads in this period upon big homes and estates, company-financed parties, and hunting lodges were poor public relations also; but these tycoons were not alone, then or now, in their extravagance.

Because utility services are a necessity, the public feels a sense of helplessness when faced with a rate raise because it can secure no alternative supply. Increasing the price of butter a few cents provokes no great outcry, because people feel that using margarine or using less butter is an answer, whether they actually do so or not. But there is no easy way to get along with less electricity, less gas, less water, or less telephone service nowadays; in fact, modern living demands more and more of these services all the time; automatic controls and labor-saving devices multiply as suburban living expands. Despite more efficient production, rising costs on the post-war wave of inflation have forced utility costs upwards (even though the advance has been perhaps less than for other cost-of-living items); and, in any event, more services used mean higher bills. Every one of these rate raises and higher bills involves potential political danger.

The public relations solutions to these problems attempted by private public utilities have been numerous and largely successful.

Employees are carefully selected and are trained and promoted from within the ranks. Long service, steady pay, and resulting loyalty are the rule. Employee information services are excellent, and good citizenship is encouraged and rewarded.

Utility stockholders are sought from local service areas where their interest in dividends and in company growth will help counter their customer interests in the lowest possible rates. Stockholder information services are excellent.

A complete financial picture is presented to the employees, the stockholders, and the general public. Since utilities are semipublic institutions anyway, with relatively low dividend returns upon their securely invested capital and are required to report their affairs in detail, a complete report is a natural step, not revealing anything that would not be generally known.

Plans for expansion and the continuance of good service are always well publicized. Low rates and the many benefits obtained from public utility services are stressed.

Good citizenship and the boosting of local service areas are continuous. Typical activities include advertising campaigns advocating the location of a business in a certain state, and the erection of large highway poster boards outside service-area towns telling about their outstanding advantages and welcoming visitors. Awards may be given for civic improvements or for the use of modern agricultural methods; schools may be aided and worthy causes assisted generally. Many of these efforts could also be performed by local chambers of commerce, by service clubs, and by other groups of interested citizens, but the fact is that often no such responsibility would be assumed if the utility company did not take the lead.

Both from necessity and long practice, public utility companies have become among the nation's best practitioners of public relations.

The Problems of Public Transportation

Trains, buses, airlines, ferries, and a few steamer services are public utilities also, but the conditions under which they operate are very different from those prevailing among the gas, electricity, or telephone service companies.

A public bus line in a city may have a franchised monopoly, and a suburban railroad may enjoy a similar privilege; yet in these days of automobile travel and decentralization, both companies probably face low profits or losses. Many people have alternatives to using their services, and such transportation companies are no longer the sole suppliers that they once were.

In intercity travel the competition can be even greater. Railroads, buses, and airlines compete with other similar ground or air services and with each other, and all battle the private automobiles for passenger trade and the trucks and waterways for freight haulage. They undergo regulation, but except in isolated instances, have no monopoly. Also, in contrast to the services of electricity or gas utilities, those of a transportation company are visible and differ in quality: This airline is felt to be better than that one; this train has a more convenient or scenic routing; the waiters are more polite on this railroad diner; or the meals are better on that airline. Although feelings may not be so keen as they once were, people develop strong attachments or dislikes for particular railroads or airlines and for types of transportation service, such as buses or subways. Public transportation has character, color, and occasional accidents—a physical being and public presence not shared to the same extent by water, gas, or telephone services. Travel plays a great part in customers' life experience as is shown by rail-fan clubs, steamboat buffs, the tears shed at the departure of the last streetcar, and transport museums maintained by enthusiastic amateurs

Public carriers have two main problems—getting customers and obtaining government approval for adequate routes and rates. The private business of transportation is hopelessly intertwined with government through the public interest, the use of publicly built or maintained highways and waterways, postal and other subsidies, a qualified right of eminent domain in the construction of routes, and a great effect upon the "public interest, convenience, and necessity." On the highways and waterways, government shares its routes with private operators ranging from yachtsmen and small-car owners to farmers' trucks, fleets of Great Lakes ore ships, and foreign-flag shipowners who also ply the inland seas, rivers, and harbors.

The main contacts which the public has with transportation companies come in the fields of equipment, employees, and information.

A stainless-steel streamliner train to maintain daily service on a transcontinental railroad line may cost more than 30 million dollars (see the Canadian Pacific Railroad streamliner-launching case cited in Chapter 9). Modern attractive equipment, well cared for and publicized, is fundamental to good public relations in transportation.

Employee courtesy and efficiency also contribute to favorable public reaction to a transportation system. They can be developed through careful selection of employees, training, rewards and recognition, a supply of general background information, and specific informational help as needed. A breakdown on a railway commuter line, for example, may make thousands of office workers late getting home for supper and is certain to result in scores of inquiries addressed to conductors and brakemen the following morning. These employees should have answers or should at least know what to do or say if they do not have the answers.

The public has so much interest in transportation that it should always be fully informed. It should be told particularly about accidents and their causes, changes in equipment, and route changes. (The American Airlines case reported in Chapter 12 is a good illustration of this policy and its result.) Press relations should be open, and informative publicity releases and advertising should be used frequently.

The Public Relations of the Media of Mass Communications

Newspapers, radio and television stations, and magazines are generally thought of in connection with their own communicatory content—their news stories, entertainment, and advertising. Yet they are also institutions in their own right and have public images of their own. Readers may feel that one newspaper is reliable but dull, and that another, perhaps less trustworthy, is more interesting. A listener may criticize a television station for making pots of money although it contributes little to the community. One magazine may seem to speak with authority while another is ignored.

Why? In the past two or three decades, progressive publishers and broadcasters have become aware of these differences, and public relations departments, or promotion departments which concern themselves to a large extent with public relations, are now almost standard on all larger American newspapers, broadcasting stations, and magazines.

Newspapers. What is newspaper public relations?

Most American newspapers today are published in one place, usually a city, and most are also monopolies in their home territory—largely because publishing two big newspapers in any but the very largest cities would be as economically wasteful as supporting two light companies or two telephone companies. Although newspapers provide an information service almost in the nature of a public utility, they cannot be regulated as utilities are, because they have the right of free speech—"freedom of the press." Newspaper employees come into contact with the public frequently. If the news staff turns out a good publication, if the circulation department distributes it well, and if the advertising people are accurate and enterprising, what more does the publication need to do than to be satisfied and to count the dollars?

Quite a bit! Readers expect their newspapers to do the expected things well and complain sharply if they don't, but to achieve the greatest public respect and liking, a newspaper must go much above and beyond the ordinary call of duty. A newspaper is a personality, and a planned public relations effort helps to invest it with the strongest and most attractive character. A newspaper speaks for itself only to a degree; it also needs to be spoken about and to act. People do not necessarily know all about a newspaper because they read it and because the paper itself is a medium of communication. Readers usually ask certain questions.

1. Who works for the paper? What kind of people are they, and why should a reader feel confident in relying on them for information?

2. What does the paper do to better its community, the nation, and the world, beyond distributing news? Vital as this function is, it should imply an obligation of leadership—provided it is not carried to the point of domination.

3. What is the history of the publication? What is its personality?

Such major needs of newspaper public relations go far beyond the best standard operating procedure of simply producing a good product and selling it well.

But why attempt newspaper public relations at all? Won't virtue (in a communications medium) be apparent and speak for itself? The best answer is to engage in research. Get public-opinion surveyors to go around the streets, stores, and homes of a town talking to people. Find out how many are suspicious of newspaper motives, convinced that news is being suppressed or altered, resentful of the power of the newspaper, and unaware of its citizenship and service. Ask the same questions of young people in high schools or colleges. See how many would consider going into journalism as a life work. Talk to their teachers.

A newspaper cannot expect to be popular with all of the people all of the time. Publishing the news in itself brings out enough unpleasant facts to make enemies, and errors and mistakes inevitably creep in; but there is no good reason why a newspaper's vices and failures should always be apparent and its virtues unknown. It might profit by trying to be understood and respected.

A good newspaper is expected to report the facts as fully, accurately, and completely as its own income and area of service allow it to do; to express its own editorial opinions but to keep them in plainly recognizable editorial space; and to present also the reasoned opinions of others upon various sides of important current issues. Then it is expected to go an extra mile or two by aiding others to achieve community and world betterment in many ways and by being a unifying force and spokesman for its people, the readers.

Newspapers today no longer operate in the news vacuum they occupied almost alone in the early 1920s. Readers can listen to or look at many other conveyors of information, and the advertiser can usually spend his money in a wide variety of ways. A newspaper today, though it can succeed without planned public relations, cannot be so well read, so much respected, so influential, and so profitable as it might be.

Radio and television differ from newspapers in that they usually face heavy competition from other broadcasting stations; they have no physical being which people can look at and feel as they do a newspaper or a magazine; and they are usually largely devoted to entertainment. In addition, the content of radio and television is principally sponsored by advertising and can frequently be heard or seen from several stations in the same form by the same listeners; even news and public-service programs frequently come from national-network sources rather than from a local source. Most stations, also, do not express editorial views, and both their function as a common carrier and the FCC regulations, will probably make this reticence more the rule than the exception.

For these reasons, establishing a vital personality for a local broadcasting station is somewhat more difficult and perhaps less immediately necessary than for a newspaper; but it is often vigorously and sometimes successfully attempted. To the listener, however, the personality of the station lies to a great degree in the content of its broadcasts, and public relations faces a problem influencing this public image and in going beyond it. The main problem is to make a nonmaterial broadcasting signal into a real personality by means of visual devices, background information, public activities, and promotions which demonstrate effectiveness and service. The more "real" a popular station can be, the easier it is to sell advertising and to exert local influence. Getting listeners, however, depends primarily upon good programming and promotion.

Magazines are usually directed toward special reader audiences and are not rooted in a place as are newspapers, or even so localized as broadcasting stations. A fishing magazine, for example, selects a sportsman audience from over a wide area; a farming magazine goes to farmers; and a machinists' magazine goes to machinists. Like newspapers, magazines have a certain physical being; they look and feel a certain way. No one is likely to mistake *Holiday* or *Fortune* for *Successful Farming* or *True Confessions*. Each is right for its audience.

Because of these specialized audiences, magazines should by nature have more personality than any of the other printed media. With the exception of the few large weeklies of truly general national circulation, like *Look, Life,* or the *Saturday Evening Post,* magazines should express themselves more fully and be more active within their special fields than other journals. Their public relations should be an extension and personification of this magazine character in visible ways, so that readers and advertisers can be aware of their personality. It should create reader loyalty and interest, aid renewals, and prepare the way for the constant problem of successful direct-mail solicitation of subscriptions over a wide area—a matter which grows increasingly expensive and difficult as competition increases. Yet surprisingly little is done in effective public relations by many magazines, perhaps because of the diffusion of the audiences or perhaps because of the hard struggle for circulation which absorbs all their energies.

Magazine public relations often takes the form of reprint books of previously published content, award programs within the magazine's field of special interest, and general publicity about writers and articles. Much more could be done—for example, sponsoring seminars upon problems suggested by the magazine's preoccupations, aiding the education of young people, and developing new areas of interest or of profit for readers and advertisers.

The Public Relations of Agriculture

The phrase "public relations of agriculture" does not refer to the problem of how to reach and influence agricultural people, which was discussed in Chapter 4, but rather to the problems of relations with the general national public shared by American agriculture and its associated activities, such as food processing, the manufacture of agricultural machinery, and agricultural education.

American agriculture today is far different from what it was only a generation ago. The great changes affecting the practice of public relations in the United States in that period have also greatly affected farming. As machinery, new crops, and new fertilizers have increased yields and lessened the need for manpower, farms have become fewer and larger, subsistence farming has diminished, and its operators have drifted off to the cities to become factory hands or gasoline service-station operators. Many farmers are now part-time factory employees themselves, with divided interests. Cities have penetrated rural areas, and new highways have brought city and country close together. The amount of capital required to establish a large farming operation has become so huge (perhaps hundreds of thousands of dollars, if a farmer starts from the beginning in a typical Midwestern corn-hog operation, for example) that it is no longer possible for a young man and his bride to begin real farming with a few thousand dollars, build their own house, and raise a family to grow up on the land they have cultivated.

Farming has become a large and complex business, as efficient, in a less apparent way to city people, as the impressive automated factories which have been so much discussed. Every year fewer farmers turn out more crops, and the percentage of farmers in the United States declines. In 1910, for example, there were 32 million farmers in the United States, or 34 per cent of the nation's total population. By 1960 the number had shrunk to 21 million farmers, or only about 12 per cent of the nation's total population of about 180 million. At the same time the prices of farm products rose only about 2½ times, while nonfarm income rose much more rapidly. The consumer in the United States now expends a smaller proportion of his income upon food and a larger proportion upon housing, cars, and vacations.

Yet this most commendable progress has brought with it much trouble for the American farmer. Farm operation is a continuous, long-term program. If a dairyman has a surplus of milk, he cannot just close down the factory, lay off the hands, go into another line, or wait for better times. He has to keep producing (in fact, he is driven into producing more at lower cost) or go out of the dairy business entirely, sometimes at considerable loss—as many have done. His cow factory is geared to nature, and production depends upon rainfall, temperature, and other factors which he cannot control. Moreover, many American farm products compete with those from other parts of the world which supply identical quality at sometimes lower production cost. Farming is an atomistic business, composed of many millions of operators who, unlike a smaller number of industrialists, would find great physical difficulty in getting together to agree upon what prices to charge and what amounts to produce. The farmer's wages are his profits, and the organization of farm unions and of strikes is ordinarily not a satisfactory means of increasing farm prices. If wheat growers should strike, consumers would simply turn to other foods; if any strike were effective enough to threaten the nation's health, the Federal government would step in.

Under these circumstances, American farmers early turned to political ways of bettering their lot and getting what they considered to be a fairer share of the national income. In 1910, for example, the large numbers of farmers and their even larger political representation, based upon our governmental system which represents land as well as people, were able to gain great power. The need of farm products in the two world wars shored up their position. But now they find themselves in increasingly difficult circumstances. The pattern of national and state representation in government is changing, and farmers are in danger of becoming an exploited minority. Their probable fate might be like that of the peasantry of industrialized countries in Europe and Asia during the various social revolutions.

Alliances between farmers and labor groups have succeeded very little, since farmers want higher prices for the food they sell and lower prices for the farm labor they buy and for the many manufactured products—the tractors, fencing, or fertilizers—which go into farming; and laborers want lower prices for food, higher wages, and perhaps less of their taxes spent upon farm-price supports. Many industrial interests are at variance with farmers' goals also, preferring lower prices for food or raw material, and higher prices for manufactured goods. Often labor and industry have combined to raise wages and prices together, at the same time complaining about government efforts to regulate farm production and to keep up farm prices.

Thus the agricultural problem in the United States increasingly involves public relations and public understanding. City people are often ignorant of the changes in modern farming, of its efficiency, and the size of its investment. The conditions of individual farming force American farmers to engage in political action for the regulation and pricing of their production which is comparable to that possible in many industries through the actions of large companies and industry-wide unions. The facts about American farming are not well told and are little understood, and a farm stereotype arises in the public mind in which a robber baron in a solid gold Cadillac succeeds the bucolic hick, with resulting danger for the future understanding of the national economy. Even if farmers today constitute only about 12 per cent of the population, they are a very important 12 per cent and mean much more than this figure would suggest in total purchasing power, stability, and influence upon the national well-being.

The farm public relations problem has only recently begun to be tackled, and that very hesitantly.

The Public Relations of Trade Associations

Every important type of businessman in the nation from furrier to plumber, from dog breeder to small retail merchant, belongs to one or more trade associations, each with its secretary and staff, its publications, meetings, and goals. The fact that trade associations exist in such profusion indicates that they serve a need in a modern democratic economy which could not be met in any other manner.

Trade associations exchange information, promote the sale or development of products, establish standards, regulate the activities of their members, and enable their membership to speak with a united voice on economic, social, and governmental problems which may affect their general welfare.

In many cities, for example, when a charity solicitor approaches a downtown merchant for a donation, he will be referred to the secretary of the Downtown Retail Merchants Association, who will then give him an amount that the members have previously decided upon, take the matter under advisement, or say "no." In this way, individual merchants avoid being whipsawed by implied threats of pressure against their businesses. Or an association, such as the California Fruit Growers Association, may become famous for developing a high-quality orange produced by its members and then advertising and promoting it so well that oranges become a standard breakfast food and the brand name "Sunkist" achieves national acceptance. Or an association of plastering contractors may try to defeat a change in a city building code which would permit dry wooden walls, instead of fire-resistant plaster, to be used in basements or attached garages.

Much of an association secretary's time is taken up in public relations activities, both internal among his own members and external. An association secretary has to keep members informed and enthusiastic about the organization's progress and activities. This internal publicity requires meetings, presentations, booklets, letters, perhaps motion pictures, and usually magazines or newspapers to communicate to the membership what is going on. Recruiting new members is often also a major activity, because some members are always lost through deaths and resignations.

Externally, the work of an association may be even more important, since often only an association can do the big job of telling the public about the merits of a general type of product. The per capita consumption of candy in the United States, for instance, dropped from 20.5 pounds in 1944 to 16.8 pounds in 1959—caused, in large part, by dietary fads and fear of tooth decay and adolescent acne. In the physical defects candy was not at fault, or no more at fault than other foods, and there was no reason for it to be singled out as a whipping boy. Late in 1960 five separate groups of candy manufacturers got together to organize the Candy, Chocolate, and Confectionery Institute with a $250,000 public relations program. This task was beyond the scope of any single manufacturer, but together they could reap the benefits of a common solution to a common problem.

Associations also busy themselves with less immediate public relations activities such as awards programs, exhibitions, general publicity, and a mixture of product and institutional advertising. In small associations the general secretary is a Jack-of-many-trades, including public relations; in large associations, several people specialize in areas such as membership, legislative representation, labor relations, and public relations. But however handled, public relations, involving research into public attitudes, actions, communications, and evaluation of results, either formally or informally, is an important associational activity.

ADDITIONAL READING

In Special Areas of Practice

Association of American Railroads: *Public Relations and the Railroads,* the Association of American Railroads, Washington, D.C., 1946.

Center, Allen H.: *Public Relations Ideas in Action,* McGraw-Hill Book Company, Inc., New York, 1957. (Case studies.)

Henderer, F. Rhodes: *A Comparative Study of the Public Relations Practices in Six Industrial Corporations,* The University of Pittsburgh Press, Pittsburgh, Pa., 1956.

Hill, John W.: *Corporate Public Relations, Arm of Modern Management,* Harper & Row, Publishers, Incorporated, New York, 1958.

Lindquist, Robert: *The Bank and Its Publics,* Harper & Row, Publishers, Incorporated, New York, 1956.

Mahoney, Tom, and Rita Hession: *Public Relations for Retailers,* The Macmillan Company, New York, 1949.

Patterson, John C.: *Association Management,* Harper & Row, Publishers, Incorporated, New York, 1952.

Perry, John: *Human Relations in Small Industry,* McGraw-Hill Book Company, Inc., New York, 1955.

Rucker, Frank W., and Bert Stolpe: *Tested Newspaper Promotion,* The Iowa State University Press, Ames, Iowa, 1960.

More Special Users of Public Relations

6

The motivation for public relations activities by profit-making organizations is quite clear. Many other groups, ranging from doctors and architects to union heads and from government bureau chiefs to public school superintendents, are equally interested in public understanding and appreciation because the fortunes of each member of the group rise and fall, to a considerable extent, with the prestige and success of his fellowship. While perhaps two-thirds of all public relations activity is practiced in behalf of the area generally called "business," a large and growing proportion is practiced in behalf of professional associations and labor, welfare, religious, and governmental groups. Some of these groups are discussed in this chapter.

The fact that public relations is not exclusively a child of business should occasion no surprise, because its uses in the fields of religious persuasion and the support of governments, although somewhat obscured in modern American society, are historically among its oldest and strongest manifestations and are today more important abroad than in this country.

The Public Relations of the Professions

What is a "profession"? There is no easy answer, because with the proliferation of specialized knowledge, the number of highly skilled and learned human occupations has increased so much in recent years that the former simple listing of the professions as the clergy, law, medicine, the military, and a few others has become obsolete.

There are, however, several hallmarks of a profession. One is its possession of an organized body of special knowledge which cannot be acquired except by long and difficult study. A layman seeks the services of a professional man—a lawyer or doctor, for example—because of what he knows that the ordinary layman cannot know: the rights of citizens under the law or the effect of medicine upon disease. Another hallmark is the requirement of a recognized standard of competence to practice. Sometimes this may be schooling alone; often it includes examination and licensing or certification by the state or by an association of the profession involved. Another professional characteristic is independence. The professional man does not have to work as part of an organization. He carries his assets primarily in his head and can practice anywhere that his services are in demand, either as an independent practitioner or as a hired part of an organization. Finally, the professional man undertakes a responsibility to use his talents for the public welfare. The doctor vows to assist whenever his aid is needed in an emergency. If he makes a discovery, instead of hiding it, he shares it with his fellows and with the world by reporting it in a medical journal or elsewhere.

The independent professional man, say the lawyer, is free to take a client or to reject him; yet it is a rule in the courts that every man should be helped to obtain legal counsel if needed in criminal actions. Although the clergy are usually closely organized into associations, they do not strike as a means of protesting and fixing their compensation, but instead negotiate individually. Almost always codes of practice prevent professional men from advertising their merits directly; they must become known by their good works and by actions which might be called public relations.

What are the goals which the professions usually seek to attain by means of public relations?

Two of the most common are the attraction of new capable entrants into the profession and the provision for their proper education. Obviously, the profession must not die out or be unable to provide adequate service. British lawyers (solicitors), for example, have been concerned because the number of young men wishing to enter the practice of law in that country today is about the same as it was in 1914, despite a great increase in population and fields of practice. To attract promising young men, pamphlets are issued, meetings, and scholarships are arranged, and members show their keen personal interest in candidates.

Professional groups are also concerned with legislative actions which may raise or lower their standards. What qualifications should be required of men appointed as government "engineers," for example? Or who should be legally eligible to practice pharmacy?

Definitions of the proper boundaries of practice are also of concern. Prescribing and making eyeglasses may be done by optometrists. But who is responsible for contact lenses which fit directly over the eyeball? The ophthalmologists (doctors of medicine) feel that the latter prescriptions should be their function because contact lenses may exercise an actual physical effect upon the eye itself. A law or legal decision may be needed to embody the answer.

Freedom of private practice, as against government-supported medicine are goals in dispute. Tax laws, to equalize the advantages and privileges of professional and businessmen in computing income tax deductions and payments are much desired. General public esteem, which will cause their services to be more sought after and better rewarded, is another goal of professional groups. All these can be obtained largely through public relations methods.

An illustration of the ways of creating greater public appreciation of services is the work of the many chapters of the American Institute of Architects. Many of the new stores erected by businessmen in a middle-sized Western city, for example, were ugly because of their unimaginative cracker-box lines; not only were they unsightly but they were destined to last for years. How could the business community be imbued with a desire to make a better-looking city? How could builders be made more aware that good architecture is a business "plus," attracting favorable attention and conferring personality upon the stores which are well-housed? How could church or school groups be led not only to plan beautiful buildings, but also to make the greatest use of available space and sites and to plan for expansion? The architects' answers to these questions lie largely within the field of public relations.

The Public Relations of Labor Unions

Outside of the ranks of their own membership and those closely connected with it, American labor unions notoriously suffer from extremely poor public relations. Why? The truth seems to be that their publicity creates a worse rather than a better impression. In a strike, for example, by the nature of events the union is usually cast in the role of the aggressor, wanting more money or other benefits; its demands are news. The company merely says "no"—an attitude which is somewhat less news. If a strike begins, the inconveniences of a great many people provide even more news; and if any violence occurs, the news reaches the headlines. Finally, if the strike is won and pay raises are granted, the company may promptly increase its prices, and the higher cost to the public is news again. In an inflationary period it may be necessary for a union to seek wage increases, but the actions needed to get them usually result in a very poor press.

Electioneering for office within a union also creates a press problem because the campaigning is conducted in the limelight, with a publicity that corporation managements seldom meet except when dirty linen gets washed in a proxy fight. To get elected, a union official may have to make promises loudly, plainly, and belligerently, often expressing more hope than he really expects the final settlement will justify. These extravagant statements may all get into the news, while his company counterparts, working quietly with a small board of directors and officers, are seldom heard by the public except in prepared statements.

Racketeers have also disfigured the faces of several unions, and the evil and arrogance of these unsavory parasites get more than their full share of attention.

Many nonunion citizens fear the political power of unions or regard them as special-interest groups, solely out to benefit their own members at the expense of society. Unions have, for the most part, done an excellent job of selling unionism to their own members; they are often still feared and disliked by other segments of society. What can unions do about this problem? In many cases they supply their side of information about economic matters fairly well, but their arguments fall far short of persuading many citizens that unions are interested in improving the products of industry, in greater productivity, and in other contributions to the general welfare. If they are thus altruistic, they should demonstrate their good intentions.

Unions have a difficult course to steer. They can hardly control government and are in danger of being further controlled by it, to the detriment of their freedom to bargain. Although public understanding and liking are essential to union freedom, unions have not fully accepted the fact. The public relations of business are almost always ahead of union public relations because businessmen understand the value of communication with the public and are more willing to pay what it is worth. Unions frequently incline to pay hired intellectuals only what the average union member would regard as right on his own scale—something below the market price. This parsimony, coupled with insecurity and lower social status, has not attracted many of the best public relations men to union representation.

As American economic life grows more complex and more influenced by world events, constantly greater government intervention may be expected. This means that take-home pay may be decided at the ballot box rather than at the bargaining table, and that therefore public support is vital. Both unions and businessmen see the handwriting on the wall, but their reactions thus far have not been clear.

The Public Relations Problems of Social Welfare

The Red Cross, the Cancer Society, the League for the Hard of Hearing, the local Community Chest, the YMCA, and a host of other organizations which minister to the needs of the American people depend for their support entirely upon successful public relations. Big givers are important, but thousands of little givers and volunteer workers actually carry forward the activities of these organizations. When the public is informed, urged, and encouraged, it gives to the tune of about $\frac{1}{2}$ billion dollars a year in Community Chest drives alone. Nowhere else in the world is there a phenomenon comparable to this American charitable instinct.

The public relations men and women who promote these causes are in an enviable situation in many ways. The worthiness of their goals is usually beyond question. Everyone wants less cancer, better hearing, or the development of youth, and the promoters find great personal satisfaction in assisting these causes. It is usually easy to find good friends and willing allies in the work.

The American press is also unusually kind to the publicity which emanates from social welfare sources, sometimes almost too much so; usually all that editors ask is that the stories approach reasonable standards of news interest, and often the standards are somewhat bent. The suspicious eye that greets commercial news releases is largely absent, and often the welfare personnel's chief problem, particularly in small cities, is to find time to supply all the news and pictures that the papers are willing to print.

Broadcasting stations are also generous, although the nature of their medium, which is largely sold and devoted to entertainment, places more limitation upon their practical aid.

A great deal of advertising for welfare causes is frequently available through donations of unsponsored time on radio or television and of billboards by outdoor-advertising companies. Portions of their regular advertising space or gratuitous notices are frequently given also by business firms in their newspaper ads. Show windows are easily obtained if there is good material with which to fill them. City authorities are lenient about the use of posters, banners, and other street decorations. In fact, publicity is so readily available that many people who inform the public about social welfare are inclined to depend upon it too much, forgetting that being known is not necessarily the same as being understood or being liked.

As business and labor organizations and professional groups have become more conscious, in recent years, of the value of public relations, they have also become very willing to lend their manpower to welfare efforts for the sake of the public good will which this type of activity returns to them. This is particularly true of show people, of the utilities, of large department stores, of local big industries, and of large service organizations such as insurance companies, in which someone from the large staff can be assigned to help without too much loss in operating efficiency.

Unpaid volunteers are the backbone of all welfare drives. They come from the local welfare group and from other people whom it is able to contact through clubs, civic associations, women's groups, schools, churches, and similar organizations. Almost always a sponsoring "letterhead committee" of the leaders of these organizations is used to give validity to the group's participation.

With complete penetration of factories, offices, and professional organizations, American welfare drives frequently resemble a voluntary system of taxation, having quotas, offering payroll deductions, and exerting considerable social and business pressure to ensure compliance. It may be argued, of course, that such voluntary taxation is better than that imposed by government.

The resemblance to taxation is particularly marked in United Fund or Community Chest efforts, in which the business and other interests of the city get together to limit the nuisance and ineffectiveness of a large number of separate drives by combining them into one major effort which they and their employees pledge to support. "Tin cup" street-corner collections every other day dull the edge of charity to the point where only nickels and dimes are collected, whereas payroll deductions, pledged once a year, get dollars. In united drives, the less glamorous but useful welfare organizations, such as the rehabilitation of injured workers or aid to broken families, tend to get a fairer share, while the tear-jerking drives for the relief of human ailments which excite the most sympathy are perhaps somewhat handicapped, since their stronger human interest appeals are submerged in the general effort.

Yet united drives, although logical, also face some serious public relations problems.

Because united giving bears some of the marks of taxation, it lacks the spiritual uplift of more personal donation to specific causes or needs in which a more personal interest may be involved. How can such satisfaction be supplied?

Unpaid volunteers may make zealous fund solicitors, but they can also be clumsy and hard to control; they have been known to apply open pressure or even to insult those whom they ask for gifts; sometimes they are not well informed as to the uses of the money and show their ignorance. Obtaining, educating, and rewarding volunteers is a big job, closely related to the public relations success of the organization involved.

The public frequently misunderstands the activities and goals of welfare organizations. Part of this misapprehension springs from garbled stories given out by welfare recipients who may be ignorant or emotionally unstable; part arises from the natural spitefulness of human nature, which likes to report evil or folly in those supposed to be doing good; and some is a compensation mechanism. Those who do not wish to give often excuse themselves by saying that the cause to which they have been asked to contribute is not worthy anyway, charging wastefulness in the collection of funds, carelessness in their use, or even misappropriation. Frequently the very size of welfare budgets is misunderstood because they look so huge that small-money thinkers have difficulty in accepting them. There are also critics who persist in transferring charges of government-welfare wrongdoing to the private-agency field.

To meet these problems, public relations people in social welfare organizations must:

1. Conduct valid and adequate research studies to determine public attitudes which may affect the success of their efforts—studies which are often more complex and difficult than those required by industry

2. Interpret the work of their organizations in human terms both to inform the public and to give a feeling of satisfaction to those who participate in its support

3. Whenever possible, correct misconceptions immediately

4. Develop and support their campaign organizations, both the small paid staff and the large number of unpaid volunteers, with information and with aid in meeting the public by such assistance as plans for open houses, meetings, and informal conversation

5. Be alert to changes in basic public attitudes

The Special Public Relations Problems of Hospitals

In recent years American hospitals have unfortunately had to depend for their necessary growth almost completely upon the good will and understanding of the public under conditions which have tended to make their public relations bad more often than good. The dice have been loaded against them for several reasons.

Hospitals are not profit-making institutions. Few, if any, have stockholders, and they are not in the habit of declaring dividends. Operated as a public service, hospitals have usually been established by churches, welfare associations, or communities, and are dependent upon gifts or taxes for all of their expansion and often for much of their daily operating costs. Although growing national population has made necessary continual expansion of facilities, bed capacity has often lagged behind needs. The result has been long waiting lists, worry, and ill will. In spite of overcrowding, hospital rates are high—disastrously so for people of moderate or small incomes who may be caught without the help of hospital insurance. Both inflation and increased services have contributed to much higher per day costs, although because of better treatment, the average patient spends much less time in a hospital now than formerly, when hospitals were largely "lying-in-bed" establishments.

The turnover of hospital help has been high, and training has been a serious problem. Patients and their friends and relatives are often in an abnormal state of mind, prone to be upset at even minor faults and inclined to take the word of anyone from a sweeper to an orderly as the latest medical gospel. There are also some inevitable losses of life and even some errors in hospital procedure, and these lamentable occurrences are magnified out of all reason and remembered while the high percentage of success is accepted as commonplace.

A natural friction exists between hospitals and the press, which wants to know facts about patients that doctors may not wish to release or seeks interviews that administrators are not willing to permit. Photographers wish to take pictures that hospital administrators feel interfere with their work or invade the patient's right of privacy. The press is usually ready to magnify hospital errors to the entire public.

Finally, behind each private hospital lurks the possibility of government control, either through a take-over made necessary by financial collapse or through public dissatisfaction with its operations. The possibility is particularly distasteful to the medical profession.

It is fair to assume that if things are left to themselves with no planned effort, the public relations of most hospitals will at least be somewhat ineffective. This unenviable condition hospitals share with such diverse bedfellows as labor unions, police departments, public utilities, and public education. What can be done about it?

Obvious first steps in hospital public relations would include analysis of the opinions of important publics, public information about goals and methods, more careful employee selection and training, staff indoctrination with the principles of public relations, constant efforts to achieve good relations with the press upon a basis of mutual understanding, efforts to give patients greater participation in activities, and the favorable involvement in the work of the hospital of as many persons and groups in the community as possible. Because of the turnover of the staff and patients, this continuous program should be as much a part of standard operating procedure as cleanliness.

The Special Problem of Convalescent Homes

There are a great many old, infirm, ill, or senescent people in the United States today. The expectancy of longer life, the spread of social security payments and of pensions which give at least small amounts for support, and the changed housing and living habits of the younger generation have all altered the picture from that of a half century ago. Then, when grandfather became infirm, he usually got the northwest corner bedroom in the big white wooden house of the son or daughter who was least burdened with a large family. Other children contributed to his support, if need be, and he was fed and cared for to the best of his family's ability. Low-cost, readily available domestic help often eased the burden. But since today's houses have almost no room and little domestic help is available, other solutions must be found.

The chief answer is to be seen all over the country in the many old hotels, mansions, and more modest houses which have been converted into nursing or convalescent homes. Some are run well and some poorly; the costs vary and so do the degrees of efficiency; and all share the same serious public relations problems.

Many of the relatives who place their kin in these homes suffer feelings of severe guilt because they are not personally taking care of the older people, and they may take out their feelings upon the home management. The inmates themselves often complain to their children when they visit, out of the need for human sympathy or because of illness. When things go wrong in these homes, when cases of mistreatment, injuries, or fires occur, they always make the headlines. Worst of all, because life in such a home leads to the unhappy end of the road that all humanity dislikes so much, the bitterness of human mortality and decline overshadows the whole atmosphere of nursing homes.

What can be done—not to meet the whole problem of care for the aged of which the present rather haphazard system of nursing homes may or may not be an adequate solution—but rather to obtain the best public understanding and support for those nursing-home operators of today who are doing an adequate job? There is, of course, no substitute for adequacy, trained skill, kindness, and a sincere desire to do the best with the resources at hand.

Standards of practice should be adopted by nursing-home associations and made public, so that they come to mean something in the identification of well-run nursing homes. Homes which cannot or will not adhere to these standards should be excluded from the association. The interest of local communities in nearby homes should be enlisted through contacts with churches, schools, sororities and fraternities, women's groups, and civic groups, so that elderly people will not feel forgotten and also so that the public can see both the good and the bad of the system. Further, community interest should be enlisted by feature stories about interesting people in the homes or about their present accomplishments and needs. Even some kinds of open houses might be arranged, and better plans for excursions or visits by patients off the grounds might be worked out. A system of regular communication between patients and home management and also between patients and their relatives and friends should be provided as needed.

The Public Relations of Churches

"Aren't the activities of churches already pretty much public relations?" some may protest. "Aren't churches concerned with attracting members, creating a favorable public reception for their messages, and doing good in their communities and the world? What more can they do?"

It is true that these typical public relations activities constitute a large part of church work, but many churches carry them out only on a word-of-mouth, person-to-person basis. As far as any single individual is concerned, the personal approach is most effective; but in these days of large, mobile populations, some more modern methods of general communications might well be added. In a way, the minister, his assistant, or the laymen making personal calls may be likened to salesmen calling upon prospects;

they will be much more effective if the product which they are selling is already well known and respected.

This introduction can be made by disseminating information about the beliefs, activities, staff, equipment, and program of the church, and by working hard in the community to attain desirable social goals. If the minister of a church is elected to national office in his denomination or to another post of responsibility, or if a new program is established within the church, the local newspapers should be supplied with a story. Much, of course, depends upon the size of the city. In a small town almost any activity of a church will be news; in a big city, only the most important. Letters, illustrated folders, and news bulletins can be mailed; and many other ways of reaching large groups of the public are familiar to good ministers. None of these media will do the job alone. They are simply preparation, in most instances, for personal contact; but as parishes grow larger and more fluid, the extension of communication through public relations methods becomes both necessary and helpful when handled fittingly. The apostles, after all, used the best means of communication they had at hand in their day, and church evangelists in the twentieth century can well do the same.

A Word about Interfaith Movements

Despite their differences, all branches of the Christian and Jewish religions share many things in common—a belief in God, common standards of morality and justice, ideals of the brotherhood and sanctity of man, and social idealism. The likenesses among their members are much greater than the differences; yet only a few short centuries ago the whole Western world was convulsed by religious wars, and only two decades ago the Jews of Europe were being slaughtered in the gas chambers of Dachau and other horror camps.

We are all now much concerned about freedom of religion, mutual respect, and a common social morality, because we know that what benefits one benefits all. Attaining respect and cooperation is a public relations problem which has been vigorously tackled in the United States by the National Conference of Christians and Jews and other organizations.

Public Relations and Race Relations in the United States

Eventually the race relations problem in this nation will not be a legal problem but a public relations problem. Without question, all citizens of the United States have equal rights under the Constitution. These legal rights have been demanded, as they should have been, and are largely being attained; but even after they are won, there will remain the problem of obtaining the *human* rights of members of a minority group, which no court action can give and no policing system can enforce.

No laws can be passed which will make people friendly, willing to give others a fair share of good employment, advancement, or promotion, willing to vote for a man instead of for his color, and willing to be good neighbors. The bestowal of human rights cannot be enforced; they can only be given because of understanding, a sense of fairness, and the honest desire of a majority group (influenced by its leaders and by its own social pressures) to do the right thing. The race relations problem of the United States today is rapidly passing into this stage if, indeed, it is not already there. Enforcement by public action may still be needed in certain places and at some times, but the big problem of such a minority group in the future is to convince the majority of its high standards of personal worth, its value to the common society, and its loyalty; and also to lead the majority to recognize the justice of fair and generous treatment.

This obligation puts a great burden upon such a minority group. It is asked to be much better than the majority in many ways, to see that the majority is aware of this merit, and yet to steer a careful course between assertiveness and subservience. Every time that members of a minority group do something well and with becoming modesty in any field—sports, music, art, the Armed Forces, education, business, or science—they advance the respect in which all their fellows are held; and every time that they do something bad, they hurt all their fellows, because unobserving majority publics do not readily distinguish among individuals. To gain public esteem, the members of a minority group require more wisdom, self-control, social control, and cohesiveness, plus a better public relations sense, than do the members of a majority which is not forced to work uphill.

But this progress, hard as it is, can be made because Americans have a conscience, take their vows of government seriously, and, when they are encouraged and reminded, are always generous to those who need help. But progress in public relations requires good sense and planning, followed by a program of deeds. The next best step for groups interested in the advancement of colored people or other minority groups in the United States will be to utilize more frequently thoughtful and experienced public relations counselors.

The Continuing Problems of Local Public Education

Once there was an elderly school-system superintendent who had been in the same town for forty years and who had done his job by the simple expedient of spending almost no money and continually assuring the taxpayers that they had the best schools in the country (whereas in fact they had almost the worst).

That same man, using the same technique, would hardly last more than a few years in his job today, for a very good reason: Rising operating costs and booming enrollments would force him to go to the voters for building bond or operating millage votes with regularity whether he wanted to or not, and if he couldn't get more money, the whole school system would start falling to pieces! The modern school head's situation is something like that which the grocer would face if every time he wanted to raise the price of butter, he was forced to seek approval at a public vote; yet it is inescapable, because in inflationary times the cost of teachers' salaries, custodial wages, repairs, supplies, and new buildings goes up and up; the number of students mounts; and in new suburban areas these problems are doubled by an exodus from the older cities.

But rising costs and the population explosion are not the only problems facing American public schools today. The school is not only expected to teach; it is also expected to overcome juvenile delinquency, to act as a baby-sitter and to provide a social hall in a period when, as a rule, both mothers and fathers work and when more youngsters drive their own cars and there is less parental supervision than ever before. Parents gladly turn more and more of the load over to the schools and then complain if it is not always successfully handled.

There is a constant dispute over what should be taught in the schools. Parents' groups are full of advocates of greater emphasis on the sciences, foreign languages, or English; but at the same time they cannot agree on what should be thrown out to make room for the additional hours to be spent on these fundamentals. The less academic activities, such as basketball, football, swimming, glee club, sewing, woodworking, and senior plays, all have their own ardent advocates. Not many have agreed so far that the school day should be expanded, say from 8 A.M. to 12 noon and then from 1 P.M. to 5 P.M., with corresponding increases being made in teaching staff, and time-and-a-half pay provided for teachers who do night work or lunch-time work—for instance, supervision or grading.

Local school districts find themselves in a lively (and losing) competition for tax money with the U.S. Internal Revenue Service and other major tax agencies, which go around like vacuum cleaners, sucking all before them. After income taxes, sales taxes, and excise levies have exacted their due, the remaining local property tax cannot usually be increased. It is about at the limit of toleration. In some suburban, nonindustrial areas, each new home is so full of new children that the cost to the community of their education exceeds the household's tax payments. Yet at the same time, when local citizens have a chance to vote "no" on a local school bond issue, they often do so, because this is the only chance that they ever have to vote "no" on any tax—the Federal and state taxes usually being beyond their reach in Congress or a legislature.

Schools must constantly compete for parent and student attention with television, picnics, bridge, bowling, magazines, newspapers, worrying about the Communists, appointments at the beauty parlor, and a host of other bids for interest and time.

Under these circumstances, the able public school superintendent does not have a choice of whether or not he will practice public relations; he has to practice it. At the same time he has to deny that he does it; he is usually not well trained in the subject; he is hindered from spending any public money on really expert assistance; and he has a host of needling and conflicting volunteers at his elbow.

The school's publics are (1) the teachers, who must be informed, encouraged, and advised on how best to contribute their efforts to the common cause; (2) the students, who are often enthusiastic but naturally fractious and shortsighted; (3) the parents, who increasingly seem to know all the answers which have escaped the educators thus far; (4) the press, which can be a good ally but sometimes lacks understanding; (5) business groups, which often have a decided leaning toward paying lower taxes, teaching the three R's, and beating the Russian sputniks with many brilliant physicists, all at the same time; (6) professional groups, which are interested in making good future lawyers, doctors, nurses, engineers, or accountants; (7) sports fans, who want the home team to win all the time; and (8) the general public. The last group consists of all groups not previously named. It gets its information secondhand through the mass media and word of mouth, distortedly remembers school as it was thirty or forty years ago, is vaguely anti-intellectual, and gets tired of being constantly asked to vote more money for a cause in which it often has no direct, apparent stake; but out of the goodness of its heart and the great American belief in education it finally does so most of the time anyway.

To reach these publics, the superintendent can use both personal and mass media methods. Personal methods include home visits by teachers, notes, conferences, open houses at schools, parent assistance in school affairs, and parent-teacher and other meetings. Mass media may include newsletters to the staffs, school newspapers sent to students and parents, yearbooks, annual or quarterly reports to taxpayers, broadcasts, news releases, and speeches.

Typical news stories, for example, might include accounts of graduations, curriculum and program developments, new staff members, retirements, enrollment and financial figures, pupil and project activities, honors, and interviews with successful graduates. One of the biggest needs is for the warm, human type of feature which shows how lives are changed by education, a fundamental which we are now all likely to forget since free public education has become almost universal.

Higher Education—the Troubled Halls of Ivy

American colleges and universities have faced not only a doubling of population within the past fifty years but also a great increase in the percentage of young people who go to college. Whereas in 1900 only about 4 per cent of high school graduates entered institutions of higher learning, in 1960 the national average was about 37 per cent and the average in certain sections of the country was much higher.

At the same time, we have seen a great proliferation of the desirable subject matter to be studied and a change in its nature. Compared with the same subjects as studied in 1900, today's chemistry, physics, biology, medicine, business administration, foreign languages, social sciences, and journalism, are not only more complex in content and theory but bear little resemblance to the simpler college subjects of a generation earlier. A few years ago a great university expected to turn out experts in only a few fields, but today it must prepare for many, because in "our expanding universe" many more areas of knowledge must be explored.

In early days, widespread public support for American colleges and universities was not so important as it is today because only the elite planned to attend college and they expected to pay for it, but today, when a college education is increasingly necessary to all higher-level job opportunities, most higher education has become state-supported. Private funds handle less of the educational load; the states themselves find their sources of revenue increasingly absorbed by the Federal government; and the problem becomes one of gaining popular support for the increased costs of a higher education that almost half of the families in the nation now expect their sons and daughters to have.

At the same time an obsolete, stereotyped image of college education lingers on in the popular mind, compounded out of the good old Siwash stories of years ago—when college was nothing but a great big happy lark for many well-to-do undergraduates—flickering motion pictures, old-graduate tales, sports pages, and exaggerated reports of panty raids, riots, and general subversion. Why should anyone wish to be taxed for this— or to contribute to it?

Obviously, a considerable communications job needs to be done, and to accomplish it, college public relations men resort to various means.

News bureaus supply the press and broadcasters with complete coverage of events at institutions of higher education. Such coverage is necessary because most newspaper staffs are not big enough to deliver a complete report from a university without aid and left to themselves, would often cover only the student indiscretions, football victories, and trustee squabbles which regularly seem to rise to the top.

College news bureaus are often well staffed with able and dedicated men, but the results of their earnest efforts are not necessarily good promotion. They may not report objectively on the whole work of a vast institution or create a generally favorable public image. Communication between college and public cannot be established by reliance upon the naturally haphazard selection of stories released to newspapers or the equally peculiar ways in which their readers snatch impressions out of the melee of daily events. Such publicity is often valuable, but it is not public relations, because while people will certainly learn more from it, they will not necessarily like universities better or admire them more.

Alumni work is another common approach, probably most useful in small, long-established homogeneous institutions where alumni bonds are tight and can be reasonably maintained. With the great recent growth of all colleges, their varied curricula, and the dispersion of their graduates all over the world, communications to alumni in many large schools are not so effective as they probably once were.

Events such as anniversaries, graduations, conferring degrees and honors, speeches by notable persons, concerts and art shows, and engineering or science exhibits are other ways of personifying the work of an institution.

Involvement of parents, friends, professional groups, government groups, and others in the activities of the university as guests, visitors, conference attendants, lecturers, and advisers furnishes another opportunity for contact and communication.

But these rather standard approaches are obviously not going to be enough to accomplish the enormous public relations task which must follow upon the great expansion of American higher education today, both because of the number of students and the diversity of their needs. The aim at the publics to be reached must be more sure; the means employed to reach them must be more refined and more intelligently used; and greater effort must be expended, more commensurate with the greater task.

Effective new approaches may include greater concentration upon the specific publics of which the general public of higher education is composed and greater personal contact with individuals. Only certain groups or persons have the motivated interest to listen to and to understand the complex messages which must be conveyed; others will either ignore or misinterpret them to suit their own desires and preconceptions. All too often educators bask in the delusion that they are communicating with important publics when, in fact, they are only talking to other educators (who admittedly constitute an important public in themselves).

It is important to consider some of the specific publics closely related to higher education.

Students of the callow freshman type of the good old Siwash days are still to be found upon American campuses, but they are exceptional. Most students today are older and more sophisticated; many of them are married and are parents; frequently they have extensive military or work experience; and often they are engaged in graduate study for advanced degrees in highly specialized areas. Student support can be enlisted both in representing their particular institutions and in speaking for higher education in general. To convey a message to others, students need information, participation in university affairs, and a knowledge that freedom is inevitably accompanied by responsibility.

Parents may or may not have been to college. (If they have, they probably share many old-graduate delusions.) Since many parents are under severe financial strain and are making sacrifices to send their children to college, information about the work of the institution, personal reporting, and recognition at some time other than the end of a term or graduation day seems only their due.

University faculty members may be assumed to be competent within their own disciplines, but also sometimes incompetent and, unfortunately, vocal in other areas. Academic freedom, like other freedoms, has its concomitant responsibilities to society, its fellows, the nation, and world. A discharged professor once remarked bitterly (and with some truth) that a university teacher had less freedom of speech than a ditchdigger. The limitation is inevitable; few people care what a ditchdigger says, but a professor carries a much heavier load of responsibility.

The fact that university faculty members are highly intelligent does not mean that they will be *ipso facto* well informed upon the whole state of the university and the role of higher education in society today. Many teachers might be more confident, more tactful, more kindly, and more closely connected with the mainstreams of economic, social, and cultural life flowing through the world if they were better informed about subjects beyond their specialties. The old stereotype of the university professor as a hopelessly underpaid recluse is quite out of date, but the full potential of today's new-style teacher has not yet been enlisted upon many campuses.

High school contacts are increasingly important as larger numbers of high school students seek admission to colleges and more of them find difficulty in getting in.

Professional and occupational groups are interested, not only in the development of their own successors, but also in their own professional updating on campus. Usually they can both learn and contribute.

The new alumni provide an opportunity to show what higher education can do for individuals and for the public welfare. Concrete illustrations will reassure a public that is in danger of being swamped in statistics and vague generalizations.

The communications media, such as the press and broadcasting stations, must be considered carefully. A spate of minor items or an overwhelming preponderance of sports news may now be of less value in creating public understanding than it used to be. Today's need is for appreciation of educational efforts in human terms, and this can be achieved only when the editors, reporters, and broadcasters themselves are in full rapport with the institution they are discussing. If *they* think of university news primarily in terms of protest marches and touchdowns, the case is almost hopeless. How many major universities, for example, take key newsmen individually through their establishments so that they may learn the work of the institution and meet faculty members informally?

Government is of primary concern to the tax-supported majority of higher educational institutions. How well do government people understand educational problems and aspirations? How outdated or distorted are their stereotypes? How responsive are they to the needs and wishes of their home constituencies in regard to education? Could they be more sympathetic? Although personal connections influence political action, the fundamental university problem is one of public support; it is imperative that the public supply information to its elected representatives in government. Last-minute, put-out-the-fire campaigns are often useless, or even harmful, unless a sound foundation has first been laid.

Groups such as business corporations and labor unions (or smaller groups), women's organizations, and churches are examples of special areas of interest which have their own terms of reference in relation to the work of a university and can be approached in appropriate ways.

The list could be multiplied, and if the huge public relations task of higher education is to be accomplished, help will be needed not only from college public relations staffs but also from the administrators, faculties, student bodies, and their friends. No public relations task was ever larger in modern times.

The Public Relations of the United States Military Services

Wars, past, present, and future, are the American people's biggest government investment, accounting for about 80 per cent of the Federal budget. Not only do the military services ask support from taxes; they also seek sons, and, in time of war, all the life of the country.

With the great need of recruitment and of citizen support during the past two world wars, and with continuing heavy financial demands and constant changes in weapons, the United States Army, Navy, Marine Corps, and Air Force have all developed large, effective public relations machines totaling perhaps 3,000 persons and spending perhaps 3 million dollars a year to place their needs before the public to which they look for support. They direct most of their efforts toward certain sections of the public.

Men now serving in the Armed Forces. The understanding and liking of men in the service are the keys to the reactions of their parents, relatives, and friends throughout the country. Since some men have chosen the service as a career while others have been drafted, their attitudes are likely to vary. Good treatment, good food, adequate information, opportunities for recreation and advancement are primary, of course, in determining the attitudes of the men. A sound public relations program in which the men of the armed services serve as ambassadors of good will for their organizations can be built only upon the facts.

Reserve forces need recognition and encouragement for the hours they put in, without much public appreciation, in times of peace. When they are called to active service because of an emergency situation short of war, their reactions may present many problems.

Civilian employees of the military forces (such as those in the many river and harbor projects of the United States Army Corps of Engineers) need to be considered just as are groups of industrial employees.

Communities near military posts offer many special problems. Men in uniform on leave arouse the herd instincts in both civilians and their own military brethren. Each group can be distinguished by its dress, and Tom, or Joe, or Bud in civilian slacks and shirts are magically transformed into "those damned soldiers" when wearing their country's uniform. Special forbearance is necessary to prevent friction when women, traffic, and civil police are involved.

Near big bases, schools, housing, and sewage become problems; near air bases the public worries about loud noises and falling objects; and missile bases make even more uncomfortable neighbors. All these inherent problems provide much opportunity for the local staff PIOs (Public Information Officers) to practice their foresight and skills in public relations.

Industry is another major public of the military services because it furnishes most of their supplies.

Higher education is almost a prerequisite for the recruitment of many officers and enlisted men. ROTC programs have had many public relations problems in recent years.

The press presents a continual problem, because it is not only a gate-keeper to broad public contact, but itself wants to know everything that goes on, especially accidents or other trouble, which unenlightened or fearful base commanders would sometimes like to hide. Because the boundary line of real military-defense secrecy is hard to draw, and because it is frequently drawn too fine, newspapermen often feel that "national security" is being used as a cloak for incompetence or errors.

The Congress of the United States is the ultimate military public because it determines which branches of the service will get how much money and for what purposes. Only a few men at the top levels at the Pentagon in Washington work with congressmen directly, but the efficacy of the general public relations programs and the activities of all military operations with which a congressman may come into contact, including those within his home territory, may do much to influence his attitudes.

The United States Government and Politics

Within the past generation the United States government has grown so large and so complex that its scope is now beyond the comprehension of all but a very few American citizens. Like the sands of the sea, its personnel and functions are numberless, and its costs are calculated in figures like those of interstellar distances. Some conservative citizens violently oppose this development as a matter of principle, but it does not seem very likely to change, and in view of the great number of services which the people now expect from their government, probably most voters really do not wish it to change very much.

In a democracy in which citizens are called upon to understand and to direct their government from time to time, this swollen size presents many communications problems. How can an individual citizen know what is going on in his government? For that matter, does the press know? Most newspaper and wire-service staffs are hopelessly inadequate to the reporting of much beyond the activities of a few key persons. In addition, the citizen is often called upon for willing and intelligent compliance with government requests instead of being forced by law. Savings bond sales drives, assistance in preventing forest fires, cooperation in civil defense, and even proper payment of taxes are all greatly aided by willing citizen effort.

The need for public information about government doings and for public cooperation with government projects has given rise to the development of public relations practice within government; but for a number of reasons the activity is hedged about with fear, and people engaged in publicity are often disguised under other titles, such as "assistants" or "service bureaus."

The basic trouble is that the power to communicate is a great asset to political success in a democracy, and those who enjoy this power, particularly through being in office, have an advantage which their opponents abhor—until they attain the same position. In our form of government, such public relations communication is usually an arm of the executive branch (the President, Cabinet officers, and bureau heads) and is much less attached to Congress; official communication is therefore frequently attacked by congressmen because the executive uses it to maintain public favor. In fact, in these days of great newspaper coverage and of instantaneous television communication, an appeal to the people can be the American President's strongest weapon. The built-in feud between the American executive and legislative branches of government finds its most painful point of contact in government public relations.

The American press itself has an ambivalent attitude toward government public relations sources. On the one hand, the press realizes that internal news releases are necessary, because no newspaper or news service could possibly be equipped to cover the vast machinery of United States government, at all levels, without material assistance from the inside. But, on the other hand, such open dependence is often felt to be contrary to the best traditions of the press in that it exposes the press to possible omissions or distortions at the source of the news. (It is hardly to be expected that a government agency will go to any great effort to dig up facts about itself which may be adverse to its own interests.) Secrecy, also, may be used to hide governmental ineptitude, and as America's foreign involvements grow increasingly complex and secret, the mantle of state security is, rightly or wrongly, thrown over an ever larger area. The press's "right" to know is increasingly confronted with questions as to the "ability" to know or the "wisdom" of telling. Boundaries between right and expediency are uncertain, and surely no one will ever be satisfied in such a fluid and complex field.

Political public relations may be defined as getting candidates or parties elected, or perhaps obtaining public vote support for specific objectives such as bond issues, referendums, or constitutional changes. These activities are difficult for public relations people because prestige is laid squarely on the line; if an election is lost by only one vote, it is just as much a public failure as if it had been lost by 10,000 votes, except in giving reason for future encouragement. Time to work for political issues is limited, and a single campaign is a promotional rather than a developmental effort, often played by ear, and all too seldom with long-range planning. The haste is unfortunate because the real build-up of a political issue or figure involves careful planning and time in which to work, as well as the arts of publicity and showmanship. Too often the ballyhoo is applied long after most minds are already made up.

Pressure groups of all sorts (for better schools, lower gasoline taxes, more roads, and different labor laws, for example) employ general public relations methods in addition to their special efforts directed at lawmakers personally. The way to attain a major political or economic goal in the United States seems to be to organize strong citizen support outside the framework of a political party. When the cause gains sufficient strength, either the party in power will adopt the program in order to stay in or the party out of power will adopt it in the hope of attaining a majority. (Sometimes both adopt it.) When success has been achieved for their particular demands, such citizen groups tend to melt away and do not remain behind to clutter up the political landscape as voter attention moves on to new issues and needs. In this way American political parties become *registers* of public opinion rather than *creators* of it. The system has many advantages because it avoids freezing party loyalties and platforms to long-outworn issues and allows for fluidity in crystallizing and facing new problems. The common criticism of American political parties for not "standing for anything" may well be somewhat beside the point; perhaps they are not supposed to stand for anything, and it may be better that their platforms are expressed in very general terms.

A Summary for Chapters 5 and 6

With the increasing complexity of modern life, the list of special areas of public relations practice becomes greatly extended, and it will continue to grow as more and more groups find such planned persuasive communication necessary to their existence and progress. But although each of these special areas has its own particular problems, the fundamentals of successful public relations practice remain the same. There is no need, at least to begin with, to learn one type of communication for banks, another for schools, another for railroads, and so on. The best evidence of the essential unity of principle in this field is seen in the manner in which the big public relations counseling firms of the United States handle many types of accounts with success; they obviously have the advantage of greater general experience and a fresher viewpoint than those that specialize too narrowly.

For the future practitioner, a study of the list of possible applications of general theories and techniques is valuable because it indicates the wide scope of communications problems in today's rapidly expanding and complex world and stimulates thinking toward further applications. But before expertness within any area is attempted, mastery of the basic principles of public relations practice which are covered in Chapters 9 to 13 is essential.

ADDITIONAL READING

Special Areas of Practice

Bryan, James E.: *Public Relations in Medical Practice,* The Williams & Wilkins Company, Baltimore, 1954.

Grinnell, J. E., and Raymond J. Young: *The School and the Community,* The Ronald Press Company, New York, 1955.

Kelley, Stanley, Jr.: *Professional Public Relations and Political Power,* The Johns Hopkins Press, Baltimore, 1956.

Levy, Harold P.: *Public Relations for Social Agencies,* Harper & Row, Publishers, Incorporated, New York, 1956.

Mills, Alden B.: *Hospital Public Relations,* Physicians Record Co., Chicago, 1939.

Schoenfeld, Clarence A.: *The University and Its Publics,* Harper & Row, Publishers, Incorporated, New York, 1954.

Stoody, Ralph: *A Handbook of Church Public Relations,* Abingdon Press, Nashville, Tenn., 1959.

Tinkham, Richard P.: *Public Relations for Bar Associations,* the American Bar Association, Chicago, Ill., 1953.

U.S. Army: *Handbook for Public Information Officers,* Office, Chief of Information, Department of the Army, Washington, D.C., 1951.

Images—Corporate
and Otherwise

7

The word "image" implies to most people something unreal, illusory, or transient. But Webster's *New International Dictionary* (second edition), offers as one definition of the word "a mental representation of anything not actually present to the senses; a revival or imitation of sensible experience, or of sensible experience together with accompanying feellngs; the reproduction in memory or imagination of sensations of sight, touch, hearing, etc.; as, visual, tactile, auditory *images;* a picture drawn by the fancy; broadly, a conception; an idea."[1]

The definition leads us away from illusion. There is nothing unreal at all about the image of a corporation because to the man who has the image in his mind, it *is* the corporation. Whether the image be true or false is quite beside the point; the man who has it thinks it is true and will act accordingly. Images exist; they are more or less forceful according to the degree of contact and interest which the holder has with the organization image; and they can be measured and changed, although such change is often a slow process.

The more usual meaning of the term "corporate image" would be that given in the third edition of Webster's NID as one of the definitions of "image": "a mental conception held in common by members of a group and being symbolic of a basic attitude and orientation toward something (as a person, class, racial type, political philosophy, or nationality)." [2] The word "corporate" would refer to the group holding the image in common rather than to the *object* of their thinking. (See Webster's definition of "corporate" as synonymous with "aggregate.") But the phrase has been

[1] By permission. From Webster's New International Dictionary, Second Edition, copyright 1959 by G. & C. Merriam Co., Publishers of the Merriam-Webster Dictionaries.

[2] By permission. From Webster's Third New International Dictionary, copyright 1961 by G. & C. Merriam Co., Publishers of the Merriam-Webster Dictionaries.

ambiguously applied so that it seems often to mean, at one and the same time, an image *by* a group and *of* a group (a corporation). The latter meaning had by 1958 reached a point of acceptance which prompted the Opinion Research Corporation of Princeton, New Jersey, to engage in a study of corporate images and of their possible development and change. Writing in *Public Relations Journal* in September, 1959, Dr. Claude Robinson and Dr. Walter Barlow of Opinion Research said:

> Our thesis in this article is that the corporate image is a bright new con-
> cept that is extremely useful to thinking about company communications;
> that the usage of the image concept will grow and become common in
> the language of communications; in short, we submit that the corporate
> image is by no means a conversational fad. It is, in fact, the *real McCoy*.
>
> Words have no inner or inevitable meaning, but are devices for com-
> munication. They are carriers both of meaning and of feeling tone. And,
> as all of us know, the cargo of meaning carried by any one word is con-
> stantly shifting and undergoing change. The test of the acceptability of a
> word or concept is very simple. It is this: Is the word or concept useful
> in visualizing, or as we might say, mentally imaging the world?
>
> The idea of the corporate image passes this test with high marks. It is
> a convenient and helpful way to visualize people's ideas about companies.
> It lends itself to measurement and analysis. A corporate image situation
> can be diagnosed, programs can be worked out to deal with it, and results
> can be measured. Or, in other words, the concept of the corporate image
> fits very practically into the working day world of operations.
>
> By corporate image, then, we mean simply the mental pictures that
> people have in their heads about companies and corporations. These men-
> tal pictures may come from direct or indirect experience. They may be
> rational or irrational, depending on evidence or hearsay, appear in an
> infinite number of patterns.
>
> The fundamental reality of mental pictures in people's heads is evident
> to all.
>
> Columbus practically had to shanghai men aboard his three-ship con-
> voy to the New World, because of the belief that the world was flat, and
> that if you sailed far enough west, you would drop into the Abyss.
>
> Standard Oil Company changed its name in part because Ida Tarbell
> fastened upon it the mental picture of monopoly.
>
> A major eastern employer still has difficulty in recruiting top-flight labor
> because the idea is still afloat in the community that it is a "butcher shop"
> despite the fact that old hazards have been so successfully removed that
> the company has won industrial safety awards.
>
> The railroads today are being regulated on the basis of their "monopo-
> listic position" despite the emergence in recent years of strong competition
> from other forms of transportation.

Even in the above explanation two definitions compete for acceptance. The fourth paragraph is clearly slanted toward the object imaged—a corporation; the sixth paragraph, toward the tendency of men to hold an image corporately.

The word "image" is similar to the term "stereotype" and is associated with "prejudice," which in its Latin form simply means "prejudging" a matter before the evidence is in. It is obviously impossible to have an image of something with which one has no contact, and images about remote things are generally quite feeble and susceptible of change. The concern about images in modern times springs from the fact that people today are supposed to have valid images of a great many things—the United Nations, Soviet Russia, Latin American industrialization, labor union B, or corporation X—about which they really know very little at first hand. A man finds that these images, once established, are often very hard to change. He has to make a distinct effort; he is likely to upset other closely held values; and his independence of thought may alienate him from friends who are to some extent friends because they hold the same opinions. Altering images is a painful, wrenching process, often leading to great unhappiness. Many persons, under certain conditions of age, health, or emotional conflict, simply give up even trying to alter their images; they have even been known to stone or to crucify those who persist in disturbing them.

Ascertaining the Nature of the Corporate Image

In the April, 1958, study referred to earlier, Opinion Research Corporation sought to find out about corporate images by the following means:

1. Motivation research using lengthy taped interviews to see how closely connected people are with corporations and to determine what image areas are real enough to justify measurement
2. A pilot test consisting of 307 interviews in the Trenton, New Jersey, area
3. Depth interviews nationally to examine the effect of distance upon perception
4. Tests upon a panel of persons in Hopewell, New Jersey
5. Field testing scattered over the United States to see if the survey method really worked in practice

In the completed survey itself, respondents were first given a pack of twenty 3- by 5 inch cards, each with a company name on it, and were asked to sort the cards into five different piles according to their degree of familiarity with each company. The choices were: "Never heard of company or company name," "Heard of company but know practically nothing about it," "Know just a little bit about the company," "Know a fair amount about the company," and "Know the company well."

The names of companies which were totally unfamiliar were discarded, and overall favorability and unfavorability were then checked by the same method. Following this came a more detailed survey in which respondents had the opportunity to express their reasons for opinions in fifty different ways. More than 3,000 interviews were conducted in respondents' homes.

Among the major findings about company images flowing from this study were the following:

> The bigness of a company does not ensure a widespread or favorable image.
>
> Better-known companies are almost always more favorably known.
>
> The public is quite selective in what it considers good or bad about a company.
>
> Companies manufacturing consumer goods have an advantage in image building; but producer-goods companies can also use advertising in print or on television to achieve a better-than-usual response.
>
> A company may be profitable yet unknown to the public.
>
> People may praise a company's products, yet consider it a bad citizen.
>
> Employee opinion contributes greatly to reputation, but often only as an employer and not in relation to products.

Doing Something about the Corporate Image

In effect, "doing something about the corporate image" is the whole point of this book (if we expand "corporate image" to include images of many kinds of organizations). The recommendations of Opinion Research in July, 1958, after further analysis of the survey, are therefore of special interest.

1. Map out the strengths and weaknesses of the corporation's existing image. This obviously calls for valid study and also some questions about what publics one is most concerned with.

2. Consciously plan and write out a definition of the corporate image which it is wished to project. Here some soul-searching may be necessary, because if the image desired is too far away from the facts, its projection will be difficult or even self-defeating. Questions such as "Who are we?" "What do we stand for?" "In what ways are we distinctive?" and "How would we wish to be thought of?" are in order.

3. Create selling themes for projecting this image to the publics. One problem is to refine a whole list of qualities and goals to a few simple things which may be understood. Depending upon the degree of their existing connection, publics are only *somewhat* interested in what one has to say, since they are exposed to a great many competing messages.

4. Utilize *all* means of contact to build an image—advertising, employees, salesmen, letterheads, product, slogans on shipping cases, everything possible. The favorable image increases with the number of contacts.

What Can You Expect from a Favorable Corporate Image?

A conservative (and realistic) answer to the above question might be: to be better off with it than without it. An unfavorable image is more of a handicap than a favorable image is an assurance of success, because numbers of companies have reasonably favorable images. An organization with an unfavorable image may find it hard to get good new employees and may have more sales problems, more labor difficulties and more governmental friction. It may have more difficulty in obtaining money and enjoy less stockholder satisfaction.

But while an unfavorable corporate image may rightly be thought of as a handicap, a favorable image is no substitute for good products, good selling, progressive research, and good all-round company management. Favor will not ensure that a firm will never have a strike, never be investigated by a Senate committee, or never face a falling sales curve. Favor is simply money in the bank against the time that these things may happen, and it is also capital upon which an enterprising management may build more soundly.

The Public Image of "Business" versus Specific Businesses

An interesting point in the public-opinion surveys referred to earlier is that while people frequently feel quite well disposed toward individual companies, many still fear and dislike "big business" in general. Apparently the efforts of individual concerns, even the very large ones, to be understood and liked often meet with considerable success, but the group efforts of businessmen as a class have been far less successful.

The explanation probably lies in the fact that every time business attempts to speak as a social group, it sets itself off from (and in opposition to) other American social groups. The phenomenon is not new and applies equally to other American groups, such as farmers or laborers; yet for many reasons, business people feel it necessary to engage in political activity and often talk too much. Increasingly their business success is determined by political factors, and in the climate of the economic democracy of the 1960s politics can scarcely be ignored.

The Proper Role of Businesses in Political Activity

At the close of the nineteenth century, in the days of Hanna and McKinley, it was accepted as a matter of course that businessmen should have a strong influence in politics. In getting a street-railway franchise approved, arranging for a tariff boost, or fighting against an eight-hour day, the purse counted heavily, and there were frequently close and only slightly concealed alliances between business bosses who could deliver the cash and political bosses who could deliver the votes.

With the coming of the trust-busting and muckraker days, however, and with political upheavals and politically strong labor unions, the pendulum shifted to the other extreme, and business firms eschewed open political activity as if it were poison. Known business support became a "kiss of death" for many candidates, and company sales managers preferred that their firms should not take sides for fear of retaliation in the market place.

In a way, this divorce from politics was something of a relief to many businessmen—because the plain fact is that, for a number of reasons, most businessmen are not very good at politics. Because of necessary advertising and sales promotional activities, large businesses are usually well known to the public. They are assumed to be rich, powerful, and interested in money. By comparison with the relative obscurity of the individuals who may oppose them, their motives are shining targets.

Businessmen themselves are often singularly obtuse when it comes to dealing with other people who are not in the business world. They often do not take into account the fact that other groups of people in the world may have quite different value systems, and they may consider other value systems wicked or lazy.

Even worse, business people have a great propensity to associate only with other people of the same standing in industry; their exclusiveness leads to a mental inbreeding which soon causes them to believe that the opinion of this peer group is the true voice of the people.

It is not easy for the typical business executive to engage in politics, even if he wants to. He has little time; he is accustomed to issuing orders and having them obeyed, rather than to palavering and compromising; and if he runs for office and should be so unfortunate as to get elected, there is a good chance that while he is away for a year or two serving his state or nation, the ranks of his organization will close behind him and upon his return he will not find his original position open; someone else has moved up the company ladder while he was absent. And frequently he may find his fellow corporation members practically forbidding him to seek offices which might implicate the firm even by indirection.

For these reasons, most United States legislative bodies are about two-thirds filled with lawyers, who find their value enhanced when they return to their firms or partnerships after a tour of duty in the state or national capitals, and by an assortment of other people whose activities permit them to campaign and to serve. Major businessmen are conspicuously absent.

Yet this abstention from politics today leaves business in a dilemma. In the bad old days of the nineteenth century, business was often in un-ashamed, direct control of government to its own advantage. In the past few decades, business has been largely cast out of the governmental fold, where votes count more than money (although money is needed to buy media time and to seek votes), and has contented itself with concentration upon technological improvements, expansion, and a struggle with labor organizations. But this no longer suffices. With inevitably increasing government control business will be influenced by political actions more and more, whether or not it makes any endeavor to control them.

The question for business interests is, what to do.

In most instances, when business openly, and *as business,* enters the political arena, it gets licked. Although a profit motive may be unimpeachable, it makes a poor platform from which to campaign, unless large groups of people outside the business can also be shown to benefit. It may be argued that labor or farm groups are also interested in a profit motive (their own profits), but their case is somewhat different, because these numerous groups of people easily succeed in convincing themselves that their motives are disinterested and for the good of the country. Besides, they have many votes, while major businessmen arc few in number, and with the expansion of the size of corporations every year, the ranks of proprietor-owners continue to diminish and the proportion of wage or salary earners to expand. If businessmen wish to win political battles, they must take with them into the campaign a sizable proportion of wage earners or other groups who can see their advantage also in the management's goals. The problem is, how to do it. A strictly "business party" in the United States can hardly expect to get to first base, and by arousing strong antagonism might bring about the very trends toward socialism which it wishes to avoid. Business people might with more wisdom penetrate deep into the ranks of existing political organizations, where issues are fought out at the primary or at a previous level before they ever see the light of public vote.

This idea of infiltration into political parties is not new; it gained ground under the leadership of the United States Chamber of Commerce in the late 1950s. A definite demonstration of the results is yet to be seen.

In 1961 Earl P. Johnson, Director of Industrial Relations of Frederick & Nelson Department Store in Seattle, Washington, said:

> (We) also have a responsibility to encourage the staff members, as individual citizens, to participate in the political party of their choice. . . . In the field of politics there has recently been a great hiatus. In the past, there was an unwritten law in most businesses that perhaps it was best not to get into politics too much because it is a controversial area. If it is controversial an individual might find that top management would be unwilling to let him participate because he works in a company that caters to the public. . . .
>
> We have now said that it is not only our responsibility to encourage staff members to become active in the party of their choice, but that as a company we will do what we can to assist them to become effective.
>
> With this statement of policy, we have assured our staff members that their political activities are the same as though they were active in some charitable or cultural program where some time away from the job is needed, that we would work out a program whereby time would become available. . . . We would not draw the line if someone decided they wanted to become a candidate for office. We would take a good look at

the dilemma in which the individual might find himself and would try to work out a program for him. If a company is to encourage its staff members to get active in the political party of the individual's own choice, then the company must go into the program wholeheartedly.

The Frederick & Nelson program not only included encouragement of staff members and time allowance, but also contained an indoctrination course in the free enterprise system (United States Chamber of Commerce material) and in the operations of the department store itself.

Another program upon a large scale is that of the Ford Motor Company, which in 1950 established a Civic Affairs Office and in 1959 greatly expanded it to include eight regional offices. Here the program stresses encouragement of political participation, an eight-session Effective Citizenship Course, setting up a voluntary political contribution plan for all employees, promotion of voting, and coverage of political contests in plant newspapers. Particular attention is paid to the relations between plant and city and between plant and state, to tours by public officials, to presentation locally of company views on current issues, to a service-awards program for employees who have made exceptional contributions to civic and governmental affairs, and to presenting to employees a record of legislative activity as it affects the company and business in general.

The success of such a program depends upon the individual's freedom to act as he sees fit and upon the company's loyalty to issues rather than to parties. If these conditions can be met, and if business groups can be imaginative enough to think in terms of human reactions instead of dollars, then there is a good chance that, over the years, business people may again exert considerable influence in political decisions; but they will do so primarily as people and only secondarily as representatives of firms.[3]

The "Corporate Image" Is Not a "Corporations Image"

The building of a corporate image which may work so well for a single company often breaks down when thoughtlessly transferred to "business" as a group interest. Most people see individual companies primarily as sources of benefits—employment, payrolls, products, and the like. They see business groups as a menacing form of control.

Perhaps the best public relations for a business group is to forget its self-consciousness as much as possible. Its members should stop gathering in clusters at luncheon and country clubs; they should include students, scholars, farmers, laborers, and housewives in their social structures without condescension, should stop talking about what is good for business and instead concentrate upon what is good for the nation or the world, and

[3] See also Dan A. Kimball, "Politics for Corporate Employees," *Public Relations Journal,* August, 1959.

above all should stop making pronouncements upon subjects in which the businessman's competence is neither greater nor necessarily less than that of many other persons. The attempted deification of any group in an outspoken, individualistic, democratic society is likely to have adverse results and should not be sought but rather avoided. Businessmen's organizations would frequently be well advised to be inconspicuous (except among their members and by their good works) while their members become well known by many segments of the rest of the public through activities that all enjoy in common, such as recreation, education, welfare, religion—and politics! Business has many good ideas to present and a vital role to play; but it does not have the voting power or the attractiveness to be dominant by itself.[4]

[4] See "The Political Impotence Of Business," a talk delivered by Robert L. Bliss at the annual convention, Public Relations Society of America, Miami. Fla., Nov. 4, 1959.

The Tools of Public Relations

8

One reason why the practice of public relations may be called an art or perhaps even a science is that it requires knowledge and expert skill to use the tools of mass communication effectively. Since most people are not proficient in the field, such knowledge sets public relations men above the amateurs whose winning personalities can charm a few persons at a time in face-to-face meetings. Charm is always useful and often highly desirable, but even applied during a whole lifetime, would scarcely be enough to change the image of a big corporation, to succeed in a major welfare drive, or to win a big election.

This chapter, therefore, will concentrate on an explanation of the effective use of the mass media—press, radio and television, motion pictures, and other means of reaching large numbers of people at one time. Men who work in the mass media fields spend their lives becoming expert in the use of these tools of communication, and a single chapter in this book can do little more than point out how to begin. Many good detailed books are available upon the nature and uses of the mass media. The serious student is referred to the short list at the end of this chapter and to many other books which can be found in any good library.

What Is Said Is Most Important, but It Must Be Well Said

Expertness in the use of the mass communications media such as newspapers, posters, booklets, or motion pictures is not, in itself, enough to ensure success in communication. *What* is said is as important as *how* it is said. But expertness is still essential; we know that a surgeon's capable diagnosis must be accompanied by sufficient skill and dexterity to enable him to perform the operation successfully. A poorly written news story never gets past the desk of a keen editor to see the light of day in a good daily newspaper's columns; a poster which attracts no attention carries no message; a badly designed booklet may repel and discourage a reader; and an ill-planned, poorly produced motion picture is a waste of time, money, and opportunity. Skill in handling these media does not lead inevitably to communication, but it makes it much more possible!

Once, before people were bombarded with so many messages every day of their lives, their tolerance of dull, clumsy, or even ugly communications was reasonably high. They are no longer so patient. Readers, listeners, and viewers have become sufficiently sophisticated, from wide exposure to good techniques, to demand excellence without even being conscious of the basis of their judgment. Readers may not expect a company magazine to look like *Life* or *Better Homes and Gardens,* but they do expect it to be well designed and illustrated, colorful, lively, and interesting. To offer them less is to court rejection as a rank amateur. Viewers may not expect an industrial motion picture to meet the most lavish Hollywood production standards, but it must be well photographed, well written, and well paced. Amateur film scrambles belong only in the privacy of family reunions.

But expertness in the mass communications media can be its own trap through "the illusion of communication," which develops when a publicity man totals up the many inches in his press clippings without asking, "Who read these?" and "What did they think?" or when a board of directors of a firm departs, oozing congratulations after seeing the preview of a new motion picture about its own company, without asking coldly, "Why should a stranger be at all concerned with this?"

The best writers, magazine editors, artists, and graphic-production experts are often the most likely to suffer from these illusions of communication because, to them, a well-written story, an attractive magazine, a beautiful picture, or an award-winning film are often ends in themselves, whereas to a public relations man, they are a means to the end of conveying thought to other people. This is why a good newspaperman or a good broadcaster may sometimes fail to be a good public relations man; he may be too easily satisfied with the high quality of his methods and not enough concerned with their real effects upon people.

In fact, the very phrase "mass communication" is in itself a trap. There is no such thing as *mass* communication; there is only the mechanical multiplying of single messages by mass means—by the printing press or broadcasting station—to produce many identical messages which go to many single persons at the same time. In each such mass communication the writer or speaker tries to communicate with individual receivers at the other end of the line. Very seldom do receivers get together in interacting groups to receive communications. They might do so at a pep meeting or in a mob, but usually receivers read alone, listen alone, see alone—even in the midst of others.

THE NEWS FAMILY OF THE MASS MEDIA

The Press and Publicity

American newspapers, because of their size, frequent appearance, and universality, provide probably the best way of reaching large numbers of people at the same time. They are not so useful in many other countries where a large proportion of the population is illiterate, newspaper circulations are scattered, the papers are small, and the standards of journalism are low. In the United States, until broadcasting came along in the 1920s, the press was the only large medium of news communication. American public relations first sprang out of press-agentry, which was the practice of supplying newspapers with free stories in the hope that they would see fit to print them.

Since it was natural for firms that wanted press agents to hire men who were already skilled in press methods, most early specialists in communication were former newspapermen, and even today about 60 per cent of the public relations men in this country still spring from newspaper backgrounds. The percentage is diminishing, but it may always remain high because press experience, entirely aside from the fact that it makes a man expert in news writing, also develops qualities of alertness, enterprise, and good judgment, which are valuable to a public relations man under any circumstances.

American newspapers have certain special characteristics. They are issued locally; they tend to play up local news to a relatively greater extent than national or foreign news (although this tendency has changed); they are read by almost everyone within their circulation areas; and though they differ in many ways, they all use similar wire services, syndicated features, and much the same formulas and patterns of editing.

Advantages: As a medium of communication in public relations, newspapers have certain advantages.

They are timely. Stories can be taken to them, mailed, or wired, and then released very quickly.

Newspapers are inexpensive to use. Almost all American newspapers are honest and would scorn an offer of pay for running genuine news coming from public relations sources. Such news, in fact, is of advantage to both promoter and paper, since it supplies the material which a newspaper is in the business of selling. The only cost to a public relations man of such newspaper publicity is his time in obtaining, writing, and delivering the news.

Newspapers are precise. Their facts are detailed carefully in a manner which readers can study at the time or refer to later.

Newspaper news implies belief in its importance because in running it, a good newspaper says to its readers, "We believe this to be true, or we shouldn't have presented it to you."

Disadvantages. Newspaper stories must be brief and of wide appeal. Long, complicated reports, of interest to only a few people, cannot be carried in most newspapers and should usually not even be submitted.

News stories are subject to editing. The editor has the full right to change them as he desires, and their size may be cut or the emphasis of the contents changed.

News stories may not be used at all even if submitted. All big newspapers and many of the smaller ones are deluged every day with far more stories than they can print; the best, in the editors' judgment, are used and the rest are thrown away.

News stories may not always be read or understood. Readers are not supposed to read *all* the items in a large newspaper every day, and a story which scores 20 per cent recall is doing very well. But in a daily of 500,000 circulation this per cent would mean at least 100,000 readers (and really far more than that, since newspapers are usually bought one to a family), which is quite a large figure.

However, just because a news story runs and is reasonably well read, we cannot conclude that the important readers have seen it. Those who are hostile or little interested—and they may be the very ones whose attention is most sought—will probably ignore a news story. A whole battery of similar stories would not affect them much more; they could ignore them all.

"Thinking like the editor" is the key to success in writing news and feature stories for American newspapers. This adaptability often comes naturally to those who have been reporters or editors, but even persons without this practical advantage can try. The way to start is to forget the kind of stories *you* want to run and, instead, consider what the editor might want to run.

Good public relations men make a habit of reading and understanding the newspapers to which they send releases. Nothing is more insulting and exasperating to a newspaper editor than for a public relations man to try to foist off on him stories which are obviously not suitable to his readers' interests. The kind of stories that a newspaper wants in every department is plain for anyone to see in every day's issue. Editors are naturally flattered when those who offer them news stories give evidence of having read and appreciated their paper. Stories should be written, for example, for readers with the special interests of people in the editor's own town or area.

Knowing the editor and being his friend cannot fail to be of some help, simply because the friendship creates better understanding, if for no other reason. At the least, the editor would like to know who is responsible for the public relations news, how capable he is, how reliable, and where he may be reached for further facts or for verification of a story.

Our advice, then, is: Send the editor the kind of story he is most likely to use—accurate, timely, and in the best news style. *Accuracy* is always the first requirement; when an editor accepts a news story from a public relations source, he trusts that it will be correct to every last name, address, or minor fact. If it is wrong and if readers complain, they will complain to the newspaper, because they do not know who supplied the story in the first place. When the editor receives these complaints, he isn't likely to forget where the blame belongs and may be little inclined to do business in the future with that source of misinformation.

News is news because it is *new* and timely. If a company's president is to make a speech and the public relations man has a text of what he is planning to say (perhaps he helped write it), it is a good idea to give the text of the speech to the newspapers a day or two in advance, especially if the delivery of the speech is slated to be close to their news deadlines. (Afternoon papers usually go to press from 11 A.M. to 3 P.M. and should have news items by at least 9 A.M. on the day of publication and usually much earlier if possible. Morning papers usually go to press between 6 P.M. and 11 P.M. and should be supplied by at least noon of the previous day. Sunday papers often close some of their sections several days in advance, and weeklies may close the day before publication date. It is always well to ask newspapers when they would like material, if there is a choice.) Make sure that the speech was *actually* delivered as scheduled. Telephone the paper if there are any changes; if the speaker departed materially from his text or, worse yet, if he didn't even appear, the people who were in attendance might be highly amused by a newspaper report of an event which never happened—although the editor wouldn't share their amusement!

If the date of a coming event is known, a release date can be placed upon a story submitted well in advance. Play fair with news releases. If there are morning and evening newspapers in one city (not a common situation today), be sure that first release dates are divided somewhat equally between the two papers except, of course, for spot-news happenings that cannot be controlled. When a daily newspaper is surrounded by weeklies, which are usually issued on Wednesdays or Thursdays, don't always release stories for the daily on Friday, for example, leaving the weeklies to wait for a whole week while the news spoils. Above all, don't expect a newspaper to print stale news; get it to the editor quickly.

Anyone who can write the English language well can write a decent, even if not an inspired, news story if he tries. To do so, read many good news stories analytically and study a good basic journalism text for style. Remember that news stories are distinguished by certain characteristics.

Brevity. How long a story should be depends somewhat upon the publication. The story of a new-plant dedication, which in a small town might run a column in length or might even occupy a special section or page, in Chicago might be worth only two short paragraphs. Length also depends, on any given day, upon the local importance of news in relation to other items and also upon the total news space available. But in any case, a good news story keeps on the track, avoids long-windedness, and does not wander or digress. It has an informational mission to accomplish and is not a literary essay.

Inverted order. Newspaper readers are skimmers who want to get the essence of what happened as easily as possible. Hence the writer should put the main news facts into the first few sentences—usually the answers to the ancient questions of who, what, why, when, where, and how.

Objectivity. The writer's opinions generally do not belong in news reports because the reader is paying to learn the facts, not to hear what some reporter thinks about them.

Timeliness is, of course, essential.

Accuracy, as mentioned earlier, is fundamental in every respect.

Mechanical conformity. A news story should always be typed (or duplicated similarly), should be double- or triple-spaced with ample margins, usually on white or light-colored paper. The source's name, telephone number, and address should appear in the upper left-hand corner of the first page. The word "More" should appear at the bottom of the first page if the story is continued and should be repeated at the bottoms of any other pages preceding continuations. Second and subsequent pages should be numbered in the upper right-hand corners and should also be identified by a slugline based on the essence of the news, such as "Jones's speech" or "fire." The end of the story should be identified by a crosshatch ($\#$), "30," or some other indication of conclusion.

Don't beg or carp in dealing with editors. If a single story fails to appear, you may have misjudged its news value for that publication, or competition for news space may have been unusually intense on that particular day. Such competitive news pressure arose when the president of a leading American university died just before Pearl Harbor Sunday in 1941. Two days earlier his obituary would have been worth a column, but on that particular day most newspapers considered it worth only one short paragraph. But if a string of submitted news stories fails to appear, it is time to check. See if the material with which the paper is being supplied is of genuine news interest. If you think it is, then perhaps you should ask the editor whether it is being prepared in the right way and sent in at the right times. Never, however, make the mistake of insinuating to an editor that you know better than he does what his readers need and want.

In dealing with reporters, it pays to shoot square. Getting news is a reporter's business; you may help him, but you must not expect too many favors. Don't ask a reporter to suppress a news item, because his first duty is to give it to his newspaper. Generally, don't ask an editor to suppress a story either (although you may discuss a possible change of timing to avoid anticipation of a bigger story or to prevent injury to someone); the decision of the press is final. If you have a complaint about the way a story has been written by a reporter to whom you have supplied the facts, tell the reporter before you run to his superiors. If you have a valid complaint about the distortion of a mailed or wired release, then see the editor to whom it was directed.

There are right and wrong times to see newspaper editors. Getting out an afternoon daily newspaper is a periodic crisis which in times of stress becomes almost theatrical. Generally, the critical period is from midmorning until press time, and then for about a half-hour thereafter, while the debris and the mistakes are being cleared away. (Any large paper which runs tens of thousands of words daily is certain to have errors in its first edition.) Finally, later in the day, comes a period of relative bliss in which long-range efforts (for tomorrow, perhaps) can be thought of. This is the best time to see an editor or a reporter in the news room.

There are all sorts of editors on large newspapers—city editors, responsible for local news coverage (the "editors" generally referred to thus far), sports editors, business editors, financial editors, women's editors, school editors, real estate editors, church editors, editors of the editorial page, and editors in almost any other field of particular interest in which the paper specializes. A publicity release concerning a new food usually should go to the women's editor, but if it refers to the expansion of a local plant, it might well go to the city editor, or to the business editor; a charity football game would, of course, be reported to the sports editor, but the story of a ladies' ticket-selling tea in connection with the game should be directed to the women's or society editor; a company's annual financial report is destined for the business or financial editor. It pays to get acquainted with all the special needs of these editors, because they all value good news sources which help them in their coverage and make them win the approval of the managing editor, who is in charge of the entire news department and is usually immediately under the publisher.

The news standards of these various newspaper editors and their departments may differ considerably. The city editor deals with important items of general local interest and may not be at all interested in an item concerning a new use of plastic sheeting in covering building excavations. He would either throw it away or send it to the real estate or financial editors, to whom it should have gone in the first place. They might, perhaps, welcome it, especially if they were struggling to fill a quota of news space on a dull day or if they faced the production of a big special section devoted to one of their areas of interest.

Editors also usually welcome knowing about the availability of helpful authorities in news related to their fields. Frequently a man handling public relations news releases for an oil company or a chemical firm knows (and should know) more about oil or chemicals than the business or perhaps even the science editor of a newspaper. One public relations man for a French oil company has not only become an expert in his field but has also assembled a great library of facts and pictures about world petroleum production and processing. When an oil crisis breaks out in the Sahara or in Iran or in Venezuela, reporters for many French newspapers call upon him first for factual material.

A public relations man is ill-advised to attempt to use advertising as a club to "persuade" a newspaper news staff. On most good newspapers the news staff is well insulated from such attempts to bargain with advertising. Editors and reporters resent any attempt to apply pressure and will often punish those who try to do so by ignoring even good material later. In fact, advertisers sometimes need the use of space in monopoly newspapers more urgently than the newspapers need the money of the advertisers.

A public relations man will do well, too, to be careful about gifts and lavish entertainment of the press. Newspapermen are busy, and free cocktails or dinners are no novelty in their lives. They do not usually mind being fed or being given a few drinks when business is to be done, but they will not be bought in this way. On the other hand, it is not a bad idea to give a press party sometimes, just to get better acquainted. It should be purely social, with no suggestion of commercial motives.

If minor gifts, such as a fifth of whisky at Christmas, have been customary, the habit should be continued; but if you start giving away fifths or cases more often, consciences will start hurting and relations will be impaired rather than improved. Major gifts arouse the suspicion of news heads, who understandably want their men's first loyalty to be to their newspapers and to honest reporting rather than to a set of personal benefactors. In general, giving gifts to the press is a dubious practice which has not been favored greatly in recent years and should be looked upon with suspicion.

Press Conferences

There are a few occasions on which an organization may legitimately wish to invite the press to send representatives to hear an important announcement or to engage in an interview with an important person. The inauguration of a new company president, with whom news reporters might wish to become acquainted, or the announcement of a new product which requires considerable explanation would warrant an invitation. The main advantages of a press conference from a newspaper's point of view (which is all that should be considered) are that it permits each publication to develop an individual story, facilitates questioning, and releases a news opportunity to all at the same time.

It is customary to prepare complete press kits for everyone at a press conference in order to save time. For the inauguration of a new president, for instance, such a kit would probably include his biography, his picture, a prepared statement, facts about any other staff changes, and perhaps material upon the retiring president and the company as a whole. A kit on a new scientific discovery might be almost a book in itself and might be sent out several days in advance with a "hold for release" date, which the press will always honor.

If, from the newspapers' viewpoint, the news given out at a press conference could just as well have been obtained from a prepared release, then the press conference probably should not have been held. Newsmen are busy, and once having been fooled by a newsless press conference, they do not tend to return to the scene of their disappointment.

Another question to ask in considering the desirability of a press conference is: Is the organization really willing to answer all questions which might be asked at such a meeting? A man who holds a press conference offers to tell the whole truth, as if he were taking the witness stand in a court; if he has anything to hide, he may find that the suspicious circumstance will be brought to light.

Handling Bad News

Some bad news is just the report of an unfortunate occurrence for which no one is to blame. An oil-refinery fire, for instance, does not necessarily reflect unfavorably upon the efficiency of the company which suffers the loss. In a case like this the company public relations staff should be well prepared in advance to help the press do the necessary job of covering the major news break. The company must have the basic facts ready to give out to reporters; must designate company spokesmen to describe accurately the damage, dangers, time needed for repair, and other details; must provide space in which reporters can work, typewriters, and telephone facilities; must supply guides and perhaps also darkrooms to aid photographers; must provide transportation around the scene—and perhaps even food. These arrangements must be mapped out well in advance and should be filed as carefully as a battle plan, since there will be no time to improvise coverage once a disaster strikes. The rewards of foresight and helpfulness to the press can be a chance to get across the company's side of the story, that is, to emphasize the smallness of the loss, the continued solvency of the company, the brief interruption of production, the assurance that orders will continue to be filled, the humanity of the company in caring for its workers and for volunteer helpers, and expressions of thanks. A final reward may be the expectation that those who help the press to do a good job in their work of covering the news will most likely themselves receive help from the press sometime.

Bad news, however, may also be somewhat disgraceful—as, for example, the absconding of an insurance-company official with a large amount of money, or carelessness in the manufacture of a product which results in death or injury to users. In these instances a company public relations man will hardly seek out the press and call the unhappy facts to their attention. Yet bad news is often passed to the press for two reasons:

1. Auditors' reports, customer suits, or government orders will bring such matters to light before the public soon, and it is better to be sure that the whole story comes out at one time.
2. Complete honesty with the press, even when it hurts, is much respected by newsmen.

In any event, there is no use trying to deny the facts or to cover up bad news. A public relations man, in effect, works for the press as well as for the organization which employs him. He cannot expect to lie to the press and still preserve his usefulness as a source of news. The very least he can do is to say, "I don't know" (and this is not very satisfactory because he should know, and if he is ignorant, he loses the esteem of the press). Or he can say, "I can't tell you" (which is taken to mean "Yes—but you'll have to dig higher"). In *no* case can he say, "The truth is this," when really it is something entirely different.

Nor can reporters be easily kept from a story once they are on the scent of it. At one time the airlines, following the theory that accident news was bad for air travel, tried to keep newspapers from getting or running pictures of air crashes, and the personnel of the United States Air Force has covered up news of disasters many times, sometimes alleging security needs when none existed. Company guards at strike scenes have been known to rough up cameramen and break their cameras, and labor goons have done the same. But the press always has the last word, and it is better for an organization to accept inevitable news coverage with grace, since it cannot expect favorable treatment one day if it withholds its own favors the next.

Publicity Photographs

Paradoxically, photographs are both easier and harder to get into large daily newspapers than are news stories. Photos encounter more difficulty because the competition for pictures is great on a large paper. The picture editor of a big metropolitan daily may be able to run perhaps forty pictures in each issue as compared with several hundred news stories. Some of these forty pictures are "mug shots," plain face pictures of people involved in crimes, accidents, political campaigns, speeches, honors, and other events; others are necessary news shots of fires, floods, and so forth; and society and sports photos account for many of the rest. Not much room is left for publicity.

Photos are *easier* to get into a newspaper than stories because many news pictures are so routine that anything unusual or interesting in itself is welcomed. Every spring, for example, the city editor says to the picture editor, "I think we ought to run a spring shot." Then the photographers try to think of something "different" for a spring photograph. Lambs? No. Flowers? No. Little boys wading in the rain puddles without their rubbers? No. Young couples walking down a farm lane hand in hand? No. All these have been worked to death.

On one large Detroit newspaper a photographer, confronted with this annual problem, reasoned like this: "What does spring suggest? Romance. What does that suggest? Necking. What creature could do the most necking? A giraffe." So he went out to the zoo to get a picture of necking giraffes. When the zoo keeper told him that giraffes had never seemed to find necking romantic, he decided to try for kissing giraffes. He started two giraffes eating simultaneously at the ends of a tasty green vine, and when both reached the middle—click! The kissing giraffes made a most unusual spring shot.

Not everyone can be so ingenious, but because *good* news-feature pictures are hard to come by, newspapers often use them when available. Standard ordinary subjects which are likely to be used include new buildings, new products, new personnel, and newly promoted employees. These have a value "for the record"; their use depends upon the size of the city and the importance of the organization. Feminine beauty, babies, and animals are subjects which are more interesting in themselves and though much overworked, still are popular. Since the public pays attention to newspaper pictures and remembers them, public relations men will find them well worth working for.

A few mechanical points should be noted about supplying pictures for newspaper use. Photographic prints for newspaper use should have good, but not extreme, black-and-white contrast and clear object outlines, since printing reproduction is only fair in quality and the pictures may be reduced in size. "Busy" backgrounds should be avoided. Hotel lobbies, for example, seem always to be adorned with floral wallpaper. When the president of the company is photographed against this background, flowers may seem to be growing out of his ears. Even amateur photographers should know that a contrast between object and background is important.

Waste space should be avoided in planning the original composition of a photograph. When one man hands another an award scroll, for example, both men should be pictured standing shoulder to shoulder instead of at arm's length. In a picture of a house a great foreground of lawn is needless, unless the lawn has something to do with the story.

Most large newspapers want photos in 8- by 10- or 5- by 7-inch size upon glossy paper so that retouching, if necessary, may be done more easily. Exactly square or very tall pictures or pictures wider than they are tall are hard to fit into a newspaper page—although size may not be a difficulty if the subject and print are excellent.

Since weekly newspapers sometimes cannot find good photos to fill up their pages at reasonable cost, mats are welcomed. A mat is a hard cardboard impression of a metal picture printing cut which can be cast up into a duplicate cut reproduction by simply letting molten type metal flow against the hard, impressed cardboard. Other weeklies, using offset printing, may prefer good original glossy photoprints. In any case, weeklies are likely to have relatively more picture space available than larger dailies and they welcome pictures of local interest or simply attractive, not-too-commercial feature pictures. Good pictures, supplied in the form in which the paper needs them, are often most helpful in livening up the content.

Just as every public relations man needs to be able to write a competent news story, so he also needs to be able to judge and perhaps to obtain adequate news pictures or feature pictures by his own efforts. Some kinds of photographs, however, are better left alone. Taking personal portraits is a specialty outside the province of the amateur public relations cameraman. People are sensitive about their appearance and it is better to let them supply their own photos themselves or to get the pictures from a professional portrait photographer. Fashions, food, architecture, and large groups of people also need special photographic methods, and the amateur should not attempt them. But if he excludes these and perhaps a few other types of pictures, he may experiment at will. Reasonable mastery of a reflex or 35-mm camera is a skill well worth attaining, if for no other reason than that it frees a public relations man from the necessity of depending upon the services of professional photographers all the time, and from the resultant problems of expense, travel, and arrangement.

However, it is wise to keep out of the darkroom, since developing and printing photos take an inordinate amount of time which might better be spent otherwise. Arrangements for handling developing and printing may be made in any large city by working with a good commercial photographer who will not only save time and do a better job but can also give the amateur much good advice about exposure and composition.

Feature Stories Yield the Greatest Reward

The difference between a news story and a feature story is easily illustrated. Suppose that a company is having an award dinner for its employees who have had more than twenty years of service with the organization. The fact that the dinner was held, that certain persons attended, and that so-and-so spoke is news, though not very important news, perhaps, except in a small town, because these dinners occur all the time. But suppose that one of the persons receiving an award has been with the company for forty-five years, is the inventor of a process upon which the company of 20,000 employees was founded, and is going to retire next week. His history is surely the basis of a feature story. What sort of person is he? What does he recall of the early days, and how have things changed now? What does he foresee in the company's future? What does he plan to do after he retires?

Such feature stories are usually longer than news stories. They start with an interesting point instead of trying to cram their essence into the first paragraph, trot along pleasantly, and then try to end with a "twister." Feature stories are almost always illustrated, and their purpose is to entertain and to inform the reader at the same time.

Since no newspaper can carry many feature stories (perhaps two or three a day at the most and several more on Sunday), they must be well written and must justify the considerable expenditure of work and space they demand. At the same time, because of their length and usual human interest, features can make a strong impression upon readers. In today's great flow of communication, features may perhaps be read less often than formerly, but they make a deep impression upon those who do go through them, and they are remembered more vividly than small news stories just because they are less usual. Features, thus, are big game, well worth stalking with great patience and care.

A first rule about features might be: Don't write them yourself. In *news* stories, except for the comparatively rare press conference, the best procedure usually is just to write down the facts in proper news style and then to take or send the story in to the paper. Unless a public relations man is an expert *feature* writer, he would do better just to jot down the facts, add photos and supporting evidence, perhaps suggest a lead, and then submit the whole effort to the editor, a reporter, or sometimes to a free-lance writer. Doing this well in advance of possible future use often makes it possible to tie the feature into a handy news event. Several feature ideas may be suggested to an editor for each one that is accepted; but when an editor does once assign a reporter to handle a feature, the story will probably appear. Too much effort and money has been invested to warrant scrapping the product.

As we remarked about press conferences, the proposer of a feature should be sure that he *wants* to be investigated. If, for instance, a major newspaper or magazine is persuaded to do a feature upon a corporation president, once the investigative process has started, the company has little control over it, since reporters will ask their own questions and write in their own ways. The company may be permitted to check upon factual accuracy, but their supervision is granted as a courtesy, not as a right.

Trade-magazine Publicity

Just as every profession and occupation in the United States has its associations, so it also has its trade or professional magazines and newspapers which serve the needs of specialized reader interests. There are many thousands of such trade publications, ranging in size from large weekly magazines such as *Business Week,* which takes as its field the whole business world, down to the *Pigeon Breeders Journal.* Some are the size of very large magazines, well written and profusely illustrated. Others are flimsy little publications, struggling to make a living, and printed on cheap stock in inexpensive country printing shops. Some have news standards as high as any in the world, pay well for their stories, and hire first-class staff men. Others exist on a precarious advertising income from small, poor, or overcrowded fields, are easily subject to pressure for free news plugs, and may even solicit such material for a fee. A few are strictly puff sheets with no legitimate circulation to speak of, playing upon the vanity of space-hungry tycoons, and the gullibility, carelessness, or venality of public relations men who wish to make a good impression on their superiors by exhibiting a large number of column inches published rather than by choosing a reputable vehicle.

Good trade papers, however, represent an excellent outlet for public relations news and features. Such stories can be aimed directly at interested audiences and can go into a degree of detail which general-interest publications could hardly allow. In many highly specialized fields, such as scientific products or office machinery, general mass publicity is of secondary value only, since the general public is not a direct purchaser of these items; but good trade-magazine stories, reaching scientists' or businessmen's own interests, may result in immediate, recognizable sales. Trade-paper stories are much easier to place than general-magazine stories because their audiences have much more exact information and are good critics, whose opinion can often be important in their fields.

The editorial content of trade papers, like that of most magazines, is usually planned well in advance. But since some of the weekly and even daily trade papers pride themselves upon the speed with which they rush trade news to their readers, it is well to inquire carefully about deadlines. Pictures, particularly those of a technical nature, are more likely to be wanted by trade journals than by more general publications. Trade-paper printing quality may be so good and technical interest in detail so keen that much more intricate photos may be submitted than would be suitable for general newspaper use. Editorial staffs, accustomed to dealing with public relations people in their special fields, often welcome help because of the complex job they face in covering large, rapidly changing industrial, commercial, or professional projects.

General Magazines

There are only a few truly "general" magazines in the United States, such as *Look* or the *Saturday Evening Post.* The rest of the many hundreds of American magazines are aimed at specific audiences—at hunters and fishermen, women who are interested in homes and household furnishings, hot rodders, boat enthusiasts, and almost any interest group large enough to support circulation and attract advertising. Most of these audience appeals are apparent in the magazines themselves. A writer should stick to their patterns, because the chance is small that they will use anything unfamiliar. If America's daily newspapers represent the *places* where they are published, most American magazines represent their *audiences*.

In writing for a magazine, a public relations man will find that it pays to study its readers and how its editors try to appeal to them. The larger and more general a magazine becomes, the tougher is the competition it offers to writers. Not only do more writers attempt to sell to it because of its fame and higher rewards, but when its circulation reaches several million, it can and should be quite selective in using only material of interest to its subscribers. If a half dozen stories have to be thrown away in the process of selecting one, the waste (in the author's opinion) matters little to the editor, faced with the absolutely vital task of interesting and holding readers.

But if breaking into the large general-magazine field is not at all easy, the rewards are correspondingly great for products, services, or causes which can benefit from such widespread publicity. Articles for large publications are often written either by staff members or by free-lance writers. Whereas for smaller trade magazines it may be a good idea to submit whole articles and pictures already finished by a public relations source, the approach to a larger publication may need to be less direct; the magazine may want to write or to buy its own stories. A man engaged in publicity work may do well to offer an idea for a story, completely outlined or roughly sketched, to a free-lance writer who may be interested because of the opportunity for a story sale. The practice of some free lancers of getting paid twice, first by a public relations source and then by the magazine to which they sell their stories, is not unknown; but its doubtful ethics sometimes results in the ending of relations between the magazine and the free lancer.

Since most of the nation's larger magazines are published in New York City, connections there, including feature-placement bureaus, can be most helpful.

Radio Publicity

Most radio stations today stress local interests in the content of their programs, thus offering a useful medium for local publicity. Radio news is shorter than printed news and should be of more general interest than expanded newspaper accounts, since the radio listener does not have the same choice of selection that the newspaper reader enjoys. He can turn the set on or off or switch stations, but can only partially select what he hears or does not hear when the station is on.

Broadcast news is even more timely than printed news. It can be put on the air rapidly and is of value in emergencies. Radio newsmen cannot be ignored at press conferences and other events, but their ability to disseminate news ahead of press deadlines is irritating to newsmen, who have to move more slowly. Radio is always in a position to make a "scoop."

Radio can be especially useful for special features such as short on-the-spot recordings, longer news reports like those describing ski-resort snow and weather conditions, and interviews with interesting persons.

Television Publicity

The amount of time available for television news is even more limited than that for radio news, since there are fewer broadcasts, and fewer items can be used in each broadcast. But television's great need for *visual* material in its news broadcasts opens up many opportunities for public relations entry. Many TV stations do not spend money for consistent hire of local news cameramen and therefore welcome short, immediate film exposures showing meetings, speeches, openings, contests, sports, awards, and similar public relations events. Feature material—fashion shows, home shows, travel, and hobbies—is often useful also. The film coverage supplied by welfare organizations, associations, and educational institutions is particularly welcome, and its impact may be great.

Longer "sustaining" films of a low-key, feature-service caliber are also welcomed by stations to fit into unsold time, to provide substitutions in the event of sudden cancellations, or to help fill the odd intervals of time left after sports events and other irregularly timed programs. High standards of production are expected, in contrast to the jerky or overexposed shots tolerated on local news broadcasts. Resort-area promotion, interesting processes and people, sports, and social activities are typical subject matter. The commercial angle should be almost nonexistent, or at least not very apparent; when promotion is obvious, the station properly feels that it should be paid for the time.

Merchandising Publicity for the Greatest Results

Every public relations man who engages in publicity work also keeps a scrapbook of clippings, not only to see how he is doing but also to impress his employers. Often these clippings are duplicated and circulated to other company officers or to salesmen to show them how much attention is being paid to their organization by the press. This useful aid in buttressing a public relations man's value to his organization also has its perils. His superiors may say, "This is fine—now get us lots more!" and if the press becomes aware of such a trophy bag, it may think it is being imposed upon and curtail the number of news items and other stories. A sounder procedure for a public relations man is not to display every single clipping but instead to select significant typical stories to serve as demonstrations of "This is what they're saying about us." A deeper danger is that public relations people may oversell the value of publicity (always easy to do), which is only part of the job, sometimes not even the major part, and then find themselves chained to their company's impossible expectation of more and more mentions. In fact, clippings, rather than the achievement of understanding or good will, may become the managerial measure of success.

Another aspect of merchandising of publicity is found in the advertising pages of *Editor & Publisher,* the newspaperman's trade-paper Bible, and in other magazines devoted to the mass communications media. Here the public relations department of a company or other organization may offer its informational services to the press in whatever field of expertness its experience encompasses. "If you want to know about space communication," it may say, "call us up. We're glad to help." For those who have a genuine store of expert aid available, this is a worthwhile practice and also reflects credit upon all releases which proceed from such a source.

Publicity, however, can never be considered the equivalent of all public relations activities; while publicity can make an organization known, publicity alone cannot determine what people will think of it.

THE ADVERTISING FAMILY OF THE MASS MEDIA

Public Relations Advertising

Any advertising not aimed at the reasonably immediate sale of a product or service can be called "public relations" advertising. It is fairly common and has increased greatly in recent years.

Advertising, in contrast to publicity, appears in space purchased in a newspaper or magazine or in time bought on the air; in it the buyer may say what he wishes—as loudly, persuasively, wisely, or foolishly as he wishes. Such space or time is expensive, but it often provides the quickest and surest way of speaking to many people at once. Large space in a daily newspaper can reach almost all the people reading the paper within its circulation area, and in a magazine it can reach all the types of persons who constitute its reader audience.

Public relations advertising may be used to make an *announcement,* for example, of the position of a company in a labor dispute; to make a statement about a new product or a merger with another company; to contradict rumors; to thank those who helped in case of a disaster; to dedicate a plant; to invite to an open house; or to announce a closing because of the death of an official.

Advertising may be used to build a *corporate family image.* The du Pont Company, the General Electric Company, and General Motors Corporation make many products and advertise them all as individual items. But these companies do more; they also sponsor quality television shows and printed advertising designed to make customers think better of the company and of all its products because they come from that company. As many similar products develop, made by many other companies, this institutional type of advertising becomes more and more important because real, valid, individual product differences are constantly harder to find. Also, although people will refuse to buy a product whose maker is not known to them, they will take a chance on buying one of which they have heard.

In the discussion of high-quality products, particularly, the boundary between *sales* advertising and *public relations* advertising tends to blur. In Great Britain, for example, the public relations director and the advertising manager of Wedgwood Chinaware are the same man. Wedgwood *is* its reputation!

Advertising which is used to promote *causes,* such as opposition to taxes, anti-inflation drives, fighting foreign competition, seeking a larger share of the market (as when railroads compete with trucks), or presenting economic viewpoints and governmental philosophies, is also definitely public relations advertising. In today's increasingly complex world, where many arguments seek to influence public opinion, this advertising abounds and will doubtless spread still further. A question of tax deduction enters in at this point, however. Sales advertising, regarded as a necessary part of doing business, may be deducted from a corporation's profits before taxes are levied. But should a similar allowance be made for an electric power company which takes space in a paper to argue against the desirability of public ownership? Or how about a machine-tool-products company which constantly uses space to preach the virtues of the American free enterprise system? The question is far from settled.

Community understanding and good will are often the objectives of public relations advertisements. They may seek to explain the economic contributions of a business, to humanize the image of its management, and to recognize the good work of its employees. Even brief forms of annual financial reports are often published in this way.

Influence upon legislation is sought by many ads which run in state capitals and in Washington as well as in some other large cities.

Financial public relations goals are often sought by advertisements in newspapers such as the *Wall Street Journal* or magazines such as *Forbes* or *Business Week.*

Many other public relations advertisements are run as *consumer services,* for example, the long-standing magazine series on health by the Metropolitan Life Insurance Company of New York or the distinguished career series of the New York Life Insurance Company.

Public relations advertising not only appears in newspapers and in magazines, but is perhaps even more important on television, as is illustrated in its use by firms such as the United States Steel Company and Aluminium Ltd. of Canada.

Large, well-designed outdoor posters on highways announcing that a nearby city is the home of a certain factory also are a common form of public relations advertising. When an electric light company erects poster boards at the edges of its service-area towns telling passing motorists about the histories and merits of the towns, there is no doubt about the public relations slant, nor is there at the other extreme when an organization sponsors an "attend church" or "support the Community Chest" board with only its name below as sponsor identification.

TOOLS OF DIRECT APPROACH

In both press publicity and in paid advertising space, the primary vehicle for a public relations message is operated by someone else. A publicity story in a well-respected, widely circulated newspaper owes some of its effectiveness to the effectiveness of the newspaper itself. A public relations advertisement in a magazine directed to physicians, for example, is effective only to the extent that the magazine reaches doctors and is read and believed by them. Both the originators of publicity releases and the buyers of advertising space can judge the vehicles which carry their messages, but they do not control them. However, when an organization starts making speeches, showing motion pictures, taking visitors on tours, constructing exhibits, mailing out company magazines, erecting plant reading racks, designing pamphlets, or writing letters, the public relations source assumes full responsibility for both the message *and* the vehicle that is to carry it. The very list of possible media conveys some idea of the complexity of the public relations man's job. He need not be an expert in all these fields (although he will be in at least several), but he *must* be able to judge their good and bad points—their beauty, suitability to the message, and effectiveness—and to hire people who can best do the job of preparing or using them. He must be skilled in the use of the graphic arts, including typography, photography, color, and design; must know good radio and television material from bad; must be able to originate an exhibit which will stop the crowds streaming through a bewilderingly large fair and tell its story; and he must do well in many other means of communication.

Company or Organization Magazines and Newspapers

Nobody knows how many organization magazines and newspapers there are because no recent census has been taken and because they keep constantly springing up and disappearing, but estimates indicate that there are at least 8,000 in this country with a combined readership of perhaps 20 million people and an annual publication cost of about 140 million dollars.

A publication is the most common form of organizational communication and may range in size from a single-page mimeographed sheet to a large, elaborate, four-color magazine resembling the best general commercial publications on the market. Editing organization publications is almost a profession in itself, and company magazine editors are nationally organized into two strong professional associations.

The greatest number of these publications are known as *internals* because they are aimed chiefly at reader audiences already closely connected in some way with the organization, such as employees, stockholders, dealers, or suppliers, and on the outer fringes, perhaps community leaders and friends. A smaller number of publications, called *externals,* go to customers or possible customers, leaders of general opinion like educators and legislators, and have as their objects selling company products, informing readers of their uses, and creating general prestige, good will, and understanding.

Whenever an organization of any sort gets so large that spoken communications are no longer sufficient, it publishes printed literature of some kind. People will always communicate, since humans inevitably think and talk, and there can be no such thing as a communications vacuum among employees or stockholders, or in any other group. These people will think about their vital concerns, and they will get impressions and information from one source or another. The organization has no choice as to whether it will or will not communicate; it can only decide how it will communicate, to what extent, and about what.

There is no single right way in which a company publication should be designed, since what is proper for one organization may be not be fitting for another. Publication appearances and contents may properly differ greatly, but there are certain basic principles common to all good editing, and the right way is to apply all these properly to the particular situation of the organization in question.

Internal publications have among their frequent objectives:

1. Informing and persuading readers about company policies and goals, ranging from efforts toward better safety records to more productivity, lessened absenteeism, or conservation of materials. A publication should not only tell readers the facts or hand down management edicts, but should also find and explain points of coincidence of interest between employees and management. For example, both employees and management share an interest in greater productivity; producing goods may preserve jobs because it enables the company to maintain competitive prices with foreign products in American overseas markets.

2. Encouraging good work by recognition. Because of unionization, many workers draw identical paychecks and are classified in the same jobs; yet some of these employees do much better work than others. How are they to be rewarded and others encouraged to emulate them? Public recog-

nition in the form of pictures and stories in a company publication is one form of reward which may be unusually important in a big city. In a large metropolitan daily newspaper, for instance, the ordinary citizen is fortunate to get even three lines of type in his obituary notice. Only the quite famous or infamous, or those who end in some spectacular way, such as jumping off the Empire State Building, are much more noted. Yet even in a faceless world people still crave recognition and personal warmth.

3. Preventing interdepartmental friction. Built-in feuds are common in too many organizations. The sales force could always sell more if it had a better product; the production staff could make a better product if it had more money; there would be more money if there were more sales— and so forth. Such disputes are natural, and to a certain point the ambition and aggressiveness of each portion of an organization are beneficial; but when too much energy is expended upon bickering, the resulting rash of accusations, excuses, and alibis, the shirking of forward thinking, and the general unhappiness leads to a cessation of company progress. Better personal understanding of the whole program of the organization can be provided by a company publication, and is often a partial answer to the problem of creating greater cooperation and enthusiasm.

4. Diminishing labor turnover. It takes both money and time to train new help, particularly skilled workers or executives; it is therefore worthwhile to find out what makes men think well of a company and want to stay with it. Among the causes of good will certainly are information, confidence in the future, both for the employee and for the organization, and a realization of the advantages enjoyed, the social life, work benefits, and pensions.

5. Aiding company public relations. What do employees tell others about their organization? Ill-informed or little-regarded employees are likely to be gripers, more so than those who are taken into the confidence of management. "I call you not servants; for the servant knoweth not what his lord doeth: but I have called you friends," said Jesus to his disciples.

6. Aiding sales. When numbers of employees in a large area are engaged in making general consumer products, they are a major market in themselves, and their word carries weight with many other possible customers.

7. Gaining acceptance for the division of earnings. Every company slices its earnings pie at least four ways—*wages* to employees, *salaries* to management, *dividends* to stockholders, and *plow-back* into the business for expansion or development. While most people agree that profits are necessary and desirable, their proper amount and uses are often subject to dispute. Employees often have an exaggerated idea of profits, and think that they should receive a larger share of the total income. If a company has a good case to present to its employees, it should publish the facts.

8. Protecting private industry. Among the public utilities or transportation companies, the need to protect private industry may be urgent. Public ownership of utilities is common in many places in the world and also in this country. Urging the merits of private ownership as a basic economic philosophy is necessary in any event—certainly to industry and probably to the country as a whole.

Such a list of objectives might be extended, but it should be noted that these objectives are all primarily those which belong to the organization issuing the publication and are not necessarily those of its readers. Company objectives will be listened to only in so far as the interests of the organization and the readers can be made to coincide. There is no such thing as a captive audience for a company internal publication; the magazine may be issued and mailed free to the homes of employees, but there is no assurance that it will be read or will have any effect. Its influence depends upon the skill of the editor and the wisdom of his superiors, usually including the public relations director. Their work will decide whether the publication will be respected and liked or whether it will sound pompous, pushing, and careless of the employees, perhaps doing more harm than good. Nothing can be more important than selecting a good editor, since a publication is no more than the thinking of its editors and writers compressed into print, and cannot possibly be any better than its origin.

The editor must have the technical skill and training to write well and also have a good understanding of photography, art, layout, and printing. The ability to interpret a company and its management to employees requires intelligence and a desire to understand both the company and its people. In a large company which makes many specialized products in plants all over the country and employs people ranging from Ph.D. scientists to barely literate mill hands, such adaptability and impartiality are not at all simple. A man needs poise and study to be able to talk to the president or the production manager in his terms, to mingle with the country-club set one day and then to cover an employee picnic at plant Number 9 tomorrow with equal grace and friendliness. He needs wisdom to avoid offending people by making mistakes and humor to take well-meant but often oblique advice. He needs patience to understand complex situations and humility to realize that *comprehension* of someone else's work is not the same as being able to perform it well. And, above all, a man in the editor's post requires unfailing accuracy, zeal, and the determination to put out such an interesting publication that readers cannot possibly avoid going through it from cover to cover.

Finding such an editorial paragon isn't easy. In most companies he cannot be trained easily from the ranks of salesmen or production workers because good editing is a specialized art. In a very small organization, a bright secretary might do the job under supervision, but in a large company a trained editor is a necessity. A young college-journalism graduate might work as an editor's assistant and eventually take over his job. A newspaperman might be hired, and if he could change his thinking from the objectivity required of a good newspaperman to the persuasion expected of a company editor, he might do well. Or an editor might be hired from a smaller company publication. In any case, a new person will take months to learn enough about a large company to be able to speak authoritatively. He has to be given freedom, encouragement, patient guidance, and proper payment. The work, though highly instructive and enjoyable, has a natural wage ceiling, and the upward route for the company editor is often into broader public relations practice itself, for which publication editing is an excellent training.

Getting out the publication. It is important that the format of a publication be suitable for its audience and main objectives. A small plant, located under one roof and with limited funds, would probably find an offset-printed, monthly, informal newspaper or semimagazine about right, probably set in typewriter type or something similar. But a bank, with the same number of employees in a large city, would perhaps want to issue a small pocket-size magazine, more formally edited and set in regular printing type with a more dignified appearance. Perhaps neither of these publications would be exactly "right" for the most effective communication, but they would be what readers and onlookers would expect. A huge, elaborate publication for a small industry, or a breezy gossip sheet for a bank might well be criticized for not properly mirroring the character of the organization. Informality is fine for Smith's Machine Works but would be out of place for the City First National Bank.

A large company with 20,000 workers under one roof might well find that a five-column tabloid-size newspaper on coated stock, appearing every two weeks, with plenty of pictures would best fill its needs; another company with four widely scattered plants of 5,000 workers in each might find that a single magazine and four modest monthly plant newspapers was the right prescription; and a shoe company putting out an expensive line of women's shoes would probably want to send its dealers a brief, but very finely designed and printed monthly or quarterly publication which would reflect the high fashion of its product.

The really important thing, however, is not how a publication looks but what it says. A good appearance may gain an audience, and a hard-to-read, uninviting appearance may drive it away, but only good content can satisfy readers and keep them returning to absorb the ideas which the organization wishes to convey.

Among the important factors in such content are news, pictures, and human-interest features. But what, for example, constitutes "news" for a company publication?

News is anything of timely importance or interest which affects a significant portion of a reader audience. Election of a new company president is obviously news, but the fact that a new mechanic has joined the maintenance force in plant Number 3 is not news to the same degree; the mechanic may be just as good a human being as the president, but his hiring does not affect as many people. The retirement of the mechanic in plant Number 3 after twenty years of service, however, is much more news than his first employment because after twenty years many more people know him and are interested in him.

When employee Joe Blow goes on a week-end fishing expedition, hooks three fair catfish, and Mrs. Blow takes a picture and sends it to the company paper, the editor has to think twice before running it; if he does, next month a half dozen employees are likely to bring in pictures of similarly undistinguished strings of fish and expect these photos to appear also. A possible working rule might be that if Joe catches a 60-pound catfish, the picture will appear because that is sufficiently unusual to be news anywhere.

In a small plant where people know each other fairly well, trivial items may be legitimate news, just as they are in a small-town weekly newspaper, where a child's birthday party may be worth at least three or four lines of type. But for large, scattered plants, news standards must be more restrictive because people do not know each other so well. An editor makes a dull paper for most of his readers if he tries to please everybody by filling it with trivial personal items which interest only a few individuals and their friends. More genuine news should have a broader appeal. Reports of outstanding personal achievements, service records, promotions, transfers, and new company developments would be of general interest. A standard news policy should be adopted and maintained so that the editor does not find himself favoring one person's report over another's. He may run news to please people, to recognize their achievements, and to get reader interest, but he must also ask himself the question: "How much does this item benefit the organization which is paying the costs of producing this publication?" Answers should be in terms of information, good will, and more direct benefits, but there should be answers.

Where does internal publication news come from? Certain sources can be organized for regular coverage; the records of promotions, transfers, retirements, illnesses, hiring of new employees, and vacations are available in company business or personnel offices. Other news items can sometimes be obtained through department heads, who will know about new production equipment, sales-drive plans, and advertising programs. Other news items may be obtained through a network of departmental or plant correspondents, whose work can be rewarded with recognition, an annual dinner, and perhaps Christmas gifts. All news items must be carefully checked for accuracy, and clumsy attempts to be funny (and certainly to play malicious pranks) must be guarded against. With all its great power for good, a company newspaper also has the capacity to hurt individuals.

Photographs and other illustrations are an important part of almost every company publication. When an item in type is hard to read or does not seem particularly interesting, the reader will ignore it completely; but a picture is at least always looked at, and viewers take meaning from it according to their abilities and interests. A photo of a complicated piece of chemistry laboratory equipment will cause the layman to say simply, "What a complicated gadget!" while the scientist will grasp its every significant detail. But if a verbal description of the same equipment is presented, the layman will understand exactly nothing and even the scientist may be somewhat baffled. Most potent, however, is a *combination* of words and pictures, because readers first look at the pictures and then read the type under them to learn the meaning of what they are seeing. Many a story can be told in pictures and cutlines which would get absolutely no attention in straight type.

Many pictures, however, can be as dull as poor prose, and their dullness often lies, primarily, in the way in which they are displayed in a magazine or a newspaper. A common failure is to run too many pictures in such small sizes that the many details in each cannot be seen or appreciated. This crowding may be excusable in a series of service-anniversary dinner-group photos because these are "record" pictures. But in covering a company picnic, the editor often commits the same sin, trying to please everyone by cramming in six photos showing ten people in each, rather than by using one or two decently large pictures and omitting or playing down the rest. If many pictures have to be used, at least they should not all be of equal size. Even though company magazines and newspapers are usually printed on good paper stock with good engravings and can usually reproduce crowded small pictures successfully from a mechanical viewpoint, good reproduction still does not make them interesting.

Very often, also, the company-publication editor will have to be his own photographer. He will need to follow the general rules about photo taking previously mentioned in connection with other newspapers or magazines. Photo negatives cost so little that it pays to shoot a great many pictures. An editor should be careful, however, not to lead people to expect that he will necessarily use every picture he has taken. He must remember, too, that people are sensitive about their appearance, and must give them a chance to look their best. Personal portraits, such as those for service-award photos, are usually better left to professional photographers, as are also large group shots in which adequate lighting and negative size are important. The editor's camera, however, can be a great icebreaker, getting people to talk and cooperate more quickly than any other means.

Artwork is important to lighten a publication and to give a change of pace; the soft grays of many photographs tend to become visually monotonous and to blend in with each other. Drawings such as humorous cartoons can add greatly to reader interest.

There are numerous good books on company-publication planning and layout, and a public relations man should be familiar with them. If, to his other duties, he must add that of an editor, he will find that allying himself with a good magazine designer, a good printer, and a good photographer can do a great deal to get him off on the right foot. But the real test of ingenuity and purpose will come in what he puts into the publication.

Features constitute the third main part of the content of company publications. They are relatively more important than in commercial publications because they frequently achieve great success in getting across the information about an organization which can be illuminating and persuasive to readers. Suppose, for example, that an editor wishes to convince employee readers that the company has a good pension plan. What better way could he choose than to interview several recent retirees, taking their pictures and finding what interesting things they are doing? Such a feature not only is full of readable human interest in itself, but since many present employees know these people, it also shows indirectly the merits of the company pension plan. Or a company might wish to encourage its employees to take a leading part in civic-improvement programs in plant cities. For example, an employee who has just served as chairman for the local United Fund drive, might be mentioned and his work described; and perhaps, incidentally, information might be given about the types of people assisted by the United Fund and the reasons why the company supports it.

Some interesting features, of course, may have no direct purpose of any sort. A story about an employee who takes an unusual vacation, or a service feature on how to prepare your income tax, or on how to tan while avoiding early summer sunburn may have a place. Although a company has good reasons for spending money on a publication, not every item should have an overt purpose or the paper will be like a friend who can discuss nothing except his business.

Soft Sell versus Hard Sell

By sound tradition, most company publications try to build good will and understanding by example and encouragement rather than by direct exhortation in which their self-interest is quite apparent.

There is a difference, however, between avoiding preaching and ducking the mention of facts because they are unpleasant or controversial. Labor union papers are often filled with exhortation and controversy. Because of legal restrictions, the company press must be careful not to tell employees what to do in a labor controversy or to seem to threaten them under such circumstances, but this does not mean that the company press must be silent. Dignified, factual reporting of news of such keen employee interest as an industrial dispute would seem to be a part of necessary coverage of what is going on.

But even so, the strongest statements might best be left to direct letters, to bulletins, and to newspaper advertisements, where they will get the greatest immediate attention anyway. A long-established company publication has often become a friendly institution. It is sometimes the most popular project undertaken by the company, and its readers may enjoy it better and continue to depend upon it longer if the most bitter elements of economic controversy are not introduced. They may prefer the usual run of stories of babies, vacations, old pensioners, and company progress. Issues come and go, but organizations and their publications can go on indefinitely. The respect and friendship which have been earned over a long period by a good company publication should not be sacrificed in the heat of perhaps one day's conflict.

A really successful internal company publication is not only read and accepted by the employees; it goes to their homes and is read by their families and friends as well. It is consistent, friendly, reliable, and frank in its purposes. It is edited from the viewpoint of those who read it. Its editor needs a good sense of communication, and the ability to understand "what I should like if I were in my reader's shoes, with his background, his interests, his hopes, and his problems."

External Publications

External publications differ from internals because their readership and their purposes are different. In general they are better-looking magazines, directed at customers or leaders of opinion outside of the organization. They may exist to further sales or to obtain good will in influential quarters. Since their readers have less direct connection with the issuing organization, the publications must compete for their attention with more commercial publications and do so without the advantage of personal contacts. Readers compare external publications directly with big general magazines or newspapers. For that reason their news must be of compellingly wide interest, as are the presentations of scientific or financial subjects in any semipopular magazine; their features must approach *Look* or *Reader's Digest* quality; and their pictures must be noteworthy in themselves. Sometimes external magazines are so well edited and successful that they outgrow their original purpose and become almost general national publications, as have *Arizona Highways* and *Ford Times*.

External magazines can be of great value to a company dealing in specialized products whose use must be explained in detail to customers too widely scattered for salesmen to reach personally; to an organization making many varied products which it wishes to group under a single sales banner; and to an organization which needs good will because of its political or social situation. An external magazine, as a rule, should be well done or it is better not attempted, because its reading public gives it no quarter.

Open Houses and Tours

Surprisingly, many of the wives and children of employees have never been in the plants or offices where the men of the family earn their living; farmers selling wheat or milk to a processing plant have never seen what goes on inside of it; users of electricity have never seen a generating plant; and parents of school children have never been inside a schoolroom. Such a separation of life and work makes for easy misunderstanding. Those who do know something about where people work and what they produce have a personal interest in their industrial environment and an intelligent comprehension of it.

Setting up a good plant or office visit, however, is not simple. Some factories are too noisy, too dirty, or too dangerous to be suitable visiting locations. Other places offer little to see because the machinery is hidden or, as in company offices, because the work is largely mental and clerical and there is nothing to observe except people at their desks. It may sometimes be necessary to set up exhibits and pictures to show what cannot be seen.

Since people give their time and attention to a tour of a plant, the conduct of their visit should be perfect. Guides must be courteous and well prepared, routes carefully laid out, explanatory signs posted as needed, rest and refreshments provided. An opportunity to make friends can easily be soured by thoughtlessness. Among the most common tour groups are employees and their families, townspeople, and special groups composed of students, scientists, salesmen, dealers, and suppliers.

Some visits to a plant are handled en masse on special occasions. For example, an open house might be held in connection with a new-plant opening or a plant-addition dedication. Such a program might include three days of tours—an opening day for employees and their families, a second day for opinion leaders, and a third day for the general public.

Tours may be arranged to other places also upon special occasions. When the Pet Milk Company of St. Louis, Missouri, reached its seventieth anniversary in 1955, it was decided to hold an open house for all office employees and their families of the St. Louis headquarters and of a nearby plant, at the farm home of the original founder of the company, Louis Latzer, about 35 miles east of St. Louis. Several hundred people attended, most of them coming in their own cars, although buses were provided without charge for those who wished to use them. Because Louis Latzer had come from Switzerland, a busload of employees from the Pet Milk Company plant at New Glarus, Wisconsin, a Swiss settlement, attended, dressed in traditional Swiss costume, to put on a program of yodeling, flag throwing, and alpenhorn blowing.

Staging a visit like this required a planned tour route, road maps, road signs, directed parking and policing, guides along the route of the tour through the big old farmhouse, large tents for luncheon and refreshments, another large tent for rest and shelter in case of rain, hundreds of folding chairs and tables, favors for the children, first-aid facilities, insurance, fire protection, printed programs, and extensive coverage in the next issue of the employee magazine. The inside of the house had to be rearranged to enable hundreds of people to walk through it. A small museum of exhibits was constructed. Its preparation included collecting objects, labeling them, and placing them in suitable glass cases which had to be built for the occasion. Every contingency was anticipated and adequate volunteer and paid help provided for. The reward was that the people who participated enjoyed themselves and got an idea of the history of the company and of the nature of the people who founded it which could have been obtained in no other way. In these days when all of us receive a constant flood of vicarious experience through many mass media, the two words "I saw" are stronger than ever. Every plant open house should have a reason. Such events cannot be held very often, but when held, they should be perfect and memorable.

Regular visitor tours through plants are another problem and opportunity. Large plants, making well-known products, located in or near major cities and on main highways, have the greatest opportunity to attract visitors. The flow can be stimulated by plant identification signs, highway billboards, and promotion in other company advertising and communications. Almost any reasonably interesting and important plant can obtain many groups of visiting students and members of clubs or of professional groups, if it makes an effort to do so. Such tours can be either perfunctory or meaningful.

A number of years ago the *St. Louis Star-Times* discovered that about 6,000 students a year were touring its downtown St. Louis office and plant. Since conduct of the tours had been haphazard, steps were taken to improve their management. Young men and women from the circulation and want-ad departments, located on the first floor near the building lobby, were trained as guides. To help them in their task, a tour route was laid out, areas in which guides could stand and talk to groups were marked, and a script was prepared for them.

At the conclusion of each school tour, the guide gave the students' teacher a tour booklet, then showed it to the children, and asked if they would like to have a copy mailed to their homes. Those who wanted it (almost all, as a rule) then filled in a small gummed address label which was later affixed to the envelope in which the booklet was mailed. A duplicated letter of appreciation for the visit accompanied the booklets, which were received at the homes of the children and were probably read by several family members. Thus the memory of the visit was revitalized. Previously, booklets given to children at the newspaper plant were frequently found in nearby street gutters.

After obtaining the teacher's approval, the guide would also announce that if the members of the class wished to write brief essays on the aspects of the visit which interested them most and would send them in to the newspaper as a group, a large world globe would be awarded to the class in the name of the student who submitted the best essay. On a plate at the base of the globe the student's name and the date of the visit would be inscribed. There was no obligation to write an essay, and the announcement was never made unless the teacher agreed in advance. Reading the essays not only gave the guides a good idea of what most impressed the students, but also led to improvements and served as a check upon the guides themselves.

The values of plant tours can be endless. In one company, a new public relations man discovered that new salesmen coming into headquarters for their initial two-week training period had, until then, never been taken on a plant tour to see the manufacture of the product they were supposed to sell. In fact, many veteran salesmen had never been inside a plant, although they had been selling for many years and had many times visited headquarters, near which a plant was located. A plant visit was immediately made a standard part of introductory training, since the process of production was excellent and gave increased confidence in the product itself.

In another case, farmers who had been selling milk to a processing plant had had no opportunity to see what happened to their daily output once it left their farms. Since the size of their checks partly depended upon butterfat, bacterial, and other plant laboratory tests, it was well worthwhile to plan tours which would enable dairy farmers to see the careful scientific testing and the expensive laboratory equipment, and to satisfy their natural interest in other aspects of milk processing.

Exhibits

There is little doubt of the communications value of well-edited company magazines or of carefully planned open houses and tours, but exhibits such as those at fairs or professional meetings present a greater problem to the public relations man. What should be told? How can there be any assurance that adequate traffic will justify the investment? How can viewers be stopped and an exhibit be made memorable even if there is such traffic? In many instances the cost of an exhibit per viewer is extremely

high, not only for the exhibit space, which is often sold upon a charitable
or sandbagging basis, but also because the competition for attention is
intense, the costs of construction high, and the labor costs of manning
an exhibit much beyond the probable benefits.

But these problems do not constitute reasons for giving up the attempt
to get the utmost value out of every dollar which must be spent. The
ideal exhibit is colorful, pictorial, and unusual. If possible, it includes
action and participation on the part of the spectators. Can the viewer
push a button, for example, and see something happen? Can he get an
answer to a question? Can he see a step in a process or distribution on
a map? People remember best what they take part in.

Some years ago the *Des Moines Register and Tribune* purchased a new
airplane which could fly from Des Moines, the capital of Iowa, to any
major city in the state and bring back news in a few minutes. To dramatize
this fact, the newspaper used Iowa State Fair exhibit space that year to
install a huge map of Iowa with all the main cities of the state indicated
by opaque glass circles on the map. "How long does it take to fly to
your city for *Register and Tribune* news?" said the overline. At the rail
in front of the big map was a row of push buttons labeled with the
names of the towns and a sign: "Push the button. See how long it takes
for the airplane to fly to your home town." When the button was pushed,
the correct number of minutes lit up in the correct glass circle on the
map, and an illuminated white line indicated the flight course. The only
flaw in the exhibit was that the buttons were pushed so hard during the
day that the electricians had to replace them every night.

On another occasion, at the same state fair, the newspaper hired a
group of itinerant tintype photographers for the week of the fair. An
enlarged copy of the front page of the newspaper was made, with the
headline CELEBRITY VISITS FAIR and a blank space, as if for a picture,
cut out beneath it, into which a visitor could stick his face from behind.
This was set up at the exhibit, and as soon as a visitor's picture was
shot, it was developed, and in a few minutes the visitor could depart
with a tintype photo showing his picture, supposedly, upon the front
page of the state's largest newspaper. This exhibit, which combined participation with selling the newspaper, was a great success; crowds lined
up in a block-long queue, and the exhibit produced about 15,000
pictures in the five days of the fair.

If a public relations man knows that his organization is going to be
called upon for numbers of small exhibits which may be of questionable
value, it may be worthwhile to prepare colorful, pictorial, but unmanned
displays for certain locations and to concentrate most money and effort
upon exhibits at the events which are likely to be well attended, and where
prestige may be gained or lost.

Several other types of display activity are related to exhibits, including parade floats and exhibit museums at construction scenes or at historic sites. Parade floats, like outdoor advertising in general, should be attractive and confined to the impact of one single idea. If other organizations in a parade spend money to look attractive, your organization must do so also, but the actual public relations value of these expensive floats in relation to their cost is often dubious.

Informative signs and museums at building construction sites are another matter, because there is usually keen public interest in what is happening, and signs, plans, and preview photos can capitalize upon it. In some instances the exhibits can become quite elaborate and effective. At the Monroe, Michigan, atomic-power plant constructed by the Detroit Edison Company, a small museum building at the site along the highway attracted many thousands of visitors who could not go through the installation itself but learned about it from models and pictures. A similar installation was exhibited in 1961 for a different type of reactor being erected by Consumers Power Company of Michigan at Big Rock Point, Michigan, as the plant neared its completion planned for 1962. Located at a scenic point on U.S. Highway No. 31, it attracted thousands of visitors and provided self-guiding viewing platforms of the new power installation.

Meetings

Getting a group of people together and talking things over is one of the oldest communications media in history, yet one which is often neglected today because it seems so simple. Because it is a personal experience, rather than a secondhand sensation, a meeting has great power for either good or ill.

One plan is simply to get everyone together and then to tell them something in lecture form, perhaps enlivened by visual aids. An annual-report meeting for stockholders or a mass meeting of employees to announce a new policy is an example of a lecture meeting. Its weakness is that it is one-way communication. The audience's interest cannot be assumed unless attendance is entirely voluntary, and achieving two-way communication in a large meeting of this sort is not easy because questions are likely to be long, trivial, and digressive; yet denial of questions is not a good policy either.

One alternative is a number of small group meetings, such as those used by du Pont and described in Chapter 12, "Communications Cases." Here two-way communication avoids the sense of rebellion caused by the imposition of one-way lecturing. Although the cost in training time and man-hours of work lost is great, perhaps the effort is worthwhile if communication is well established.

Another type of meeting is the voluntarily attended lecture on some subject related to the business or simply of general interest. The employees, their families, and friends are invited, but it is made clear that attendance in no way affects an employee's job. At a chemical plant, for example, the visit of a noted scientist might provide the occasion for such a semipublic lecture. On a newspaper, the Washington staff correspondent might report to his home-town people every year. Promotion of the business can be touched on lightly in the remarks of the chairman and in questions from the audience. An informal social hour may well be combined with this type of meeting.

Organized Social Activities

Company picnics, Christmas parties, bowling leagues, and golf tournaments may not, at first, be considered communications devices; but to a large extent that is what they are because they say something about the people who put them on and who take part in them.

The question as to how much togetherness is desirable in running a business or an organization depends on the size of the organization and the city in which it is located and also on the expectations of the persons involved. Generally, in larger Eastern and Northern American cities, the separation between the job and social life is virtually complete, and here a few well-produced formal events with a pleasant atmosphere, to which *all* employees (or those within a certain area) are invited, convey the impression that the management is thoughtful and interested. More frequent (or wilder) parties are better left to the employees themselves. The development of political cliques based upon prowess in company card playing, golf, or bowling can be disruptive to the morale of other employees who want to get on with the business but to run their own lives at the same time.

In small places, especially in the South, work and private life tend to run into each other more indistinguishably, and a greater amount of planned social activity may be expected of an organization. But the dangers still persist, and management must be careful not to seem to play favorites or to be too paternalistic. Social arrangements are often better left to the employees themselves with only cash and blessing bestowed by management.

The entrance of a company into the social activities of an employee's family is of even more uncertain desirability. In this area of half knowledge on the part of wives and other relatives, strong feelings may be aroused or explosions set off by the most trivial things. The company is invading a very sensitive region, like that in which political jealousies abound or like the mined fields on faculty row in college campuses or among officers' wives on an army post.

Participation in Local Events

How much should a company take part, or encourage its employees to take part, in efforts for community betterment? Should employees be encouraged to serve on local school boards, to lead charity drives, to be elected deacons in their churches, to head the local Kiwanis or Lions Club, to lead farm youth groups, to help neighborhood-improvement associations, and even to engage in politics?

The answers depend upon the nature of the company. An organization which sells service, as does an electric light company or a bank, should pay more attention to these local activities than a shoe manufacturer. On the whole, American business has encouraged its people to be active local citizens, often at considerable cost in lost time to the company and even, on the part of some employees, in lost interest in their jobs.

More than this, companies often supply speakers and contribute heavily from their own funds and time to local efforts, in which the public relations director is usually the prime mover. When such activity says something about the nature of the company which supports it, it is a justified form of public communication.

Action Programs

Not strictly a communications medium, "doing things" is closely related to communication because actions sometimes speak louder than words, and they provide the material which can later be communicated to others by speech or writing. Actions are discussed more fully in Chapter 11, "Action Cases," but it may be noted here that the fundamental nature of many public relations actions programs is communicatory. Awards for town betterment or for accomplishment in work demanding expertness reflect the interests of the donor; giving scholarships and aiding schools in the development of their curricula communicate an attitude toward education; and holding seminars in which scientists can discuss their problems is an act of leadership.

The Motion Picture and Its Uses

One of the most complex and expensive means of communication, the motion picture, offers a great opportunity to influence viewers in a way which no other medium can match—and also to waste money and time prodigiously. Next to its uses in entertainment and in education, the motion picture finds its greatest value in public relations, and the development of television in the past two decades has greatly extended its possible influence. Books have been written upon the successes and failures of motion pictures in public relations endeavors, and the reader is referred to them if he is seriously thinking about the subject. In the meantime a few guidelines may be valuable.

Advantages of motion pictures for covering public relations. Appealing to the eye and ear simultaneously, the motion picture is the most powerful communications medium short of direct experience. Films can hold the sustained and exclusive attention of receivers for long periods of time and can show motion, sequences of development, and details of actions in a way that cannot be seen by the unaided human eye. Time can be collapsed, objects enlarged, and cartoons made to move. The motion picture can convey ideas quickly and lastingly with subtle emotional overtones, and in today's television era people are getting more and more used to receiving their information this way. Motion pictures can be beautiful and exciting works of art in themselves.

Disadvantages. Motion pictures are primarily limited to showing external aspects and often become insincere when trying to portray ideas. In many processes of importance, for example, legislation or scientific thought, little appears on the outside, and in the absence of concrete evidence, the motion-picture maker is tempted to resort to oversimplification and undue dramatization. Not everything makes a good visual story or spectacle. As we said earlier, television news broadcasts frequently suffer from the same deficiency.

Motion pictures proceed at a set pace, allowing the viewer little opportunity for reflection or questioning while he is watching the film. He often wants a clarifying two-way conversation after "The End" is flashed on the screen, but his desire is usually not satisfied. Nor is there ordinarily much opportunity for him to review what he has seen and to ponder its significance.

Problems. Despite its power, the public relations motion picture is an expensive medium for the small organization, with a median production cost of about $1,200 per minute of shooting time, or about $26,000 for the average 26-minute noncommercial film, according to a 1954 Association of National Advertisers survey of 157 important business films. A good rule of thumb, also, is to budget about as much for extra prints and for distribution costs as the original cost of the film; these additional expenditures would bring the median total cost to about $52,000 per film. Since the life of a film would have to be at least five years to amortize this cost (except in special instances), the subject matter is usually limited to relatively undated activities.

The most economical distribution in the 1954 ANA survey, from which the preceding figures were drawn, was achieved with a combination of commercial organization and sponsor distribution of films; the median cost per viewer was 4.6 cents. When television use of films was added, the cost fell to 1.6 cents.

The biggest audiences obtained were from schools, for which 89 per cent of such films were intended. Eighty-two per cent were also intended for clubs and the general public, 80 per cent for business and industry, 62 per cent for employees, 61 per cent for churches, 57 per cent for company managements, 52 per cent for television, 41 per cent for social agencies, and 12 per cent for stockholders. These figures seem to indicate that an organization should ask some precise questions before venturing to produce a public relations film. Who wants it made? Is this the best communications medium to do the job, considering the film's cost and its distribution possibilities? Is the story it tells good film material? At whom should the film be aimed?

Several conclusions often emerge. The public relations film with a general aim at a broad market and expectation of a long life is a blue-chip proposition, best suited to the long-range public relations objectives of a large organization. To be used on television, except in paid time, and in the schools, its "sell" must be subtle or almost nonexistent. Film production standards must match Hollywood's best, and subject matter should be of keen public interest. Such a film will also be useful in giving general information, explaining a public-service concept, or recounting history rather than in promoting a specific firm or product.

There is also often good use for the lower-budget, more specific type of motion picture which seeks to present to a more compact technical or special-interest audience material which could not be conveyed so well in any other manner. For example, several years ago the Baden Street Settlement House, serving poor people in a mixed neighborhood in Rochester, New York, decided to get out a motion picture showing the work of the House. Since no money was available for professional help, a highly skilled amateur on the staff of the agency planned and shot the 16-mm picture. The film, musical scores and recording, printing, lights, and many other items were contributed. All in all, perhaps three hundred persons helped. The roles of the persons shown in the film (settlement-house workers and a Negro family) were all played by the actual people portrayed. The consummate artistry of the film moved its audiences and told the story of the work of Baden Street Settlement House better than any speech, printed brochure, or even tour of the facilities could have done.

A number of years ago the Dow Chemical Company of Midland, Michigan, spent a great deal of money installing equipment to end whatever pollution its wastes might be contributing to streams in the area; yet, because it is a large and well-known chemical manufacturing establishment (and therefore an obvious target for criticism) it still found itself being blamed for downstream pollution. This contamination was actually caused by a combination of circumstances, among them waste from other industries and untreated city and town sewage. Instead of taking a defensive and useless attitude of simply denying guilt, several Dow employees produced a good 16-mm color film showing how such stream pollution arose, illustrating Dow's successful efforts to remedy the situation in its own watershed, and urging, over the sound track, that other industries and cities, nearby and all over the nation, join in a clear-streams effort. The film received wide showing in the Midland area among engineering, industrial, and conservation people, as well as the general public; and it has also been in demand all over the United States. This story could have been told as well in no other way; in fact, it is doubtful if duller methods would even have held many audiences.

A third general use of motion pictures is in communication, at an admittedly high cost per viewer, to very specific groups such as stockholders (in which General Mills films have been outstanding) and to limited regional publics. A power company, for example, might find it advantageous to show its industrial-development activities to groups of business men, or a concrete-paving association to show progress in new concrete state highways before engineering, political, or news media men.

Sometimes a film must be made to do the job simply because the use of a film is expected. The necessity was apparent in a United Fund drive in a Midwestern city some time ago. The success of the drive hinged upon the way the employees in one large industrial firm would contribute, and a film had been shown as a part of the solicitation drive in this plant for several years previously. Since no one was willing to take a chance on using an old film over again or on abandoning a film entirely, a new one had to be made. If it had not been made and if the drive had failed, the lack of a film would have been blamed.

The biggest thing to remember about public relations films is that they must be workmanlike. Since few public relations men are expert film producers, it is the part of wisdom to obtain the aid of someone who is. Examining past work and talking to past clients will serve as a guide in selecting the right film producer for your needs.

Summary

A great many other communications tools—direct-mail letters, booklets of all sorts, bulletin boards, posters, information-booklet racks, suggestion programs, speakers bureaus, and meetings—are often used by public relations men in talking to various publics. Each one is a tool which the skilled practitioner handles as a matter of course, always using the right means of communication in the right place, in the right way, and at the right time. The tools themselves should be perfect and their employment without a flaw. But excellence in their use is simply a means to an end and not a goal in itself.

The public relations man is not satisfied with asking himself, "Wasn't that a beautiful motion picture?" or "Wasn't this a handsome booklet?" Instead he is more concerned with those who saw the effort and what they thought as a result of their experience. Mastery of tools is but the beginning of success.

ADDITIONAL READING

About the Tools of Public Relations

Association of National Advertisers: *The Dollars and Sense of Business Films,* Association of National Advertisers, New York, 1954.

Baus, Herbert N.: *Publicity in Action,* Harper & Row, Publishers, Incorporated, New York, 1954.

Bentley, Garth: *Editing the Company Publication,* Harper & Row, Publishers, Incorporated, New York, 1953.

Chester, Giraud, and Garnet Garrison: *Television and Radio: An Introduction,* Appleton-Century-Crofts, Inc., New York, 1956.

Dover, C. J.: *Effective Communication in Company Publications,* Bureau of National Affairs, Washington, D.C., 1959.

Haas, Kenneth B., and Harry Q. Packer: *Preparation and Use of Audio-Visual Aids,* Prentice-Hall, Inc., Englewood Cliffs, N.J., 1955.

Stephenson, Howard, and Wesley Pratzner: *Publicity for Prestige and Profit,* McGraw-Hill Book Company, Inc., New York, 1953.

Wilson, Wm. H., and Kenneth B. Haas: *The Film Book for Business, Education, and Industry,* Prentice-Hall, Inc., Englewood Cliffs, N.J., 1950.

Public Relations at Work

PART II

A Formula for Successful
Public Relations Practice

9

The distinguishing mark of a successful public relations man is that he knows where he is, where he wants to go, and how to get there. Like an explorer, he has a map of the terrain always in his head. He knows that far more time, money, effort, and opportunity have been wasted through lack of an objective or unfamiliarity with the route than through inability to travel.

This map, or plan of action, can be reduced to a formula. Red Motley, publisher of *Parade* magazine and once president of the United States Chamber of Commerce, said that "no man is smart enough to remember all he knows." This is the justification for the existence of formulas: They remind us of what we ought to know but often forget. They are an aid to thinking, not a substitute for it.

In the advertising world an ancient formula called "AIDA" has served many a beginning direct-mail or other ad writer well by reminding him that he ought to get *Attention, Interest, Desire,* and *Action* into his copy for surest results at the sales till.

In the public relations world a new formula using the letters R-A-C-E can accomplish the same result. These letters stand for a sequence of words used in attacking a public relations problem—*Research, Action, Communication,* and *Evaluation.* Remembering these words won't make a dull man bright, but orderly consideration of them will prevent many mistakes and omissions. Detailed one at a time and illustrated by actual cases, they form a large part of the content of this book.

Research in Public Relations Practice

When called into public relations responsibility, a person must first ascertain the expectations of those who have asked him to do the job. What does the organization want? What are its resources? How much time will he have? Can its wants be fulfilled by public relations aid?

161

Some years ago, an Englishman went to work as public relations director for a large British industry. He stayed there only about eighteen months. "I failed to ask the right question," he explained to a friend later. "When I was being interviewed for the position, I answered all the questions that were put to me satisfactorily, and then the pause came which meant that it was my turn to ask questions. I should have said, 'And Mr. Doe, what would you say that public relations is?' Since I didn't ask this, it took us many months to find out that our understandings of the subject were really quite different."

Often employers have unrealistic expectations. They may think that in some magical way public relations can gloss over bad situations and by much favorable speaking make them seem good; they may simply desire widespread publicity regardless of its effects; and sometimes, although they will seldom admit it, they may simply seek a sop to their vanity by getting their names and pictures into newspapers and magazines or onto programs. Or they may have only the vaguest picture of what they want. Public relations, they think, is supposed to be a good thing; others are doing it.

Sometimes employers are unwilling to allot adequate resources to attain the goals they have in mind. Brains and enterprise in public relations cannot be bought by the pound as one would buy steel scrap or sugar, but a public relations man who is too burdened by necessary routine tasks will probably not be so fully productive as one more adequately subsidized, who has more time to think. And again, an employer may expect results too quickly. A public relations campaign composed of a flood of news releases, booklets, speeches, tours, exhibits, and motion pictures may look huge to the company president, who sees it all outward bound; but dispersed among millions of people and scattered into millions of competitive messages, it is usually reduced to a trickle when it reaches its public. But that trickle may still bring a flood of results if given time.

The *first* step in necessary research is for a public relations man to look into the minds of those who plan to employ his services. Often one of the biggest helps that he can give to his prospective employers and to himself is to enable them to clarify their objectives and to understand the role that public relations can play in attaining these goals.

The *second* step in research consists in assembling all the existing available information on the situation. This might consist of careful inspection of all newspaper and magazine clippings over a long period of time, of examining an organization's correspondence files, of reading sales and promotional literature and advertising, of reading the minutes of past meetings, and of having conversations with people who know the story well.

Such research often goes even further into examination of the history, economics, and sociology of the business, area, or institutions involved.

Personalities, politics, and feelings have to be known well, since before a public relations man can do anything wisely, he must know and assess all the facts. This sounds like a big assignment, but it can be easily accomplished with a little work.

The *third* step in public relations research is more difficult. It consists in finding out the opinions or attitudes currently held by the groups of people toward whom one wishes to direct persuasive communication. This investigation is vitally necessary, because if the practitioner does not know how people stand on important issues, he may find that he is needlessly antagonizing some persons, trying to convert those who are already converted, or even wasting effort upon others who are not really concerned. Many good books have been written on opinion research, and the reader can inform himself in greater detail at any good library. At this point it is worthwhile to examine two aspects of the manifestation of public opinion.

1. *Existing evidence.* This might consist of press clippings about an organization, comments in letters received in the normal flow of correspondence, the reports of salesmen, staff members, and others, and the opinions of friends and relatives. Such informal evidence is pertinent and often gives highly significant tips, but it is too haphazard to be representative, and it is usually highly subjective. We remember what we like to hear, and our friends (if they wish to remain friends) tell us what we like to hear, although occasionally a confirmed pessimist will make a point of recalling the damaging evidence. Only a very well-balanced observer can arrive at truth through hit-and-miss surmises about existing public opinion.

2. *Planned investigation.* Planned investigation usually means sampling, by some reasonably scientific method, the opinions of groups with whose thought one is concerned. Such sampling might take the form of a cross-sectional survey, a survey panel, depth interviews, mail surveys, or other methods—each with its strengths and limitations. There are numerous possible sources of error in such samples: Questions or interviewers may be biased; answers may seek prestige; returns may be inadequate or unrepresentative; and since opinions change frequently, time also may invalidate such a survey. The investigator should be aware of the limitations of opinion research and of its proper use. In a large involved program it is usually better to hire the services of a firm which specializes in opinion research; yet even so, much of the burden of answering "Is this valid and significant?" and "What does this mean to us?" remains a public relations responsibility and cannot be escaped.

Scientific opinion research can do much to clarify management thinking as to needs in public relations and to obtain support for a program in a manner which no amount of personal persuasion could ever accomplish.

In addition, it may help by enabling the investigator to pretest communications media and appeals before they are launched on a grand scale.

But opinion research is a foundation for creative thinking rather than a substitute for it. It measures public opinion of what *has* been done or *is* being done, but cannot ordinarily tell one what *might* be done! Respondents can tell how they feel about existing conditions but can hardly anticipate their reactions to some possible future event. One cannot expect them to vote intelligently about what should be done, nor should one always be guided by what they seem to wish. Public relations is not to be confused with gaining favor at any cost, and public relations people must sometimes try to promote unpopular or unpleasant programs.

The Importance of Sound Research Cannot Be Overemphasized

The things that you don't know or the things that you think you know that aren't so usually have the capacity to hurt you most. Public relations men are naturally enthusiastic, and natural enthusiasts are often inclined to get on with their jobs without any critical appraisal of *how* or *why*. Influencing human opinion by means of public relations is a serious thing because it is indelible. A mistake can't just be erased and a fresh start made. If an impression takes root at all, it may remain in the minds of its receivers for many years to come, perhaps for their lifetimes.

Large companies frequently spend a great deal of thought and money on opinion research. In Chapter 10 you will see how a state hospital association found out what newspaper editors really thought about hospital services; how a major Western oil company shared the results of its consumer research with its employees; how a large communications organization kept in touch with the opinions of its stockholders; how a large Midwestern chemical company used research to start to solve its community relations problems; and how a United Fund drive in a large American city was established upon a sound understanding of public opinion. None of these things could have been accomplished without first ascertaining the facts by the use of shoe leather, planned, persistent questions, and the notebook—all three, synonyms for research.

The best-laid plans concocted in an office far away from the reality of the assembly line, the town council chambers, or the housewife's struggle to feed, clothe, and corral her youngsters are often wide of the mark, and only down-to-earth research can set them right again. Only after the true situation is really *known* is the public relations man ready for *action,* the next step in the R-A-C-E public relations formula.

Action in Public Relations Practice

We sometimes think of public relations as primarily a process of telling people about an institution, but before we can discuss something, we must be sure that it is there to be discussed; if things aren't happening, they may have to be made to happen.

Sometimes actions already exist. Consider the public relations efforts of the United States Marine Corps, for example. The bright uniforms and the stirring band music of the Marine Hymn are present realities, and the tradition of gallantry represents a history of continuing action. If these things did not exist and one faced the problem of popularizing the Marine Corps, they (or some equivalent) would have to be created.

Action may take the form of changing a situation. If a bus company is getting complaints about slow service on a commuter run, it is useless to argue that the service is really fast. Before the public relations problem can be overcome fully, the service must be speeded up, and the riding public must be informed of the change.

Actions, too, may be contrived to express externally in some way an inward quality which is abstract or invisible. We do this all the time in our daily lives. An American who once visited Argentina came back with a new word, "exteriorization." In the Spanish language this means simply to show on the outside how you feel on the inside. Latin Americans are somewhat better at exteriorizing than most North Americans, whose Anglo-Saxon tradition makes them regard "deadpanism" as a point of honor. But North Americans must learn that exteriorization is practical in public relations. How may a company that makes high-quality merchandise *demonstrate* this high quality instead of just telling about it? How can enterprise in scientific research be shown in actions as well as in words? These are practical questions.

Another opportunity for action lies in giving evidence that one is *listening*. As will be shown in the discussion of communications in Chapter 12, most organizations are fairly adept at telling things to people and then in *saying* that they are listening to their responses; they know that two-way conversations are the most effective means of gaining conviction and co-operation. But how does one *show* that he is listening? What actions can be taken to organize channels of communication upward as well as downward? Organized listening should be dramatized in much the same way that outgoing messages are frequently dramatized.

Finally, actions in public relations are frequently needed to make news and to gain public attention. The safe operation of an airline for ten years without an accident is only minor news because this is the way airlines are supposed to operate. The papers will hardly give such routine safety a line, and this treatment is negligible, compared with their coverage of one crash. But what sort of action could be organized to make safe operation *news?*

The insistence upon *action* as a vital element in public relations practice is one of the main things that has made public relations into what it is today—a broad-gauge art, or profession, far-removed from the old-style press-agentry which simply tried to whitewash events and never took a hand in their development. Action makes public relations a part of management, because action is primarily a management responsibility. Actions not only speak louder than words; they also provide the basis upon which many words can properly be written.

Chapter 11 presents many examples of effective actions engaged in by various public relations people from among organizations as diverse as a city water company, Rockefeller Center in New York, a moving-van line, a bank to which a little girl wrote a letter about her longing to buy a horse, a manufacturing concern which sent an intrepid outboard motor-boat struggling across the stormy Atlantic, the Chicago Board of Trade, an automobile company helping train boy mechanics, an electric company educating young scientists, a railroad giving each of its commuters a chance to be an engineer-for-the-day, a large company holding a dramatic annual meeting of its stockholders, a professional group focusing public attention upon its work, and a group of clothing manufacturers trying to get a larger share of men's and boys' spendable income. In all these cases what a public relations man could have *said* about the organization on its own behalf would have been weak compared with the statements made by others because of what it *did*.

The public relations man thus becomes an expert not only in saying, but in doing. He influences the course of events by instigating action as well as by writing about it, and sometimes his influence can be very great indeed. This broadening of the concept of public relations adds interest to its practice. It is not just a mirroring of events but actually a creator of them. As a researcher, the public relations man delves into reasons and causes; as a communicator he tells about them; but as an activator he is a man of affairs who knows the thrill of setting up events and gambling upon their success or failure, of making policy, and of personifying organizations by their deeds.

Communication in Public Relations Practice

When the layman thinks about public relations practice, the first thing to come to his mind is *communication,* and his instinct is right, for facility in spreading information is still the backbone of publicity efforts. Ability in communication alone, of course, isn't enough to make a man qualify as an expert in the profession; certainly a capacity for research, for promoting action, and for evaluating the results is also vital to the practice of public relations upon an executive level. But the fact remains that communication is the one area in which a working public relations man *must* be good, and that is why so much of this book is devoted to the communications aspect of the R-A-C-E formula.

There is very little chance that communications will be underemphasized. Yet there is a chance that the essential ability of the good communicator may be overlooked. He is not just a spokesman or mouthpiece; he is also highly skilled in at least two ways:

1. Understanding the nature of the many communications media which he may use
2. Understanding the communications process itself, so that he will not confuse the transmission of a vast amount of material with its successful reception —will not fall victim to the "illusion of communication" that regularly trips those who are sure that their "much speaking" has made them heard and understood

Both of these simple-sounding aspects of communication have commanded the lifetime attention of very capable men; scores of books have been written about them; and we are still far from understanding them well. The subject of communication is not at all simple!

Yet, despite such complexity, communication is often quite well accomplished, and in the detailed discussion of communication cases in Chapter 12 you will find examples as varied as the following: a gas company which decided that it needed a personality; a telephone company which turned the problems of a disastrous hurricane into a communications asset; a large chemical company which invested thousands of dollars in a program of small-group discussion to aid two-way communication among its employees; an airline which decided that forthrightness in publishing the news was the best way to apprise the public of steps taken to improve a faulty airplane after a series of crashes; an important government agency which couldn't get anyone to listen to its story because it was too disagreeable in telling it; and another large company which decided that its corporate name was too long and confused and selected an entirely new one. Of course, not every communication effort is a success. Chapter 12 also discusses some failures.

There is very little danger that anyone engaged in public relations will forget to attempt to communicate, but there is a good chance that he will omit the final step in the public relations formula, which is *evaluation*.

Evaluation

When actions have been taken, when messages have been sent out, what has happened in people's thinking? Who listened? How much did they listen? What did the message mean to them in their own terms? What effect did it have upon their attitudes? Their actions? These are questions which could be asked in evaluating the results of public relations. They are important to the practitioner not only because they measure his success, but also because the answers provide the basis for his next moves.

Yet important as evaluation is, it remains the least developed and most tantalizing of all the areas of public relations work. Trying to estimate the results of efforts to change human attitudes and opinions is within the province of the social sciences, whereas the effort to change material things belongs to the physical sciences. Controlled experiments are possible in solving many problems of the physical sciences. If, under known conditions, a chemical is added to a substance and a change occurs, there is some reason to suppose that the new factor was the cause of the change, especially if the experiment can be repeated numbers of times. But human beings are much more complex than the physical elements which compose their bodies. One cannot know exactly what natures and experiences they bring to an experiment; no two of them are alike; and in any complex civilization people are exposed to many influences, while an experiment is going on and also immediately afterwards while a scientist is trying to measure the results. The methods of estimating opinion change are crude at best compared with the weights, measures, and litmus papers of the physical sciences.

It is no wonder, then, that social sciences have progressed much more slowly than physical sciences; they started later, and their field is much more complex. Public relations, through its kinship with the social sciences, shares their tardiness and uncertainty. This difficulty sometimes causes scientists or hardheaded businessmen (both of whom are accustomed to dealing with exact measurement) to decide that a statement about something which cannot be measured easily is either unimportant or mumbo jumbo; and it must be confessed that some public relations men have taken advantage of this difficulty in measurement to peddle rather vaporous wares themselves, clothing their lack of exact knowledge in vehemence and big words.

Most public relations men, faced with the difficulty and cost of evaluation, forget it and get on with the next job, relying upon common sense, which often serves well enough, to assess their results. In this they have been joined by employers who are willing to take results for granted. Perhaps their confidence is fortunate, because if all important human efforts had to await exact definition and substantiation, then not much would be accomplished. One may not be able to see the wind, but any intelligent mariner knows that it is there and that he can sail with it.

As a rule, only large companies with continuous problems engage in persistent evaluation; some of these efforts are described later in this book.

Closing the Circle

Evaluation is evidently very close in its nature to the first step in the public relations formula, *research*. It *is,* in fact, another form of research, conducted at the end of a job instead of at the beginning. At this point

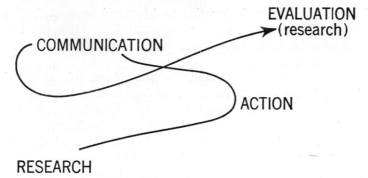

Figure 9-1. In ongoing public relations programs the R-A-C-E formula is really a spiral leading to the next step, since *evaluation* also serves as *research* for future programs.

the R-A-C-E public relations formula will take on the appearance of a spiral. Each step leads to the next, and the conclusion leads to renewed action.

EXAMPLES OF THE R-A-C-E FORMULA IN USE

1. Launching a New Streamliner[1]

Several years ago, the Canadian Pacific Railroad decided to put a new stainless-steel streamliner train into service between Montreal and Vancouver—2,881 miles. This major investment involved the expenditure of many millions of dollars, because the maintenance of daily service on such a long run as this requires several complete trains westbound and several more eastbound, moving all the time, plus extra equipment for cleanup and turnarounds at the terminals. The train, two years in construction, was built by the Budd Manufacturing Company of Philadelphia.

The railroad knew that the success of this new train would give a strong impetus to the development of other parts of the C.P. transportation empire, which includes numerous hotels in Canada, a transatlantic steamship line, and airlines. The problem was to publicize the attractions of the new train so well that it would be solidly booked from its very first run.

Approaching this problem with the R-A-C-E formula in mind, a public relations man would have to ask a series of questions.

Research. Where are passengers for this new train likely to come from? What sort of people will they be? What will interest them? How may they be reached?

Action. How can this new train be made different from other streamliners operating in the United States or Canada? Made in the United States,

[1] *Public Relations News,* July 18, 1955.

it will have to go through America to Montreal to start its first trip. Does this part of its career offer any opportunities? How can the actual start of service be made memorable? What about cities along the way, like Toronto or Winnipeg?

Communication. How can people be told about this new train? By methods now in use, such as present timetables or calendars? By purchase of advertising? By bulletins, booklets, movies, open houses, or tours? By alliance with other institutions which might also be interested in telling people about the train? What approach is best in the stories? Serious appeal to business travelers or to vacationers or to women—or to all three? Describing the train or describing the scenery through which it passes, or both? How can a visual image be developed?

Evaluation. How many prospective travelers are aware of C.P. communications? What effects has the publicity had? *What has been the patronage of the railroad?* Why (judging from their comments) did patrons choose this new train? What do they like or dislike about the streamliner now that they have traveled on it? Will they recommend it to their friends? These are just a few of the questions that might be asked under the R-A-C-E headings.

The Canadian Pacific Railroad carried out a very interesting experiment in public relations, in their successful launching of the new train. Most of the passengers, it was thought, would be from the upper or upper middle class in the New England or Middle Atlantic areas of the United States or in eastern Canada—vacationers, families, women. Business travelers would be more likely to fly than to take the train because of the time involved in this long run.

Concentrating their efforts on travelers obviously in holiday mood, the Canadian Pacific translated their ideas into *action.* Observation lounges of the train, "scenic domes," were named after Canadian national and provincial parks, and prominent artists were chosen to decorate them with murals. Sleeping cars were named "Manors" after famed English-Canadian historical figures or "Chateaux" after similar French-Canadian persons. Dining cars were named after famous C.P. hotels and were decorated with the crests of these hostelries.

Since department stores are often willing to use a new promotion in their windows and stores if it will help them to sell women's clothing, the railroad proposed a set of traveling displays to illustrate the proper wardrobe to wear on a Canadian vacation in the new train. The exhibit was introduced at a breakfast fashion show in a leading New York department store and was used by 112 stores. A promotion program was added: The 500 people who attended this breakfast (130 of them news, radio, TV, and newsreel representatives from the United States and Canada) were taken by the train from New York to New Hope, Pennsylvania, near where the train was built. New Hope was declared Canadian territory for the day, and a flag was raised to the music of a Scots piper band. Another fashion show was put on at the famous Bucks County Playhouse by the John Wanamaker Department Store of Philadelphia.

When the new train first left Montreal on regular service, it was launched with appropriate speeches by dignitaries and greeted in the Dominion capital, Ottawa, by government heads and again at main points all along the line.

The train was featured for months in many media of communications. It appeared in advertising of all kinds, especially newspaper advertising before the train made its first passage through major towns; in newspaper stories as it progressed, written by a corps of newsmen who were taken along; and in pictures shot from a helicopter hovering above the train.

Evaluation showed that the campaign had been a great success. Stories and pictures appeared in more than 3,000 publications. The train was sold out months in advance, and bookings for the next year were from 50 to 75 per cent ahead of those of the preceding year.

This public relations program was successful because the research into the peculiar nature of the problem was sound, the actions were exciting, and the communications were numerous and interesting. Besides the C.P. railroad public relations staff, many organizations contributed to its success. Budd Manufacturing Company made the train and benefited by joining its forces with C.P.; the department stores tied in with public interest and sold more merchandise; and the many news media which carried stories and pictures tapped reader interest for themselves.

2. The Case of the Shredded Clothes

Very different was the problem which the American Institute of Laundering faced some years ago. When the public takes clothes to a laundry and they are accidentally torn, faded, or shrunk, the laundry gets the blame and customers want their money back, plus restitution for the damage to the clothes. Sometimes the damage is the fault of the laundry, and this the American Institute of Laundering could try to prevent by getting all its members to use only the best equipment and methods. But sometimes the fault lies in the poor quality of the customers' clothes; laundries annually pay millions of dollars for losses which never would have happened if the clothes had been sturdy in the first place.

To help overcome this problem, the Institute established a large testing laboratory and gave garments, sheets etc., that passed the test a "certified washable" seal of approval which manufacturers could place on their garments and display with them. But why should garment makers attach the label? Only to give an added recommendation to their clothes. If the seal was to constitute a "selling point," then, both manufacturers and the clothes-buying public would have to know about the laboratory and value the testimony of the seal to such a degree that most manufacturers would want to submit their garments for testing.

In this problem *research* was already inherent in the facts given. The laundries knew what they were losing in damaged goods and why. *Action* lay in the setting up of standards of good procedure for the laundries themselves and in the establishment of a testing laboratory which would award its seal of approval to certified-washable garments. The next problem was *communication*—how to let both manufacturers and users know about the laboratory and seal and impel them to value the scientific tests. This might involve further actions. Finally came *evaluation,* perhaps in the form of a survey among manufacturers or customers to see how many knew of the laboratory and seal and what they thought of them; or perhaps in a checkup of garments coming into laundries to see how many actually had the seal; or perhaps also in a checkup of manufacturers' advertising to see to what extent the seal was being promoted. And, of course, damage-loss figures in relation to the volume done would be the final test.

3. Moving an Automobile Manufacturing Plant[2]

In the 1930s, Ford Motor Company built an assembly plant at Edgewater, New Jersey, across the Hudson River from New York City. It was a multistory building in the middle of town, which in time became inefficient. As the demand for cars increased, it could not be expanded easily; as assembly-line techniques changed, large horizontal in-line plants were found to be much cheaper in operation than buildings with stories piled one on top of another. Ford found a larger new plant site in Mahwah, New Jersey, some 26 miles away. Ford public relations people were called in to help plan the move.

Research showed that many of the 2,900 Ford employees at Edgewater had spent years with the company. Their skills were valuable, and the company wanted to keep them. The loss of the Ford plant would hurt Edgewater, but not too badly since there were many other industries in the area and the old Ford building might be turned to some other purpose. Besides, Mahwah was within commuting distance, and many older Ford employees with homes in Edgewater would probably continue to live there, especially if they were within a few years of retirement. The main problems were to expedite the move, to keep employees, to build good will in both towns, and to cash in on the publicity value inherent in such a major industrial shift, for it was not intended to shut the plant down in the process of moving.

[2] *Public Relations News,* Sept. 19, 1955.

This plan for continuous operation provided a basis for a special *action*. Why not publicize the unique feat of moving tons of machinery and thousands of people 26 miles without skipping a beat in the production of Ford automobiles? Surely this achievement would be spectacular and newsworthy. Plant whistles could blow farewell to the factory at Edgewater; a welcoming delegation could be at Mahwah; and in between, a caravan of trucks and railroad cars escorted by police could be seen hauling the machinery. The move would get the attention, not only of the towns involved, but also of the New York metropolitan area and the nation as a whole!

Of course there were many other actions to be taken—a new plant tour in advance of the move for employees, open houses for opinion leaders in Mahwah, and a campaign to find new occupants for the plant at Edgewater. The oldest employee was to drive the last car off the line at Edgewater (and when it was discovered that she could not drive, the town's mayor drove instead). The first car off the new line in Mahwah was specially fitted for amputee use and was given to a hospital. But the action inherent in the move itself lifted the change to regional and national importance.

Communication flows naturally in a situation like this. Employees must be informed before anybody else. Provision must be made for listening to their problems and aiding them. Management must know the story and carry it to opinion leaders in the area. The local public must know what's going on. The press must be kept aware of events and supplied with material.

Evaluation was carried out in many fields. Only 10 out of 2,900 employees left the company because of the shift, and these were elderly persons who decided to accept accelerated retirement instead of moving. Coverage in various media all over the New York metropolitan area was of outstanding quality. Many people doubtless admired the enterprise of the Ford Motor Company in its smooth transfer of production and by implication valued Ford products more highly.

Many other examples of the use of the R-A-C-E formula in solving public relations problems could be cited, and other, perhaps equally useful, formulas could be devised. The most important thing is to develop an orderly pattern of thought, to face the truth squarely, and to think, not about what you would want to hear, but about what others would find interesting. Then with a dash of the unusual, you have the beginning of a good public relations program.

Research and Research Cases

10

Suppose a man calls in a doctor and says, "I don't feel well, but don't bother about making a diagnosis. My relatives and friends all assure me that my symptoms are exactly the same as those which my Uncle Otto had when he suffered from an inflamed appendix. I know that you're a good surgeon, so get busy. Take out my appendix and send me the bill later." If the doctor then operates, you may rightly conclude that he isn't much of a physician, but rather some kind of charlatan.

But in public relations, many may try to practice the art who are often shockingly inexperienced. Some men are quite willing to admit that they may not be able to write a really good magazine feature article, prepare a well-paced television script, or produce a good motion picture; few will claim to know how to produce an attractive exhibit for a great world's fair or even how to plan an effective youth-talent show; but a great many people will assume, without second thought, that they are completely competent to identify public relations problems, decide their weight and severity, know what other people think about them and why they think it, and then prescribe all sorts of effective remedial communications. Sometimes they may be right; often they are not.

A Framework for Public Relations Research

The general objectives of research include probing basic attitudes, measuring actual (not supposed) opinions, identifying leaders of opinion, reducing costs by concentrating upon the most valid targets, testing themes and media, timing, discovering the strength of antagonistic views, achieving two-way communication, revealing trouble before it develops, and using opinion research as a communications tool in itself.

Much research is done by amateurs, but even amateurs should know its limitations and be able to judge rightly the validity of what they are doing. Mistakes made in amateur research are quite often serious because whole sets of plans are built upon the foundations laid by research, and a user who is convinced of something untrue is worse than an ignorant user. In

174

addition, since amateur research men are often responsible for the selection and hiring of professional research firms and for judging the value of their findings, some knowledge of the research field is absolutely essential, even for those who have neither the time nor the desire to become really expert.

Examples of Basic Public Relations Research Questions

In approaching a public relations problem, any organization might ask itself some fundamental questions.

Who are we and why do we exist? What do other people think of us? Who are these "other people"? The image that an organization has of itself may be quite confused, and before much can be communicated to anyone else about that image, perhaps the possessors of it need to engage in some objective introspection—if that paradox is possible.

Can others be criticized for not having an accurate image of an organization if it has done little or nothing to communicate it to them? We must always remember that as far as others are concerned, their image of the organization *is* the organization in their own minds—even if it does not happen to coincide with the facts.

Often the problems of an organization are really not what the men of that organization think they are. For example, when an industrial plant was being enlarged in a Southern city, the work had to be held up temporarily because of the objections of nearby residents to the noise. Since these complaints did not appear to represent a valid criticism, a survey was made to determine whether noise or some other reasons lay behind the efforts to block the proposed expansion.

In the survey-research interviews, only 5 per cent of the respondents volunteered any criticism of the noise at the plant. When those being interviewed were questioned directly about their reaction to noise, common answers were, "The noise doesn't bother me" or "It's sometimes noisy, but that doesn't happen very often." Several volunteered that the noise from nearby railroad trains was much worse than any noise from the plant construction. "We have forty-four trains a day pass by here, but I never notice any noise from the plant," was a typical remark.

It seemed apparent that the criticism of noise at the plant was not serious, but further probing brought out complaints that the company should "do something to cut down the dust on the street leading to the plant." Accompanying these complaints were more practical suggestions: "The company should sprinkle or oil these two streets that go from the highway to the plant, especially when they are hauling materials, because the dust is simply fierce," or "The trucks and traffic are terrific; our streets will be all broken up and we shall live in a cloud of dust all summer." There were also complaints that better provisions should be made for parking the cars of construction workers, which had to be left on the street in front of homes all day.

When action was taken to meet *these* complaints, objections disappeared, and it was possible to proceed. What had prevented people from complaining openly about the parking and the driving before? Probably they were reluctant to be critical of the construction workers who were of their same social and economic class.[1]

Recently, when the Michigan Hospital Association wanted to find out the opinions of twenty-nine of the editors of the state's leading newspapers, who constituted a small but very important public, an experienced newspaperman was hired to make the interviews.

He found that twenty out of the twenty-nine editors thought that the most important hospital public relations problem was costs and that nineteen of the twenty-nine felt that access to information from hospitals by newspapers was the second most important problem. The two major problems observed by the editors were entirely different in character. In mentioning the cost problem, the editors were reporting on community feeling. The information problem, on the other hand, was one with which they were professionally concerned as newspapermen. To solve the problem of public irritation with costs, the editors suggested such things as simplified annual statements released to the newspapers, more information and breakdowns on statements given to the patients, greater emphasis in releases to all media on the fact that payrolls (what the patients paid for services by others) were the big cost in hospital operation, explanations that a hospital is a community-based service and that the biggest part of a dollar spent in a hospital returns to the community, and using hospital personnel in an enlightened way to tell the hospital-cost story.

On the problem of the blocks in getting information for the press from hospitals, the suggestion was made repeatedly that an educational program be started inside the hospitals to inform the personnel on how to give out information while at the same time preserving the traditional privacy of the patient. One frequent suggestion was that someone on the hospital staff should be empowered to serve as a press contact twenty-four hours a day to provide coverage when the chief administrator was not present.[2]

There was nothing startling in the information gained by either of these simple forms of research. Yet if the company which was building the plant addition had assumed that the complaints of noise represented the real trouble and had tried to correct it, while at the same time neglecting the dust and parking problems, the hostile feeling would have continued; and if the hospitals had assumed that their main public problems (in the eyes

[1] Charles E. Parker, president, Central Surveys, Inc., Shenandoah, Iowa.
[2] "Hospitals and the Press," a survey of the opinions of Michigan editors by the Michigan Hospital Association, Lansing, Mich., 1961.

of the Michigan press, at least) were poor quality of service and lack of public confidence in their skill or facilities, they also would have spent much time solving unreal problems.

Public relations research is nothing more than planned, carefully organized, sophisticated fact finding and listening to the opinions of others. It becomes necessary when human relationships exist upon such a big scale that some form of organized, scientific feedback is necessary to find out what is in the minds of other persons. When one man talks to another or to a small group, he can get some idea of reactions simply by watching other people's faces and by listening to their comments. But when a public relations practitioner, addressing an audience at long distance in news stories, booklets, or television programs, wants to know what impression he is making, he has to devise some planned mechanism for listening and to establish ways in which two-way communication can be achieved. Otherwise his efforts to communicate are likely to be misdirected and ineffective.

Common Objectives of Research

1. *To probe the basic attitudes of groups.* What predispositions exist to accept or to reject ideas, and to judge favorably or unfavorably the sources from which they might come? If a railroad, for example, wishes to talk to Kansas wheat farmers, it will profit by knowing in advance what these wheat farmers think about railroads in general and about their rates, practices, and history in particular; and by knowing what feelings they have about road building, trucking, gasoline taxes, and anything else pertinent. Our own estimates of what others think are often misleading, because we project our opinions into their minds. The old saying "If I were in your shoes, I should do so-and-so" is not so useful as "If I were in your shoes and had your background and interests, I should probably do so-and-so."

2. *To measure the true opinions of groups.* How can you tell what a group of people really believe? This is often a complicated question because the loudly expressed opinions of a vocal minority within a group may not be at all the same as those of a silent majority. Who within a group holds certain opinions? How intensely do they hold them? And how are trends shifting?

3. *Identification of leaders of opinion.* Where do people within a group get their ideas? From immediate friends and neighbors? From those a notch or two above themselves in the social scale? Or from the top brass which they read about in newspapers or see on television? Who spreads opinion? Who are the first to adopt new ideas or practices, and how much are these innovators then copied? What is the role of gatekeepers—editors, broadcasters, teachers, and preachers, who pass on information and opinions to others, although their own viewpoints may or may not be reflected in such conveyance?

4. *Reducing public relations costs by concentrating upon valid targets.*
Trying to reach too many people and reaching them ineffectively through
a poor medium of communication may both be extremely costly efforts.
A number of years ago, a California company began the manufacture of
pepper mills. They made pepper mills easily and placed them in the hands
of retailers by the hundreds. And then nothing happened. The buying
public did not know what pepper mills were, and they did not want them.
So a public relations campaign was entered into, concentrating upon the
food editors of newspapers and magazines who controlled space in which
the public regularly expected to find new ideas about food. This was a
natural alliance, because food editors are constantly pressed for something
new to present. Pepper mills appeared in pictures of table settings, in motion pictures of famous restaurants, in descriptions of salads; and after a
time, when people had learned about the purpose of pepper mills by seeing
them, reading about them, and hearing about them, the contrivances could
be sold by means of regular small-space advertising which had previously
failed.[3]

5. *Testing themes and media before placing all bets upon them.* Public
relations advertising may cost hundreds of thousands of dollars for magazine space or broadcasting time. Often it is only prudent to test public
response through a representative sample before risking all on a major
effort. A company magazine may be costing thousands of dollars for each
issue. How well is it being read? What items are most read or least read?
What ideas do readers gain from the magazine? The best way to know is
to ask questions in a scientific manner. The answers may not be complete
or final, but at least they will be a guide.

6. *Timing.* The American commander at the Battle of Bunker Hill
warned his untried troops to hold their single-shot musket fire until they
could "see the whites of their eyes." This good advice prevented scattering
musket fire at ranges too distant to be effective and ensured that every
bullet would count when the concentrated blast came. But in public relations conflicts, withholding fire often doesn't work. People are usually much
more susceptible to persuasion *before* the battle has been clearly joined.
Later, when they have chosen their side, they tend to stop listening to anything which might shake their faith, and their ears are closed to reason.
Rapid opinion research can often tell whether thoughts have solidified upon
issues and to what degree, and in this way can separate areas in which appeal may be vain from other areas which still may be cultivated.

7. *Ascertaining the strength of the opposition.* In the heat of a political
campaign, for example, a certain idea injurious to your side may seem to
be catching on. Should forces be diverted to answering it right away, or
should they continue with their original plans? A quick survey might show

[3] *Public Relations News,* Oct. 15, 1956.

that the apparently widespread strength of the idea has been greatly exaggerated. Some newspapers and strong partisans of the opposition may be giving it great play, but the great balance of the public may be quite apathetic. Changing communications strategy at once to meet this minor threat may dislodge the adherents you have been gaining upon the present tack and will profit nothing.

8. *Achieving two-way communication.* Simply finding out what recipients think is not really two-way communication; such research is done for the benefit of the sender, and if only a small segment of the recipients are sampled, very few of the total number will be aware that their opinion is being sought. A small cross-sectional sample may be adequate from a scientific viewpoint, but a large well-known survey can also become a means of two-way communication for the respondents who are interviewed, giving them a chance to express themselves and to talk back. A good example appears later in this chapter in connection with the Western Union stockholder-survey program.

9. *Revealing trouble before it happens.* Effective public relations work often never shows itself openly because it consists in ascertaining difficulties before they ever come to the surface and in correcting problems before they ever break out into public view. Opinion surveys, especially those taken at intervals to show trends, constitute one of the most effective ways of raising warning flags, since before people act in a certain way, they must first have done some thinking. The strike that didn't happen, the plant changes that were accomplished without a protest, the stockholders who regularly returned a management to power, were probably the result of intelligent actions and communications which were themselves preceded by careful public-opinion research; without the research nothing might have been communicated because the need for it would not have been so clearly realized.

10. *Opinion research as a weapon in itself.* Showing valid evidence of public opinion upon an issue can be very effective when used in groups outside of an organization. A survey, for example, taken by an impartial research firm showing fairly the opinions of a city population, might be a decisive factor in the decision of a city council.

Inside an organization, fact-minded people such as treasurers or production men frequently dominate company boards of control. These people sometimes need to be shown the reality and true nature of a problem. Frequently a public relations director, because his antennae are more attuned to outside human contacts and reactions, may see danger or opportunity in a public attitude and yet be unable to move his colleagues who do not have a similar responsiveness. In such a situation it is both difficult and dangerous to insist upon action solely upon a basis of unsupported hunch; more evidence is needed, and this is best supplied from the findings of organized opinion research, to which the hardest-headed will usually listen.

The History of Modern Opinion Research

Trying to find out what people think about things is certainly as old as democracy itself. Putting issues to a vote is the ultimate test of public opinion, and although from time immemorial kings and tyrants have snooped about by means of agents to discover the sentiment of their subjects, the final revelation takes place at a general public election.

Modern public-opinion research, however, using samples of public opinion before the formality of a mass vote, is largely a creation of the past thirty years—a period which seems almost absurdly recent. In the 1930s, for example, public-opinion research methods moved from the inaccurate system of taking big "chunks" of popular sentiment (samples which, no matter how large, were not necessarily representative of the whole group from which they were drawn) to a serious effort to ascertain mass opinion by cross-sectional samples which would truly reflect the feelings of various groups and might thus safely serve as a basis upon which projections could be made about the entire group.

One fiasco which helped to kill unscientific chunk sampling as a serious research device was the *Literary Digest* poll of 1936 involving some two million responses from users of telephones or similar upper-economic-level lists and predicting a landslide sweep for Alfred Landon, GOP nominee for the Presidency, just before Franklin D. Roosevelt, Democrat, in fact mopped the floor with the remains of the Republican party. There were several reasons for the failure of the *Literary Digest* poll.

In the midst of the Depression, when every dime counted, telephone service was more largely restricted to the upper classes, who would be likely to vote for Landon, than it is today. At that time also, as George Gallup, later to wrestle with some polling problems himself, noted:

> Before 1936 you were as likely to find Republicans among workers as you were among people who owned telephones. The controlling factor was still the Civil War; my grandfather was worse than any Southerner, only he'd fought for the North. He was an immovable Republican. Social class bias in your sample made no difference—until the New Deal stratified the people of America politically.

In other words, an inaccurate chunk which had fortunately served well enough as a sample previously had ceased to be at all representative.

To avoid the trap in which the *Literary Digest* had been caught, Gallup and the other polltakers developed "quota sampling" to a point of some refinement. Each interviewer was given certain types of people to query, the combination of types being planned in all *important* aspects of the whole universe to be surveyed. The problem still remained, however, of what was important.

Even quota sampling had its limitations, for a number of reasons which will be discussed in more detail later, such as last-minute shifts in opinion and the inability of respondents to tell what is really on their minds. This inaccuracy made necessary further development, and the very late 1930s and 1940s saw the beginning of "motivational research," an attempt to probe by psychological means not only what people *say* they believe, but also whether they really believe it or something else, and why they believe as they do.

Types of Research Used in Public Relations

1. *Fact gathering.* Much of what a public relations man may need to know about his audiences is available just for the gathering from the United States Census reports, *Sales Management* magazine surveys, and other sources. He can easily find answers to such questions as: How many cars do people have? How far do they drive? How do they vote? What is their race, age, and sex? How much do they spend for different varieties of merchandise?

In addition, many newspapers, broadcasting stations, and magazines are prepared to give more or less reliable profiles of some other characteristics of their audiences, such as where they shop, go on vacations, send their children to school, and (of course) what they say they read or listen to.

The interpretation of the facts is up to the person who assembles them, and the proper conclusions are not always so obvious as they seem. But carefully chosen sources of information can be relied on. If one has something to publicize to boat owners, for example, boat registrations and the readership of a boating magazine would seem to be pretty good guides to interested personnel; and if one has a resort to promote, the people who habitually visit the region would seem to be worth following up and questioning.

2. *Opinion research* is at least two steps deeper in complexity (*a*) because opinion research concerns itself with what people say they think rather than with the much more easily verifiable record of what they do and (*b*) because an opinion survey almost always must depend upon a sample and is misleading unless that sample is representative of the whole. Some dangers will be noted in the paragraphs following. One of the best uses of opinion surveys is to show trends rather than absolutes.

3. *Motivational research.* As we have mentioned before, motivational research attempts to probe into the reasons why people believe and do things, often seeking reasons which they cannot, or will not, tell an interviewer in response to simple questions.

Motivational research takes a variety of forms, including "depth inter-

views," in which those interviewed are encouraged to talk freely and seemingly almost at random, although the interviewer has in mind a planned
pattern in the conversation; "thematic apperception" tests, in which respondents are asked to write or speak freely about situations imagined in
pictures; "projective techniques," such as asking people to describe an
imaginary scene glimpsed through a keyhole; "psychodrama," in which
people are asked to take part in and to interpret plays; and a variety of
multiple-choice tests including the "semantic differential," by which degrees
of response toward pairs of polarized words can be expressed.

A weakness in motivational research efforts to peer into the human
mind sometimes springs out of the necessity of creating hypotheses, both
in setting up the studies and in interpreting their meanings. A number of
years ago the writer witnessed an instance of such misinterpretation. A
number of Cadillac owners and De Soto owners were asked to tell their
reactions to a picture which showed a car passing another car on a hill;
just over the crest of the hill, on the passing side, could be glimpsed the
upper works of a large truck. The question was: "What does the passing
car most need to do?" Most of the Cadillac owners said, "Step on the gas
and clear the car being passed to get back into line." Most of the De Soto
owners said, "Stand on the brake and fall back into line behind the car
alongside."

From these answers the researchers concluded that Cadillac owners as a
class were more dashing and venturesome than De Soto owners. This may
very well have been so, but the test did not prove it. The De Soto model
that year was an extremely underpowered car with a "slushy" transmission,
and any De Soto driver knew that when caught in such a passing trap
there was no solution except to fall back into line as quickly as possible.
Whether De Soto owners as a class were more cautious by nature in advance of purchasing their cars was not shown by the research. It was clear,
however, that they soon became so after a little experimentation with their
vehicles!

Research Pitfalls

Mark Twain once referred to a man "who knew more things that weren't
so" than anyone else he'd ever known. Despite the great and necessary
use of research, the unreliability and gullibility of the human beings who
express opinions and of those who employ opinion sampling and motivational research as a basis for public relations practice still make the basis
shaky and dangerous. The typical public relations man seldom becomes a
formal research expert (this particular vocation seems to be more of a
"calling") but will certainly be involved in buying opinion research and in
judging its validity. For this reason he needs to understand the chief pit-
falls, without flying to the other extreme of being antagonistic to well-

conducted research or feeling that in some way it hampers his creative intuition.

1. *Nonrepresentative listening.* All of us tend to associate with people who are similar to us in their tastes and habits and in their wealth and social positions. Businessmen tend to spend their spare time with other businessmen at clubs, professors with other faculty members, and laborers with other laborers, each of the same rank and type. Furthermore we tend to remember only what pleases us, and other people tend to tell us what they feel we would like to hear. Even more, we hear only what is spoken, and the louder and more persistently it is spoken, the more we note it. If ten people are silent and one is speaking, we are likely to assume that the speaker expresses the sentiments of the other ten, although there may be many reasons for their silence.

All these tendencies make random, unplanned observation of popular feeling highly unreliable. We are all familiar with the businessman who is convinced that everyone is as conservative as he is (or that they would be if only they had the "facts") and with the liberal who is appalled by the conservatism of the "masses." As the poet, Robert Burns, once said:

> Oh wad some Power the giftie gie us
> To see oursel's as ithers see us!
> It wad frae monie a blunder free us,
> An' foolish notion . . .

But the probabilities are that even if we were to receive this gift, we would be inclined to discount such insight heavily in favor of our preexisting feelings.

2. *The advisory committee.* "Letterhead" committees are one of the oldest devices used by drives and causes. Sometimes keen individuals within such committees are able to feel the public pulse; but the main function of advisory committees is to give support and testimonials and to create involvement. An advisory committee is always drawn from the ranks of those who are at least somewhat favorably disposed toward a cause, because otherwise they would not be willing to serve. In addition, they are usually drawn from the top ranks in whatever groups they circulate among, and since they are thus more aggressive, vocal, and wide-ranging in their interests, they may be helpful; but they are not typical. They are not chosen for their valid reflection of public opinion.

3. *The representative panel.* The representative panel reflects an attempt to set up a somewhat permanent cross-sectional body from which, at intervals, a realistic sample of opinion can be obtained. The device is not a bad one in some respects, since it permits deeper probing than can be done in offhand interviews and also enables a researcher to have greater knowledge of the peculiar characteristics of the panel members. Its weak-

ness is that the longer a panel is kept in touch with a given situation, the less it becomes really representative, because familiarity with the subject matter alters the panel's reactions. As the old saying has it, "No man can step into the same river twice."

4. *Field reports.* "Our salesmen say so-and-so" is one of the most frequent and invalid clichés which research-minded public relations men encounter. It's worth knowing what salesmen think (sometimes it's all-important), but salesmen are necessarily favorably disposed toward the company which they represent or they wouldn't be its salesmen, and in any case, they are usually prudent enough to tell the boss what they think he would like to hear. Nor is there any assurance that the outsiders they contact are at all representative of the whole group whose opinions are sought. This applies also in the case of their reports upon dealer opinions, since salesmen prefer to call upon and to listen to dealers who like them and who receive them well. Even when field reports from salesmen are not intentionally misleading, the reporters are often self-deluded.

5. *Improper sampling.* Improper sampling may be of several sorts: inadequate, unrepresentative, or badly timed. Although huge samples are not necessarily representative of the whole, tiny samples involving only a few people are likely to be misleading because they may easily have happened upon nontypical persons. The danger is particularly great when an adequate large sample is broken down for analysis into smaller subsections, some of which may include only a few respondents; the inadequacy of the subsections may be masked by the adequate size of the main sample.

Unrepresentative sampling can occur, for example, when telephone checks on broadcast listening are made only within the city limits because of the cost involved in reaching rural listeners by long-distance telephone. In this way the differences in taste between rural and urban listeners may be obscured, and with some programs, such as mystery dramas or church music, their true ranking with the total audience is altered.

Timing errors arise when something happens to alter the validity of a sample between the time it is taken and the time it is used. In the 1948 presidential election, for example, one of the major national sampling polls predicted a victory for Thomas E. Dewey on the basis of a poll taken in September. The actual vote in early November came out quite otherwise, and the pollsters believed that the trouble lay, not in the sample, which was accurate enough, but in the voters' last-minute unrecorded swing to President Truman. The fact that results of periodic sampling polls may show definite, consistent variation over a period of time indicates that changes do occur in public opinion and that plans based upon outdated research may be inappropriate and dangerous.

6. *Biased interviewers.* To biased interviews we might add careless, lazy, and dishonest interviewers. Fortunately, this error is usually easily checked

by comparing the work of one of several individual polltakers against that of the others. Any undue variation in what should be adequate sub-samples will bear careful investigation.

7. *Foggy response* may spring from the respondents' simple inability to understand what is being asked, often accompanied by a cheerful willing-ness to make a stab at answering anyway so as not to lose face by an ad-mission of ignorance. Akin to this is the common desire of those interviewed to look good in the eyes of the interviewer.

Some years ago, when a soap company's researchers went about asking people how many baths they took each week, a prodigious amount of bath-ing was reported. Taking frequent baths has social prestige, and those who seldom went near a tub could scarcely be expected to admit the fact. A similar prestige response occurs when people are asked whether they read the editorials in a newspaper or whether they subscribe to certain high-class magazines. Many respondents will answer "Yes," but will fall down on further specific checks of readership of the exact contents of yesterday's editorials or last month's magazine.

Often related to this desire for prestige is a simple desire to please the interviewer. "The young lady obviously wants me to say that I use Blotzos, so I'll say that I use Blotzos." There is also, sometimes, a fear or caution reaction. "This fellow is asking me about my reading the company maga-zine. He *says* the survey is anonymous, but how do I know that he won't tell the boss if I say I don't read it much? So I'd better play it cool and say that I read it most of the time." Or: "How do I like the *Tribune*? Well, it's the town's only newspaper, and if I ever wanted to run for office or get anywhere in business, I'd hate to have it against me, so I'd be a chump to say that I think it's a lousy rag!"

8. *Undue recall of the prominent.* Modern Americans are exposed to so many communications every day and every week that it is hard for them to remember where they all came from, often only a few days later. This helps to explain why it is possible to paste an ad of a prominent product into a newspaper or magazine in which it never appeared and still get a fair number of interviewees who will remember having seen it there the day before. They are not intentionally lying—just remembering the ap-pearance of the ad the week before or even in some entirely different medium.

9. *Exaggeration of minor differences.* If twenty items are recalled to a person's memory, he can probably tell you, with considerable accuracy, the few he likes best and also those he likes least—if there is any real variation between them. But his comparative rankings of Number 12 versus Number 13 and of Number 11 versus Number 10 are not particularly im-portant. In broadcast listening, very high ratings or very low ratings are doubtless important, but a small rise in percentage in the middle ground

based upon a small sample is not earth-shaking and should not cause undue jubilation or alarm.

None of the difficulties listed above are intended to imply that since research, like walking, when carefully examined is found to be an enormously complicated process, therefore research and locomotion are impossible. After all, since the biggest part of public relations practice is understanding and influencing public opinion, it behooves all public relations men who wish to be more than witch doctors and hacks to use all the weapons of social science to make their understanding as exact and scientifically valid as possible. It is only a partial basis for criticism that social science still has a long way to go in this field. Practically all progress in social science, in the modern sense at least, has taken place within the past hundred years, whereas the physical and biological sciences have been busily at work on what may be a less complicated assignment, during the several centuries covered by the lives of Galileo, Copernicus, Newton, Harvey, and Darwin.

The liaison between the social scientist and the working public relations man is not very good, because neither of them really speaks the other's language or shares the other's goals. The primary burden to establish a better connection, of course, lies upon the public relations fraternity because public relations men hope and expect to be the practical beneficiaries of the many new ways of understanding what people think and how they are influenced. Public relations men have good reason to want to know, and sometimes also have the money with which to support research.

Both sides need to have great patience. The working public relations man must try not to become exasperated at the slow, detailed analysis of the psychologist or sociologist of what often seems obvious; and the social scientist must not become upset by the "let's get along with the fight and hang the details" attitude so common among active public relations people. Neither side can afford a holier-than-thou attitude. Enormous progress has been made since the 1920s, but the increase in problems, needs, and knowledge is so great that the difficulties now seem even greater than they were forty years ago.

The modern public relations practitioner needs to remember that, after all, he is simply another kind of teacher, preacher, editor, or politician and that he shares with all these persuaders a common interest in the development of the art or science of communication.

Relationship between Research and Public Relations Planning

Even within the limitations of present research methods, it is still possible to make some marvelous discoveries. In a 1958 survey of the images of some twenty major American corporations, for example, Opinion Research

Corporation of Princeton, New Jersey, compared the standings of two large retail-trade companies and found that figures corroborated impressions.

On "believable advertising" the first company was ranked high by 34 per cent of the respondents as compared with 22 per cent for the second company; on "pleasant to do business with" by 41 per cent as compared with 24 per cent; on "tries to keep prices down" by 43 per cent versus 24 per cent; on "good record for steady work," by 28 per cent versus 15 per cent; on "excellent employee benefits," by 22 per cent versus 7 per cent; and on "shares prosperity with employees," by 19 per cent versus 5 per cent. The needs of the second company, compared with those of the first, are apparent and provide the basis for some sound public relations planning.

Valid research helps to answer the question "What do we want to do?" *How* to do it is the next step.

All effective public relations programs begin with careful planning. Where are we? Where should we like to be? How shall we get there?

Answers must be written out convincingly, clearly, and logically and must be buttressed by facts. Planning cannot be done in a vacuum; the public relations man plans not only to provide a blueprint for his own actions but more importantly, to convince others and to obtain their support. By himself he can do little, because he does not occupy a position of line authority from which he can command people farther down the line to do what he wishes. Instead he must explain, inspire, and gain cooperation. It is possible to make public relations plans without research, but they usually have a wild-blue-yonder, unconvincing quality.

Some Public Relations Cases in Which Research
Is a Dominant Factor

The Standard Oil Company of California.[4] Beginning in 1944, the Standard Oil Company of California started the practice of running an opinion-research audit of its public standing every few years. Following a 1955 survey, the company had another survey taken in 1957 which involved 2,170 personal interviews. Work was done by the Field Research Company of San Francisco, and the main results were published in five issues of the company magazine, *The Standard Oiler,* in 1958.

In May, 1958, an article beginning the series was headed "What the Public Really Thinks about Us." After telling how the survey was conducted, it said:

> The results were not heartening. All oil companies and big business seem to be subject to increasing public criticism. Favorable opinion of our company, according to the survey, has shown a decided decline since the previous sampling in 1955. . . . Public relations will use the results

[4] T. L. Ansboro, executive assistant, Public Relations Department, Standard Oil Company of California, San Francisco, Calif.

What the public really thinks about us

Personal interviews of a cross-section of Western adult public give clues to recent changes in attitudes about our Company

EVERY year or so, our Public Relations Department enlists the services of a public opinion polling organization to find out what the general public thinks of our Company and our industry. The latest survey was conducted throughout the seven Western States at the close of last year. It was based on 2170 personal interviews of a cross-section of the adult public.

The results, in general, were not heartening. All oil companies and big business seem to be subject to increasing public criticism.

Favorable opinion of our Company, according to the survey, has shown a decided decline since the previous sampling in 1955. But the shift has been more toward a neutral position rather than toward actual dislike. It's now a stand-off between those who like us and those who are neutral. The "dislikers" are still a minority.

Many questions were asked in an attempt to find out specifically what bothers people about our Company. The most significant complaints seem to be four: They claim we're (1) too big and powerful, (2) too large to best serve the public, (3) a monopoly, and (4) charging too much for our products.

Public Relations will use the results of this latest poll in planning future programs and projects to help correct these impressions. But *you* can help, too. Much of our public's attitude is formed by chats with Standard Oilers, so you can help by becoming familiar with the facts about your Company and sharing them with your friends wherever appropriate.

Next month, THE OILER will begin a series of articles offering up-to-date facts to refute the main complaints of the public as revealed in this poll.

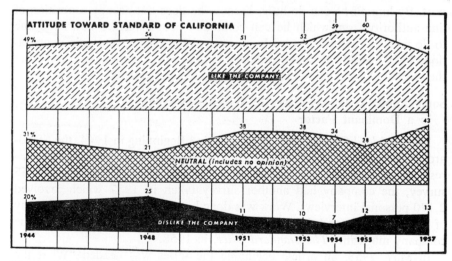

Figure 10-1. A company magazine, *The Standard Oiler,* begins a series of articles reporting to employees the results of research into public opinion of the company.

of this poll in planning future programs and projects to help correct these impressions. But *you* [employees] can help too. Much of our public's attitude is formed by chats with Standard Oilers, so you can help by becoming familiar with the facts about your company and sharing them with your friends whenever appropriate. . . .

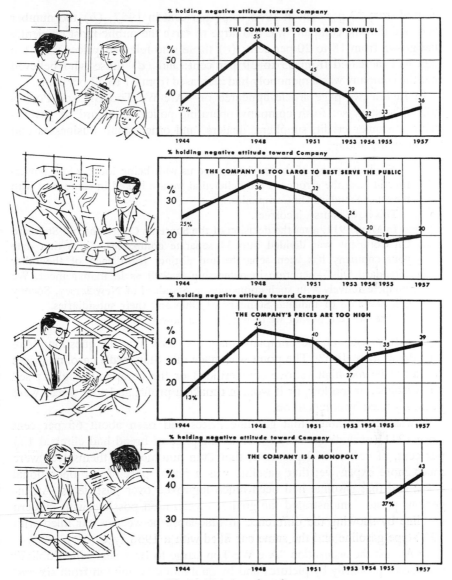

Figure 10-1 (*continued*)

The charts which followed showed that the percentage of the survey respondents who said that they liked the company had dropped from 60 per cent in 1955 to 44 per cent in 1957; "neutral" had increased from 28 to 43 per cent; and "dislike" from 12 to 13 per cent.

A breakdown of negative attitudes toward the company showed that (*a*) the number who said that the company was too big and powerful had in-

creased from 33 per cent in 1955 to 36 per cent in 1957; (*b*) the number
who said that the company was too large to serve the public most efficiently
had grown from 18 to 20 per cent; (*c*) those who felt that prices were too
high had increased from 35 to 39 per cent; and (*d*) those who believed
that the company was a monopoly had increased from 37 to 43 per cent.

In June a two-page article appeared on "Are We Too Big and Powerful?" The story set forth company operating policy in regard to government, customer credit, suppliers, dealers, and other small businesses and
wound up by noting:

> No doubt many of those who charge us with being too big and power-
> ful still have the erroneous old belief that we are linked in some way with
> the other Standard Oil Companies.
>
> This is, of course, incorrect.
>
> In May, 1911, after the decision of the Supreme Court, the old Standard
> Oil Company was divided into 34 separate companies. Since that date
> your company has been separate and distinct from each of the other
> "Standard Oils"—separate in ownership as well as in management. We
> compete actively with such companies as Standard of New Jersey, Socony
> Oil, Standard of Indiana, Standard of Ohio and their subsidiaries.
>
> Sure, we're big—but we're not big *and* powerful.

The July issue of the company magazine took up the question "Are
Our Prices Too High?" The point was made that Standard's gasoline prices
could not be *too* high (above competition) or the company wouldn't sell
any gasoline, or too low, or it wouldn't make a profit, and that prices were
primarily fixed by competition.

It was further noted that gasoline prices had risen about 65 per cent
since 1941 (excluding taxes), whereas the price of bread had climbed 123
per cent, of coffee, 330 per cent; that even automobiles themselves were
much more expensive; that gasoline was a minor part of car operational
costs; and that gasoline had been much improved over past years. An ingenious photo demonstrated the greater acceleration possible with modern
gasoline by showing the difference in time-lapse between a car filled with
1930-type gasoline and the same car filled with a 1958 type.

In August the accusation "Are We Too Large to Best Serve the Public?"
was faced, primarily by pictures and by quotations of opinion from six employees ranging from salesmen and chemists to the company president. The
strong assertion made by all was that size was necessary for oil exploration,
the risks of drilling exploratory wells, large, efficient manufacturing facilities, and on-going research into the field of new products and improvements
in existing products.

The final article, in September, tackled the question "Are We Really a
Monopoly?" and stressed competition in the oil business. The two photos
used as illustrations showed a street lined with filling stations of various

companies and a crossroads on the oil-producing desert with signs leading to five competitive leasing areas.

The Western Union Telegraph Company.[5] Prior to World War II, the Western Union Telegraph Company instituted a program of calls to be made by company officials upon stockholders of the company. The war and a series of unprofitable years immediately afterwards brought a hiatus in the program, but in 1948 it was stepped up under the direction of a new company president, and by 1961 a total of about 60,000 calls had been made upon Western Union shareowners in the twenty years since the program was instituted. There are about 40,000 shareowners, and in a typical year perhaps 2,500 of them will be called upon personally by company officials.

These personal contacts represent a rather high percentage of shareholders visited each year. Only independent holders owning 100 shares or more are called upon. Excluded from the program are Western Union officials, directors, employees, and members of their families; banks; attorneys and banks holding stock as executors, administrators, trustees, and guardians; stock brokerage firms; stockholders who say that they do not wish to be called upon; those whose physical condition makes a visit inadvisable; those who cannot be seen during the general routine of working hours; and those whose residence is too remote or hard to reach.

Particular attention is paid to new stockholders; and the intent of the program is that one-third of the "active" stockholders shall be interviewed personally every year. Interviews are spaced out as evenly as possible over the year. About 250 top-management people in 100 key cities take part in the calling program. Ninety-eight per cent of all shareholders interviewed have appreciated the idea of a personal call and have said so.

The interviews and the reports of them are well planned. The interviewer introduces himself by name, title, and the office in which he works. He then usually opens the conversation by asking the shareholder if he has received the latest annual report, the quarterly report, or any other recently issued special reports to stockholders; and whether the regular reports which he has received give him the data he would like to have. Each interviewer is equipped with a copy of the latest annual report, the latest remarks of the president at the annual meeting of stockholders, the latest quarterly report, any special reports, and some explanatory booklets.

Interview forms containing a report of the conversation are filled out after the interviewer has left the presence of the person to whom he has been talking.

The length of the interview is left to the discretion of the shareholder, who is encouraged to ask questions or to make any suggestions that occur

[5] Edward F. Sanger, vice president, the Western Union Telegraph Company, New York.

to him. Interviewers are all experienced men and have been specially briefed, but if they encounter questions beyond their ability to answer, they are instructed to wire (appropriately) the New York public relations headquarters of Western Union for a reply. The manual for interviewers says,

> For obvious reasons, [we] must not, under any circumstances, express opinions on these matters: (1) whether Western Union stock (or any other stock or security) should be sold, held, or added to; (2) whether the market price of any stock is likely to go up or down; (3) what future earnings or dividends will be (in the absence of any published reports from headquarters).
>
> Any decision respecting the first matter must rest with the shareowner's own judgment. We cannot properly venture an opinion or give advice which, conceivably, could later be taken to have influenced a stockholder's decision. Nor can we give opinions as to stock market prices, because these depend upon many variable and often unpredictable factors. As to the third matter, revenue and earnings figures and dividend declarations are factual matters that are made public as soon as possible in formal reports or in releases to the press.

What are the values of this program?

Western Union feels that the program, conducted since 1939, has three main objectives:

1. To give shareowners complete and up-to-date information about the company and its operations
2. To give the shareowners full scope and opportunity to express their opinions and views and to ask questions freely
3. To permit management to keep currently informed concerning the thinking of stockholders about the company's operations, policies, earnings, and so forth, and their reaction to reports issued to them.

The program met with a cordial response from shareholders. In one year, for example, 424 complimentary statements (12 per cent of all the comments obtained during the interviews) expressed thoughts such as:

> "A call like this makes me feel that I'm really part of your management."
> "I've got stock in thirty companies, but you're the first ever to call on me."

Information obtained from stockholders has enabled annual reports and other material to be tailored accurately to their needs. The number of stockholders has steadily increased, and their support of company programs is to be relied on.

Favorable articles have appeared in a number of national magazines and the New York Stock Exchange magazine, and press comments have noted the value of this program in spreading greater information about the American business system to shareholders.

There are also secondary benefits in spreading the word of Western Union's available services (which go far beyond the old concept of telegrams only) among an influential group which passes it on to others. Shareholder calls are an indirect way of selling.

Wyandotte Chemicals Corporation puts a survey to work.[6] The largest employer and biggest taxpayer in Wyandotte, Michigan, a city of 42,000 persons 12 miles downriver from Detroit, is the Wyandotte Chemicals Corporation. The company pays about 40 per cent of the local taxes in Wyandotte, where about three-fifths of its 3,500 employees live.

For the first sixty-five years of the company's seventy-year operation, Wyandotte Chemicals was family-owned, and little or no information was available on earnings, capitalization, or corporate affairs. Five years ago, when some of the stock was sold publicly, this policy was changed substantially.

Over the years the owners of the company had given the city of Wyandotte its hospital, library, and a marina for the community rowing club. The company maintained an employees' club with gymnasium, bowling alleys, and kitchen, all of which were made available for local community functions and youth organizations. In addition, the company and its employees were generous contributors to Greater Detroit's outstanding United Fund. Yet all was not well.

Until the company adopted a modest communication program a few years ago, the general attitude of a vast number of residents was that Wyandotte Chemicals made nothing but money and contributed only smoke and smells to the downriver area. The trend of retail buying to outlying shopping centers hurt the more compact, older city of Wyandotte; stores were left vacant; and the diminished volume of business tended to reduce local tax revenues. At the same time the company felt obliged in principle to oppose the validity of certain local taxes in the courts, where the company was finally upheld, one year's decision resulting in the loss of $40,000 anticipated tax revenue by the city.

Air pollution remained a vexing problem. Although the company had invested more than a million dollars in equipment to help solve the problem and annually spent more than $200,000 to operate the equipment, the company's big twin stacks, which were extremely conspicuous, frequently received all the blame for smog in a heavily industrialized area where the polluted air came from many sources.

The interests of the Wyandotte Chemicals Corporation and its city were so closely intertwined that something had to be done to verify facts, clarify the issues, and improve mutual understanding. A task force of middle-

[6] Carlton E. Spitzer, director of public relations, Wyandotte Chemicals Corporation, Wyandotte, Mich., "Dual Purpose Survey Helps City and Company," *Public Relations Journal,* June, 1961.

management people from all divisions of the company was formed to consider certain broad questions.

"Should the company encourage more employee participation in civic affairs?"

"Should management take a stand on political issues?"

"Should the community be better informed about the company's problems, policies, and objectives?"

"Is the company doing all that it can to be a good citizen?"

After months of discussion, since the group considered that it did not have enough real information to come to a valid conclusion, Opinion Research Corporation was retained to develop a study which would provide a valid analysis of employee and public opinion upon a wide range of subjects. The eventual cost was about $25,000.

Of the large sample of 725 anonymous personal interviews in the town, 225 were from Wyandotte employees and 25 from a special opinion-leader group. Personal letters to employees and newspaper advertisements and releases informed the community that a survey was to be taken and promised to reveal its results in full, whether favorable or unfavorable.

The questions concerned the company's and citizens' reactions to life in the city in the following general categories:

1. Residents' appraisal of the city
2. Company-community relations
3. Sources of information about the company
4. Appraisal of the company by residents who were also employees

Though the questions covered both the plant and the community, city officials, merchants, and others in the city were enabled to get a true picture of citizen attitude toward the town which would not have been available otherwise.

In spite of the fact that survey findings were generally favorable to the company, problem areas were revealed. Seventy-five per cent of those replying believed that air and water pollution were the biggest problems, and 40 per cent felt that no progress was being made in solving them. Some merchants were incensed because 60 per cent of the respondents made some criticism of the downtown shopping facilities (a criticism unfortunately published about the time that Christmas decorations were going up). Significantly, 80 per cent of those interviewed said that they wanted the management of the company to speak up more on public and community problems.

In presenting the findings, community officials and merchants were first invited to a special meeting to discuss the replies to questions with company representatives. Then a series of six advertisements in the two local weekly newspapers was prepared entitled "Citizens Report on Wyandotte." Advance copies were mailed to the homes of all employees, blowups were displayed in a vacant store's windows downtown, and a booklet was prepared containing a discussion of the matter based on all six.

Advertisement Number 6 of the series, a summary of the first five, spotlighted the following disclosures:

1. Most residents recognized that tax contributions by local industries substantially reduced individual property taxes.

2. Industry received the most blame for odors and smoke and the most credit for trying to solve the problem.

3. Wyandotte Chemicals was rated as a good employer and an important taxpayer; but the report revealed criticism about the company, misinformation about some of its activities, and a limited awareness regarding the amount of local taxes paid by the company and the reasons for its tax appeals.

As a result of this opinion survey, the city developed a blueprint for its future development, in which Wyandotte's people assisted as good citizens.

At the same time, the company stepped up its employee communications in magazine, newspaper, and letter form; started to cover new subjects such as union negotiations; began to brief editors and other local opinion leaders in advance upon company positions on such things as taxes; commenced planning a speakers' bureau; and planned to analyze the effectiveness of its new communications program regularly. Employees were encouraged to take a greater part in civic activity, and the company expressed its views publicly when speaking out seemed advisable.

A survey to determine whether Minneapolis should have a United Fund drive.[7] In the summer of 1959 the people of Minneapolis and the various health and welfare groups which solicit funds from the public in the area were considering the advantages and disadvantages of grouping as many of these solicitation drives as possible into one United Fund effort.

It was decided to find out what the public thought about the subject. A 600-person set of interviews was conducted, based upon a probability-type multistage sample. The questionnaire for the study was designed by a local research corporation with the advice and assistance of a citizens' committee. The sample took into account such things as residence in the city or suburbs, sex, age, family income, and occupation, all of which might be expected to make a difference in response. The main findings were these:

1. In answer to an open-ended question, "How do you feel about these drives to raise money for health and welfare organizations?" 46 per cent of the people interviewed in the city of Minneapolis and 64 per cent of those in the suburbs volunteered that there were too many drives, although 53 per cent in the city and 44 per cent in the suburbs also felt that all were for good causes and that the money was needed. About 15 per cent suggested that appeals should be

[7] Bert Russick, president, Mid-Continent Surveys, Minneapolis, Minn.

combined. The spontaneous suggestion showed evidence that they had been thinking about the subject, since the interviewers had made no comment previously. About 10 per cent questioned the wise or proper use of the money—a "wiseacre," defensive reaction which is not uncommon in these discussions. About 5 per cent disliked being asked for funds at several places, such as at home, at school, and at work; and an average of about 3 per cent felt that such drives should be government-supported. There was a difference in response between men and women; women felt more strongly that there were too many requests, yet also that the money was needed. Those with higher incomes complained more strongly about the numerous requests than did those with lower incomes.

2. In answer to a question about the *way* in which health and welfare organizations raised their money, about 36 per cent felt that no other method was possible, but about 10 per cent felt that a united appeal would be better.

3. Respondents were then shown a list of funds and were asked if they had been requested to contribute to them, and if they had been asked, where and by whom.

As a check, a nonexistent fund, "The National Pancreas Research Fund," was inserted along with the agencies actually soliciting in the Minneapolis area within the past year, and about 5 per cent said that they had given to it also.

Identification of other funds and claims of giving to them, however, were about in proportion to the known activity of these organizations within the area and nationally.

4. Citizens were then asked how much they had given to these various causes. The great majority (usually about 70 per cent) said they had given under $25, and almost all were under $5.

5. About 94 per cent of those interviewed stated that neither the respondent nor a member of his family had served as a volunteer worker in collecting charity funds during the preceding year; but 88 per cent felt that such activity was highly commendable.

6. When asked if there were "more," "about the same," or "a smaller number" of money-raising drives now than formerly, 82 per cent of the people in the city and 92 per cent in the suburbs felt that there were more, and almost half added unhappy comments. When, at this point, a question about their reaction to a combined drive was broached, 70 per cent favored a combined effort. The biggest reason for preferring separate drives was that they enabled the giver to select the organizations he favored. Those preferring a combined drive felt that it was more economical and efficient, and that the money went where it was most needed.

A survey such as this provides an answer to those who insist, "But this city is *different*"; encourages those who are in favor of a project and disarms those who oppose it; and points out ideas which should be incorporated into a program, such as the prime point that spoken opposition to the unselectivity and impersonality of a United Fund drive could be counteracted by allowing givers, if they wished, to specify the use of their donations.

Several "Public Opinion Index for Industry" Reports[8]

When several companies combine their efforts in a research field which concerns them all they gain a number of advantages. Not only is the cost lowered, but, more importantly, each organization sees how it stands in comparison with others in its own and other areas of business. Such a service has been provided for many years by "The Public Opinion Index for Industry" surveys of Opinion Research Corporation of Princeton, New Jersey. Typical examples of some of their monthly studies are illuminating.

1. A study of the "corporate image" of twenty-two leading American concerns showed a great variation in the degree of the general public's knowledge of them, ranging from 59 per cent for a retail-trade organization to only 9 per cent for a chemical company. In this instance, companies selling consumer products have an advantage, but even so, while the first retail-trade organization was well known by 59 per cent of the respondents, a second was known by only 43 per cent; and while the chemical company mentioned was recognized by only 9 per cent, another in the same category scored 28 per cent—three times as much. As companies get better known, they almost always become more favorably known. A company may be liked for its products, but feared for its bigness and strength; but bigness alone does not necessarily breed dislike, for some big companies are better liked than smaller ones.

2. The great impetus given to science education and research in the late 1950s led to a number of interesting studies. One, for example, sampled the opinions of 622 scientists and engineers as against those of 105 managers in the same companies.

The findings showed that despite generous pay and privileges, scientists and engineers were one of the most disgruntled groups on United States industry payrolls; they felt that companies forced them to overspecialize, misused their talent, and paid them less than they paid other similar groups. The men designated by their managements as having extraordinary talents shared these sentiments to only a slightly smaller degree than the whole group. Scientists and engineers felt that managers had political skill, but placed little value upon it, and because there was no easy way to identify their degree of managerial ability, such as an academic degree, doubted their competence. In general, scientists considered themselves highly intellectual and very important to social progress, while they were little concerned with money, power, or short-range objectives.

Team rewards that attracted management people had little lure for scientists, who wanted to be recognized personally. In the same vein, most of them rejected unionization as a way to improve their lot.

3. College students and teen-agers have come in for attention also. A 1960 study sought the answer to "Why are so many college students economic illiterates?"

[8] Walter Barlow, president, Opinion Research Corporation, Princeton, N.J.

To get the information, a 39-question survey test was given to 3,391 freshmen and 1,138 seniors in twelve Midwestern liberal arts colleges. The essence of the findings might be stated as follows:

> Seventy-one per cent did not know that workers' real wages had risen 75 per cent since the 1930s.
>
> Sixty-six per cent didn't realize that in an average year many companies make no profit.
>
> Sixty-four per cent believed that owners, rather than workers, had received the lion's share from productivity increases due to mechanization.

Freshmen scored only 49 per cent of the correct answers to all the questions, and four years later seniors who had not taken at least one economics course still scored only 52 per cent, whereas seniors who had taken an economics course rated 63 per cent. By comparison, economics majors scored 72 per cent. Interestingly enough, freshman sons and daughters of businessmen scored almost no better on the test than did children of manual workers, union members, or noncollege parents.

Those who studied college economics were found to be more conservative than their fellows, though one could not conclude that the studies produced the conservatism.

In a similar study, high school students were queried on their views toward business and government. Whereas only about 30 per cent of the adults, of whatever age, favored a larger role for government in life, about 43 per cent of the teen-agers were inclined to approve of it. Much of this opinion perhaps springs from school study of the "robber baron" and muckraker eras in United States history. In the words of the survey report, "Young people know that this portrays a by-gone era, but they do not have an up-to-date image of modern capitalism to put in its place." (One is tempted to wonder whether the very word "capitalism" might not be better replaced with another.)

Teen-agers know very little about many large American companies. The chief source of their impressions is television. Though they are seriously concerned about the direction of world developments, they are personally more concerned about academic pressures. They are idealistic and not so cynical about the sin and selfishness of governments as were the Founding Fathers of America, who had just had some unpleasant experiences and foresaw more. Teen-agers would like to know more about business, but would prefer to get the information in a personally participating way, such as through visits or demonstrations, and not through preaching.

Summary

Sound research underlies most effective public relations work. Among common research objectives are:

1. Probing basic public attitudes
2. Measuring true opinions
3. Identifying leaders of opinion
4. Reducing costs by concentrating upon valid targets
5. Testing themes and communications media
6. Achieving good timing
7. Ascertaining the strength of opposition
8. Achieving two-way communication
9. Revealing trouble before it happens
10. Providing facts which can be used in public relations programs

Modern opinion-research methods have been largely developed within the past thirty years, and their use has been marked with increasing success but also by some notable failures.

Among the main types of research used by public relations practitioners are (1) simple fact gathering, (2) opinion research, and (3) motivational research.

Knowledge of possible errors in common research is important. Among the more common of these errors are the following:

1. Nonrepresentative listening
2. Undue reliance upon advisory groups
3. Weakness in planning representative panels
4. Field reports
5. Improper samples
6. Biased, untrained, or dishonest interviewers
7. Foggy responses
8. Undue recall of the prominent
9. Exaggeration of the importance of minor differences

Every public relations man needs to know the fundamentals of valid research. But research is a highly developed discipline in itself. When confronted with a major problem in this area, an investigator should usually seek the help of those who are highly trained and who have had wide experience.

ADDITIONAL READING

Dichter, Ernest: *The Strategy of Desire,* Doubleday & Company, Inc., Garden City, N.Y., 1960.

Experience with Employee Attitude Surveys, National Industrial Conference Board, New York, 1951.

Hyman, Herbert: *Survey Design and Analysis: Principles, Cases, and Procedures,* The Free Press of Glencoe, New York, 1955.

Martineau, Pierre: *Motivation in Advertising,* McGraw-Hill Book Company, Inc., New York, 1957.

Osgood, Charles E., et al.: *The Measurement of Meaning,* The University of Illinois Press, Urbana, Ill., 1957.

Parten, Mildred: *Surveys, Polls, and Samples,* Harper & Row, Publishers, Incorporated, New York, 1950.

Action and Action Cases

11

The English language is full of sayings to the effect that "actions speak louder than words" or that "what you are speaks so loudly that I can't hear what you say." Their popularity tends to indicate that, as a people, we are by nature somewhat suspicious of rhetoric and are much impressed by deeds. Words alone are often regarded as feeble or downright harmful when the claims they make cannot be justified, and even the best advertising cannot sell a bad product twice to the same customers. For these reasons, public relations men approaching a problem of popular persuasion think primarily not in terms of "What can we *say?*" but in terms of "What can we *do?*" Action is an essential ingredient in successful relations practice.

Public relations men do not always create the actions to which they seek to direct attention; many times the action is inherent in the very nature of the organization which strives for greater understanding and good will. Trains which run on time; water that spurts merrily out of the tap, clean and pure; and banks which take good care of your money and pay generous interest for its use, are all engaged in actions typical of the standard operating procedures of good railroads, reliable water companies, and sound banks; but such actions are not news, and organizations can say only a limited number of things about them without seeming to brag about the obvious. Public relations practice goes beyond the worthy performance of everyday duties. Like the public itself, public relations assumes that such efficiency is to be expected and seeks to go an extra mile in demonstrating the value of a service, the characteristics of those who produce it, and its worth in the public interest. Public relations thus operates not only as a spur to the maintenance of already good performance (which is assumed), but also as an incentive to the creation of better products and services.

A FRAMEWORK FOR PUBLIC RELATIONS ACTION

The number of important actions which can be shown to the public is limited. One cannot do too many things and get attention for all of them;

the net effect of too many busy actions is likely to be confusion. The public relations man finds that the choice of good actions demands even more care than the choice of telling words.

Actions may be inherent in the existing situation; they may arise out of the opportunities created by facilities or events; they may be carefully planned to focus attention upon certain aspects of an organization; they may be created to serve the public welfare; they may be cooperative with other groups; they may be created primarily to serve communication needs; or they may consist largely of organizing people into a common effort, itself an action and a means of communication (creating something in common).

Public relations actions may be either large or small: as large as a national science-talent search or as small as allowing the public to fish in a company lake. The instigators of an action should almost never call attention to its virtues. The onlooker is supposed to draw conclusions for himself (with the aid of proper publicity). The best actions are those which the onlooker hears about indirectly, usually those which meet some need very much in the social interest, and which make it possible for others to achieve *their* goals. Trivial actions should never be proclaimed as important, and the big ones will speak for themselves if well known.

1. Action Inherent in an Existing Situation

Sometimes the facilities and operations of an organization are set up so well that, with ingenuity and imagination, they may easily be converted into actions which will earn public good will and appreciation.

The Indianapolis Water Company[1] has two large reservoirs upon which it permits boating by free special permit. In 1960, the company initiated a "Fireman Citizen of the Year" award to honor outstanding firemen, not only for performance in the line of duty, but also for their extracurricular activities in the public good. (The fact that firemen are great users of water at fires can scarcely go unnoticed!) The company also sponsors a TV weather program (related to rain) and such fitting events as television sports coverage of swimming meets.

The company has used a long series of water-company newspaper advertisements, several of which have been cited by the Bureau of Advertising of the American Newspaper Publishers Association for their outstanding quality. A recent copy theme has been "Water, water everywhere . . . but—" followed by the fact that "Your Indianapolis Water Company Has to Inventory It" (or distribute it, or make it safe to use). A new motion picture was developed in 1958 for use by schools, churches, libraries, and other groups. Radio broadcasts of high school sports have been sponsored along with billboards, participation in various civic events, and employee activities.

[1] John E. Kleinberg, director of public relations, the Indianapolis Water Company.

Figure 11-1. A public relations advertisement of the Indianapolis Water Company stressing the investment and labor needed to supply a large city with water.

One of the main efforts of the water company has been to keep the press thoroughly informed of all news, good and bad; not only plans to construct new mains or to save the city money by helping to pave a street, but also news of how long service will be shut off when a pump breaks down or when a contractor, bulldozing the head off a valve, creates a small flood in one spot and a complete drought elsewhere.

Community relations at Rockefeller Center, New York.[2] The world's largest privately owned business and entertainment area, Rockefeller Cen-

[2] Caroline Hood, director of public relations, Rockefeller Center, New York. (From a paper delivered at the Second World Congress of Public Relations, Venice, Italy, May, 1961.)

ter, supports sixteen skyscrapers built on 15 acres in the heart of New York City, where 40,000 people work and an estimated 160,000 more visit every day. Its reputation came first from its size and from the fact that when it opened in 1933, the Center was a pioneer in its construction, concept, and land use. But its further reputation for quality and primacy has been carefully fostered over the years by a well-planned public relations program, which has as its objectives: (1) projection of the Center's corporate personality through newsmaking events, exhibits, and visitors; (2) communication of the corporate story to all media; (3) close association with the tenants from whom its income is derived; and (4) an integrated personnel who contribute heavily to the community program.

The policies which govern the Center's special events and exhibits are good taste, civic responsibility, appropriateness, and consideration for both the tenants and the public. Within this context an amazing variety of newsworthy projects has been possible: ice skating and folk dances; dog shows and vintage cars; singing and speechmaking; philanthropic rallies; international ceremonies; and gatherings to honor achievements, ideas, and personalities. The setting for these events is the 95- by 125-foot recessed lower plaza which serves as midtown New York's "village green."

Because of the publicity value of this location, the public relations personnel of the Center, although they say "yes" to many requests for events, have to say "no" to an equal number. Among them have been plans as varied as rigging up a cable car from the observation roof of the seventy story RCA Building to Central Park some eight city blocks away; a request from a waning opera star to sing from the top of the Center's big annual Christmas tree; and a demonstration of a new parachute by an ex-fire chief, who proposed to jump from the top of a high building and guaranteed to float to the street at the pace of 9 seconds per floor.

Seasonal flowers, shade trees, benches, a skating rink, flags, murals, mosaics, and sculpture, plus guided tours, are among the attractions for visitors. Regular contact is also kept with the building tenants and with the more than 2,000 employees who service the buildings and are recognized by management as its front-line public relations emissaries.

The influences of Rockefeller Center reach far beyond its 15 acres and have been reflected in the refashioning of communities across the United States and overseas. When new buildings are erected in Philadelphia, Pittsburgh, Caracas, Paris, New Delhi, or Sydney, the newspaper clippings are apt to describe each new project as "another Rockefeller Center." The value of consistent, careful public relations planning in connection with the operation of the Center has been incalculable and has added greatly to the net worth of the buildings, far beyond their steel-and-concrete dollar evaluation.

Atlas Van Lines, Inc.[3] A study undertaken by Atlas Van Lines, Inc., though on a completely different scale, still shows public relations inherent in the operation of an organization.

Moving day probably comes for Americans more often than for any other highly civilized people upon the earth. Corporate shifts and opportunities to seek new jobs cause the big vans to be backed up to the doors of houses in almost every neighborhood every few weeks. Adults have been through upheavals before and take them in their stride; but what is merely sadness to them may be an almost catastrophic uprooting to their children, particularly to teen-agers, who may have their deep and often their only roots firmly fixed in the neighborhood.

This problem is peripheral to the physical job of the long-distance, over-the-road movers in bundling furniture from one city to another, but it is inherent in their business and offers an opportunity for useful public relations action in aiding adults to solve the problems of their children in adjusting to a move.

The *action* taken by Atlas Van Lines was to commission the Association for Family Living of Chicago to make a special study for the moving company of the emotional problems of children of families involved in cross-country moves. This study was then distributed to Atlas agents as a sales tool in dealing with customers, furnished the basis of publicity in newspapers and trade publications, and was made into a reprint booklet. A sample of its flavor can be obtained from portions of the general publicity release upon the story.

> Of all the events which can occur in a family—from a new baby to a new job for father—moving day stands out as a time of upheaval. . . . The Association for Family Living, Chicago, pinpoints some of the problems and possible solutions in a special study made for Atlas Van Lines, Inc., Chicago. . . .
>
> "Toddlers and pre-school children demand, more than any other age group, familiarity and predictability in their daily routine," the study stated.
>
> "Between the ages of one and four, a child learns to recognize the physical characteristics of his surroundings and takes comfort in their stability and permanence."
>
> "Any drastic alteration in these surroundings will be accompanied by a correspondingly diminished feeling of security."
>
> Family Living's study detailed the experiences of one typical young family—the Garfields—in moving from one city to another.
>
> The couple had three children—David, six months; Bobby, three years old; and Jane, 11. Like more than 60 per cent of all moves today, the

---

[3] The Public Relations Board, Inc., Chicago, Ill., public relations counsel.

Garfields' was necessitated by a job promotion and transfer for the father, Henry.

The new home was too far from the old to permit frequent trips back and forth. However, on one visit that both parents made there, the Garfields traveled on a week-end so that the oldest child, Jane, could accompany them. Henry also took many pictures of the house, both inside and out, which all could consult at any time.

The Garfields decided to include Jane and three-year-old Bobby in as much of the preparations as possible, but without overburdening them with a mass of detail. . . .

It was decided that Jane should be permitted to help select the color scheme for her room and to arrange the furniture as she wished. Mrs. Garfield knew that Bobby did not fully appreciate the fact that he was leaving his old home, so she decided not to change any of the furnishings in his room and to decorate his new bedroom just like the old.

Jane was quite worried about the changes ahead. What would the children be like in the new neighborhood? Would they like her, and would she like them? Would she fit in easily at the new school? Would the teachers be as nice as those she was leaving?

Mrs. Garfield took pains to explain to Jane that they had selected a house and neighborhood with these thoughts uppermost. This served to give Jane a measure of reassurance. . . .

The story then went on to tell how actual packing was not done until the last moment to avoid a sense of loss among the children, how three-year-old Bobby went on a visit to friends the day of the moving so that he would not see strange men upsetting his familiar home, and how family understanding and participation in planning could make the day of departure an adventure into a bright future rather than a day of tears.

The story received good play in the press because it was authentic, human, and helpful and dealt with a situation familiar to a great many urban newspaper readers. It was not contrived, but was an action which grew very naturally out of the regular activities of the moving company.

Career secretaries.[4] The American Photocopy Equipment Company, which is in the highly competitive office-machinery field, realized that the attitude of secretaries was often decisive in (1) determining whether a copying machine should be bought at all and (2) suggesting which type and make would be most efficient. The problem was to provide a service to the career secretary which would attract her attention and good will.

This was accomplished by a study based upon 247 interviews with bosses and secretaries in seventeen states. The purpose of the study was, first, to find out what sort of persons bosses wanted as their secretaries, what duties they expected them to perform, and how anxious they were to keep them

4 *Ibid.*

satisfied; and, second, to ascertain the personalities, education, and habits of successful secretaries.

The feature stories resulting from this action appeared in *The Secretary* and *Today's Secretary* (top publications in their field), in *Business Week,* and in several wire-service stories which were carried in newspapers across the country. The research demonstrated that APECO's interests extended beyond sales of its product alone into the problems and interests of its users.

The American Institute of Certified Public Accountants.[5] Most public relations cases involve many activities, and the classification of any particular case may be somewhat arbitrary when research, action, communication, and evaluation are all present. But the program of the American Institute of Certified Public Accountants in providing its 40,000 members with a mass counseling service in public relations for their profession certainly involves a strong element of action.

The trial run of the program began in the state of Louisiana in 1961 and consisted of the following steps:

1. A questionnaire mailed to all members of the Society of Louisiana Certified Public Accountants to serve as a study guide and to ascertain public relations practices existing among CPA firms in Louisiana

2. A survey based upon depth-type interviews among the members of the business community in Louisiana to determine their attitudes toward CPAs in the state

3. A three-hour lecture-discussion session with Louisiana CPAs, consisting of some theoretical background in public relations, examination of the public relations problems of Louisiana CPAs as revealed by the businessman surveys, and discussion of the current public relations activities of CPAs within the state

4. A pooling of common problems and public relations procedures among CPA members and sharing of this information among all

5. Surveys evaluating progress or regression set up at about three-year intervals

Similar programs have been conducted in other states of the union.

International Harvester acts on a smoke problem.[6] The public relations value of "do well and then tell about it" is sharply illustrated by the actions taken by the International Harvester Company in connection with a smoke problem at its Memphis, Tennessee, works some years ago. Starting in the dark, negative atmosphere of smoke, public relations efforts created a clear

[5] John Ashworth, public relations associate, American Institute of Certified Public Accountants, New York City.

[6] John W. Kenney, International Harvester Company, Chicago, Ill., and an article by James Robert Massey, public relations manager, Memphis Works of the International Harvester Company, in *Public Relations Journal,* September, 1954.

and positive spirit of good will. The company was willing to spend the money for actions which were right, but without proper handling of communication, it is doubtful whether they would have been properly understood.

Immediately after World War II, International Harvester built a new plant just outside Memphis near the community of Frayser. Because it was almost entirely surrounded by open fields and because there were no nearby residential neighbors, the company did not anticipate any smoke-cinder-soot complaint problem.

But soon homes were built near the plant, people moved into them, and complaints began—faint murmurs of unhappiness which penetrated to plant management. Neighboring homeowners could have been told, "We were here first; you shouldn't have bought your homes so close to our plants"; or an accusing finger could have been pointed at real estate developers who created the problem. This procedure would have established who was right, but it would have done nothing to change a hostile attitude, which, with growing population and its potential power upon taxation and local regulations, could have become serious.

Instead, the company's public relations department met the growing problem head-on with a personal touch. Company representatives made calls upon housewives in the affected neighborhood, saying that the company had had a few complaints and that they were investigating to get the facts. Samples of the offending dirt were taken from homes, yards, and laundry on the line. When the samples had been analyzed, letters to all the homes informed plant neighbors that Harvester was convinced that the soot, cinders, and bits of coal came from the plant powerhouse. No promise of relief was made, but sincere concern for the situation was expressed with a promise to search for a solution.

Three years passed. Numerous control-equipment manufacturers made tests, but none of them could promise more than about 70 per cent removal, which the company did not consider adequate for the cost involved. Other steps to alleviate the condition were taken in the interval, including the installation of some gas burners and of smoke indicators on the stacks to warn plant firemen when they were getting poor combustion, the spraying of oil and water on the coal, and the purchase of a 17-acre tract of land between the plant and the nearest subdivision, which was planted with trees and grass to catch low-level debris. The total cost of these improvements was more than $68,000.

During this period, these activities were reported to nearby homeowners, and a special committee of residents met with the works manager for regular progress reports. There was no open public complaint because people were convinced that the company was doing its best to find a good solution to the problem.

Finally, after prolonged tests, the company was convinced that a new type of air-control equipment it had developed could trap from 85 to 95 per cent of the residue from the powerhouse. It was installed at an additional cost of almost $72,000.

Immediately upon company approval of this work, the works manager invited neighboring homeowners and community leaders to a meeting in the plant conference room. A vice-president from the company's national headquarters came for the occasion and opened the meeting by thanking the group for their patience and understanding; he then announced the new improvement and noted that Harvester had spent more than $140,000 to solve the air-contamination problem. A simple nontechnical explanation was given of how the equipment would work. No promises were made that it would be absolutely effective; the company stated that about 90 per cent freedom from contamination was the best that engineering science could provide. Questions were answered, and coffee and doughnuts followed the discussion.

Press coverage was excellent, one headline reading, "IH Spends $71,900 to Be a Good Neighbor." But more important was the reaction of the homeowners, many of whom volunteered expressions of appreciation. In the words of the works public relations director:

> They seemed to be just as impressed by our efforts to keep them informed as by our efforts to provide relief for them. The fact that a vice president journeyed to Memphis to talk to them made a deep impression. . . .
>
> It seems to us that industry can turn bad into good when smoke mars their community relations by (1) recognizing the serious public relations aspects of the situation, (2) being willing to spend the money to provide relief, and (3) maintaining frank, honest and consistent communications with the community. . . . All the control measures would have been authorized had there been no public relations man on the staff. We do, however, take credit for seeing that the company got credit for its efforts by maintaining the flow of information to the neighbors and the community.

2. Action Capitalizing upon an Existing Facility or Event

Action which makes use of an existing situation reaches a shade farther into the field of public relations actions. It involves the imaginative utilization of a facility or an event which otherwise would not have been put to work.

Interestingly enough, our two illustrations come from the field of big-city banking, an area in which both competition for depositors and enterprising public relations practices have developed greatly within recent years.

Manhattan Savings Bank[7] has one of the top midtown locations in New York at 47th Street and Madison Avenue. Resources of the bank stood at more than 420 million dollars in 1961, and deposits between 1953 and 1960 grew at a rate more than double that of all savings banks in New York State.

"The progress of the bank in recent years, particularly the extraordinary deposit growth attained without the establishment of additional offices, has been due in large measure to an imaginative public relations policy," said Willard K. Denton, president of the bank.

The bank's main public relations effort has taken the form of attractive displays and holiday presentations in the bank's Madison Avenue lounge, where they have been the source of much favorable comment on the part of leaders in advertising, public relations, and communications industries within the area.

A city boat show, for example, inspired a display of nine boats in the lounge, accompanied by water-skiing equipment, fishing tackle, and an advanced radio-communication system. Coast Guard personnel gave a demonstration of safe boating procedure.

Other activities have included water colors painted by artists on the staff of a major nearby advertising agency, prize-winning photos of the New York Press Association, a bridal fashion show, a special dog show following the one at Madison Square Garden, and a concert by a noted Japanese pianist.

Christmas really sees activity in the MSB lounge, beginning at 9 A.M. daily, when the area is transformed into a miniature Central Park with features such as four pretty girl ice skaters, a singing clown taking children on rides in a sleigh, a chimpanzee on ice skates, Santa and Mrs. Santa Claus (a glass blower who demonstrates the making of Christmas-tree ornaments), and the songs of the forty-odd MSB Choristers. The Choristers, incidentally, have not only given regular concerts at the bank but have also toured Manhattan on a motorized float and serenaded employees at each of the city's major daily newspapers, where the bank presented a $500 check to charities sponsored by each paper.

When nothing else is going on in the lounge, a pianist plays background music during the midday period, which is the bank's busiest time, and between 5:00 and 6:30 on Friday afternoons a string ensemble presents semi-classical selections while tea is served (an activity which has properly brought mention from as far away as London).

Relaxed atmosphere, friendly personnel, and a program of activities including many more even than those mentioned make Manhattan Savings Bank a far cry from the chilly marble palaces with gun-toting guards and cold clerks which, only a few years ago, represented the accepted environ-

[7] Gene Burke, vice president, Milburn McCarty Associates, Inc., public relations counselors, New York City, and *Public Relations News,* Feb. 20, 1961.

ment for a bank. MSB's location, of course, is ideal for this approach. Would it work elsewhere? Much of the program undoubtedly would if applied with understanding and imagination.

Hanover Bank[8] (now Manufacturers Hanover Trust Company) at 70 Broadway occupies an entirely different type of location; yet its public relations management seized upon an opportunity for news action with equal enterprise and imagination. It came about some years ago.

On December 6, 1955, the Hanover Bank, as coexecutor of the estate of the late William Woodward, Jr., a well-known horse fancier, announced that on December 15 the nation's top race horse, Nashua, and sixty-one of his stablemates would be sold through sealed bids. This was important sports news and got top play in many dailies.

On December 15, Nashua was sold for $1,251,200, and his stablemates brought an additional $615,000. Again, sports editors gave the news top billing.

On December 16, shortly before noon, the Public Relations Department of the Hanover Bank was notified by the Personal Trust Division that the following letter, accompanied by a color sketch of Nashua, had been received:

> Dear Sirs:
>
> I read in the paper today that you are going to sell Nashua and his friends. If you have a horse that no one will buy, I would like to. You can send him or her out to the following address: 22 Rutledge Rd., Valhalla, N.Y.
>
> The horse will have a good home, 1½ acres of woods and fields and loveing care. I would like a horse that would grow old with me. My sealed bid is $24.03, but maybe by the time you have opened the bids I have earened some more money, I can pay a little higher.
>
> Sincerely yours,
(SIGNED) Karen Ann McGuire
>
> P.S. My place is called Bramble Hill.

The Personal Trust Division could not classify this letter as a firm bid. Therefore it was treated as a communication and was not processed with the legal bids that were submitted.

The bank's public relations director saw in this letter an opportunity to show to the public that bankers are human and to associate the Hanover Bank with a heart-warming project that would, through the happiness of a child, give the public vicarious pleasure. Action had to be rapid and most steps were consummated within seventy-two hours after the letter first came to his attention. Here is what was done:

[8] Donald R. Hassell, public relations director, the Hanover Bank, New York City.

Figure 11-2. Quick action, imagination, and friendliness were evident when the Hanover Bank of New York City presented a horse to a little girl who had written a letter in response to a news story about the sale of an estate.

1. The director recommended to management that a horse be given to Karen and gave assurance that such action would meet with public approval. Bank funds were not used for this purpose, but a collection of about $600 was obtained by gifts from bank officers who contributed personally.

2. He ascertained, before proceeding further, that the gift of a horse to twelve-year-old Karen would be acceptable to her parents and that they would and could house, feed, and care for the animal.

3. He obtained the services of a reliable horse auctioneer to help Karen select a horse for the amount donated which would be suitable to her riding abilities.

4. He arranged a press conference with some thirty newspaper, magazine, radio, and TV people to announce the project and to give the newsmen an opportunity to interview and photograph Karen, her parents, and the auctioneer who would buy the horse. The conference involved ordering photostats of Karen's letter, photographs of her sketch of Nashua, and writing a 500-word news release approved by bank officials and Karen's parents. A letter was written to Karen from the president of the bank; and the director arranged for a letter of responsibility to be signed by Mr. and Mrs. McGuire accepting the horse and absolving the bank from responsibility for the animal's future actions.

This first press conference was only the beginning. Media representatives were kept informed of Karen's progress in selecting a horse. Before the actual presentation was made, about a week later, the horse had to be bought and equipped with saddle, bridle, halter, and blanket; felt lettering was affixed to the blanket, one side reading, "Karen Ann McGuire" and the other "Hanover's Wishing Star"; a veterinarian was engaged to examine the horse and to issue a certificate of health; and an even larger number of media representatives were invited to the second conference than had come to the first. An additional complication was the fact that the conference actually began forty-five minutes ahead of scheduled time because all the participants got there early! The first press conference had been held at Hanover's midtown branch bank because of its greater convenience for both the press and the McGuires; the second was held at the riding stables in Greenwich, Connecticut, where the horse had been housed until presentation. The bank's president, who made a thirty-two-word presentation talk, passed the bridle to Karen, and remained out of the scene while press, magazine, and TV photographers took pictures for nearly two hours. The bank's own photographer was on the scene and took additional photos, which were later sent to banking trade magazines with a story which told, from the bank's viewpoint, something of the public relations thinking behind the event.

The coverage of this story by the press was extremely heavy, including front-page pictures in the biggest American newspapers of both the East and the Midwest as well as editorial mention.

The outstanding characteristics of the action (which received a well-merited American Public Relations Association award) were the quick recognition of opportunity by the bank's public relations head, the speed with which it was handled while it was hot news, and the thoroughness with which every detail was covered—all essentials in good public relations actions.

3. Action to Display the Existing Characteristics of a Product or an Organization

Johnson Motors.[9] Demonstration is one of the oldest devices of salesmanship. It is feeble and commonplace simply to *assert* in advertising and elsewhere that a boat motor is dependable; it is quite another thing to show that it is so under the toughest conditions.

One of the main public relations goals of Johnson Motors has been to develop more public confidence in its products. To help attain this goal, Johnson in 1958 cosponsored the crossing of the Atlantic Ocean by a small boat in cooperation with the Botved Boat Company of Copenhagen, Denmark, using two Johnson V 50-horsepower engines.

[9] M. L. Prentiss, public relations manager, Johnson Motors, Waukegan, Ill.

A public relations representative from the J. Walter Thompson Advertising Company of New York was sent to Copenhagen to oversee details of the kickoff along with the company's own photographer. One of the details was an alliance with the Thorden Steamship Lines, through which fuel would be pumped to the small boat from the decks of one of Thorden's transatlantic freighters, which could also serve as a mother ship in case of real trouble.

Several severe storms did cause trouble. Although the small boat was able to ride out the weather, it was obliged to reduce its speed so materially because of the rough seas that it had to be picked up by the freighter, which

Figure 11-3. Persistence can salvage a public relations failure! A transatlantic crossing by a small boat powered by two outboard motors failed when it encountered rough weather and had to be hoisted aboard the mother ship. But the boatmen's insistence on continuing when the seas calmed made an even better story in itself.

carried perishable foods and had to maintain its ten-day schedule to New York City.

At first glance the project appeared to be a failure, but two things saved it:

1. The small-boat men insisted on being put back into the ocean with their tiny craft as soon as the weather had calmed sufficiently to enable them to keep up with the freighter. The same loading derrick which had plucked them from the sea launched them back upon it.

2. The company photographer recorded every step of the project, including both removal and replacement of the small boat, in still pictures and colored movies.

Because the boat men refused to quit and the photographer did his job, what was first thought to be a failure turned out a sizable success. The press, including the important boating-trade magazines, chose to regard even the initiation of the project as highly significant. The achievement of the three boat men in piloting their small craft over most of the several-thousand-mile journey by themselves was a solid foundation of fact. Wire services carried the story; the boat men upon their arrival were logical subjects for newsreel, network radio, and national television broadcasts; Johnson advertising exploited the fact of the crossing; and a motion picture based upon the exploit, known as "Three for Adventure," became a basic film in the Johnson library. The boat itself was displayed at boat shows, and the project was an undoubted success in demonstrating the reliability of the motors which had powered the boat on its long voyage.

Demonstrating public response. Several years ago, advertising salesmen for the *St. Louis Star-Times* found their going tough because their newspaper was the third in circulation rank among St. Louis dailies. Although its actual circulation was more than 170,000, both of its competitors were larger and spread the word that it had little power to get response in the community. Some tangible demonstration of *Star-Times* reader response was necessary. But a demonstration involved considerable risk, since to get reader response meant public promotion of an event, and failure to attract a big crowd would have provided dramatic confirmation of the rivals' charges. Whatever was attempted had to be both gigantic and successful.

It was decided to risk an outboard motorboat race in the Mississippi River between the famed Eads Bridge and the next bridge about a mile downstream, known as the "Free" Bridge. A huge cobblestoned levee, hundreds of feet in width and sloping down into the river along the St. Louis side of this mile-long stretch, made a natural viewing stand for thousands of people.

Making the race possible involved cooperation with local boat-racing groups in sponsorship and prizes; promotion for contestants; renting river barges and a steamboat and arranging them as a temporary harbor; coast guard clearance; rescue craft; fire and first-aid provision; insurance; policing, parking, and first aid for spectators; drinking water and toilet provisions; a public-address announcement system; food concessions; judges; stands for dignitaries; and many smaller details extending over several months' preparation. Promotion of crowd attendance included everything possible, and when a crowd estimated at from 60,000 to 100,000 turned up for the event and stayed almost all afternoon in 100-degree-plus August heat, the event was judged a success in demonstrating *Star-Times* readership.

Later, an air show was staged, which attracted an even bigger crowd, creating a traffic problem which got completely out of hand in blocking a main four-lane highway. After this proof that the newspaper had power in the community, such spectacular demonstrations were dropped in favor of youth, educational, and religious activities of smaller size but of unquestioned value.

Miniaturization awards.[10] The work of Miniature Precision Bearings, Inc., of Keene, New Hampshire, was the exact opposite of a huge or spectacular achievement. The company manufactured extremely accurate tiny ball bearings, the smallest of which is about the size of the period at the end of this sentence. Miniaturization in general has become of importance in an air and space age when complicated machinery, reduced to very small size, must still preserve its complete accuracy. Precision Bearings, Inc., wanted to be better known and to be more closely identified, in the industrial and scientific worlds, with the rapidly growing field of miniaturization. The company went to public relations counsel for advice.

The result was an annual awards contest for the most distinguished examples of miniaturization in any industrial or scientific field in the United States during the year.

A capable judging committee was selected; a sculptor was commissioned to prepare an unusual and attractive award statuette; a descriptive circular was prepared and mailed to the entire MPB customer and prospect list and to leading research institutions, editors of scientific journals, and government bureaus; the company magazine featured the contest and company advertising was devoted to it for a month; and salesmen made a special effort to encourage entrants. As a result, fifty-four entries were submitted, many of them from leading United States companies.

The winner the first year was the Diamond Ordnance Fuze Laboratories of the U.S. Army Ordnance Department with a complicated electronic subassembly which had previously been reduced to the size of the palm of a man's hand and then further reduced to the size of a fingertip (it used no ball bearings at all). Presentation of the award was made at the Institute of

[10] *Public Relations News,* Feb. 9, 1959.

Radio Engineers' annual convention and was followed later by excellent publicity and a touring exhibit.

Through this promotion, Miniature Precision Bearings, Inc., not only helped the development of its field, but also assumed, in association with other strong companies, a position of leadership.

Futures trading seminar of the Chicago Board of Trade.[11] Much public misunderstanding and hostility exist in regard to the practice of trading in future price contracts upon grain and other commodities, the main activity for which the Chicago Board of Trade provides a setting. Despite the stabilizing effect upon the market of contracting to deliver an amount of Number-2 yellow corn at a stated price at some future time, its social utility is not readily apparent, nor is the social justice of a speculator's making or losing money thereby. Political capital has been made of this ignorance, and more may be made in the future.

"Why," asked the directors of the Chicago Board of Trade, "is the public willing to accept futures trading in magazines or newspapers, for example— the purchase of subscriptions for several years in advance—yet not understand the business need for contracts to deliver amounts of commodities at some future time?"

These thoughts, coupled with unfavorable publicity, impelled the directors to make a survey of the attitudes of key publics, such as farmers and economists. The findings of the research led to the establishment of annual educational symposia designed to acquaint college-level educators with commodity markets and their functions. Eleven such meetings were held, reaching more than five hundred educators. At that point, in 1959, the Exchange and its Educational Advisory Committee decided that a new need had become more urgent—that of stimulating new research into the nature of futures markets. More effort was needed to encourage inquiry and the development of comprehensive knowledge.

A futures trading seminar was set up, at which four leading economists presented papers which were discussed vigorously by a panel and members of the audience. Manuscripts of the main papers were furnished the panel in advance and were duplicated and given to the audience; and a court reporter recorded the question-and-answer session. These formal papers and their discussion contributed greatly to the body of available knowledge about futures markets. The Exchange produced 1,500 copies of the proceedings in hard-cover book form, of which 1,200 copies were quickly distributed to libraries, government officials, and agricultural economists.

Specialized trade magazines covered the meetings in some detail, and there was widespread but generalized mention by the press. Future plans of the Exchange include similar approaches in other related areas.

[11] Irwin B. Johnson, director of public information and education, Board of Trade, Chicago, Ill.

Public relations action in this case was used to expand a general field of knowledge in which the very existence of the Board of Trade was involved. There are many such areas which could be illuminated by understanding in our increasingly complex world today.

The public relations of employee retirement policies.[12] Generous and well-planned retirement programs are now a characteristic of most American businesses and other organizations; yet through lack of information and of common public relations sense in handling, they are often not widely understood, even by those involved in or related to them. Some of the actions which may be taken to aid this situation may be seen in the following examples:

Several years ago, the Bell Telephone Company of Pennsylvania surveyed 1,840 employees who were within a few years of retirement, and 460 who had recently retired, to find out whether those still working wanted help in planning their retirement and what the actual experiences had been of those who had just retired. The surveys indicated that those about to retire were concerned with money, their use of leisure time, living arrangements, and personal health. Those who had retired felt, in retrospect, that adjusting had been much easier than they had anticipated.

Actions flowing out of this information included a series of booklets and articles in the employee magazine, followed by employee group discussions with experts in the various fields.

Dan River Mills, Inc., of Danville, Virginia, noted a few years ago that 600 out of its 715 retired employees continued to live right in the plant town and that they constituted an influential communications group in the public relations of the company.

The main action then taken was to establish a "Retired Workers Club," without dues and with its headquarters in the company's recreation building. The club not only used the sports, park, woodworking, and training school facilities of the company, but also engaged in a vigorous charitable program of its own for hospitals and nursing homes, for invalids and others who needed care.

Another event was originated several years ago at the Norton Company in Worcester, Massachusetts, when a combined luncheon and open house was established at the plant for a "Retirees' Homecoming Day." Outside publicity was reduced to a minimum so that retired workers would not feel they were being exploited. Mimeographed invitations to 700 retirees drew 375 acceptances. Sixty active employees who were known to most of the retirees assisted as hosts at the luncheon. The program started at 10 A.M. with a half-hour coffee period to give all the visitors time to arrive, to pick up their stick-on badges (printed in jumbo type), and to chat with old

[12] *Public Relations News.* Bell Telephone Company of Pennsylvania, Feb. 11, 1957; Dan River Mills, Inc., Feb. 23, 1959; and Norton Company, Nov. 4, 1957.

friends. The chairman of the board (84 years old) gave the welcoming address, followed by six 5-minute talks by division heads describing company developments. A chicken barbecue lunch in the company cafeteria was then followed by visits to any plant areas the old employees wanted to inspect. Most of them went to departments in which they had formerly worked, but many turned also to new areas. Meeting old friends and departmental visits ranked high in favor in a survey response taken some days after the event was over.

4. Actions Which Show the Character of an Organization through Service in the Public Welfare

The best public relations actions, of course, are *related* to the nature or background of the organization which supports them, but they may also be *created,* at times, with the specific intent of showing something about the organization's character. They are, in the best sense of the word, "window dressing" because they display some of the wealth of the science, or technology, or interests of the organization which developed them. Like the windows of a great department store, they show the passing spectator a few of the many things on sale inside. No one expects that the windows will exhibit a completely representative sample of the entire contents of the store but only that they will be characteristic of the store and that the merchandise displayed there *is* to be found within. Like good windows, good, creative, public relations actions demand both artistry and imagination along with a sure sense of spectator interests.

The Plymouth trouble-shooting contest.[13] In 1961, after a dozen years of growth, nearly 1,500 automobile-mechanics students, representing more than 500 high schools, took part in thirty-five Plymouth automobile trouble-shooting contests throughout the nation. The idea, which started modestly in Los Angeles in 1949, was simple but served many purposes well.

The program was directed at high school students who were in vocational classes training to become auto mechanics. In competition for awards and prizes, each high school within an area sent a team of two students to a regional meet, where perhaps a dozen to twenty other high schools would also be represented by teams. Here the young men confronted a group of Plymouth automobiles which had been deliberately "bugged" with a dozen or more malfunctions. Starting at a signal, under the supervision of judges, each boy's assignment was to get his assigned car going and to drive it a specified distance. The winners (in perhaps 25 to 35 minutes of working time) received trophies, awards such as tools, and perhaps scholarships or other prizes. Runners-up received smaller awards.

The program worked well as a cooperative effort made by the Chrysler

[13] Gil Benedict, N. W. Ayer & Son, Inc., Detroit, Mich.

Figure 11-4. For more than a dozen years Plymouth Motors has sponsored a trouble-shooting contest through which young mechanics can display their skill and win prizes.

Company (which provided know-how and promotional material), dealers within an area (who provided manpower, promotion, and prizes), and school officials (whose permission and cooperation was necessary).

From the automobile company's viewpoint the publicity was important, but even more important was the contact established between Plymouth dealers and future good mechanics. In 1950, for example, the United States had one auto mechanic for every seventy-five cars on the road; by 1960 it had one for every hundred cars. As the result of only one contest, fifty students were hired as mechanics by dealers.

From the school viewpoint, the program furnished boys in shop courses motivation and recognition comparable to the stimuli which might have urged them on as members of an athletic team. Representing the high school at a regional trouble-shooting contest paralleled the importance of being a basketball or football star, and the regional newspaper and broadcast publicity about winners reflected credit upon the quality of shop courses within a school, and was good for teacher morale. In addition, the contest performed a national service in the public welfare; in an age of multiplying mechanical contrivances, good repairmen are always in increasing demand.

The Plymouth trouble-shooting contest is a good example of an action created to serve numerous public relations purposes successfully.

The Kroger-Westinghouse junior cook-of-the-year search.[14] An unsolved

[14] Merle J. Thomas, Public Relations Department, the Kroger Company, Cincinnati, Ohio.

problem in today's American business is how to distinguish among grocery supermarkets. Carrying similar or identical merchandise at close to identical prices, located in the same types of buildings, surrounded by identical parking lots, and usually using very similar advertising techniques, the markets offer the customer no good reason other than location to prefer one store to another. Under these circumstances, imaginative public relations activities might be of more than usual importance to any one store. Kroger, a very large Midwestern and Southern grocery chain, showed considerable imagination in devising an individuality for itself.

In 1959 Kroger teamed up with Westinghouse in the junior cook-of-the-year search, which has been held annually since then. In the fall of each year, girls and boys between the ages of twelve and twenty (in two divisions, twelve through fourteen and fifteen through twenty) are invited to submit their original favorite recipes in several classifications. These are judged by home economics experts, and the fifty top winners from various regions are brought into Cincinnati, Kroger headquarters, for three days to compete in a "Cook-off" in which they actually prepare dishes from their own recipes.

All those who compete in the Cincinnati finals receive full expenses for the trip, including the expenses of their teacher or group leader accompanying them, a $100 check, a Westinghouse range, and the cook's costume which they wear in the final competition.

The grand prize is $5,000 plus a ten-day trip to Europe for the winner and his or her mother and teacher. The other prizes are $2,000 and $1,000 for top rank in both age classifications, and many lesser awards in merchandise. Because of the generosity of the basic $100 award and the gift of a range to all contestants at Cincinnati, there has been no problem of disappointed losers.

The publicity has been excellent, beginning with the mailing of entry blanks to more than 26,000 schools, 4-H clubs, and girl scout troops, as well as store displays. By the second year of the contest more than 2,000 stories of the cook-off, many of them in generous space, appeared in newspapers from coast to coast. Sixteen Wirephotos were sent out by Associated Press and thirteen by UPI. Fifty-five food editors, radio-television women's directors, and leading national home economists attended the cook-off finals. Five national and regional magazines were represented.

There were hundreds of newscasts on radio and TV, a nationwide telecast of the grand-prize winner's picture on a network program, a nationwide interview on NBC Monitor, an Arthur Godfrey interview on CBS radio, and more than 4,000 requests for the five prize-winning recipes. (The winning recipes that year, by the way, were: (1) "Hot 'N Hearty Sandwich Loaf," a sort of Americanized pizza on toasted bread; (2) "Walnut Wonder" cake; (3) Chicken Royal; (4) Candy Bar Cake; (5) Lemon Fluff Tarts.)

The Westinghouse science-talent search.[15] The Westinghouse science-talent search, which began in 1942, has been a soundly conceived program and has also profited from the increasing impact of science upon American life, particularly since the postsputnik era began in 1957. A record 29,000 students entered the search in 1959. From 1942 through 1960, 307,552 high school seniors participated, and of these, 56,841 completed the exhaustive final requirements. In that period Westinghouse scholarships and awards of $278,750 went to 585 young men and 175 young women; more than $5,000 students were named members of the honors group; and more than 5 million dollars in scholarships and financial aid from other sources was awarded to winners and honor members as a result of their standing in the search.

Some of the early winners, now grown, have distinguished themselves in science in the Army, in medicine, in nuclear power, in chemistry, in geology, and in teaching, both at home and abroad.

The program was conceived in the fall of 1941, when G. Edward Pendray of Westinghouse, Dr. Harlow Shapley, director of Harvard Observatory, Mr. Watson Davis, and Miss Margaret E. Patterson of Science Service met to decide how a fund available from the Westinghouse Electric Corporation could best be spent to aid young scientists. They sought a means of selecting students with an unusual aptitude for science as early in their school careers as possible, and the structure of the program decided upon then has been continued with only minor alterations.

Announcement of the search is made each year to more than 50,000 high school principals and science teachers, who urge students to begin working on their individual science projects. In December the entrants are given a 2½-hour science-aptitude examination which is designed to test their scientific potential. These tests are then sent to Science Service in Washington (a national association of youth science clubs), along with the students' project reports, scholarship records, and written evaluations of their abilities as seen by their teachers.

Careful inspection and judging of the entry materials is done by teams of educators and scientists, who in a series of eliminations select the top 10 per cent of the entrants for the honors group, and finally the forty national winners.

At the Science Talent Institute in Washington, each finalist is interviewed by the two presiding judges and an adjunct judge to determine the top five scholarship winners. To the most promising boy or girl scientist goes the highest honor—a four-year $7,500 Westinghouse grand science scholarship. Second place is a $6,000 scholarship; third, $5,000; fourth, $4,000; and fifth, $4,000. Each of the other thirty-five winners receives a $250 award.

---

[15] Dale McFeatters, vice president, Westinghouse Electric Corporation, Pittsburgh, Pa., and Gilbert H. Furgurson, New York Public Relations Office, Westinghouse.

All former search winners have attended college, and all but 1 per cent are studying some branch of science. Of those who have finished college, 93 per cent have bachelor's degrees, 60 per cent have master's degrees or the equivalent, and 45 per cent have doctor's degrees.

The five-day visit to Washington takes the forty winners on a busy round of activities. They meet socially with many of the leading scientists of the country and with their congressmen, stage their own science exhibit for themselves and hundreds of invited guests, engage in panel discussions, and see the historic and scientific sights of the nation's capital. Many of the groups have been received by the President in the White House. The final evening of the Institute is climaxed by an awards banquet at which the five top scholarship winners are announced.

Science fairs. The Westinghouse science-talent search confines itself to high school seniors. Yet many teachers have observed that scientific ability manifests itself at a much earlier age and could well be encouraged among younger children, even in elementary schools. This observation led to the rise in the 1940s of local "Science Fairs," which have coalesced under Science Service into an annual National Science Fair in Washington. This is not competitive with the Westinghouse effort, but rather complementary to it.

The first local science fair of which the writer has record began in Providence, Rhode Island, in the mid-1940s under the sponsorship of the *Providence Journal-Bulletin*. It was visited by a St. Louis, Missouri, high school science teacher, who upon his return home, approached the *St. Louis Star-Times* (of which the writer was then promotion manager) with the thought that such an event might be developed in St. Louis. Its quick success demonstrated the truth that cooperation in which several groups and the public all benefit is the best kind of public relations for all involved.

The partners in the venture were:

The Star-Times, which provided money for publicity mailings and entry forms, advertising and news space in the paper and on the radio, several dinners, and organizational assistance.

The science teachers of the St. Louis area city and private schools, who joined together to provide manpower for the promotion of the exhibit, supervised its actual conduct, and obtained judges, award money, and scholarships for the winners.

Washington University, which provided the use of its field house as an exhibit space, janitorial and maintenance help, assistance in the judging, and general sanction, including an opening address by the chancellor of the university.

Various St. Louis companies in scientific or semiscientific fields, such as chemicals, electric power, metals, and so forth, who donated prize money totaling several thousands of dollars and who also freed the time of some of their personnel to assist in the judging.

Universities and colleges, which contributed scholarships worth about $20,-000 to winners in the fair, given only to high school seniors or juniors. Lesser awards, given to a large number of entrants, consisted of cash and ribbons of merit in three classes.

The program was a success from the start, having about 1,300 entries the first year and 3,000 within three years when the size of the field house began to be a serious limitation. The quality of the entries ranged from very high for the more advanced students to amateur and somewhat amusing efforts by lower-grade youngsters, who often entered their exhibits as school class projects. (These were of supreme importance to their submitters and to their parents and teachers.) Attendance was about twenty thousand, not including exhibitors.

The most worthwhile parts of the program were its unquestioned public benefits and the close cooperative contact it established between the newspaper, the teachers, the colleges, and the industrial concerns in attaining a goal of youthful scientific development which all these interests held in common, yet which no one of them could have reached alone.

There are now several hundred science fairs in the United States, culminating in a National Science Fair to which local winners are sent, and these programs and the Westinghouse science-talent search must have exerted a considerable influence upon the scientific interests of young people within the past two decades. Since most of these efforts were begun before foreign scientific prowess astonished the American people and stung governmental programs into action, the public relations persons who were associated with them in their early days can take modest pride in their role as leaders in an important field.

Ford Motor Company's Latin-American programs.[16] Sometimes the term "statesmanship" can properly be applied to private public relations activities, and it well describes the activities of the Ford Motor Company in at least two of its efforts in Latin America—the concourse of manual arts in Mexico City beginning in 1959 and the hemispheric promotion of Rural Youth Clubs, which was announced by Henry Ford II in early 1961.

The exhibit of manual arts in Mexico City began in 1959 and was much expanded in 1960 by the setting up of regional exhibitions in seventeen Mexican cities in addition to the main event in the capital. The number of prizes was increased from 50 to 108, the first prizes consisting of eight trips to Ford headquarters in Detroit, with all expenses paid, for the four winning students and their teachers.

Exhibits consisted of some very splendid work in furniture, jewelry, toys, electrical equipment, tooled leather, sculpture, and objects of art. The first award in 1959, for example, in the secondary school classification was for

[16] Ford Motor Company, Dearborn, Mich., including John Mayhew, International Public Relations manager, and Paul F. Burns, Public Relations Services manager.

a table whose center consisted of an intricate copper reproduction of an ancient Aztec calendar. First prize in the vocational schools classification was for a perfect scale-model reproduction of a tractor and its farm implements.

The Ford Motor Company program to help support the growth of Rural Youth Clubs throughout Latin America is much larger than the manual arts program and is potentially of very great importance to the Western Hemisphere.

One-sixth of all the land in the world is in Latin America, and two-thirds of the people living in Latin America must earn their living from the land. There are 250,000 young members of agricultural youth clubs in Latin America, organized somewhat as are the familiar 4-H clubs of rural youngsters in the United States, although the initials, varying with the language, may be four C's, or four S's, or four F's, or four A's in some of these countries. Much of Latin-American rural life is still village-centered, and many of the problems which were solved in achieving the unparalleled standard of productivity of agriculture in the United States still await solution south of the Rio Grande.

Controlling soil erosion, supplying fertilizer, improving the breed of crops and animals, of sanitation and water supplies, planting new crops, overcoming epidemics, both animal and human, the development of good roads, and the improvement of rural industries are all major projects ahead for most farm people in Latin America. The experiences through which they are now passing, and will soon pass, are in many ways similar to those through which farmers in the United States passed from 1910 to 1930—the period in which automobiles and tractors arrived, horses began to disappear as a means of motive power, new strains of hybrid corn were introduced, soil-erosion-control practices were developed, artificial fertilizers became common, dairying was introduced to many areas in which it was formerly unknown, chicken raising and egg production were revolutionized, new crops such as soybeans became common, and farm electrification began to appear. The result in the United States was a great increase in farm production, a higher standard of living for those who remained upon the farms, and a freeing of farm labor for more productive jobs in factories and in services, all of which changes have raised the general standard of living throughout the nation.

A similar development will have to take place in much of Latin America within the next few years, and the more of it that can be done by voluntary cooperation and self-help (as it was so largely accomplished in the United States) the more it will obviate many of the less satisfactory methods of totalitarian state planning with their accompanying loss of liberty and initiative.

Ford's contribution to the program was inspired by the success of a 176-

page illustrated *Yearbook* of Latin American Rural Youth Club activities, issued by Ford in 1960, which reported upon projects and developments of various farm youth clubs among the 5,277 then in Latin America, most of them established in the preceding eight years. With only one rural youth club member on the average for every 245 farms (Puerto Rico, where the average is much higher, is not included), the great need was for leadership training and for exchange of information so that a formidably big job could be accomplished in this generation.

As a result, the Ford Company (1) issued a 30-minute documentary motion picture on rural youth club work in Latin America to help inspire and instruct future groups, (2) started work on a second edition of *Anuario Para la Juventud Rural de las Americas* (the yearbook) for 1962, and (3) established a small bimonthly magazine beginning in 1961 in Spanish, Portuguese, and English, which could supply information and ideas between appearances of the *Annual*. Copies of this material can be obtained from Ford offices in Mexico City, Buenos Aires, Santiago, Montevideo, Caracas, or São Paulo, or from Ford headquarters in Dearborn, Michigan.

How to celebrate a one hundredth anniversary.[17] There is nothing stereotyped about historic occasions—or at least there need not be—and different organizations may wish to approach them in different ways. Some may elect to throw a party featuring champagne and Hollywood starlets; others may decide to be more civic-minded and dignified. Neither way is necessarily right or wrong; the correct choice depends upon the time, the community, and the organization involved.

In 1956, when the First National Bank in St. Louis reached its one hundredth year, it decided to eschew the fireworks and plan a more informative program.

1. It gave $50,000 each to Washington and St. Louis Universities, with no strings attached.

2. It issued a beautiful 86-page booklet of old St. Louis scenes, edited by the director of the Missouri Historical Society. The initial copies were distributed to 600 St. Louis business and civic leaders and their wives at the ninetieth anniversary dinner meeting of the society, held in the historic old Federal Courthouse on the St. Louis Mississippi River front, where the famed Dred Scott case had been tried and where the society was founded in 1866. The total run of the booklet was about 45,000 copies.

3. It held an open house for employees and their families in connection with completing the remodeling of the bank.

A New York or Texas bank celebration might have been different, but the St. Louis atmosphere leans toward conservative tradition.

[17] C. Arthur Hemminger, vice president and public relations director, the First National Bank, St. Louis, Mo.

5. Cooperative Actions Stimulating Others in Work for the Public Welfare

Public relations actions may take the form primarily of encouraging others to help themselves. The participation of the stimulating organization itself is apparently very modest, but actually its expenditure of salaries and time is considerable, especially in attending meetings, offering awards and dinners, and picking up the check now and then.

The planned progress program of the Union Electric Company.[18] In the early 1950s the Union Electric Company of St. Louis, Missouri, and its two subsidiaries, Missouri Edison Company and Missouri Power and Light Company, began to be concerned about the decline of the use of electricity in many smaller rural communities as a result of depopulation and a lack of industries. Since an electric utility company can't roll up its wires, take down the poles and move, the company decided to promote a program which would help the communities to help themselves (and use more electricity).

The result was the "planned progress program," which began in 1952 with 30 schools and 36 communities participating, and in six years had grown to 100 schools and 200 communities. Briefly, the program works like this: Each fall, high school students in the smaller towns which wish to participate make a survey of their respective communities as a part of their regular classroom work. They find out what the community has, what it needs, and what it will support. Using this survey information as a basis, the students then select two community-improvement projects and prepare a precise report on how they think the projects might be accomplished by the adults of the community with the young people helping.

Each participating school submits its report to the electric company, and cash awards are made to the schools doing the best job, with the stipulation that the money be used to buy school equipment not normally available through ordinary school funds.

The second part of the program starts January 1 and calls for actual accomplishment of the community projects under the direction of a planned progress adult council in each town. This council is made up of representatives of all organized groups in the community, such as Kiwanis, Lions, PTA, churches, and so forth, as well as individuals who are interested in improvement.

After a year's work, the adults submit their report to the company on accomplishments. The contest is limited to towns of less than 7,500 population and is divided into several classifications. Top award for a class is $1,000—not a large amount except when the small size of some of the

[18] Leo J. Reid, Jr., Public Relations Department, the Union Electric Company, St. Louis, Mo.

towns is considered. It must be spent on civic improvement. In 1958 a total of 2,130 reports were described by participating communities. Typical projects include water plants, sewage disposal, community halls, fire-department organization, youth centers, and the development of new industries.

Working together to build a community park.[19] A big postwar building boom north of Syracuse, New York, stimulated rapid growth of the towns of Cicero, Clay, and Salina, which found themselves without recreational areas or undeveloped areas in which to build them. Late in 1958 an abandoned 23-acre gravel pit, whose water had become a hazard to children and a breeder of mosquitoes, was deeded to Clay. Since it bordered on another town and was less than a mile from the third, Clay officials conferred about the gift with civic groups in all three towns, and in early 1959 an association was formed to develop the area into Tri-Town Recreation Park, to which Clay deeded the land.

Plans for full development called for areas for picnics, lawn games, fishing, wading, skiing, hockey, baseball, and touch football. Land clearing was accomplished by borrowing heavy equipment from nineteen firms located in the area, with fuel donated by three oil companies. The cost was approximately $6,000 for $33,000 worth of work. The amount needed to complete the job was about $50,000.

At this point a publicity committee, headed by the public relations director of Porter-Cable Machine Company of Syracuse, was set up and obtained excellent cooperation from the news media. Mass meetings were held, a speakers' bureau set up, and a brochure prepared with the donated assistance of an advertising agency. The drive went over the top in three weeks.

In a similar program in the writer's experience, the town of Bryan, Ohio, had acquired a 40-acre plot near the town, which required drainage. Much of the necessary work was donated, and a master plan for park development was drawn up for about $1,500 by two university planning experts. The various town organizations, such as the American Legion, Scouts, Rotary, churches, and the schools, were each given particular projects—baseball diamonds, bridle trails, woods cabin, and picnic grounds—as their own jobs, designated by name. As a result, the park grew in an orderly pay-as-you-go fashion without resort to heavy taxes.

6. Actions Needed Primarily to Achieve Communication

Frequently something needs to be "done" in order to have something to talk about. This is not only the nature of news, but is also the nature of human interest because we pay attention to extraordinary happenings rather than to matters which simply go on in a routine fashion, especially if their connection with our own affairs is not very close. Thus it is often up to a public relations man to make something happen which will provide a basis

[19] *Public Relations News,* Nov. 21, 1960.

for proper news attention and which, ideally, will also be an occasion into which the reader can project himself in imagination.

Engineer-for-a-day on the Long Island Rail Road.[20] As the world's largest commuter line, moving one-fifth of all the railroad passengers in the United States, the Long Island Rail Road is America's biggest passenger carrier, and its public relations problems are correspondingly demanding. With hundreds of weekday trains running only a few seconds apart at the peak of morning and evening traffic, the slightest delay can make 40,000 to 60,000 people late to work or to dinner. In the early 1950s the railroad was in bankruptcy, equipment was run down, and no fare increases had been permitted for several years. Eventually the financial situation was remedied, but a legacy of public ill will remained along with the natural difficulties of a service in which success is taken for granted and occasional lapses are the cause for bitter complaint.

Under these circumstances, a vigorous public relations effort was needed to improve the morale of employees, increase business, and prevent constant public friction. A major information program was entered into; but something additional was needed, and after about a year, the line's public relations director had an inspiration.

What better way could be devised to make a rider familiar with a railroad's problems than to make him an honorary engineer for a day?

In the words of Long Island Rail Road's public relations director:

> Much of the criticism pouring down upon us was a result of the misconceptions most people have of how a commuter railroad operates. . . . We were convinced that all the speeches and press releases in the world couldn't correct this situation. The answer, we decided, was to find some way of giving a cross section of our passengers a behind-the-scenes look at what makes a railroad tick—or what, on occasions, makes it fail to tick—and depend upon them to pass this insight on to fellow commuters. We were pretty sure that both our operation and our employees would stand up well under such a spotlight of first-hand inspection.
>
> . . . we had a notion that . . . our passengers who hadn't completely outgrown boyhood dreams of being locomotive engineers . . . would see and learn if they were given an opportunity to ride up front with the engineer. . . . So we decided to extend a blanket invitation to all of our regular commuters to be an engineer for-a-day on their way to work some morning.
>
> Although in our fondest dreams (or our most fearsome nightmares) we never expected the 2,000-odd acceptances we ended up with, we knew from the start that this was something which might take quite a bit of doing. . . . If the program was to be successful we must have the wholehearted support of the whole railroad, not just the blood, sweat and tears

[20] James A. Schultz, director of public relations, the Long Island Rail Road, Jamaica Station, New York.

of the two-man public relations department. . . . We moved slowly and cautiously. The idea (never before tried elsewhere) was thoroughly chewed over at a couple of President's staff meetings and suggestions were encouraged from all departments. From an original it's-strictly-impossible reaction, there evolved not only a feeling that the thing might be made to work, but also a genuine enthusiasm. . . . Then, and not until then, were we ready to shove off.

Invitations to be an engineer-for-a-day were sent to ticket agents (they included a return self-addressed business reply card) . . . and simultaneously a press release announcing the program was distributed to all media.

There was no time to sit back and wonder whether or not the thing would catch on. The response was instantaneous. Within a few hours after the first invitation had been passed out . . . the cards began pouring in. The cards were carefully filed in order of receipt, and each would-be Casey Jones received a letter from the railroad president and a little booklet about the line.

Two weeks after the first invitations were distributed our first guest engineer climbed into the cab . . . selected by lot from the 37 reply cards received in the first mail after the program was announced. . . .

Organizing the program took extreme care. To avoid distracting the working engineer, an officer or supervisor of the railroad met each guest at his station, escorted him to the cab, rode with him, and answered all his questions. Fifty-eight persons volunteered for this job. They phoned personally to four people a week. Hosts, such as lawyers or accountants, who were not familiar with actual operating details of the line, were provided with a five-page briefing sheet.

In commenting on the results of the program, the Long Island Rail Road public relations head said:

> One of the many surprises of the program was the unexpectedly large number of letters from those taking the cab rides. More than half wrote in to say "thanks"—there wasn't a single criticism.
>
> These letters, with a penciled "thank you" note from the president were sent to the host and the train crews involved. . . .
>
> Any publicity we might get from the program was secondary in our decision to undertake it. The emphasis was on the person-to-person contact that would be possible. Even so, the volume of publicity many times exceeded anything else we'd ever attempted.
>
> Every daily in New York City and on Long Island, for example, carried full and favorable stories on the initial announcement. The story was also featured on virtually every radio and television station . . . in the metropolitan area and in approximately a hundred weekly newspapers on Long Island . . . also widely used over the country.
>
> We had our fingers crossed the morning of the first ride. Engineer-for-a-day No. 1 had been picked by lot and we had no way of knowing how he would handle himself with the 20-odd reporters, photographers and

radio and television people who were waiting at the end of the line in Long Island City. The results couldn't have been better if we had hand-picked him and coached him for a week in advance.

. . . the continuing publicity was very gratifying. Weekly newspapers, for example, carried stories and pictures in virtually every issue of local residents who had been engineers-for-a-day during the preceding week, and more than a score of employee publications . . . carried similar stories on their own people—from presidents down through secretaries and stock-room clerks—who made the trip.

An important by-product . . . was strengthening the morale and pride in the railroad on the part of employees. Capsule comments from letters were carried in each issue of our biweekly publication.

. . . although it took six months . . . and hundreds of man-hours of time by officers and supervisors . . . we're still convinced, almost five years later, that this was by all odds the most successful public relations program the Long Island Railroad has ever undertaken. . . .

Ford Motor Company's national teen-age press conference.[21] Press previews of new models are a somewhat well-worn feature of the Detroit automobile promotion scene, but in 1957 the Ford Motor Company came up with a new twist. Why not invite some teen-age journalists to the party? The program was an immediate success, and within a few years more than 150 high schoolers were annually attending Ford's new-car previews, considerably outnumbering the adult working pressmen—from whom, however, they were kept strictly separated, except at the actual time of the unveiling of the new annual automobile models.

Selection of the junior journalists was left up to the sponsoring newspapers, which picked them within their areas, although popular methods included competitive news writing based on a press conference or other event, an essay contest, or selection by school heads on the basis of student records and school newspaper work. General scholarship was also taken into account, because the Ford Company considers it important in giving awards to those who write outstanding stories at the national press conference in Detroit.

The high school regional winners were given all expenses of a trip to Detroit and back and of a three-day stay in the fall of each year. While there, they embarked on a program of activities, of which the following would be an illustration:

Wednesday evening—Meet with seven college journalism heads for a panel discussion of newspaper careers.

Thursday—Preview the new Ford truck line by watching five National Truck Roadeo champions put new trucks over an obstacle course at Dearborn proving grounds; ride in cabs with the drivers.

[21] Paul F. Burns, Public Relations Services manager, the Ford Motor Company, Dearborn, Mich.

Thursday evening—Join with 36 other high school students from the
United States and Mexico, winners in Ford's Industrial Arts Awards
Competition, in a salute-to-champions banquet at which three Olympic
champions will tell of their experiences abroad.

Friday—Join the adult working press in a preview of The National Automobile Show at Cobo Hall in downtown Detroit. During the press conference the teen-agers will write for their sponsoring publications and
compete for five college scholarships ranging in value from $800 to
$8,000. (Winners are announced about six weeks later, after their stories
are judged by a panel of journalists not connected with the company.
The identity of every writer is disguised.)

The young writers returned to their homes on Saturday.

The program has grown from year to year and has resulted in good press
relations, a reasonable amount of publicity, increased interest on the part
of youngsters in the American automobile industry, and perhaps in the encouragement of some junior journalists to pursue careers in the newspaper
field. It has also certainly given a new twist to an otherwise somewhat stand-
ardized piece of automobile news coverage.

Brunswick makes annual stockholder meetings into news! [22] There are a
number of ways of holding company stockholder meetings. The law doesn't
say much about procedure except that they have to be conducted properly
on a duly announced date. A number of years ago one of the country's
largest oil companies was still holding its annual meeting in a 2 by 4 room
over a filling station. But in 1958, the Brunswick Corporation of Chicago
conceived the idea of holding its annual stockholder meetings in a setting
which would be appropriate to its main products, would dramatize the expanding nature of its business for stockholders, and would also make news.

Brunswick started out as a pool-table manufacturing concern a century
ago, and then became dominant in the United States in the bowling-ball
field fifty years later. A little more than a decade ago the company introduced a new automatic pin-setting machine whose popularity combined
with the bowling boom to start a period of fantastic growth and acquisition
in the sporting-goods, boating, medical-supply, school-furniture, defense,
and international fields.

In 1958 Brunswick gathered its shareholders into a lavish Chicago bowling emporium, where they heard of the fabulous success of the company's
then-new automatic pin setter.

The following year Brunswick invited its owners to a suburban Illinois
high school (along with seventy seniors majoring in economics), where
company executives focused attention on the organization's growing role as
a major contributor to the advancement and modernization of the nation's
expanding classrooms.

[22] R. K. Creel, director of corporate public relations, the Brunswick Corporation,
Chicago, Ill.

Figure 11-5. Stockholders' annual meetings don't need to be dull. When the Brunswick Corporation bought a boat company to diversify its line, it put on a show in Chicago's McCormick Place which dramatized its new enterprise and made headlines.

The next year stockowners went to Chicago's plush South Shore Country Club, where 1,200 of them were treated to news of the company's new acquisitions in the sports field, particularly of MacGregor sportswear and equipment. Colorful tams were worn by Brunswick executives (MacGregor tartan, of course) when they went outside the club to putt golf balls into a hole whose greens flag carried the clearly visible figure $275,099,000—the company's annual sales for the year just past. Lessons were then given by golf pros to those who wanted them, and each departing guest was presented with a box of three Tourney golf balls as a sample to convince him of their quality.

In 1961, after the acquisition of several boat companies, Brunswick Corporation held its annual meeting at Chicago's McCormick Place show hall and was attended by 5,000 stockholders. In the words of the *Wall Street Journal*:

> Brunswick Corp. announced a year-to-year gain in first quarter earnings at a six-hour annual meeting, held in a nautical atmosphere of yachts, swim-suited girls, and an hour-long water ski show on the rolling surf of Lake Michigan.
>
> The remains of Sunday's 7-inch snow storm and chilling 40-degree weather failed to halt the water-skiing program. A dozen skiers in red,

black and orange swept back and forth on Lake Michigan in front of Chicago's new $35 million McCormick Place Convention Hall where the meeting was held. Shareholders watched in comfort from inside the hall. The object of the show was to point up the company's growing nautical operations. . . .

Some 4,500 Brunswick shareholders filed into a 5,000-seat auditorium for the meeting, which was brightened by a seven-piece orchestra, a seashore fashion show, and a rousing quartet singing "Roll, Brunswick, Roll." Following a baked chicken and apple pie lunch, stockholders watched a water show, ambled through twenty water craft ranging up to a $28,500 yacht, and received a gift of a $3.95 boat cushion.

Details of the corporate spectacular included getting clearance from nearby Meigs Airfield for a water skier to soar up into the air lanes on a kite towed by a speedboat, and obtaining bulldozers to clear paths through the heavy snow to the parking lot. Prior annual meetings included such settings as bowling alleys and schools to emphasize these aspects of Brunswick's business.

An additional aspect of this Brunswick meeting was the presence of thirty-three student high school newspaper editors, who had been invited to attend at Brunswick's expense. Each represented a high school in a community where Brunswick has a plant.

By interesting coincidence, Brunswick's 1961 annual meeting in McCormick Place, attended by 5,000 shareholders, was followed two days later by the seventy-sixth Annual Meeting of American Telephone and Telegraph Company (the first event ever held outside of New York City) in the same location, attended by almost 20,000. The *Chicago Tribune* said:

> Preparations for A.T. & T.'s meeting almost defy the imagination.
>
> Truckloads of corporate records and displays have been brought in from New York and workmen will be busy two days setting up the equipment.
>
> Displays of the latest communications developments also will be on view including showing communications by means of satellite. These displays will be at one end of the 300,000 square foot exhibition plaza. In the center will be tables and chairs where box lunches will be served. At the other end will be 13,000 chairs and a speaker's platform. . . . If attendance is more than 13,000, the overflow will be accommodated in the center's theater which can seat about 5,000. . . . Chicago was chosen for the meeting because 17 per cent of the utility's two million stockholders live in the Chicagoland area. . . .

And the following Sunday the *Chicago Sun-Times* remarked in an editorial captioned 20,000 CAPITALISTS:

> . . . the A.T. & T. meeting—like the McCormick Place meeting Monday of 5,000 stockholders of the Chicago-based Brunswick Corp.—pointed up some encouraging facts about corporate life in the '60s. One important

such fact is the switch to goldfish bowl operations of most of today's corporations—in contrast with the secretive procedures and limitations of stockholders' rights that characterized many corporate operations in the past. . . .

7. Action as Seen in Organization for Public Relations Purposes

Often the main accomplishment in a public relations effort is to bring together scattered forces and to unite them in one positive program. This "action of organization" is largely internal within the groups involved and consists in the development of a program upon which most can agree, in its vigorous selling and defense, in obtaining the active participation of members, and then in keeping the program sold. The external program itself may be far less trouble and require far less skill and patience to actuate than the task of persuading the scattered legions all to march together, an achievement which does not show at all to the outside observer. The task is not always so arduous, of course, but all those who work with trade and professional associations are familiar, through long experience, with the difficulties of persuasion.

Law Day U.S.A.[23] Surveying the national scene in the late 1950s, farsighted men among America's attorneys had cause for alarm. At home understanding and respect for the law seemed at a new low ebb—the result of an unsettled population, lessening of parental and social influence, and a great increase in the complexity and variety of laws themselves as more people's activities impinged upon each other all the time. The practice of the law was often held in poor repute, and the quality and number of young men seeking to make law a profession was cause for concern. Abroad, in the Communist world, the very principles of law, as the free world conceives of them, were denied, and in many newer, less developed nations the actual practice of freedom and equality under the law rested upon very shaky foundations.

What to do about it? Some focus of attention was needed, some cause to which the many, but scattered, persons and institutions who respected the law could rally. The result was the establishment in 1958 of Law Day U.S.A. by proclamation of the President of the United States.

Its purposes were: (1) to foster respect for law, (2) to increase public understanding of the place of law in American life, (3) to point out the contrast between freedom under law in the United States and governmental tyranny under communism (to which might be properly added tyranny under any lawless regime).

The date selected for Law Day was May 1 of each year; and this was no accident, because May Day each year is the occasion of great Communist celebrations and riots, to which Law Day was intended to be an answer.

[23] Don Hyndman, director of public relations, the American Bar Association, Chicago, Ill.

Within three years Law Day U.S.A. had grown to a point where there were 75,000 observances across the land—school programs, speeches, dedications, and other programs mirrored in hundreds of newspapers and radio and TV stations. The Committee on Public Relations of the American Bar Association made available a manual suggesting events and telling how to put them on, a speaker's brochure containing useful quotations, explanatory leaflets to give out at meetings and elsewhere, envelope labels, mats for newspaper advertisements, motion pictures, window cards, and billboards.

Suggested programs included mock trials, citizenship examinations, and court tours by schools; speakers and panel discussions for civic clubs; admissions to the bar and naturalization ceremonies in courts; law school open houses, moot courts, and banquets; church observances emphasizing the

MAY 1 . . . LAW DAY U.S.A.

"Freedom under law is like the air we breathe. People
take it for granted and are unaware of it—until they are
deprived of it."

DWIGHT D. EISENHOWER

Men have died to leave YOU these 4 symbols of freedom—

A HOLY BIBLE . . . symbol of your right to worship as you wish.
(First amendment, U. S. Constitution)

A DOOR KEY . . . your right to lock your door against illegal government
force and prying.
(Fourth amendment, U. S. Constitution)

A PENCIL . . . Freedom to speak or write what you think, whether you agree
with the government or not.
(First amendment, U. S. Constitution)

A FREE BALLOT . . . your right to choose the people who represent you
in government—your protection against govern-
ment tyranny.
(Article 1, U. S. Constitution)

*These symbols have no meaning in countries where government controls
everything, for there the individual man or woman HAS NO FREEDOM.*

join Americans everywhere in commemorating Law Day U.S.A. May 1

Figure 11-6. This newspaper advertisement, made available in mat form to local bar associations or other sponsors, helped to promote Law Day, by which the American Bar Association hopes to develop a better understanding of American legal processes.

place of law in the Bible; window and library exhibits; radio and television discussions and speakers; and marking of historic sites.

The American Bar Association was careful to point out that law was not developed for the benefit of lawyers, but rather for the protection of citizens. The rights of an American citizen include the right to a good education, to live where he pleases, to work where he wants to, to worship as he chooses, to vote secretly, to have a fair and speedy trial, to own property, to start a business, and to manage his own affairs. The point was made that laws are developed not to be restrictive but to give freedom by the protection of the greatest number of people from violence, deceit, and pressure; that laws are in an orderly process of change; and that Americans have many responsibilities of citizenship, such as taking part in community affairs, teaching youth the nature of law, and supporting those who bear the responsibility of enforcing the laws.

"Our system," said the American Bar Association, "is dependent upon voluntary compliance with laws. The best answer to rising crime rates at home is a redoubling of effort to strengthen voluntary obedience to law through the church, the home, the school, and the community agencies. Similarly the best antidote to tyranny abroad is to demonstrate the virtues of freedom and the steady broadening of the rule of law."

The American Music Conference.[24] In 1947 leaders in the industry of making musical instruments in the United States found much to be concerned about.

First, the development of radio and phonograph records, then the Depression, and then World War II had taken people away from making music. The automobile had widened the range of things to do outside the home, and the Sunday afternoon musical get-togethers and the family gathering around the piano in the evening had disappeared. School emphases had changed, and all these alterations showed up in the sales figures of the music industry, which failed to keep pace with the population growth or the increase in leisure time. Many authorities feared that unless something was done, the American people would forget completely about making music.

So in 1947 the industry formed the American Music Conference with membership from the trade associations in the field. The AMC employed a Chicago public relations counseling firm, which conducted extensive research into musical habits and interests; obtained a staff of music education specialists; and launched a unique program of public relations designed to change, subtly but effectively American indifference about making music into permanent enthusiasm and action.

The results have been impressive. In 1959, for example, it was estimated that 34,250,000 musical instruments were owned in the United States as compared with only 20,300,000 in 1949—an increase of almost 70 per

[24] Philip Lesly, Philip Lesly Co., Chicago, Ill.

cent within the decade. Of these, pianos were the most popular (21 million), with guitars coming second (4½ million—doubtless influenced by Elvis Presley), and violins and other strings running third (3.2 million). Drums (300,000) were the least numerous (fortunately!).

The number of amateurs playing musical instruments in the nation was estimated at 18 million in 1949 and at 31 million by 1959. The proportion of musical-instrument players in the American population had risen from one in eight to one in six, and the dollar volume of retail music business had grown from 220 million dollars annually to 550 million dollars in the decade, and was almost seven times what it had been in 1939! By 1960 there were 9 million children playing musical instrument under 500,000 music teachers. Schools had more than 73,000 instrumental musical organizations, and there were an estimated 1,500 adult community symphony orchestras scattered over the nation.

Moreover, public opinion ranging all the way from *Financial World* and *Business Week* magazines to Jacques Barzun, Dean of Graduate Faculties at Columbia University and professor of history, united in noticing (and applauding) the change.

Modestly, the American Music Conference gave the following reasons for the big change:

1. Tensions of modern living demanding an emotional outlet
2. More leisure time
3. Growing parental and educator concern over youth's lack of interests and a realization that musical training builds character
4. Higher incomes and more living space
5. Improved teaching methods
6. Better instruments
7. The band-wagon appeal

To these the observer might, perhaps, add television, which, in contrast to radio, enables the viewer to *see* the musical performers and perhaps desire to emulate them.

But all these reasons would doubtless have been far less effective (if effective at all) without the public relations program of the American Music Conference, which took care to see that they were well augmented. It is questionable whether a public relations effort can ever swim successfully against a tide, but there is no doubt at all that it can certainly take advantage of a tide and go much further and faster than it would go unaided.

The main steps in the AMC program have been the following:

> Obtaining music-teaching specialists, who developed new methods of music instruction which could be utilized in larger classes and which made music more appealing. The possibilities were explained by means of articles, booklets, and workshops for music teachers all over the country.
> Boosting the interest in music through plugs on radio and TV by means

of script services to announcers and stimulation of programs about music on the air.

Hundreds of major magazine articles about musical development in America, particularly in household and farm publications.

Publicity for local newspapers.

Motion pictures and slide films to aid teachers in music instruction.

Scores of booklets upon subjects ranging from "Organizing a Community Band" to "Music in Industry Builds Employee and Public Relations." About five thousand booklets a year are sent out in response to mail requests.

A contest for display advertisements (of nonmusical products) in which musical instruments are featured.

The scope of the program can be judged by the fact that in the twelve months ending August 31, 1959, AMC representatives visited 33 teacher training colleges in 23 states to give 194 lectures before 12,072 teachers-to-be; presented 67 one- and two-day workshops to 5,115 working teachers; appeared as guests on 78 radio and TV programs in 25 states for a total air time of 1,226 minutes; assisted 20 school systems with music problems and attended 19 conventions of music teachers of which they participated in 12 programs.

The American Institute of Men's and Boys' Wear, Inc.,[25] faced a problem of its own a number of years ago. American men and boys were spending less and less of their available incomes upon clothes, fashion was becoming less important, and sloppiness (especially at the juvenile level) was disgustingly universal.

There were good, but from the clothing manufacturer's viewpoint, distressing reasons for social change. Some were:

The exodus of people to the suburbs from the city, where a man's dress was relatively more important than his home in establishing his rank; automobiles, which enable casual trips to be taken in privacy and disarray; a reaction from the enforced uniform neatness of two wars; and the youthful folk heroes, who were no longer Horatio Alger types who made their way up in the world through a combination of neatness and enterprise, but varieties of casual and careless young men who offered very little comfort to the clothing merchant.

In 1956 the AIMBW launched a "Dress UP" campaign included institutional advertising in various national magazines which stressed the importance of good male appearance, the promotion of special newspaper supplements on men's fashions, and widespread publicity of various kinds.

In 1959 AIMBW withdrew all consumer advertising and upped its public relations budget to $400,000, to which was added about $100,000 in clothing-trade-magazine advertising to keep the trade upon its toes in support.

---

[25] Dale O'Brien, Mayer and O'Brien, Inc., Chicago, Ill.

Figure 11-7. Helping servicemen to dress appropriately when off duty is recognized, as a national USO award is given to the American Institute of Men's and Boys' Wear. Servicemen who had just taken part in a GI Fashion Show look on during the presentation.

A ten-point public relations program included a motion picture showing how a young salesman was seriously handicapped by poor dress, to be shown over television and before clubs and similar groups; a male fashion service to 1,500 daily newspapers in an effort to increase coverage of men's fashions to something more nearly approximating women's; a program for high school boys; public service radio spots; tie-ins with regular TV shows; a USO booklet for the men in the armed services; material for labor union members; cooperation with industry to help get employees to dress as they should; a "how to dress right" booklet for consumers, distributed to a large extent through retailers; and cooperation with the Junior Chamber of Commerce, 4-H, Boy Scouts, YMCA, and similar groups.

Work in the schools was of particular interest, since it was felt that there was a real relationship between neat dress and student conduct. In 1961, for example, *Scholastic Magazine* sent a questionnaire to the principals of the 4,000 largest high schools in the country. Responses were received from 543 of them, and of this number 57 per cent had conducted Dress Right programs in their high schools; 98 per cent felt that they were effective in improving appearance, study, behavior patterns, and the after-school activities of students; 99 per cent felt that such programs helped the student after he finished school, either in college or on a job, and would like to see the programs continue. When asked whether they felt that teen-agers were more concerned with making a good appearance now than five years ago, 98 per cent also said "yes."

Early in 1961 *America's Textile Reporter* said:

> . . . The impact of the AIMBW program was documented by a report from the Clothing Manufacturers Association which said that the clothing sales increase during 1959 had continued right into 1960. Moreover, said the CMA, "promotion of *Dress Right* principles is almost sure to keep the industry working at near capacity in the next year and even the decade ahead."

The American Home Lighting Institute[26] public relations program provides another illustration of how the winds of chance in consumer trends can be resisted or altered at times through public communications efforts and skillful work with key groups. In the not-so-far-distant days before public relations was understood by American businessmen, there were often only two alternatives: (1) Take the swells of public favor as an act of fate, hoping that eventually the tide will turn, and (2) buy major advertising space and attempt to sway consumer opinion (not really practicable in many instances because of the cost).

When electricity first appeared in American homes in the early 1900s, the first inspiration of the lighting-fixture manufacturer was to enclose the bulb in a ball or in a glass dish and hang it up in the middle of the room, casting a pallid glow on all below; the light was not strong enough or near enough to anyone to do much good except in a general sort of way. Beginning with the vogue for floor lamps in the 1920s, central and other installed lighting fixtures began to disappear, and by the early 1950s they had shrunk to only nine per new home, the rest of the electricity outlets being handled by wall plugs.

A 1958 article in *Sales Management* magazine observed:

> The American Home Lighting Institute is a non-profit trade organization of residential lighting fixture manufacturers and distributors, as well as makers of component parts. It was launched in 1945, but in June of 1955 AHLI was about to fold its tents and disappear. Membership was down to six manufacturers. Sales of lighting fixtures were moving at a pace of $64 million a year, less than half of what the experts thought it should be. Lethargy within the industry itself was the biggest trouble. Joint action for ten years had failed to produce results. Now (in 1958) the picture is dramatically different. AHLI membership has risen to 16 manufacturers,

[26] Ted Cox, Ted Cox Associates, Chicago, Ill.

plus 110 distributors, who have been enlisted as associates. Fixture sales are up to almost $92 million a year . . . (the number per home rose from 9 to 14).

The head of the public relations counseling firm which helped bring about this change says:

> Some of the morals which can be drawn from this experience are these:
> 1. We did an honest research job to determine whether the fixtures which were not being used were actually needed in American homes. We found they were and that the market was far from being saturated.
> 2. We found that lighting, with its significant effects on the home and the human beings who live there, was a subject of interest to people. This was the basis of a dynamic publicity program. We found that editors lacked information on lighting fixtures and, as a first step, prepared a major fact book to supply quick information for story development.
> 3. We canvassed all possible allies of the fixture manufacturing industry for common interests. We patiently discussed these common interests with each ally and geared our program to them. The result was constant growing support (from major manufacturers, contractors associations, electrical utilities, and others) . . . which enlarged the entire market development program far beyond the limits imposed by a relatively small fixture industry.

Summary: Seven Aspects of Actions in Public Relations Practice

1. Action may be inherent in the existing situation, in which case it must often be made clear and be communicated.

2. Action may go farther and capitalize upon an existing facility or event which might not always be apparent at first glance.

3. Action may need to be developed to display the characteristics of a product or organization.

4. Actions may need to be entirely *created* to demonstrate the character of an organization through its services in the public welfare.

5. Action may take the form of cooperation with others to aid and stimulate them in the public welfare, while the prime mover remains relatively in the background.

6. Action is sometimes needed to provide a basis upon which worthwhile and effective communications can be built.

7. Action sometimes consists primarily of organizing various units into a common effort so that they may unitedly influence public opinion. Organization is itself a form of action.

Creating good actions involves much imagination upon the part of a public relations man. He must be able to answer questions such as: Will this be interesting to the public? Does it serve a real public need? Will it get sufficient coverage by the communications media to justify the expense and time? Is it truly representative of the nature of the organization? What will the public reaction be? Can it help other groups attain their goals? Will it perhaps grow over the years or diminish?

While a primary motive of organizations engaging in praiseworthy actions may be their own self-interest, the public good is also greatly served in a way which might not otherwise be possible. Other organizations may also be stimulated to similar actions. Selfish motivation often leads in time to a genuine altruism through association, and in any event, human motivations for good deeds, whether on the part of individuals or organizations, are seldom unmixed. So long as those having a self-interest candidly recognize it and do not fool themselves or others about their mixed motivations, no harm is done and often much good.[27]

---

[27] In the words of Heilbroner, "Public relations may be a commercial conscience— but a conscience nevertheless!"

Communication and
Communication Cases

12

"Letting people know" is the backbone of all effective public relations programs, because no matter how virtuous one's actions may be, they can have little effect until they are widely known. The saying attributed to Emerson, "If a man builds a better mousetrap, the world will beat a path to his door," may have testified truly to the fame of simple good workmanship among close neighbors a century ago; nowadays "the world" buys its mousetraps from the manufacturers who are most talked about, without examining too closely the reason for their renown.

In fact, the truly unique function, for which all sorts of organizations are willing to pay in hard cash, is the public relations practitioner's skill in communicating. This, of course, includes writing skill, knowledge of the media of communication and their uses, and acquaintance with the experts in the field. But it also involves far more! It includes the ability to approach readers, listeners, or viewers in such a way as to command their attention, to create pictures in their minds, and to obtain their interest and agreement.

This is not easy. Men communicate today, as they always have, through words, symbols, and the simple relations of friendship; but they communicate more effectively if they have a thorough knowledge of the *principles* of successful public relations communications as they have been demonstrated time and again. A completely exhaustive list of such principles of effective communication has not yet been made and is not likely soon to be made, for social scientists are continually discovering and refining them.

A FRAMEWORK OF COMMUNICATION

The cases which follow in this chapter are listed under the heading "communications," not because they illustrate this activity exclusively but because the communicating was exceptionally well accomplished.

Among the principles covered are humanization, suiting the message and the means of communication to the audience, speaking the receiver's language, timeliness, dramatization, two-way communication, reaching your own people first, facing the facts, performing a needed service, stressing positive benefits, repetition, overcoming refusal to pay attention, using leaders of opinion, preconditioning the audience, and keeping all communications in harmony.

There is no magic in any of these principles; most of them have been known for several thousand years, and varying lists could be drawn up at any time. Whole books have been written about all, or parts, of them. But in today's world of overflowing communications the important thing to remember is that while people may be easily bombarded with messages, they will pay little attention to most of them unless the communications are of considerable personal interest; and this usually means that the messages must, in some way, recall and reinforce the experiences or goals of the recipients. Since such experiences are much wider than they used to be, and since the number of communications has multiplied even more, the role of communications expert requires increasing knowledge and discrimination. Mere volume of communication is no longer the sole prerequisite to success. In today's great flow of communications, in fact, only a few of the greatest organizations can hope to beat down indifference by sheer massive assault. Aim is becoming increasingly important.

1. The Principle of Humanization

People find it hard to think in the abstract and usually attempt to give human characteristics to inanimate or even abstract things such as nations, governments, business corporations, and social or religious organizations. We identify a nation with its president, dictator, king, or queen; and the companies which stand out in our minds are those in which a colorful personality—the original Henry Ford or John D. Rockefeller or George Romney—has made his mark. This tendency has both its advantages and its dangers: Real people make mistakes, lose their tempers, and often act in foolish ways which may reflect badly upon the organizations which they personify. The ideal human symbol, perhaps, is a fictitious person who is always wise, serene, and pleasant, like General Mills's "Betty Crocker" or Quaker Oats's "Aunt Jemima." Everyone knows that these people do not exist, but they still fill a definite purpose in pleasant identification.

The Minneapolis Gas Company[1]

THE PROBLEM. Everyone agrees that gas is a clean, convenient fuel. Yet how much personality does a gas company have? We take its service for granted because gas continually arrives, quiet and unseen, in an under-

[1] R. F. Calrow, assistant vice president, Minneapolis Gas Company.

ground pipe; we notice gas only if it ceases coming and the house gets cold, or if it leaks, smells, or explodes—although the monthly bill gives us a reminder too. But what mental image can a name like "the Minneapolis Gas Company" evoke in the public mind? Probably nothing more than a string of letters in a certain style of type or the remembrance of a big downtown office building. This was the problem of the Minneapolis Gas Company; it had little personality.

THE SOLUTION. The answer was a little Indian maiden with a cheerful smile and a bright blue gas flame in her headband in the place where the single feather ought to be. Her name was Minnegasco—a corporation-coined name to be sure, but one with the local flavor of Minneapolis, Minnesota, Minnehaha, and Minnetonka, with which people of the upper Midwest are quite familiar. The little Indian girl wears an ample brown elkskin garment from under which her feet peep out coyly.

Early in 1959 gas company employees were introduced to the Indian maiden, learned how and why she was created, and were told what the company hoped to accomplish with her winsome personality. Minnegasco then met the public through a full-page color advertisement in the *Minneapolis Sunday Tribune*; next became acquainted with the company's 12,000 stockholders by arriving in the annual report; and finally visited the homes of 200,000 customers by direct mail, her initial mission being to explain how the unusually cold weather had boosted gas bills.

To make Minnegasco a fellow employee, she was featured at a company party where a Minnegasco button adorned every coat lapel and dress; the name of the employee newspaper was changed from the *Pilot Light* to *Minnegasco News*; brightly colored cardboard Minnegasco cutouts were put on display in all offices; and all new brochures and letterheads featured her prominently.

Minnegasco helped to humanize the company for customers by becoming a permanent part of a redesigned gas-service bill. She was featured with the company name on cars and trucks, and Minnegasco stickers were placed upon appliances to indicate the date of service calls. Meter readers even stuffed their pockets with Minnegasco buttons and became the favorites of the small fry.

Strengthening the company image in the community took several forms, including a series of advertisements boosting Minnegasco Land as a place in which to live and work. One ad, for example, praised the development of the arts in the upper Midwest, but others hit more closely at matters in which a gas company would be vitally concerned. A "good schools" ad pointed out that Minnegasco pays the largest single amount of school-supporting personal property tax in twenty-two of the twenty-five communities she serves. An "it's-fun-to-eat-out" ad not only scratched the backs of local restaurants but also noted that the best cooking was done with gas, and another ad proclaimed "The fresh air's fresher because greater Minneapolis goes first class with gas"—a plug for the use of smokeless fuel in homes and factories.

A full-page color ad in the local newspapers offered 300 free 21-inch Minnegasco stuffed rag dolls just for filling in an entry blank with name and address at a local gas-appliance dealer's store, and every customer received a free Minnegasco headband and blue feather.

In another newspaper ad the Indian maiden held a big pencil with which to sign up for a budget plan on gas heating, and in a summer gas air-conditioning ad she appeared as a little figure in every action picture. A press relations ad in *Page One Yearbook,* a local journalistic publication, showed the heads of the three members of the gas company public relations department with feathers in their hair, while Minnegasco herself followed close behind.

Come to Minneapolis land—the breathing's great

**The
fresh
air's
fresher**

because greater Minneapolis goes first class...with gas

The Minneapolis region is gas-conditioned: no soot, no smog, no smoke, no fog because the natural gas flame burns cleanly.

Some Minneapolitans express their appreciation of the sparkling, heady delights of the air by spending most of their spare time just *breathing* (it's a great place to relax.)

Others, galvanized by its tonic qualities, dash off to nearby lakes to tussle with

hulking wall-eyed and northern pike (there are panfish for the faint of heart.) Still others prefer the cool depths of ferny forest in summer, game trails or shooting fields in fall.

For the overcivilized, there are dozens of rolling, velvety golf courses. And, of course, Minnesota is literally the *home* of winter sports.

Within a few minutes of downtown you will find scores and scores of blue-water

lakes and bays, looked down upon by wooded hillsides—just sitting there, waiting for someone like *you* to come build a house that will appreciate its surroundings.

Come soon—it's a great place to visit, a great place to live, a great place to do business.

© 1960

Minnegasco
MINNEAPOLIS GAS COMPANY
8th & Marquette • Southdale • Robbinsdale

Figure 12-1. A newspaper advertisement featuring "Minnegasco," the little Indian maiden developed to give personality to The Minneapolis Gas Company.

Other community-wide efforts included a "Birth of Minnegasco" presentation before business clubs; special folders distributed on Business Education Day to teachers visiting the company; and thousands of memo books, paper plates, buttons, and matchbooks.

RESULTS. Minnegasco's impact was immediate. In a survey made only three weeks after her introduction, 37 per cent named her correctly or almost correctly from her picture alone, and 56 per cent associated her with the gas company.

Children organized Minnegasco Clubs and wrote in for headbands and feathers; a Minnegasco skit was featured in the 1960 Gridiron dinner of the Twin Cities Newspaper Guild; an attractive girl dressed as Minnegasco was a hit at a home-builders show; employees and customers were full of comments and suggestions; and from a gas company as far away as Chihuahua, Mexico, came a request for suggestions in developing a similar program there. The Minnegasco program won first place in the Community Relations classification of the American Gas Association Public Relations Awards for 1960.

DISCUSSION. Serious-minded people may consider this attempt to assume a personality foolish, but their scorn is unjustified. Why should a company be known only by a string of letters, spelling a word which means only the name of the city in which the company does business and another word, "gas," which names an immaterial product that the consumer can neither see nor touch?

Sometimes, of course, word names do evoke pictures, such as Lincoln Life Insurance Company, Bell Telephone Company, Hercules Powder Company, Ford Motor Company, or Edison Electric Company. Each of these names suggests a person, although it is a fair guess that the public has largely forgotten Alexander Graham Bell and substitutes for his name an image of the Liberty Bell. Other names may suggest products or may be simply fanciful, like Carnation Evaporated Milk Company or Pet Milk Company.

Often company names come to acquire a certain aura of meaning, although the words themselves are almost unintelligible to many people— the Atchison, Topeka, and Santa Fe Railway, for example, or Pan American Airways. Most companies are named after persons who are quite unknown to the general public; or they are named after the companies' functions, as is the Metropolitan Electric Company; or they present grandiloquent generalities related to their functions, such as Trans-World Airways or Continental Airlines. Only through their connotations do these names acquire meaning.

The average citizen today, faced by the vast multiplication of companies and organizations, needs more visual symbols to replace or to amplify words if he is to remember and understand names. Some observers also feel that the advent of television has made the public more symbol-minded. Symbols are the oldest form of written language; the crown, the cross, the swastika, the hammer and sickle, the torch, the shell, the snake, and the eagle are all symbols which speak often more clearly than words. Flags are potent symbols. But the best symbol is a human being, who can be responsive. A human symbol can talk to us and we can talk to it; hence the particular virtue of friendly little Minnegasco! A good symbol is often the only thing that can transform an abstract, perhaps somewhat unfriendly, name into a reality and finally into a personality.

2. The Principle of Suiting the Message and Means of Communication to the Audience

One of the most serious dangers in public relations communication is the illusion of having achieved it when in fact there has been no communication at all—only a one-way outpouring. A mass media approach is generally noticed only by those who agree with it; the rest ignore it. Yet the sender, convinced of his rightness and knowing the wide potential coverage of newspapers, magazines, or broadcasting, assumes that his message has been attended to and has done its work. People see what they want to see and hear what they want to hear, and therefore the act of sending is not equivalent to communication; to assume that it is often results in unpleasant surprises.

The case of the unhappy deer hunters

THE PROBLEM. Every fall in a large Midwestern state approximately a half million deer hunters pour into the woods to bring back the venison. About four out of five of them are disappointed (sometimes the proportion is greater than that). What a customer relations problem for the state conservation department, especially since much of the department's annual income comes from deer hunters' license fees!

To make it worse, a great number of these hunters fancy themselves experts, and this delusion is not confined to the city sportsmen who enter the woods once a year; it is probably endemic among the small-town and rural men who feel that they know all about deer through their own experience and their forefathers' life in the wilderness. Very few men are willing to blame their own lack of skill for their failure to bring back the antlers.

Actually, the management of a statewide deer herd is extremely complex, and few individuals making random observations within a limited area can know much about it. Literally tens of thousands of wooded or brushy square miles are involved. In each of these square miles a hunter may see only a few deer and may be fortunate to shoot one during the season; yet census-check drives will show that there may be thirty to thirty-five deer in each square-mile area. The total deer herd of the state is more than 600,000, and during a long snowy winter up to 50,000 deer may starve to death from lack of browsing food. Scores of experienced men are needed to estimate deer population by spot checks, to get an idea of how many are shot legally during the season, and to tramp the frozen cedar swamps to see how many deer are starving in the places where they hole up for shelter in the cold winter.

Actually the limiting factor on deer population, in most instances, is winter food and not hunter pressure; and all the grandfathers' tales about the times when there were deer behind every tree (or no deer at all) are probably true, though the dates and places may be somewhat hazy. Big pine timber stands support only a few deer because there is nothing growing in the shadow of the dark trees for them to browse on. Obviously, in the days of the first pioneers and the Indians there were not many deer in the virgin forests; neither were there many hunters. With the clearing of forests, which were replaced with tasty green brush, came a boom in the deer population. Next came fires and unrestricted market slaughter of deer for meat—and a great decimation of the deer herds, which reached their lowest numbers about 1900 to 1910. Following this period, a fire-control program resulted in a great increase in woods food available for deer, and this, together with laws preventing market slaughter, brought about a deer boom.

For some years now the state conservationists charged with management of the deer herd have felt that the herd has outgrown its food supply. The large number of deer starved every bad winter and the poor condition and small number of fawns of those surviving in the spring are evidence. The state conservation officers feel now that if more deer are killed by hunters in the fall, there will be no total diminution of the herd. Laws restricting shooting to bucks were passed in the 1920s, but the Conservation Department has, for the past several years, instituted a limited doe season.

Now for the essence of the state conservation department's public relations problem:

Last fall's deer season was very poor. Only about 60,000 deer were shot compared with about 100,000 in several preceding years. Some hunters and hunting-resort operators have made a great outcry. Bills have been introduced into the state legislature which would take deer regulations out of the hands of the conservation department and put them under the control of county supervisors—dozens of rules for dozens of counties! The conservation department is composed of men averaging more than five years' university training and about fifteen years' experience on the job. They feel that they know their business and that no one else knows it so well. They believe that a bad, rainy opening day of the season last fall was the main reason for the smaller number of deer taken and that a limited doe season should be continued. They are particularly stung by the proposal before the legislature that their carefully planned scientific study be scrapped and control be thrown into the hands of local amateurs. It is a refutation of all they have worked for most of their lives.

What has gone wrong? Why does a significant portion of the deer-hunting public seemingly lack confidence in the ability of their own state conservation game-management department? Has there been a failure to communicate? What should have been done differently? What is the next step?

This is a public relations problem—a persuasive communications problem. Laws cannot solve it; in fact, law right now seems to be in danger of going the other way.

SOLUTIONS. In the past the state conservation department has relied mainly upon the following ways of telling its story to the public:

The press. The department has maintained a steady flow of good releases to daily and weekly newspapers of the state. The articles have been widely printed and, generally speaking, press contacts are favorable. Many editors and outdoor writers are willing to go out of their way to support the knowledge and positions of the conservation department officers, even at the risk, sometimes, of personal unpopularity.

Department publications. The department publishes a magazine and booklets. They are well written and attractively illustrated with photographs and cartoons and contain all the facts a man would need to be well informed.

Conservation clubs and schools. State conservation officers make numerous appearances before clubs and schools, frequently showing motion pictures or slides of their work.

Other methods of public contact have included some radio and TV broadcasting, although conservation department members are unhappy about the controversial situations in which they have been placed by some broadcasters who are more interested in "conflict" and a "lively show" than in true reporting. Department scientists are not so articulate on the air sometimes as they would wish to be, and even a man who knows his field well may suffer when contrasted with an impassioned opponent who may ask more questions than can be answered with absolute certainty.

DISCUSSION. The methods just described seem to be missing the target. Is the method of communication used suitable to those for whom it is intended? Obviously not, or the conservation department would not be in danger of having its authority stripped from it by the pressure upon the state legislature exercised by disgruntled hunters and resort operators.

The trouble seems to be that the news stories, booklets, and club and school appearances have been doing a good job of informing and influencing the segment of the public which is *already* well aware of the ability and devotion of the state game-management department. More news stories, more newspaper support, more booklets, and more speeches to schools and conservation clubs will not succeed in communicating with those who do not read a great deal, who have their own minds already firmly set and will ignore printed material, who fail to attend talks, or who will take their opinions primarily from a circle of similarly minded friends rather than from what some distant, aloof, scientific expert may say. A new approach is needed, if these people are to be reached.

The key to contact with the opposition may lie in asking two questions: To whom do these people turn as leaders of opinion? How do they arrive at their opinions? It seems probable that they draw their opinions primarily from their circle of friends. Primarily these opposition groups consist of rather close-knit, small-town sportsmen. Leaders of opinion in these circles tend to "know from experience" and to distrust or ignore other sources.

If the aid of the key persons could be enlisted, other members in the group might be willing to open their ears to thoughts which run contrary to the presently prevailing norms in their cliques. One solution might be for conservation officers to ask their help in going into the woods in late winter to count deer-starvation kills or to help in checking browse conditions. This would have to be done with care, because one thing which may be causing some local leaders to assert their own knowledge strongly is a feeling of inferiority in the presence of the irritating assurance of the supposedly scientific, highly educated professional game-management men. Much of the communication with key people in these groups must be managed personally; only then will other media of information and persuasion have a chance to be heard.

Another useful solution might be to set up demonstration areas where game-management methods could be shown in outdoor museums. The conservation department controls several large sites adjoining main highways. A walk-through or drive-through plan with signs, a small zoo, and rest and picnic facilities could tell the story of deer-herd management in an interesting and convincing way to those who have to be *shown* because they are "from Missouri." If local labor and advice is solicited in arranging these museums further participation will be gained. Promotion of these places and the attendance of large crowds would doubtless be gratifying to local resort owners, and might answer, in part, their question: "What does the state conservation department ever do for us?"

Other efforts to encourage participation and favorable two-way communication along the lines suggested could be arranged. The important thing is to suit the message and the means of communication to the predisposition of the audience which they have thus far failed to reach.

3. The Principle of Speaking the Receiver's Language

Even when a communication is directed toward the right people, it may still fail because its words are outside their range of understanding or because they convey meanings to the receivers quite different from those which the writer had in mind. The danger of misunderstanding is not the only cause for concern. The writer may be under the illusion that words wh'ch are reasonable and familiar to him have done their work and that he needs to make no further effort. He may be suffering from the "illusion" of communication.

The case of gobbledygook[2] employee communications[3]. Failure of communication, to a large extent caused by different understanding of words, created widespread interest among public relations people during and after the nationwide steel strike of 1959. Two organizations, Group Attitudes Corporation, a subsidiary of Hill & Knowlton, the public relations firm which was representing the steel companies, and, later and independently, Opinion Research Corporation of Princeton, New Jersey, conducted extensive surveys to discover how well workers understood words commonly used in the negotiations and what their reactions to them were.

THE PROBLEM. Opinion Research surveys have shown that only about 12 per cent of the employees reading typical economic messages addressed to them by business really grasp their meaning. Much of this material is written on a high school–graduate or college level, and many of the employees have not progressed thus far in school; or sometimes their memory of technical terms has faded through disuse.

Words affect our intellects and our feelings. To impart *information,* the writer and the reader (or hearer) should not only know what a word means, but should both have the same meaning in mind. To provoke the *feeling* desired, a writer must use a word that awakens the right emotional overtones or connotations in the mind of the receiver. Neither one of these achievements is easy.

Consider the word "capitalism," for example. Out of hundreds of workers who were carefully interviewed by Opinion Research in late 1959, only 55 per cent claimed that they knew the word, and only 26 per cent could describe its meaning. Those who did attempt a definition often came through with quite unfavorable emotional reactions, such as "The wealthiest people take over," "Big business has so much money that they freeze the little fellow out of business," "A dictatorship by the rich."

It is quite obvious that to the exponents of capitalism the word has one meaning and that to most workers it either means little or arouses hostility. How a word acquires unfavorable connotations would be difficult to discover, but we might suspect that while American workingmen unequivocally reject communism, they have picked up some of the meanings of the word "capitalism" given to it by Karl Marx and his followers. Words can serve

---

[2] A word devised by Congressman Maverick of Texas to describe high-sounding, meaningless government communications.

[3] John W. Hill, chairman of the board, Hill & Knowlton, Inc., in *Public Relations Journal,* August, 1960, and from a January, 1960, study of Opinion Research Corporation of Princeton, N.J.

equally as instruments of confusion and of enlightenment, and agreement can be achieved only when we are talking about the same things. "Capitalism" is not one of these agreed-upon words, although tests show that "free enterprise" comes much closer to being mutually understood. Any words, however, can become hackneyed and acquire unpleasant or different meanings over a period of time, depending upon who uses them and for what purpose.

SOLUTIONS. To convey information, writers should be sure that all the words they use will be readily understood correctly by their readers. The Group Attitudes Corporation survey at the time of the steel strike, for example, found that such words as "accrue," "contemplate," and "delete" had little meaning for the readers.

"Accrue" was changed to "pile up or collect."

"Contemplate" became "think about or expect."

"Delete" was translated into "cancel, take out, or remove."

Whole phrases were also found to be confusing or meaningless. "Changes would be sanctioned only if . . ." became "no changes would be allowed unless . . ."

"Jointly chaired" meant "took turns as chairmen."

"Reject summarily" was another way of saying "turn down flat."

The words and phrases that the Group Attitudes survey found to be most frequently misunderstood and their translations are contained in the table below.

THIRTY WORDS AND THIRTY PHRASES*

Following are thirty words and thirty phrases found by Group Attitudes Corporation's interviewers to be most frequently misunderstood by steelworkers and a translation of these words and phrases into "steelworker" language.

Thirty Words

"accrue"—*pile up; collect*

"compute"—*figure*

"concession"—*giving up (something)*

"contemplate"—*think about; expect*

"delete"—*cancel; take out; remove*

"designate"—*name; appoint*

"deterioration"—*breaking down; wearing away*

"detriment"—*hurt; damage; harm*

"economic problem"—*a cost problem*

"efficiency"—*the way it should be (e.g. operating a machine the way it should be operated)*

"embody"—*contain; include; hold*

"equitable"—*fair; just*

"excerpt"—*section; part*

"facilitate"—*help along; speed up*

"fortuitously"—*by chance; accidentally; luckily*

"generate"—*create; build; produce*

"impediment"—*barrier; road block*

"inadequate"—*not enough*

"initiate"—*begin; start*

"increment"—*raise; increase*

"inevitably"—*in the end; finally*

"injurious"—*damaging; harmful*

"jeopardy"—*danger*

"magnitude"—*size*

* *Public Relations Journal,* August, 1960.

"modify"—*change; alter*
"objectivity"—*fairness*
"pursuant"—*in agreement with*

"perpetuate"—*keep alive; continue*
"subsequently"—*later*
"ultimate"—*final; end*

Thirty Phrases

"avoid further inflationary pressures"—*avoid the things that make prices go up*

"best long-term interests"—*better in the long run*

"changes would be sanctioned only if . . ."—*no changes would be allowed unless*

"endeavored to interest Union leaders affirmatively"—*tried to get the Union leaders to agree to*

"exclusive function"—*sole right*

"fundamentally the same"—*almost exactly the same*

"insofar as practicable"—*as far as possible*

"impartial men"—*fair men; men without an axe to grind*

"in all sincerity and complete conviction as to the merit in the public interest"—*because we sincerely believe it is best for everyone*

"jointly chaired"—*take turns as chairmen*

"meet reasonable requirements of business demands"—*do our best to serve our customers*

"misrepresented these proposals as devices"—*unjustly attacked the proposals as ways*

"modify the discipline"—*lighten the penalty*

"men of outstanding qualifications and objectivity"—*fair men of broad experience*

"not justified on any basis of equity"—*all give and no take; not a fair deal*

"protection against arbitrary discharge"—*guard against being fired without cause*

"representatives of both parties"—*men from both the Union and the Company*

"retain the sole discretion to decide"—*be the one to decide*

"reject summarily"—*turn down flat*

"seek to demonstrate a cooperative attitude"—*try to be fair*

"share new economic progress"—*share in future gains*

"substantially in accordance"—*almost exactly like*

"take precedence"—*come first*

"take affirmative action"—*go along with; move ahead*

"to make it consistent with"—*to make it agree with*

"ultimate solution"—*the final answer; the end result*

"union studiously vilified the companies"—*the Union went out of its way to attack the companies*

"unnecessarily restrictive"—*too binding; too strict*

"wholly inconsistent with their professed desire"—*not what they say they want to do*

"with the objective of facilitating"—*with the idea of helping*

Words convey more than information, however. They frequently have strong emotional overtones, and sometimes a word may be familiar and understood, but not liked. In a survey late in 1959 Opinion Research attempted to delve into this aspect of word recognition by asking workers not only whether they were familiar with words and could define them, but also what thoughts occurred to them most readily in connection with them. Often words which might be considered almost synonymous had very different "favorable-unfavorable" ratings.

Management sometimes uses "work stoppage" and "strike" as if they were the same thing; yet to employees a strike is considered largely justified and has little unfavorable connotation, whereas a work stoppage has many unfavorable feelings associated with it because it can also be construed as a wildcat strike or even a lockout. Employees generally regard the term "profits" with favor but prefer "company net income." They may understand profits better but feel that an aura of "excess profits" or "profiteering" clings to the word. Both "investors" in a company and "stockholders" are regarded favorably, but stockholders is the more popular designation because investors are felt to be a distant group, bigger, and less intimately connected with the company. "Layoff" is a very bad word (though most people know what it means), but "reduction in the work force" is a little less unpleasant.

The phrase "hidden wages and salaries" provokes a generally unfavorable reaction, probably because of the possible sinister meaning of "hidden," but "pension, insurance, and hospitalization benefits" scores near the top in favorable response. "Fringe benefits" is well accepted, but "employee benefits" is more popular.

Much of this reaction to a word depends upon how you look at it. To the factory manager the money spent in hiring mill hands is "labor costs," but to the mill hands themselves, it is "money paid in wages and benefits." If the factory manager is writing to the board of directors and to other factory managers, he will obviously use one term, if to employees, another.

"Piece rate" is a bad word; "incentive pay" is much better (although less understood).

"Annuity" was understood by only 25 per cent of the workers interviewed, but was regarded favorably by those who did know the meaning of the word.

"Compulsory union membership" was only slightly favored, probably because of the word "compulsory," but the phrase "union shop" scored near the top.

"Government ownership of business" was less well regarded than "socialism" (although both are on the unfavorable side of the score), presumably because few workers have a good idea of what socialism is.

And, interestingly enough, the name "corporation" is much more coldly received than "company"—a holdover, perhaps, from the phrase "soulless corporation."

DISCUSSION. Why do so many businessmen use cold, little understood, or unfavorable "businessese" terms when writing to employees and to the general public? Their language fails completely to communicate. It is too simple to say that businessmen aren't writers. While most of them are indeed not writers (they are accountants, lawyers, and administrators), some of them are good writers, and they have the means to hire good writers (though they may not know a piece of good exposition when they see it). The same accusation of failure in communication can be leveled at scientists, educators, heads of government bureaus, doctors, and generally experts in *any* field.

Probably the main reasons for a man's inability to speak another man's language are selfishness, lack of imagination, and a desire to impress his colleagues rather than those at whom the message should be aimed. Good writing is not just a matter of knowing a great many words and stringing them together prettily; it first consists in putting yourself into the other person's shoes and saying, "If I were a steelworker in Youngstown, Ohio, how would I understand and regard this?" or "If I were a housewife in Des Moines, Iowa, what would my reaction be?" To do this takes a lively and experienced imagination. It is not a job for the boss's son just back home from a literary course at the university. The writer has to want to communicate and be interested in the people he is addressing. And finally the writer must forget about the language of his own trade or clan and write for the benefit of others, not his fellows. The erudition that impresses the company president may confuse or anger the outsider. Speaking the receiver's language is the least the writer can do in return for the gift of his time and attention!

4. The Principle of Timeliness

Probably the main reason why big recent events constitute news is that most people have a share in them. The events are a part of their common experience. It is no accident that most conversations between strangers begin with the weather, which is current and of universal interest.

Alert public relations men are on the lookout for news—the more current and commonly experienced the better—which will help them to approach their public. Timeliness is frequently the key to attention, and it offers a rare opportunity to communicate, since news that has been built up by the press has a ready-made audience. If everybody is participating in an event and talking about it, related items are certain to be absorbed also.

The case of the two hurricanes. Hurricane Diane[4] in August, 1955, drowned Connecticut more thoroughly than had any flood or storm ever before in the state's history, and the Southern New England Telephone Company faced one of its greatest emergencies. Some 80,000 of its 970,000 phones went out of service because of washed-out lines and offices.

Though a disaster is never pleasant, this one offered opportunity as well as challenge to the telephone company. The challenge was to repair service quickly, a work that crews immediately set about with characteristic efficiency; the opportunity was manifold. The first job was to inform the public about repair efforts. This was done by newspaper ads and news releases

[4] *Public Relations News,* Oct. 24, 1955.

and by radio and television coverage. Major credit was given to telephone company employees, in recognition of their work. The second job was to install emergency equipment and to let people know of its location and availability. Public cooperation in limiting phone calls was requested.

One group which needed emergency help immediately was the press itself; restoration of lines and aid to news staffers was a major order of business. Telephone men supplied reports of conditions, which were worked into releases by the public relations department, and telephone photographers supplied photos for newspapers and movie films for television stations on an around-the-clock rush basis. By prior arrangement, the telephone company had contracted with several local professional photographers to keep movie film on hand and to take pictures in case of a disaster. Work crews from other A.T.&T. member telephone companies came into the state to help. Southern New England Telephone Company seized the opportunity to point out how its national connections aided patrons in fast restoration of service.

Within five days after the floods, enough film had been processed to prepare a twenty-minute sound movie with a commentary which could be shown to employee groups and service clubs. A special issue of the com-

Figure 12-2. Hurricane Diane was a disaster for residents of Putnam, Connecticut, and for Southern New England Telephone service there and elsewhere, but intelligent public relations capitalized on the great public interest in the event.

pany's employee magazine containing fifty-four pictures of the floods was off the presses just one week after the disaster struck, and at the same time it could be announced that all phone service, except in completely wrecked homes, had been restored. Two days later a statewide newspaper ad, entitled "Picking Up the Pieces Is Never Easy," reported the renewed service, expressed sympathy for those who had suffered losses, and thanked the public for its understanding and patience. The same message was added to bill inserts and was later printed in the annual report to stockholders. Letters of appreciation and favorable editorials in the newspapers reflected public appreciation for a good job well done and well understood.

The main thing that a telephone company has to sell is service; but that subject is extremely uninteresting while the service keeps on functioning normally. But let a major disaster disrupt service, along with most other aspects of life, and the company can be sure of the keenest public interest. A capable public relations man will anticipate this condition and capitalize upon it when it happens.

Hurricane Donna,[5] which first hit in Florida in 1960, like Diane offered an opportunity and a challenge to the public relations personnel of the Atlanta regional office of the Insurance Information Institute. One of the staff members was assigned to go to Florida to see that press inquiries about storm damage there were properly handled.

A member of the New York staff was also assigned to hurricane watch, and a precaution story was telegraphed to news media in the path of the northward-advancing storm. A release was issued telling of the steps being taken by the insurance business to survey and adjust the claims in the Florida area.

As the storm hit, an estimate of insured losses in Florida was released for newspapers, radio, and TV. INSURED LOSS FROM HURRICANE DONNA PUT AT $135 MILLION; 500,000 CLAIMS EXPECTED, said the headline in the *Wall Street Journal.* INSURANCE EXPERTS FLOODING INTO DONNA-STRICKEN AREAS, proclaimed the *Miami Herald,* which also carried a two-column box listing seven steps in how to handle damage claims. INSURERS RUSH PAYMENTS — DONNA TAKES HEAVY TOLL IN NORTHEASTERN STATES, said the *Journal of Commerce.* DONNA LEAVES $135 MILLION TAB FOR THE INSURANCE BOYS TO PAY, said the *New York Daily News.*

Although insurance companies are not particularly enthusiastic about hurricanes, the publicity associated with Donna served to bring wide recognition to the Insurance Information Institute as a source of information for the press, provided an opportunity to tell the public about the extensive efforts of the capital stock insurance companies to settle losses quickly and

[5] Burton Youngman, director of research, Insurance Information Service, New York, December, 1960.

fairly, and may have been responsible for actually cutting losses by aiding in timely warnings to people farther up the Atlantic coast as the storm moved north after first striking Florida. "It's an ill wind . . ."

The case of the nonmerging bank[6]. A rumor which threatened to be embarrassing was turned into a benefit by alert public relations management at the American National Bank and Trust Company of Chicago late in 1960.

American National was the youngest member of the Chicago La Salle Street financial community, having been founded in 1933, but had grown rapidly and by 1960 ranked fifth in the city. During that year a merger was made between two other major loop banks, and rumors started circulating that American National was also going to be part of a merger. In December the *Chicago Tribune* carried a story that American National was considering joining another large bank.

Officers of American National were deeply concerned about these rumors, for one of the principal points of the bank's marketing strategy was its emphasis upon personal and individual attention for each account. Many of the bank's customers made inquiries, for they feared that if American National were absorbed by a larger bank, they would lose that valued personal touch. It was decided to issue a vigorous denial.

The denial first went to the bank's own staff, assuring them that the rumors were not founded on fact and that none of the 700 staff members need worry about losing their jobs because of a merger with another institution. Later, reporters from the four daily newspapers received the same emphatic denial. Despite the bank's efforts to contradict them, rumors continued to circulate.

At this point the bank's public relations director and counseling firm had an inspiration. For some time the bank had been considering signing a twenty-year lease for two additional floors of space in the building which it occupied, with options upon six additional floors. In normal times this would have made only slight news, but as an answer to rumors of consolidation, it would definitely be page-one material. Why not expedite the signing of the lease and with it also release news of the bank's expanded earnings and success in the year just ending?

A press conference was scheduled between the president of the bank and the four financial editors of the daily newspapers, at which the news could be released and all questions could be answered. At the same time an advertisement was prepared to run in the Chicago dailies and in the *New York Times* covering the same facts, reprints of which were mailed to 6,000 correspondent bank customers and prospects. And a direct-mailing

[6] George H. Dempsey, director of public relations, American National Bank and Trust Company of Chicago, March, 1961.

piece of a similar nature was also prepared to go to all checking-account customers with their statements at the end of the month.

News coverage and response were excellent. Not only were the rumors laid to rest by a forthright, timely communications program but in addition, many people not connected with the bank received a new conception of its size, growth, and determination to remain an independent part of Chicago's banking community. The response from many customers expressed their approval. Had this situation been left to drift, it could have been injurious; but by timely seizing of news interest, it became a benefit.

The case of automation.[7] Sometimes news interest is more gradual. A new word endowed with powerful new meanings may swim into the journalists firmament and shine there for months or years. One such term was "automation," as used in the United States in the 1950s. In 1951, for example, approximately fifteen articles concerned with automation were published in periodicals with general circulation, and by 1953 the number had increased to thirty.

The word fired the imagination of magazine and newspaper writers. A syndicated story in a large New York newspaper was headed AUTO-MATION EDGING OUT HUMANS. Another story in another newspaper carried this headline: MAN VS. MACHINE—WILL MACHINES MAKE MANKIND OBSO-LETE? And still another questioned, WILL HUMAN LABOR BE OUTMODED? Labor unions began using it in bargaining, and Congress held hearings upon the subject.

Actually there was nothing very new in the concept of automation in industry. In some ways the use of automatic controls in in-line manufacturing processes is as old as the beginnings of the industrial revolution in the 1700s. Certainly it had been commonplace in processes like oil refining or chemical production for many years. What was new was its increasing application to such industries as automobile making, where assembly lines had largely been hand-tended until then. Here automation resulted in increased efficiency and the need for fewer workers.

One of the big producers of automatic controls in the United States is the Minneapolis-Honeywell Company. The company and its public relations counsel, Carl Byoir & Associates, saw both a problem and an opportunity in the yeasty bubbles of news interest and confusion centering about automation. The problem lay in threats of attempts to hold progress back, arising from the workers' fears that automation would take away their jobs. (As a matter of fact, producing more goods more cheaply is an unequivocal benefit; and the social problems arising from change may be

[7] James H. Porterfield, vice president, Carl Byoir & Associates, Inc., at the Third Annual Midwestern Conference on Public Relations, University of Wisconsin, October, 1959.

solved by other means than attacking the beneficial change itself.) The *opportunity* lay in the desire of important audiences to understand the term better by knowing all the facts, and in the way in which Minneapolis-Honeywell could justifiably identify itself as an authority in the field.

To develop the program, a survey was first conducted to find the opinions of businessmen upon automation. A 2,000-word booklet was then prepared to sum up the facts and arguments in relation to the subject of automation; a major series of speeches by Minneapolis-Honeywell executives was arranged and mirrored in news releases and reprints all over the nation; and newspaper feature stories, and trade-magazine and general-magazine articles were also developed. A very extensive publicity program on the actual installation of automatic devices by Minneapolis-Honeywell was also carried on.

In the course of these stories, public relations people came to the conclusion that one of the sources of misunderstanding lay in the ominous and little-understood terms of engineers working with automation installations. A dictionary of automation terms was prepared, and the book proved to be immensely popular, more than 40,000 copies being distributed upon request, as well as serving as story material in 105 newspapers and 130 magazines.

The benefits of this campaign to Minneapolis-Honeywell, as a leader in automatic controls for machinery, would not have been possible had it not been for the timeliness of its public relations communication. Without such public interest no amount of promotion or advertising could have achieved the same results because people simply would not have listened.

5. The Principle of Imagination in Dramatizing Communications

Stunts have somewhat fallen out of favor among many conservative public relations people in recent years. The excesses of their fraudulent use among Hollywood and theatrical promoters, a certain country-fair flavor, and the fact that victimized editors were frequently roasted by their own readers contributed to the decline. But since so much good communication is still nonverbal, worthwhile dramatizations that are honest and in good taste often manage to make a lasting impression and to say things that words alone cannot so well convey.

The case of the paper swim suit. One such imaginative approach was put on by a major chemical manufacturing company a few years ago. The company had invented a chemical which would retard the wetting of paper so that it would not lose its strength and break easily. The product had many important potential uses, such as in making shopping bags which would not burst and other protective packaging; but simply to tell about it was very dull. The solution was a *demonstration*.

A press conference was set up at the Waldorf-Astoria Hotel in New

York City. The main feature, besides the usual press kits of releases, fact sheets, pictures, and statements by company officers, was a large and very wet bath shower spraying into a temporary floor pool in the middle of the room. At the proper moment, a beautiful girl arrived, dressed in a paper bathing suit, and skipped into the shower. Needless to say, nothing happened to the bathing suit. Thanks to the new chemical, it *was* water-resistant.

Other paper objects were also dunked, but the paper bathing suit made the biggest impression and the best pictures.

Making a railroad fashionable.[8] The railroads' troubles have been so well publicized in recent years that if you were to ask the average American what he associates with rail travel, he would probably refer to comfort, dependability, and safety—but not to glamour; yet glamour is what both railroads and steamships greatly need if they are to keep passenger patronage.

To help meet this problem, public relations people of the Baltimore and Ohio Railroad Company staged a ladies' fashion show on board one of their crack trains in the Union Station at Washington in the winter of 1960. Put on in cooperation with a major Washington department store, it was held in honor of the women members of Congress and of the wives of congressmen from the thirteen states in the area served by the road.

Four lounge and dining cars were used; but for the twenty-one models to walk down their entire length each time would mean a cluttered 360-foot trek amid the guests to their converted baggage car "dressing room." This problem was solved by placing a red carpet alongside the train, so that the fashion-show could be seen outside as well as from the cars. The use of four cars also required four commentators, to fit the spoken word to the guests' span of vision.

Five weeks before the event, engraved invitations went to the congressmen, wives, and other nonmedia guests; those who accepted were sent admission cards. A week later the press was invited by special letter. Of the 121 media people invited, 61 accepted. A press kit was assembled; power lines were provided for TV; arrangements were made to seat visitors and media representatives at tables reserved for natives of their several states; each guest was given a special corsage made of the official flower of her state; and flags of the states were displayed on poles along the platform.

The show lasted 1¼ hours. Refreshments were served to all who attended, and each guest received gifts of a barbecue apron imprinted with the B & O insignia and a handkerchief stamped with a department store's name.

Media coverage by press, radio, and TV was excellent. Although fashion

[8] *Public Relations News,* May 9, 1960.

shows commonly receive very little notice, the use of a new location made an otherwise routine event into news.

6. The Principle of Two-way Communication

In today's complex society, where people are more talked *at* than ever before, the opportunities to talk back are not very numerous. Yet two-way communication is the essence of communication itself. How is it to be achieved in large organizations where the natural flow of communications always seems to be downward and never upward? If it is not achieved, what are the psychological consequences of its neglect?

Failure to achieve two-way communication, or at least to make recipients feel that they *can* answer, results in some serious problems. One is the resentment a person feels when he is always talked at and has no opportunity to direct his own destiny, a rock upon which the paternalism of many industries (and of parents and governments too) has foundered. Companies have sometimes done everything for their employees in low-cost housing, recreation programs, benefits, and retirements only to be shocked by ingratitude. They should not have expected that good will could be bought with good works. People prefer that which they have made themselves. "A poor . . . thing, sir, but mine own," says Touchstone in Shakespeare's *As You Like It,* in a somewhat similar reaction.

Another cause of resentment arising from one-way communication is a feeling of helplessness. "I am so little and alone and the Great White Father is so big and powerful!" No one likes to be afraid or subordinate, and in today's world fear and loneliness are common feelings. This is one of the reasons why workers value a union, which gives them a feeling of equality. It is said that the steel-company magnate, Judge Gary, used to say that there was no need of a union, that his office door was always open to any employee who wished to discuss a problem. But most of us realize the inequality of the positions of the two men on either side of the desk.

Continued lack of two-way communication has another serious aspect for would-be communicators: It results in the inability of recipients to hear! Unless they have a chance to take part in some way in the communications process, they soon turn a deaf ear to sources which for them are no longer interesting. There are many other more rewarding things to attend to. Those who wish to be heard, then, must also be listeners and must show that they are listening.

Two-way communication, upward as well as downward, is a necessity to companies that wish their employees and communities to hear them, to politicians who desire real support, to school administrators who seek public understanding and votes, and to governments that wish to influence other people abroad. It is a problem of particular importance today because of the size of almost all organizations and the one-way nature of communication in the omnipresent newspapers, magazines, television pro-grams, and films, always pouring out but never stopping for an instant to listen to whatever thoughts their output may have stirred up. Only genuine two-way communication can overcome latent feelings of resentment, help-lessness, and boredom, and can win genuine gratitude for those who are willing to engage in it.

Revitalizing a suggestion program.[9] Suggestion boxes, which are fairly widespread through American industry, offer a formal, limited beginning at two-way communication. Employees often use them for voicing gripes or for submitting bright ideas which they hope will result in financial gain or improvement of status; but since they *are* available and anonymous, sug-gestion boxes do indicate that management has an ear.

Twenty-seven suggestions submitted per 100 employees is the national average in any one year in industrial plants. In 1958, when Owens-Corning Fiberglas Corporation of Toledo, Ohio, noted that its box activity was far below this level, it decided to open up this disused channel of communica-tion.

Ten key principles were applied to the system:

> Secure energetic support of top management.
> Set up awards large enough to furnish adequate incentives.
> Make it easy for employees to make suggestions.
> Open the system to all types of employees.
> Process and act upon all entries promptly.
> Make sure that each employee knows that each suggestion has received full and careful consideration and why it has been turned down or accepted.
> Pay only for constructive ideas.
> Adopt all those paid for.
> Give public recognition to all winners.
> Use every possible means to encourage participation in the program.

A suggestion-award committee was set up, and suggestions were proc-essed quickly and thoroughly. A manual was prepared to guide the com-mittee and other administrators who might be called in, and the maximum award for suggestions was raised from $1,500 to $2,500.

The name "Ideas for Progress" was applied to the new program, which was promoted among employees by an extensive cartoon-type, in-plant program including booklets, posters, letterheads, memo pads, pay-envelope stuffers, and employee publications.

The suggestion blank itself was redesigned with spaces to fill in labeled "This is the present condition," "I suggest," and "This is what will happen." The bottom part of the blank, perforated and serially numbered to match

[9] *Public Relations News,* Sept. 15, 1958.

the upper portion, was to be torn off by the employee to serve as a receipt. The numbers were intended to preserve anonymity. Boxes were repainted and located in important traffic spots in the plant near promotional posters.

At the start of the program employees received a letter from the president at their homes which described the Ideas for Progress plan and stressed not only the awards, but also the importance to the company and thus to the employee's job of steadily increasing efficiency of operation.

In the first six months of the new system, the suggestion rate increased 50 per cent above what it had been and rose 32 per cent above the national average. Awards were approximately $20,000, and savings were estimated at $100,000.

While a suggestion program has limited objectives, it also has strong intangible values in establishing that management is listening and is interested.

Harnessing the power of small-group discussion.[10] Real two-way communication which overcomes the curse of bigness and impersonality must go deeper than casual talk. E. I. du Pont de Nemours & Company decided seriously to explore employee opinion on a nationwide basis in the middle 1950s.

THE PROBLEMS were widespread in a very large company, operating all over the United States with thousands of employees in many plants, ranging from scientific workers to sweepers. It was one thing to tell supervisors and employees that costs were rising, competition for sales was intense, and the premium on high and rising productivity was never greater; it was quite another thing to get employees to adopt the problem as their own individual responsibility; to visualize their own role in solving it; to originate ideas for improving performance within their sphere of action; and to accept ideas for change introduced from outside of their own operational group. Chain-of-command orders may impart information, but they cannot create cooperation, imagination, and a genuine desire to be of help.

It is widely recognized that small-group discussions within operating areas provide one of the best ways of give-and-take two-way communication; yet such discussions have their dangers, since, unless well planned, they may be a wandering waste of time. Dominant leaders may offend participants, and ignorant or uninterested leaders may disgust them. "Getting to know you better" sometimes results in less respect and interest rather than more. Even to maintain effective small-group discussions in a large multiplant company requires the training of many adroit discussion leaders, almost every one of them converted out of present middle and lower management. How was this to be done?

THE SOLUTIONS. It was decided to hold discussions within certain departments, for example, sales, engineering, plant management, research,

[10] Opinion Research Corporation, Princeton, N.J., study, June, 1955.

and plant-personnel management. The objectives of the discussion training were to be to save time in meetings, bring out more ideas, solve on-the-job problems, build a sense of participation, improve decision making, and build acceptance for management policy. A headquarters institute was set up in which 160 men were given a forty-hour training program in discussion. Classes were limited to groups of eight. These men then returned to plants and other company locations and gave a fifteen-hour similar training program in discussion-leading techniques to more than 4,000 du Pont managers, supervisors, and foremen.

The main points stressed in the training were careful preparation for meetings, stated objectives, stimulation of full participation, keeping a neutral role for leadership, staying on the subject, and getting participants to put ideas in writing as a means of forcing concrete thinking. Through focusing on these objectives, meetings moved to results in a pleasant atmosphere, and people got to know, respect, and like one another better. The main problems remaining were for leaders to stay neutral, since the nature of supervisors who lead discussion is to be dominant, and to stimulate participation by members of the group who, either through caution or shyness or indifference, took little part. Some problems, of course, cannot be solved by such discussions. Certain personal situations demand a private approach; and certain matters of broader company policy should be recognized as being beyond the group's proper authority. In initiating this program, the company had no intention of abdicating its responsibility to run the organization, nor did employees expect it to do so.

The benefits were many. The executive in charge of one of two plants in which a pilot plan of the program was first tested said:

> We don't want people just to take orders. We want them to have a part in many job decisions. We have a lot of operators who are doing more than just working with their hands. They are intelligent people who are closest to the job. They see these problems first and often come up with the best answers.

Other means of two-way communication. Surveys of public opinion (employee, stockholder, or community, for example) are in themselves a two-way communication device. The surveyor not only learns what is thought but also gives the thinkers a chance to express themselves in telling. Reports on the results and action, if any, are usually welcomed by participants.

Letters to the editor of company publications, to which careful, considerate answers are given, are another form of response. The writers are listened to, and others with the same thoughts who might have written felt that they, too, have been answered. The editor must be prepared to respond to all sorts of questions, not just to the nice ones!

Mass meetings are a less effective form of two-way communication, because when a group gets beyond the small-discussion size of eight or ten, the opportunity for questions is limited by the patience of the mass, and only the more courageous or less wise are likely to talk much. Nevertheless, when carefully and democratically run, mass meetings are better than straight published pronouncements. Planted questions may be necessary to bring out points and to get the ball rolling.

Tours with well-trained guides, committee participation in planning and executing events, and employee representation of the company in civic activities outside the walls are other ways of achieving two-way communication.

There are many good ways of handing down orders and information (bulletins, newspapers and magazines, public-address systems, large mass meetings, radio, and television, to mention only a few), but it still remains difficult, costly, and time-consuming to devise comparable ways of achieving communication *upward*. Yet effort expended upon it will be well worthwhile because of its profound effect in producing receptive attitudes and willingness to listen.

7. The Principle of Reaching Your Own People First

The front line of communication frequently consists of your own employees or the members of your organization. Not only do they constitute a significant public in themselves, but they also engage in effective word-of-mouth communication with other publics, and their actions frequently speak even louder than words. The old saying that "a man is known by the company he keeps" is reversible into "a company is known by the men it keeps."

Moreover, employees should feel that they enjoy a special communications relationship with their employer. The relation of friendship cannot, of course, be fully achieved in the bigness of modern organizations, but an approach can be made and will be appreciated.

INFORMATION. Every employee is regarded by his friends as an expert on his company. Patients in a hospital often confuse the orderlies with the head surgeon; the man who handles a minute portion of a chemical process is supposed to be informed upon the most abstruse details of modern chemical manufacturing; and the man who refuels the airplanes may be regarded by his friends as an expert in aviation. This confusion is particularly noticeable in the large cities, where many of us now live and where private life and professional activity are so often separated.

Under these circumstances, most people are ashamed to plead ignorance of their jobs when their friends question them, and it is only kindness to provide them with enough facts about the huge process in which they are engaged to enable them to discuss their work with enthusiasm and accuracy.

Nature abhors a vacuum, even an informational vacuum. If correct information is not provided, misinformation will flow in to take its place.

The data given need not be elaborate; sometimes they can be very simple. The Kroger Company has 1,400 supermarkets in 20 states with 40,000 full-time and 20,000 part-time employees. Its 1960 annual report for employees consisted of a 2½- by 4-inch wallet card with a capsule history of Kroger and description of its size on one side and a division of the Kroger sales dollar on the other side. The 1959 report was in the form of a grocery tape 1½- by 7 inches in eight pages telling the story of the previous year's sales.[11]

Many companies distribute full annual reports to employees just as they do to stockholders, while others carry information of this and other matters in employee newspapers and magazines. Whatever the method, the objective is the same: to help employees to present a better image of their company to the public. The informed employee is likely to be a better public relations representative than the one who has to confess that he doesn't know and that no one has ever bothered to tell him.

The worst situation of all, of course, develops when outside people learn of company developments through the public press before the employee has yet had a chance to be informed, and then ask him questions to which he must confess ignorance. This really results in a loss of face!

COOPERATION. Since employees communicate with other publics by what they *do* as much as by what they *say*, it is often necessary to seek active employee cooperation in public relations efforts.

This was true, for example, at the Baylor University Medical Center in 1959.[12] The hospital, like many others, suffered from the strains of high turnover, overcrowding, and lack of adequate staff during the war years and long afterwards; it had also, naturally, all the normal stress and strain of a hospital—tensions which can wear down even the most well-adjusted and congenial individuals.

There was an unintentional loss of good temper. Brusqueness too often replaced politeness and kindness; carelessness in interpersonal relationships produced friction between hospital groups as well as between the hospital family and the public. The war was well over, and working conditions had improved; yet poor attitudes had continued. It became necessary to focus employees' attention upon the subject and to seek their cooperation.

The problem was discussed frankly by employees in a selected planning group who were asked their opinions on corrective steps. The consensus of the advisory group was that the situation existed, that discourtesy was one

[11] David H. Crooks, director of public relations, the Kroger Company, March, 1961.

[12] Marjorie Saunders, director of public relations, Baylor University Medical Center, Dallas, Texas, in *Public Relations Journal,* December, 1959.

of the hospital's greatest liabilities, and that courtesy could be one of its greatest assets.

A four-month program consisting of five main subjects of study and practice was worked out by the committee and presented in the hospital's internal magazine. (1) Each employee was urged to consider the meaning of courtesy and to put his understanding of it into daily practice. (2) Each employee was given the opportunity to write and submit an original essay on "What is courtesy?" A $25 savings-bond prize was offered. (3) Each employee was given the opportunity to submit a slogan on courtesy for which the same prize would be awarded. (4) Films on courtesy were shown, including "By Jupiter," originally produced for Marshall Field and Company in Chicago. (5) Patients, doctors, and employees were asked to help select the most courteous employee in the hospital, and ballots were made available to all.

Along with other steps taken, this campaign focused attention upon the problem and obtained employee cooperation in making a much more happy ship.

IDENTIFICATION AND PARTICIPATION. Effective employee communication involves giving workers the chance to feel a part of the company and to participate in its activities beyond drawing a paycheck. In the mid-fifties the Life Insurance Company of Virginia at Richmond discovered that it had always taken its home-office employees for granted and decided to go beyond the dull eight-hour-day relationship then existing.[13]

The retirement of a president offered the occasion for a dinner to which were invited all employees, officers, and directors with lengths of service equal to or surpassing his. Then the installation of the new president offered the opportunity to entertain all home-office employees at an informal but fairly elaborate reception.

Next, a management consultant was brought in to make a survey of employee opinion. The survey and its aims were explained by the president in a letter to each employee. Employees checked preferences on answers to more than fifty questions on printed questionnaires. The unsigned questionnaires were then deposited in locked ballot boxes, which were shipped, unseen by company officials, to the consultant's offices for tabulation. Three weeks later the printed results, with a letter from the president expressing his appreciation of the suggestions, were in the hands of every employee.

The answers embodied many good ideas and some gripes, the main criticism being that abilities were not being fully recognized and that the opportunities for advancement were limited. This problem was tackled im-

[13] John Moyler, Jr., second vice president and director of public relations, the Life Insurance Company of Virginia, Richmond, Va., in "Public Relations for Life Insurance Companies," 1958.

mediately by conducting a voluntary search-for-talent test in which over 175 employees eventually participated.

By far the most important by-product of the survey was the remarkable employee interest and participation aroused by the creation of numerous committees to study survey answers and suggestions. Committee members put in many hours of work on such problems as merit rating, job evaluation, work simplification, and standard practices and procedures. The groups, though headed by company officers, were composed largely of supervisory and rank-and-file employees.

Among the results were the formation of a club for employees of long service, reactivation of the employee recreation association, a pay-period study, improvement in the cafeteria, and modernization of the washroom facilities.

Later the company began a series of ¼-page ads in the Richmond newspapers, featuring employees selected by the opinion-survey committee. Flowers from the president were sent to all ill or bereaved employees; a birthday card and a Christmas card went to each employee. Once a month all employees with service anniversaries were entertained at luncheon in the guest dining room by the president and senior vice-president, and the occasion served as a good unofficial sounding board of opinion. A full-time editor was obtained for the company magazine, a home-office newsletter inaugurated, the suggestion-box program overhauled, employee benefits liberalized, the employee handbook revised, the entire building air-conditioned and modernized, and officers and employees encouraged to take an active part in civic affairs.

Management was entirely satisfied with the results of the program. Employees were not only happier, but were also better workers and boosters for the company. They were proud of their connection and enjoyed active participation in the firm's activities.

CARRYING THE BALL. Sometimes telling your own people is far more than a part of a public relations communication program; it is almost the entire program. This is particularly true of associations with large memberships, such as the Michigan Education Association, which has more than 50,000 schoolteacher and administrator members in the state.

Schools (and their teachers) have all sorts of public relations problems, particularly about curriculum, discipline, and money. The need for public understanding and support is great, because only through active good will can more funds be obtained. Unlike workers in labor unions, teachers cannot strike effectively, since the funds for wage increases must come out of citizen-voted taxes. More funds are forthcoming *only* if the citizens believe the schools are doing a good job. Free consent rather than economic pressure counts at the ballot box.

The 50,000 teachers of Michigan (or their counterparts in any other state) evidently constitute the first line of public relations. A state organization such as the MEA can help them; under certain circumstances it can speak for them or be their eyes and ears; but its own resources are too limited to do a public relations job alone among millions of people in hundreds of cities and towns.

To aid teachers in carrying the ball, the MEA issues a simple, clear *Public Relations Handbook,* carries articles in the *Michigan Education Journal,* such as "PR Doesn't Come in Wrapped Packages," and offers a slide film, television programs, and a host of other material available through the National Education Association. With this help, teachers must do the rest of the job for themselves.

8. The Principle of Facing the Facts (Even When It's Hard to Do So)

Uncompromising honesty in facing an unpleasant situation is usually the best procedure if communication is to be established. The American public and its news media respect forthrightness and courage. Straight talk builds a reputation for reliability, which gains attention and promotes belief in the communicator who is known to practice it.

American Airlines' response to the Electra crashes[14]

THE PROBLEM. Rarely was a new airplane welcomed with more enthusiasm than the new Lockheed Electra when it entered United States airlines' passenger service in 1959. Carefully designed and tested, it was ideally suited to be a short- and medium-range companion to the big cross-country turbojets then entering commercial fleets. It was enthusiastically greeted by pilots for its tremendous reserve power, instant response, advanced design, and unequaled ability to stop on wet or icy runways. A long waiting list of crew members wishing to fly the Electra as soon as their seniority made them eligible backed up their spoken preferences.

Then came trouble. In 1959–1960 the new Electra was involved in five highly publicized accidents, three of which could have happened to any airplane—two landing accidents at La Guardia Field in New York caused by pilot error and a gust of wind, and one caused by a flock of starlings during the critical moments of take-off at the Boston airport. The other two crashes were in-flight failures, caused by a destructive phenomenon which had not been detected in tests.

What happened, briefly, was this: At 275 knots indicated air speed, if there had been some previous damage to the engine or nacelle mountings and the plane felt the force of an impact (such as a severe gust of wind), the propeller and its shaft could begin oscillating at a specific cycle to

[14] Karl Dahlem, director of public relations, American Airlines, in *Public Relations Journal,* February, 1961.

which the wing was resonantly responsive; all three conditions had to be present for disaster. Under these circumstances the wing and the propeller-power-plant assembly could mutually drive one another to greater and greater oscillation until the entire wing structure broke up. This happened on two occasions, and the whole aviation industry joined in an investigation to find the cause of the accidents and to eliminate it.

The first step was to make a recurrence of such accidents impossible by restricting the indicated air speed and by special inspection procedures so that even the most minor damage to members of the engine mounting would be detected. Then structural changes were made in the wings so that destructive vibration could not occur.

The airplane was now safe to fly, stronger and more secure than many of its contemporaries, but the big problem still remained: how to overcome public fear. The plane's history had become notorious. The Electra was mentioned in headlines and broadcasts whenever a plane was in any trouble, while other makes were ignored; and even comedians indulged in morbid Electra jokes.

THE SOLUTION. There were two possible courses. One would have been hush-hush, to ignore the trouble and hope that it would go away, as it probably would have in time. The other was to meet it head on; and American chose the latter. The company continued to use the name Electra in all adds referring to Electra services, in timetables, and in normal conversation of agents with passengers. Some other airlines deleted the name from their activities, although they continued to fly the planes.

American's policy was the result of studied decision. The line felt that any passenger who was reluctant to fly on an Electra (no matter how wrong American might think him to be) had the right to form his own judgment and should not be misled by not receiving all the information to which he was accustomed. American was concerned about the public relations reaction of passengers arriving at an airport and finding they were about to depart on an Electra. Even though under the pressure of circumstances they might have to use the flight, they might feel insecure and fearful. Yet American felt that it would still be wise to make the usual announcements.

American went further, however.

First came a statement from the line's president: "The good reputation of American Airlines is more valuable than the property rights in a fleet of airplanes. If we believed the Electra to be unsafe, we would ground it."

Then American's best customers, frequent airline travelers, received personal letters from the president and a testimonial to the safety of the plane from the test-pilot captain.

Leading corporate accounts were visited personally by sales personnel and senior pilots to explain "the Electra Story."

Well-attended press briefings were conducted by Electra Fact Teams in all cities served by American's Electras. Top engineers explained Electra's strength and performance characteristics, its safety, and the reasons for the crashes. Veteran flight-crew members with millions of miles of flying experience told why they preferred the Electra to other propeller-driven planes. Questions were invited and answered in detail. Not only newsmen but top customers, government and civic officers, and travel agents attended.

The program to modify the Electra so that it could return to its original speeds was explained. Simplified drawings depicted the structural changes to be made and illustrated how these would prevent the destructive coupling of forces previously possible in the high-speed range.

Gen. E. R. Quesada, Federal Aviation Administrator, stated that the temporary speed limit "gave the airplane a structural margin as great, if not greater, than any other aircraft in our transport fleet today."

Arthur Godfrey, whose aviation interest was well known, personally flew an Electra and landed it with three of its four turboprop engines deliberately set at zero. Besides endorsing the Electra on his broadcast, Godfrey volunteered for a thirteen-minute television film on the Electra and the men who fly them.

Jerrie Cobb, noted woman flyer, also flew the Electra, and her impressions were vividly described by one of the nation's leading press wire services.

Editorials urging a calm appraisal of the Electra history began to appear in newspapers, and the company began to receive commendatory letters from patrons. As the campaign progressed, one point became clear: The line's estimate of the intelligence and maturity of the audience to which the program was directed was correct. People listened to the presentation, and they understood. Few who heard the Fact Team briefings had any doubt that the Electra was a safe airplane or that the operation of the Electra was safely conservative.

In the first quarter of 1961 Electra carried loads which, in relation to those of the total fleet, were well above the loads carried prior to the campaign. There were indications, too, that American was doing much better with its Electras than other lines also operating the planes which did not follow a policy of open disclosure.

The Chicago Hospital Council seeks better understanding.[15] Hospitals today belong to a class of institution whose public relations are more likely to be bad than good. Although everyone favors hospitals in the abstract as necessary centers of healing, the public complains frequently of high costs, impersonality, and carelessness; and although most people entering a hospital are either ill or in a highly overwrought emotional state, still many of their complaints are justified. Hospitals need good public relations badly, not only because they want to function pleasantly and effectively, but also

[15] Delbert L. Price, *Hospitals J.A.H.A.,* Feb. 1, 1957.

because, being almost always dependent upon voted tax money or gifts for their operation or for necessary expansion, they need public good will. Despite their high charges, almost all hospitals are not profit-making organizations. They have no stockholders—and if they had, certainly no dividends would be distributed.

Generally press and community attitudes toward hospitals are favorable, but sometimes in the hurly-burly and excitement of a big city, misunderstanding and surliness may develop. This was the situation in which the Chicago Hospital Council found itself in 1954.

THE PROBLEM. One winter day a child suffering from burns was brought into the emergency room of a Chicago-area hospital and given first aid. The mother said that she did not have the money to pay a hospital bill; the intern pronounced the child fit to be moved; and, following established practice, the hospital referrred the mother and child to a public hospital. The next day the child died.

Ten days later hospital emergency services and financial staffing practices were under violent attack by public officials. The story was on the front page of every metropolitan daily and remained there for more than a week. Wire stories got big play from coast to coast.

The Chicago Hospital Council, the coordinating group uniting all the hospitals in the Chicago area, was goaded into a realization that, among many people in Chicago, hospitals were not very popular. It was not so much the damaging publicity that concerned the Council as the evident public approval of the attacks.

The Council had no public relations budget, but it was decided to hold a press luncheon at which a prominent Chicago newspaperman would tell representatives of the hospitals what was wrong with their press relations. He did so vigorously, unloading all his feelings of frustration from many years of dealing with hospital personnel. With the insight gained from this disclosure, the Council was enabled to start a campaign. A $4,500 budget was obtained, and with the priceless volunteer help of public relations people at member hospitals, the Council got to work.

Within a year a major press luncheon was held, at which reporters, editors, science writers, photographers, and television and radio newsmen much outnumbered hospital personnel and spoke freely. As a result of this discussion, it was decided to appoint a person who would be responsible for news contacts at hospitals and for information to news media, and to appoint also a committee which was to draw up a code of hospital-press relations approved both by the hospitals and doctors and by the press.

For example: A major point of irritation had been the insistence of press photographers who wanted to take pictures of police cases in hospital receiving rooms. This involved not only good taste and patient relations, but also a person's legal right not to have his picture taken without his consent and the subsequent possibility of suits. The solution was for news photographers to obtain consent from the patient or his doctor; the hospital would exclude photographers only when the patient's condition did not permit his being disturbed, when crisis conditions existed in emergency rooms, or when other discretionary action seemed advisable. Instead of acting as a watchdog against photographers, the hospital assumed a more neutral role. At times when prominent persons were confined in hospitals, the staff was instructed to carry requests for pictures or interviews to these persons, with the suggestion that, since their location was known anyway, the best way of keeping press favor was to be cooperative.

Institutes were set up for hospital supervisors on better methods of handling both patients and the public. Those in closest contact with the public, such as switchboard operators, admitting clerks, and floor nurses, attended sessions at which public relations representatives of other activities in close contact with the public—airlines, banks, hotels, and the telephone company—told how they won good will. The public relations of fund-raising drives was discussed.

The Council public relations committee concluded:

1. There is a natural friction between hospitals and newsmen. This should not be upsetting, since each has a job to do; yet they can still cooperate upon a friendly basis. The important thing is to seek to achieve understanding.

2. Don't worry too much about getting publicity. If you are helpful to newsmen and have good material and ideas, publicity will come.

3. Reporters are well schooled and trained. Don't underestimate them.

4. Newsmen are in close contact with public thinking. They can take the public pulse for you if they wish.

5. Every major hospital needs a professional public relations worker on its payroll. The communications problems are too complex and important to be handled by amateurs.

6. The support of top management is essential.

Finally, the committee concluded, hospital public relations is a never-ending job. Because of new staffs and new publics, it will never be "done." Contact and effort must be kept up constantly if the public is to understand the work of hospitals and support it.

The unpleasant problem of raising railroad fares.[16] The public is always particularly sensitive to increased costs of living. Some, of course, cannot be escaped. If the cost of butter, of shoes, or of automobiles fluctuates, the customer merely groans and says, "I can always use less, or substitute, or make it last longer." But when the cost of electricity, water, or transportation, which are necessary to the living of thousands of people, must go up, the opposition is likely to be vigorous—and in the long run, the public,

[16] George M. Crowson, assistant to the president, Illinois Central Railroad Company.

through government rate-regulatory bodies, has the say on what these costs shall be. Gaining public consent is necessary for profitable operation.

This was the situation which the Illinois Central Railroad faced in its Chicago commuter operations beginning in 1947 and continuing on into the 1960s. Its experience is not unlike that of many other businesses in a time of rising costs.

THE PROBLEM. The Illinois Central has one of the finest commuter lines in the world, serving the south Chicago area with 108 miles of high-speed electrified track and other equipment worth about 40 million dollars. All commuter facilities are completely separate from Illinois Central main-line passenger or freight services going elsewhere into the Midwest or South.

In the years immediately following World War II, the electrified commuter line made a profit, but inflation caused soaring operating costs, while the increase in the use of automobiles and the decentralization of the city area caused railroad traffic to decline. When the 1949 operating statement showed a loss of $335,000 on the commuter service, the railroad applied for a major rate increase. Two smaller previous rate boosts had failed to meet the loss. After twenty-one months of hearings and legal delays, a raise was granted which should have provided a 3.2 per cent return on the suburban operation, the equivalent of the percentage the railroad was earning upon its main-line operations.

This rate increase failed to meet the need, and after an $870,000 loss in 1951, the railroad decided to ask for a further 45 per cent increase in all suburban fares. Since a particularly high degree of resistance had been encountered in the previous boost of fares, railroad officials knew that the public reaction might be vigorous.

THE SOLUTION. A comprehensive program was developed to explain the facts about suburban service and to make patrons aware of the problems which the railroad faced. One phase of this program was a series of five advertisements scheduled for publication in metropolitan, community, and suburban newspapers along the suburban lines. The first, for example, was entitled WHAT DO YOU DO WHEN EVEN YOUR BEST LOSES? Other headlines were HOW GOOD CAN A SUBURBAN SERVICE BE? FOR SUBURBAN SERVICE ONLY (describing the investment), THESE ARE THE FACTS (losses), and finally WE WANT YOU TO UNDERSTAND WHY WE MUST REQUEST AN IN-CREASE IN SUBURBAN FARES. The series was introduced at a luncheon to which editorial writers, financial editors, and other media representatives were invited.

After hearings, which began in November, 1952, a rate increase averaging 25 per cent was granted in June, 1953.

EPILOGUE. Public relations and advertising have no magical power to halt long-term trends. There has been a continuing decline in commuter railroad travel and a constant increase in operational costs. In 1957 and

1958 the Illinois Central was granted additional suburban fare increases. In 1960 the net operating income of the line's suburban service was $100,000, representing savings resulting primarily from economies in operation. Any black figure was gratifying after years of deficits, but the return was tiny upon a property valued at many millions of dollars used exclusively in suburban service. The courage of public relations men in putting all the cards upon the table had at least created a greater acceptance of the railroad's problems and had helped it to break even rather than to continue to show large yearly losses.

9. The Principle of Communication by Performing a Needed Public Service

Although the following cases show "actions" taken in public relations practice, they are cited here because the main element of the approach was *communication* which gained attention by being obviously in the field of general public service. The fact that it also served its originators is incidental.

Ambulance chasing in Dade County.[17] How public relations may gain attention by performing a needed public service is well illustrated in the cleanup of ambulance-chasing lawyers and fraudulent insurance claims in which the Insurance Information Institute and the *Miami News* and the *Miami Herald* engaged recently.

It doesn't matter whose idea it was. An automobile liability insurance policy which cost $71.80 a year in Miami cost only $46.80 in Jacksonville and only $33.60 in Tampa; yet the accident rates of all three cities were about the same. Why the difference? Because the high accident awards in Miami were due to frequent collusion between police and tipsters who supplied eager attorneys with the names of persons who had just had accidents. Even some doctors were willing to testify to severe, mysterious injuries. Everyone wanted a slice of whatever damages might be awarded. The insurance companies were the first sufferers from inflated damage claims, but since their rates had to reflect realistic costs, the citizens of Miami who bought insurance were also exploited. A hidden tax was draining thousands of dollars from the community into the pockets of cheats and swindlers.

The main thing needed was a spotlight upon the shady practice, and this was what the newspapers and the insurance companies jointly provided. Claim offices of insurance companies took the unprecedented step of opening their files to the press, and the reporters took it from there, doing a superb job. A Dade County Citizens' Committee supplemented the publicity and, in time, the Bar Association and Medical Society entered the fray to police their own ranks.

[17] Burton Youngman, director of research, Insurance Information Service, New York.

The newspaper stories constituted a hard-hitting journalistic crusade. The editors not only featured news reports of fraudulent claims, but also showed enterprise in exposing some of the worst offenders. For example, they prevailed upon a young woman in perfect physical condition to claim to be a recent accident victim, and, accompanied by her "husband" (a newspaper reporter), to visit attorneys' and doctors' offices. When the professional men eagerly snapped up her case, their actions and the thunderings of a local judge prodding the local bar were fully reported.

This sort of problem is never fully cleaned up, but the campaign at least abated the nuisance and loss to a certain extent, and the Miami legal climate became more congenial to the insurance business.

The soap association and dermatitis.[18] Dermatitis (skin irritation and injury caused by reaction to various substances) has long been a major industrial health problem, one of extreme seriousness where certain materials are handled. A study conducted by the U.S. Public Health Service in the 1940s revealed that the malady accounted for more than two-thirds of the ailments reported to compensations boards and was costing at least 100 million dollars a year. Since there was no authoritative textbook available upon the subject, the Association of American Soap and Glycerine Producers, Inc., saw an opportunity to perform a needed service to industry.

A former medical director of the U.S. Public Health Service and internationally recognized authority upon dermatitis was commissioned to write a booklet containing a comprehensive and impartial discussion of all types of industrial skin irritants and the methods of protection against them. Entitled "The Prevention of Occupational Skin Diseases," it was sold by the AASGP for 50 cents a copy.

To make the booklet known, a press conference was held in New York City at which fifty-five media representatives attended, and copies of the booklet were mailed to 3,500 leaders of opinion in the field. A series of feature articles ran in trade papers such as *Factory Management and Maintenance, Chemical Week,* and *National Safety News,* stressing reports of how individual companies had conquered dermatitis (not necessarily by using soap). To make managements more aware of the hazard, reprints were distributed to companies which might be interested. A new survey was made which revealed that 9 per cent of the employees in 141 plants, employing a total of 429,000 workers, were contracting dermatitis and losing a total of 18,200 hours of work a year. These data provided the basis for additional features.

No promotion of soap was necessary in any of this communication. As in so many other associational public relations efforts, if the need for the product and its uses are established, the sales are a matter for the enterprise of each individual manufacturing company.

[18] *Public Relations News,* Sept. 22, 1958.

The private electric utilities aid education.[19] Business firms have long talked about their desire to aid education, but to many a schoolman their heavy-handed efforts have suggested an intention to use education for their own purposes. True aid differs from propaganda; it consists in supplying the kind of help that both parties can agree upon, and conclusions flow from the facts as presented; they are not stated and pushed.

A program of such disinterested help to education was agreed upon by sixty-four investor-owned electric utilities during 1960 in the National Youth Conference on the Atom held in Chicago. The conference brought together 300 of the nation's most gifted young science students, accompanied by 200 science teachers from thirty-eight states for a three-day study of the peaceful uses of the atom. They met and spoke with high-level scientists and were treated to the kind of superior presentation of the subject consonant with their interests and backgrounds.

Through this program the electric utility industry was trying to show:

1. Concern for the future of this country in the atomic-power field
2. A desire to inform the public of the peaceful uses of the atom in the future
3. The electric industry's important stake in the development of the atom for peaceful purposes
4. The desire of the industry to attract the most gifted scientists of tomorrow to its work

Student participants were chosen through their contributions to science fairs and records in special-aptitude tests, and upon the recommendation of their local educators. Before coming to Chicago, many of them were invited by their local electric companies to visit their plants and to get acquainted at first hand with the processes of generating and transmitting electricity.

In Chicago speakers and leaders for discussion groups were chosen, and field trips were arranged. Some of America's foremost scientists and members of the Atomic Energy Commission participated. Sixty scientists from the University of Chicago, Argonne National Laboratory, and the Illinois Institute of Technology led discussion groups of from ten to fifteen delegates. The last day of the conference the group visited the Argonne National Laboratory and the Dresden Nuclear Power Station, a full-scale, privately financed atomic-power plant.

From this experience in providing a needed public service to education, the originators, Bozell & Jacobs, Inc., suggested several ways in which industries might be of aid to the schools in their neighborhoods:

> Opening laboratories under supervision on week-ends so that young scientists who have inadequate school facilities could progress further in their work

[19] Donald D. Hoover, president, Bozell & Jacobs, Inc., New York, in *Public Relations Journal,* April, 1961.

Tours accompanied by competent scientific help

Useful printed material for science classes

Sponsorship of science clubs or projects

Classroom visits and demonstrations by company representatives

Visual aids and films

Information about possible personnel career openings and the training needed

10. The Principle of Stressing Positive Benefits

Public relations may often be concerned with somewhat philosophical subjects, such as economic systems, types of government, public welfare, and education, but this preoccupation does not mean that its psychological approach to communications has become vague. In most successful public relations efforts, as in most successful advertising, high-flown appeals to abstract noble sentiments are usually backed up by direct answers to the receiver's unspoken query of "What's in it for me?" This recognition of self-interest should not be shocking because, properly used, it may be more honest, more constructive, and less spurious than other emotional or intellectual appeals.

The National Hardboard Association faces foreign imports.[20] In the late 1950s and 1960s the trade group concerned with the production of hardboard faced a situation which had become increasingly familiar to American manufacturers after a war-induced lapse of time. In 1950, for example, practically no hardboard was imported into the United States. By 1960 imports had captured approximately 12 per cent of the domestic market, and with worldwide hardboard production constantly increasing, the percentage could be substantially raised.

A common reaction to such a situation is to launch an emotional "Buy American" program, but to the Public Relations Board, a Chicago counseling firm which handled the account of the National Hardboard Association, hiding behind the flag seemed both cowardly and unavailing—cowardly because it was an admission that American products could not match foreign goods and unavailing because the customer today will buy what he considers the best product for his purpose, regardless of its national origin. But if flag waving was useless, what benefits *could* the American purchaser of hardboard expect from buying a product made in the United States?

Home construction and improvement accounts for about half the hardboard market in the United States, furniture construction for about 15 per cent, and many other industrial uses, such as automobile manufacture and building of promotional displays, for the balance. In all of these uses American-made hardboards were superior to imports.

There are more than fifty different varieties of American hardboards,

---

[20] Lee Schooler, president, Public Relations Board, Inc., Chicago, Ill.

far more than imports can supply. Controlled quality and the reputation of a local manufacturer stand behind each piece. The fact that the supply is dependable, and the delivery rapid precludes delay on jobs or a large investment of capital in inventory. Expert technical advice on its use is available from hardboard manufacturers anywhere in the United States. Through long advertising and sales promotion, American hardboard manufacturers have helped to persuade customers of the merits of their products; items using such hardboard are, in turn, easier to sell. The use of American hardboard assists in forest-conservation practices here and also aids the nation's economy.

To tell this story, the American Hardboard Association used a press conference followed by feature stories in general and trade publications. A twelve-page brochure entitled "A Pig in a Poke Is Not for You" was widely distributed. Salesmen used a sales portfolio and direct mail, and bundle tags and stamps were used to identify products made by American Hardboard Association members. An impressive schedule of advertising appeared in trade magazines. A featured story in *American Lumberman and Building Products Merchandiser,* for example, told how one retailer, Central Hardware Company of St. Louis, Missouri, had returned to American hardboards after a fling with imports.

To appeal to the builder or to the manufacturer to use American hardboards because of patriotism would have been relatively ineffective. An appeal to the ultimate consumer would have been pointless, for he usually neither knows nor cares where the hardboard incorporated in his house or dresser comes from. To point out the advantages to the user was the only practical way to get results.

11. The Principle of Repetition

A common failing in public relations efforts is to quit before the battle has been won. Many a good idea has been abandoned before it could take root because its weary sponsors grew tired of it before a distant, busy public even realized that it existed. What looks like a great outflow of press releases, institutional advertising, booklets, speeches, and films as it leaves an organization often looks like a few scattered spots amid a sea of other messages every day in the consciousness of recipients—if it makes even this much impression.

There is also evidence that the mere fact of repetition helps a tendency toward belief, because if a thing is heard often enough it gradually becomes accepted as part of one's mental equipment.

With repetition, of course, should go a reasonable degree of variety in presentation of the basic idea for the benefit of those observant people who may happen to become annoyed by identical repetition. The same tune should be played upon different instruments, as it were.

12. The Principle of Overcoming Refusal to Pay Attention

One of the most baffling problems of a public relations man arises when an audience resolutely refuses to pay any attention to his attempts at communication or even becomes irritated with them. Sometimes the hearers perceive no personal ground of concern with the communication, or sometimes the communication may be so unattractive that they prefer to ignore it entirely.

A classic case of unconcern occurred a number of years ago in Cincinnati, Ohio, when a tremendous campaign was put on to popularize the idea of the United Nations. A heavy barrage of newspaper stories, radio and television programs, posters, films, and speakers apparently brought no particular increase in the public awareness of the United Nations or its functions. Surveys after the campaign corroborated this impression. Evidently Cincinnatians simply thought that the United Nations had little relevance to their personal lives; almost any amount of propaganda in favor of it would have been ignored. Simply increasing the amount of promotion would have availed little and might even have served as an irritant, resulting in a negative reaction.

Mental avoidance of messages because of their unpleasant nature often seems to occur in safety propaganda. Here the tendency seems to be not to understand the message or not to consider it applicable to oneself. The "other fellow" may be a bad driver, but "not I." Under these circumstances scolding is useless, because the receiver thinks the scolding is properly aimed at someone else. Often a minor threat or an appeal to pride may be more effective than an accusation or an appeal to a serious fear.

The unpleasant task of the U.S. Office of Civil and Defense Mobilization

THE PROBLEM. Speaking before a group of public relations men at Battle Creek, Michigan, then national headquarters of the OCDM, Edward B. Lyman, deputy assistant director for National Organizations and Civic Affairs of the organization, said in late 1960:

> . . . To be perfectly honest about it, if I were back in public relations and advertising and a client brought me something like this (OCDM's problem of obtaining citizen cooperation in civil defense efforts), I'd tell him to take it back to his laboratories, for civil defense as a consumer item has almost everything against it. The very concept involves the unpleasant admission that we are vulnerable to attack and destruction almost beyond imagining.
>
> Next, we need to tell the consumer that, repulsively though our product is packaged, it will taste even worse. For to make civil defense effective, he and his family are going to have to take training, to build and stock a fallout shelter at their own expense, to volunteer for duty—and to do

this year after year, even though at times war may seem very far away.

Finally, we can't even guarantee that our product will do the consumer, personally, any good. If he is caught under the bomb or if he is in an area of intense fallout without any shelter, he may still die. All we can promise is that if he and enough like him will take this thing seriously, the nation itself will survive. . . .

But we in civil defense have no choice. *Our* product was created by the nuclear age in which we live. And for the sake of the nation we have got to sell it. . . . Let us begin our self-analysis, however, by recognizing frankly that public disinterest and even hostility to civil defense are just as natural and just as predictable today as the very same reactions were a hundred times before in the course of history under similar circumstances.

There is nothing new about it. The plain truth is that people don't *want* to be told unpleasant things. They'd rather push them in the closet. . . . That is why people walk away from us when we talk about the possibility of an attack that will involve *their* homes, *their* families, *their* lives. . . .

If we persist in our efforts to warn the people, some of them get mad. The rest take refuge in defeatism—and to me that is the only really alarming reaction we have to contend with, because it is so completely foreign to our national character and heritage.

THE SOLUTION

. . . We have got to get civil defense turned around in the public mind, so that it appears to be a positive rather than a negative concept. We have got to present it as part of something that is big and important, dynamic and constructive. We have got to clothe civil defense with the same mantle of popular respect and national necessity that our military defense traditionally wears.

To do this, Lyman suggested that civil defense must be presented in its role of making America strong, of enabling us to have freedom from fear and pressure as a nation, and of enabling the United States to speak with assurance in international councils.

. . . In this perspective, building a fallout shelter becomes more than an isolated gesture of self-protection. It becomes part of something big and important, something that is bound up with our national mission as a leader of the free world. . . .

Surveys indicate that civil defense today has long since reached the public awareness stage. Our big job now is to translate this awareness into action. . . . We have to remember to stay away from scare techniques . . . of short-range benefit in the absence of immediate threat. . . .

(For motivation to action) we are putting increased emphasis upon our work with leadership groups, for we know from experience that they can give us the face-to-face contacts we need. . . .

We feel that *security* comes closer to being a sounder emotional appeal (than fear) in today's climate. The kind of security we are talking about, however, is something more than a fence against external threats. It is . . . the preservation of our right to enjoy our freedoms and way of living. . . .

Civil defense is not like a recruiting drive. It will be with us and our children and our children's children for as long as there is a need for a military defense. . . . We can talk our way into apathy as a subconscious excuse for doing nothing, but I am not ready to admit that a *real* public apathy to civil defense exists today except on the surface. Do you know why? Because the record shows that people *do* hear. They may not seem to listen, but they hear. . . .

Less than two years afterward, American interest in civil defense seemed to have died down to almost nothing. Fallout shelters were a drug on the market and even talking about them had become again unfashionable.

Capable observers were divided in their estimates of the situation, some agreeing that "What's the use?" or "Let's not look and it may go away" reactions had completely taken over, others thankful from a practical point of view that people did not face the problem logically, because to have done so coldly might have led to panic or to a blind impulse toward a suicidal preventive war.

But while the discussions went on, the problem remained. America had never faced the danger until the late 1950s, but many other civilized people have lived with and surmounted it over the long centuries of history without defeatism or destruction of their moral values, creativity, and ingenuity. Living with the enemy outside the walls may be abnormal to Americans of the 1960s, but it was normal enough to many Greeks, Romans, Byzantines, Chinese, and medieval Europeans on many occasions.

In facing issues like these, public relations men undertake a major responsibility. They have to undertake it on faith, not knowing whether their services will be great or small, their effects beneficial or damaging. Always their value will be disputed, and the rewards will be little. But to ignore problems is not to solve them, and Americans must be awakened from lethargy.

13. The Principle of Concentrating upon Leaders of Opinion

Faced with insufficient funds to communicate with everybody, public relations workers frequently resort to the idea of trying to influence leaders of opinion, who, it is thought, will then influence others or actually direct some groups when they pass from leading opinion to holding positions of authority.

Although the idea seems sound enough, in modern times it faces some questions:

Who *are* leaders of opinion? In the relatively simple society of the 1900s they might have been the town banker, the leading merchants, the editor, the clergymen, and perhaps the teachers. But do people now really take their opinions from these local mentors (if they ever did)? If not, then to whom do they look? Are today's leaders of thought perhaps remote people —television personalities, popular writers, newspaper columnists, or national leaders in politics and labor? How much does opinion actually trickle down from leaders to the mass of the public? Or does the public make up its mind in small family or social groups which are not readily distinguishable from the individuals who compose them?

Despite the difficulty of identifying today's leaders of opinion and of ascertaining their true influence, it is still sound public relations strategy to cultivate the understanding and support of many of them because they are worthwhile in themselves and because they also, to some extent, control the *gateways of communication*. These people, whether their own opinions are particularly listened to or not, do have the power to speak or to write, and usually, are voluminous speakers and writers. Teachers, editors, preachers, broadcasters, club and group leaders all come into contact with the public regularly in situations in which they convey ideas, some of them reaching millions of auditors by way of the mass media, others speaking to scores of personal friends and hearers.

In addition, these persons and others of respected rank often serve as *validators* of reports. "It's true because I saw it in the *Journal*" or "Professor Jones said so, and he's an expert in physics."

How the Ford Motor Company reaches college leaders of opinion.[21] Beginning in 1956, the Ford Motor Company decided to hold a series of seminars on "Ideas and Automobiles," at its many plants scattered throughout the United States. The invited guests were college faculty members, who took a tour of the plant, ate lunch in the plant dining room, and then broke up into groups, engaging in discussion of science, engineering, marketing, community relations, labor relations, economics, and other such subjects. Company officials served as resource persons, making short talks and then, for an hour or so, answering questions, many of them sharp and pointed.

During four years following the start of this program, Ford officials met nearly 2,500 faculty members from 180 colleges and universities near its plant cities. The teachers learned something about Detroit and its business. Ford's gain, however, was less definable. No effort was made to sell cars, recruit employees, or press any economic viewpoint. The real value lay in better understanding alone, which could not have been achieved as well in any other way.

[21] *Business Week Magazine,* Apr. 1, 1961.

14. The Principle of Preconditioning an Audience to a Viewpoint

The most effective public relations communication usually takes place not *after* issues have been joined, but *before*. When a discussion reaches the stage of controversy, the participants are apt to shut their minds to additional information unless it happens to agree with their own convictions. It is then usually too late for any amount of communication to influence them; in fact, an overdose may have a strong negative effect.

Good public relations communication often provides the framework of thinking in which decisions are reached. Thus the ability to foresee coming issues and directions of thought becomes of extreme value and is another reason why the really expert public relations practitioner should be something more than a wordsmith.

15. The Principle of Harmony of All Communications

In today's busy communications world, filled with multitudes of symbols and words, an organization cannot afford to give a scattering picture of itself, either in appearance or in thought, if it is to be noted and remembered.

A big chemical company establishes identity.[22] In 1961 Olin-Mathieson Chemical Corporation spent 2.5 million dollars in an advertising campaign featuring a new and simplified corporate-identity system. The twelve-syllable signature of the company was replaced by a two-syllable signature— Olin.

Although the legal name of the company remained Olin-Mathieson Chemical Corporation, the signature for general use now simply became Olin in a distinctive heavy type in which the initial "O" was split like a stenciled letter, the bottom half being black and the top half in a dark color, usually red.

Brand names that had a well-established meaning were retained and joined with Olin such as Squibb Division of Olin or Olin Winchester-Western Division. When they had less identity, they were absorbed completely, Western Brass becoming Olin Brass and Frostkraft Containers becoming Olin Containers.

The fact that the company would identify itself by Olin instead of its full legal name was announced in a full-page newspaper advertisement headlined "Please call us by our first name."

More than seventy different letterheads were consolidated into one style.

In explaining the move the company said:

[22] Henry M. Hunter, Director of Communications, Olin-Mathieson Chemical Corporation, New York.

1. Research indicated that the company's full legal title was too long and cumbersome, and, in view of Olin's activities in metals, packaging, arms, and ammunition, it overemphasized the chemical aspects of the business.

2. The previous corporate mark, which was an "O" resting atop the letter "M," had the disadvantage of being a pair of initials which in a company such as Olin were not communicated often enough to be identified and remembered.

3. Having expanded through a number of mergers and acquisitions, the company suffered from too many brand names and trademarks.

4. Advertising and sales-promotion budgets were being diffused in the attempt to establish and promote too many separate products and product groups.

Summary: Fifteen Principles of Effective Communications

1. Humanize—identify in terms of people if possible.
2. Suit the message and means of communication to the audience.
3. Speak the receiver's language.
4. Be timely.
5. Dramatize communications.
6. Use two-way communication.
7. Reach your own people first.
8. Face the facts—even when it's hard to do so.
9. Perform a needed public service.
10. Stress positive benefits.
11. Repeat if necessary.
12. Overcome refusal to pay attention.
13. Concentrate upon leaders of opinion.
14. Precondition the audience to your viewpoint.
15. Keep all communications in harmony.

Look at communications from the receiver's viewpoint. The public relations man who puts out a large number of news releases and stories, holds conferences, makes motion pictures, and engages in many activities, may seem to himself and to those near him to be creating quite a bit of communications material. The receiver gets only scattered bits now and then unless he is connected with the organization in some way. The material sent out may seem both plentiful and of absorbing interest to the producers. But how does it look to the receivers?

Sometimes effective communication is achieved by the happy coincidence of accidental common interests; successful authors and editors who happen to publish at the right time feel that the gods have been propitious. But the public relations man, having more fixed objectives, cannot rely upon such fortunate circumstances and instead must actively use his imagination to seek out areas which he has in common with those with whom he wants to speak.

Evaluation and
an Evaluation Case

13

Ascertaining the results of a public relations effort is, for a number of reasons, the most neglected branch of the art. Such evaluation is difficult because it deals with that most difficult of things to measure—changes in human opinion. As Burns W. Roper, a partner in the nationally famous Elmo Roper and Associates research firm, once said:

> Measuring public relations effectiveness is only slightly easier than measuring a gaseous body with a rubber band. Unless a person is in some way personally connected with a company, he is not very much concerned about the company. When a message is beamed at him about this company, he doesn't stop everything and pay strict attention. Thousands of messages are beamed at him from other companies, the government, his wife, his boss, his kids, his friends, and many of these messages come much closer to the mainstream of his life. How can you measure the effect of a particular flyspeck in this person's life?

Because it is difficult, evaluation of the results of public relations is also expensive, and once an organization has satisfied itself that a public relations effort is reasonably successful, it is usually disinclined to spend a lot of money to estimate the degree of its success. Besides, public relations people live in a constant press of work and new challenges. The natural tendency of the business is to say, "What can we do next?" rather than to examine past results.

Many variables are involved. In the natural sciences, controlled conditions for an experiment can usually be relatively easily established; but human thought takes place in a constantly changing environment in which not all the factors may be known. It is often extremely hard to say that "this" caused "that," and yet some such connection of cause and effect must be a goal of public relations activity evaluation.

Empirical evidence of change frequently seems quite adequate, and it may really be so, for practical purposes. Scientific studies of opinion change are of the most value if done periodically, in order to keep a continuous record of change, and they are even better when norms are available for comparison. An absolute figure, such as "Ten per cent of the people said they believed this," may not tell much. Is that good or bad? If it was 20 per cent or only 5 per cent last year, and if the norm of other similar companies is 15 per cent this year, then the figures give us something to go on.

But with all these problems, the future of public relations, of many a public relations man, and to some extent of the social sciences themselves depends upon an increasing ability to evaluate the results of communications in affecting the opinions and attitudes of recipients; and difficulty is no excuse for giving up.

A Framework of Public Relations Evaluations

If a simple, 100 per cent effective way of evaluating changes in attitude or opinion is not within a public relations man's grasp, nevertheless he should make certain attempts.

The first is personal. At least annually he should evaluate the success of his work in order to measure his progress and to set new goals. If he finds this study hard, then perhaps the difficulty itself is an indication that he needs better evaluative procedures.

Next he should employ various empirical and scientific methods of research. It may be hard to get the money to carry on this work. Perhaps funds should not be spent on evaluation that could be spent on action or communication; on the other hand, perhaps nothing is more important. The choice depends upon the internal circumstances of an organization.

In any case a public relations man should be humble. If people think better of his organization than they did before, perhaps his efforts, out of a great many other stimuli, had something to do with the change. If they think worse, perhaps other factors overcame his best efforts. (No one can tell for sure how much worse it might have been with no efforts.) And once in a while he may have to mutter to himself in a moment of truth, "That set of boners really hurt"; because occasionally, though not often, public relations efforts do harm instead of good.

An Annual Audit of Public Relations Effectiveness

Just as a business measures material progress in its annual report, so a public relations management may profitably engage in stock taking at least once a year. What are employee attitudes now as compared with those noted a year ago? Did our activities have anything to do with their change? How about community relations? Press relations? Consumer relations and relations with schools and colleges? Stockholders? Government? Dealers and suppliers? Others?

Sitting down to supply the answers not only forces public relations men to account for time and money spent; it also makes them face their problems anew, ask what has changed, and consider what the course should be from here on. Evaluation inevitably creates plans; and public relations *must* be in the forward-looking vanguard of any organization.

Planning and looking to the future are not things that the alert public relations man does in his spare time; they are almost his main reason for being. His plans and forecasts may not always be accepted, but if he is not in the forefront of thinking, with his ideas well buttressed by facts showing what has been accomplished and what is still needed, he is failing in his function as the public eyes and ears of his organization. In the full circle of public relations activity, evaluation inevitably becomes the research which leads to the next steps of action and communication (unless it is a one-time program which will never be repeated).

Empirical Evaluation Methods

The whole business of asking "How successful were we?" in a field so hard to measure as the effect of persuasion upon public opinion, is fraught with peril. No other investigation brings with it a greater tendency toward self-delusion, wishful thinking, and the vanity of being overimpressed by what friends say or of thinking that because much was issued, much resulted.

Several types of empirical evaluation are constantly in evidence:

Faith. If we issue sound statements and if they are read to any great extent, we tell ourselves that they must have some good result. We can check readership fairly easily if we go about it in an orderly fashion, but we cannot assume that the desired results followed. Probably they did; usually such an empirical assumption is valid, but we cannot rest entirely upon it. For example, people who know more about something do not always like it better.

Random evidence. Column inches of publicity, mail returns, comments, field reports, requests for participation—all are valuable in showing that something is happening, but they do not tell exactly *what* is happening inside people's minds, and they may reflect intensity rather than breadth.

Associated effects. Suppose that employee turnover diminishes after the installation of a good employee communications program. Should the public relations man rush right in and claim credit? Probably not; cautiously, if at all. Too many other factors may have been at work—worsened job-hunting conditions, better earnings, increasing age of the work force, for example. The communications program may well have had a part in stabilizing employment, but other factors may have helped even more. Some year an even better program might be overwhelmed by a combination of un-favorable factors. What would one say then? *Post hoc, ergo propter hoc* logic cuts both ways.

An association of effects may appear in many fields. Suppose that management seeks an increase in the number of stockholder proxies re-turned and that after a better stockholder information program is instituted, the number of proxies returned increases. The cause-and-effect relationship is probable, but not certain. Or suppose that a series of company meetings is held, that they are well promoted, and that attendance is good. Did public relations promotion do the trick? Or could people have attended for other reasons? Suppose that a company magazine has a good response to a reader contest. Surely the enthusiasm is evidence of the quality of the magazine! True, but it may also be evidence of the trust and attachment of employees—an attitude which has been built up by enlightened manage-ment, good supervision, and benefits over many years. Suppose that the good public relations of a company seems greatly to enhance the effective-ness of its advertising (as it frequently does); again many factors may be at work. The public relations chief will be not only truthful but also politically prudent if he is modest; many other workers have had a hand in his success.

Opinion conferences. A good empirical method of measuring results is to get special groups together and to encourage them to let you have their candid views—groups such as the press, educators, and clergy. If they're convinced you really want frankness and if they are not afraid of retaliation or of hurting your feelings, such informal soundings are often highly worth-while.

Insurance. One thing we shall never know in most public relations prac-tice, because of the many factors involved, is the answer to "What would have happened if we hadn't used this program?" Any theory is bound to be speculative. The probable answer is "Nothing much—except that things would have been a little bit worse . . . and the year after that they would have been still worse . . . and in future years yet worse." The business of making human impressions is both slow and continuous. The sins of the fathers are visited upon the children down to the third and fourth genera-tion, and youngsters in school today are still damning corporations because of errors made in the Teddy Roosevelt era. Only the very wise who expect to be in business a long time look far ahead.

Scientific Evaluation Methods

Empirical methods are not all bad if their limitations are considered; neither are scientific procedures.

It is often fairly easy to measure the receipt of a message; it is much harder to measure the resulting response and attitude changes. One way is to poll comparative groups, one of which has been exposed to a program and the other has not. But if such a method is used, the test group must not know that it is being used as a test group; otherwise its interest in the subject will be alerted to an abnormal degree and will make its reaction unrepresentative. And in any case, the reaction of the test group is open to suspicion, because simple before-and-after measurements with the same people seldom work; the first exposure blurs the second attempt.

Depth interviews, semantic differentials, and other fairly complex psychological tests on selected comparable groups may often yield good results, but at great cost in arriving at a conclusion that often seems almost self-evident from an empirical viewpoint. Most corporate managements are not enthusiastic about spending so much money in after-the-fact-evaluation. They would rather use it as an underpinning to some new venture.

Select Your Own Methods—but Evaluate

In thinking about public relations, no one ever forgets the phase known as *communications*, and today almost everyone is familiar with the need for *action*. *Research* as a basis for action and communication is becoming quite commonplace too, but examples of careful *evaluation* are still rare.

Evaluation is the new frontier of public relations, and the practitioner who can present valid evaluation of his work is certain to get a reputation as a pioneer and to prosper accordingly in his own wisdom and professional standing. There is a keen hunger for evaluation, and it is in the area of development of human relations that it is most promising and important.

THE CASE OF THE BELL TELEPHONE COMPANIES [1]

Of all the businesses in the United States, the various operating Bell Telephone Companies of A.T. & T. undoubtedly do the best job of keeping their hand upon the public pulse. They not only *think*; they *know* what the public feels about more than a score of aspects of telephone service, all the time and for many years back. Because of this knowledge, they keep little trends from becoming big troubles, and they avoid major mistakes. Almost every step of telephone activity is constantly analyzed.

If this care seems excessively meticulous, consider what is at stake. Basically the telephone company has only one thing to sell—service. Telephone service is of necessity a monopoly, but not necessarily a profitable monopoly or in private hands. If service were to decline seriously, if public regard for its efficiency and good citizenship were to diminish, it could always be nationalized. Private-enterprise telephone service exists on

[1] Credit for most of these illustrations goes to Dana Rose, assistant vice president, Michigan Bell Telephone Company, and to Hale Nelson, vice president, Illinois Bell Telephone Company.

sufferance, good will, and the public conviction that it administers a
monopoly of telephone conversation at least as well as, and probably better
than, a government body could.

In 1959 the president of the Illinois Bell Telephone Company, said:

> The Bell System, together with the rest of the telephone industry, has
> a reputation for being progressive, efficient and useful to our economy—
> which reflects both our imaginative technology and traditionally superior
> service. Our communications system is looked upon as an outstanding
> business achievement representing the best of free enterprise in America.
> This is our heritage. It represents the work of many telephone people over
> more than three-quarters of a century of industrial growth in America.
> This was largely an era of individualism in business with *material values*
> playing a significant part in the philosophy of industrial management.
>
> Today we are operating in a new kind of business climate. More and
> more, people are measuring business character to the extent to which it
> respects *human values*. People in this sense include representatives in
> government, educators, the press, the clergy, our customers—in fact much
> of our population. . . .
>
> It's timely, therefore, that we appraise our concepts of management
> . . . to see how well we reflect this new order of things in our decision
> making. . . . The overall quality of our service, as we measure it, is
> better now than it has ever been. But in spite of this we are often criticized
> for the manner in which we deliver it. We are sometimes referred to as
> a cold, impersonal monopoly that has a rule for everything. And why is
> this? It may be because we do things in ways that cause people to think
> we are not sufficiently considerate of human values. . . .

The information about public attitudes to which the president referred
came, in large part, from a constant series of Bell System evaluations, some
of which are detailed below.

A Study of the Bell System Exhibit at Disneyland

The Bell System exhibit in the Tomorrowland area of Disneyland features
"America the Beautiful," the Circarama movie which was the highlight of
the 1958 Brussels World's Fair. Projected on a 360-degree screen are
scenes of a New England village, Times Square at night, the Grand Canyon,
and many other parts of the country.

While waiting for admission to Circarama, visitors are exposed to the
following exhibits:

> A direct distance dialing map which traces a call from Los Angeles to
> Washington by means of colored lights
> A three-dimensional mural showing the geographic areas of the nation,
> accompanied by seven screens telling the story of the telephone business
> A marketing exhibit displaying the latest in home and office telephone

equipment and a phone-needs computer telling the number of phones required in a home

A telephone cable, opened to reveal its structure, which serves as a railing around the exhibits

A space-communications display set up at the entrance to the theater

Evaluation. Personal interviews were conducted with about 2,600 visitors —half before seeing the exhibit and half after they had seen it. The purpose of the survey was to determine general reactions and the reactions to specific portions of the exhibit, and to find out whether the exhibit had had any effect upon viewers' attitudes toward company services, costs, and contribution to scientific research.

Almost all the visitors were pleased with the telephone exhibit. The circular motion picture itself received the highest vote (97 per cent); the latest phones for the home and the long-distance dialing map came in second in popularity with about 60 per cent each.

The significant thing is that the index of favorable attitude toward the company for those who were questioned after seeing the exhibit was 89— six points higher than for the control group, which had not been exposed to the exhibit before being questioned.

Of those who had seen the exhibit, for example, 97 per cent felt that the telephone company was much interested in assuring its customers of good service, as against 89 per cent who had not seen the exhibit. In response to a question about cost, 88 per cent of those who had seen the exhibit felt that in comparison with other things today telephone service had good value, as against only 80 per cent in the control group. Ninety-three per cent of the exhibit viewers felt that telephone users were benefiting from the technical research carried on by the company, as compared with 86 per cent who had not seen the exhibit.

It would perhaps be naïve to conclude that seeing the exhibit itself resulted in the changes noted. Perhaps the viewers were simply being nice in their answers as a way of expressing their thanks to its originators, or perhaps they were reminded of things which had not been so much in their minds when approached "cold." In a way, however, this question of source is unimportant. The mere fact that people responded more favorably *made* their attitude more favorable, because things which are expressed tend to become a part of belief simply through their expression.

In fact, any friendly contact with an organization is likely to improve the attitude toward it. Telephone people, for example, have been quite aware that the installation of dial systems replacing customer conversation with living operators, though it may improve the service rating of a system, substitutes an impersonal mechanism for a living, human link (and perhaps leads to an increase in the concept of the telephone system as being "cold" or "not interested in people").

Reactions to a Telephone Fashion Fair

Contact with even a strictly commercial exhibit may also have a good effect upon the general public attitude toward a company.

In the summer of 1960, for example, Michigan Bell Telephone Company presented an outdoor exhibit, "Phone Fashion Fair," at several large shopping centers in Metropolitan Detroit. The Fair consisted of three large tents which housed various displays of telephone equipment available for residences and places of business. There were also several exhibits of "future" telephone equipment. The purpose of the exhibit was to provide an opportunity for on-the-spot sales of telephone equipment and services and also to serve as a means of improving customer attitudes and public communication.

A total of 1,924 interviews were conducted at the Fair, 324 among individuals who purchased telephone equipment or services at the displays, 524 among people who visited the displays and talked with telephone personnel, 534 among persons who visited the displays but did not talk to personnel there, and 542 among nonvisitors in the shopping center.

The objectives of the study were to find out the sales effect of the Fair and also to see whether the attitudes of people who conversed with a company representative at the exhibits compared favorably or unfavorably with those of people whose opinions were not asked.

Respondents overwhelmingly thought that presentation of displays like these was illuminating, and they did not resent the selling, nine out of ten saying that it was a good idea. Sales were good, although a number of people, ranging from 25 to 61 per cent of the viewers, said they would have bought anyway. The most interesting difference arose in the expression of general attitude toward the company.

In response to the question "How interested do you think the Telephone Company is in seeing that its customers get good service?" 97.1 per cent of those who purchased at the Fair thought it was quite interested; 96.3 per cent of those who talked to a company representative, but did not buy, also thought so; 95.5 per cent of those who simply walked through and 93 per cent of those who did not visit at all were favorably disposed.

On a question about the cost of telephone service, 72.3 per cent of those who bought thought costs were fair, as compared with 60.9 per cent of those who did not buy.

On the question "How much regard do you think the company has for the interests of the public?" 87.7 per cent of those who bought, 85.4 per cent of those who talked, 86.2 per cent of those who walked through, and 82.8 per cent of the nonvisitors held favorable viewpoints. Again the difference is significant.

A New York City Before-and-after Study

An interesting type of test was given in 1957 by the New York Telephone Company. More than 700 questionnaires were obtained during fourteen lecture-demonstrations of an illustrated talk entitled "New York Has Everything." The slide-talk itself consisted of a presentation of pictures and facts about New York, well laced with Telephone Company promotion, such as pictures of switchboards, TV pickups, and illustrations of the part that the telephone company plays in the life of the city.

The method of administering the test was unusual, half the audience being used as a check upon the other half. The first half received an identical set of questionnaires before seeing the program and immediately afterwards. The second half, without knowing it, received an entirely different set of questions before the program, but filled out the same set of questions as the first half after the program had been seen. There were no significant differences in the "after" scores of both groups, indicating that the act of filling out the first survey had not materially altered the reaction of the before-and-after group. All other factors were kept constant as nearly as possible.

In response to the question "In your opinion, is the Company doing all it can to keep down the cost of service to telephone users, or could it do more?" 40 per cent said "yes" before they had seen the presentation and 52 per cent of the same group said so afterward. (The control-group figure was 51 per cent.)

On "What reputation do you think the Telephone Company has in your community?" the figure shifted from 47 per cent who said "good" before seeing the program, to 52 per cent who responded favorably afterward.

On "How well do you feel the Telephone Company treats its employees?" 61 per cent said "very well" before and 64 per cent afterward.

"Diamonds Are Different"

In 1960 the Bell Telephone Company of Pennsylvania ran a before-and-after check upon the reactions of 353 persons in twelve adult audiences to a soft-sell demonstration-talk entitled "Diamonds Are Different," the general nature of which was a history of diamonds and their industrial uses. In the final minutes of the presentation, the speaker mentioned several times that Western Electric, a Bell manufacturing subsidiary, used diamonds in wire-drawing machines to make better scientific equipment which lowered the cost of telephone service. Glass replicas of diamonds were used as illustrations in the lecture.

The audience showed excellent comprehension of the point about costs, the number believing that the telephone company was "quite interested" (meaning reasonably interested) in keeping down costs to users shifting from 37 per cent before the talk to 47 per cent afterward and the number saying it was "very interested" from 23 to 35 per cent.

The questions on company image, such as "reputation in community," however, showed a falling off, particularly among men, who may have considered the connection with diamonds somewhat farfetched.

The message about Western Electric came through clearly with a 12-point increase in those who thought its efforts helped keep down phone costs after they had heard the talk.

"Salute to the Handicapped"

A lecture-demonstration related to the telephone aids available to handicapped persons could be expected to have strong human-interest appeal and favorable overtones. Such a lecture was tested by the Wisconsin Telephone Company in 1960, using ten audiences, and receiving from them 271 filled-out before-and-after questionnaires. The audience got the idea quickly, the cost index improving from 75 per cent before the program to 81 per cent afterward, and the company-attitude index rising from 84 to 89 per cent. As in several other cases, the customers who had had the most unfavorable attitudes softened their judgments most noticeably.

Specific figures are particularly interesting.

Before the lecture-demonstration, 40 per cent of the audiences said they thought that the Telephone Company was "quite interested" in keeping down the cost of its services and 18 per cent thought it was "very interested." After the talk the figures stood at 49 and 29 per cent respectively. Before the talk, 40 per cent felt that the Telephone Company had an "excellent" reputation in their community, afterward, 47 per cent. Beforehand, 39 per cent felt the Company had a "great deal of regard for the interests of the public," afterward, 52 per cent—a whopping gain of 13 points! Ninety-three per cent found the talk "very interesting."

"Sage—the Electronic Paul Revere"

The presentation of the role of electronics and communications in America's national defense was particularly dramatic and timely in 1960, when a before-and-after test of 427 persons was taken from among audiences who listened to the talk presented by the New York Telephone Company. Motion pictures and other visual aids were used in the talk. Technical explanations contained relatively few and indirect, but telling, commercial references.

As might be expected, with such a "socially acceptable" subject as national defense, the scores on many subjects showed marked gains. For example, before the talk 28 per cent of the respondents felt that the Telephone Company was "very interested" in keeping down costs of service to users. After the talk 42 per cent expressed this opinion.

Before the talk 39 per cent felt that the Company had "a great deal" of regard for the interests of the public, afterward, 47 per cent.

Beforehand 74 per cent felt that the Telephone Company was "contributing a great deal" to the scientific progress of the country, afterward, 85 per cent.

"Your Yellow Pages Time"

Evaluation, of course, may be just as useful in telling you what *not* to do as in lining up success stories. A good example is the information which the Michigan Bell Telephone Company received when it tried to stretch a little more commercial mileage out of its telephone time service in Detroit in 1960.

For many years Michigan Bell had offered a service whereby customers, after dialing a specific number, could obtain the time of day. Beginning on December 1, 1959, the recorded message used in this time service was changed to "At the tone, your *Yellow Pages* time will be ———." The cost of this additional promotion was minimal, and instead of being used for yellow pages, it might just as easily have been used for selling other services and equipment such as extension lines and colored telephones.

However, there was concern within the company over possible customer irritation, especially after several letters and phone calls had been received objecting to the "commercial." It was decided to take a survey to find out how people felt.

A random sample of 1,800 names was selected for telephone interviews. Of these, 1,487 could be reached, and of this number 549 had called Time Service within the past month. The survey was made in the last two weeks of January, 1960, about six weeks after the change in the time-service message had begun.

Thirty-seven per cent of the persons who had called Time Service remembered the mention of Yellow Pages. Unaided recall was lowest (6 per cent) among those who had called within the previous month as compared with 35 per cent of those who had called within the previous week.

When asked, 25 per cent of the respondents stated that they did not feel that the use of the additional words "Yellow Pages" was a good idea. This response contrasted with that given in a previous statewide survey, in which only 4 per cent of respondents felt that it was not a good idea for the Telephone Company to advertise in general.

Interestingly enough, those who were most conscious of the message liked it least. Of those who remembered the words "Yellow Pages" without help, 29 per cent felt that the interpolation was not a good idea; of those who had to be helped to recall it, 19 per cent disapproved of it. Women disliked the addition more than men—27 to 20 per cent. Those who had called most recently liked it less than those who had called some time ago, 30 per cent of the previous-week callers opposing it as compared to 13 per cent of the previous-month callers.

After digesting these reactions, the company dropped the whole idea.

General, Constant Customer-attitude Surveys

In addition to spot checks of particular events and programs, the Bell Telephone Companies run consistent surveys of public opinion in response to a standard set of questions concerning attitudes toward telephone service, costs, and general corporate image. These are taken from time to time on a regular basis; they are also taken in particular exchanges for comparison with the company-average scores, and in the various companies for comparison with the national indices.

"What Customers Think of Us," Saginaw, Michigan, 1960

The responses of a sample of 631 respondents were compared with those noted in a previous exchange survey taken a year earlier and with a companywide index taken about six months previously. Significant changes from the town's previous record or departures from the companywide norm were noted along with verbatim comments of respondents. The same procedure was followed in most cities.

"Trends of Customer Opinion," Michigan Bell, 1960

Beginning semiannually in 1949, and shifting to annually in 1957, Michigan Bell Telephone Company, a typical member of the A.T. & T. system, has been running a constant audit of customer opinion upon service, rates, and the company in general.

About 2,000 questionnaires are obtained in each annual survey. Questionnaires to be filled in are left overnight in the homes of residence customers, and are picked up the next morning. Distribution of the questionnaires is made by representatives of an outside research agency, and customers are selected at random to obtain proper proportions from large and small exchanges and from dial and manual offices.

A similar program is carried in other operating companies of the Bell System, and the results, taken together, provide a national norm by which each member company can measure itself.

"Customer Recall of Telephone Advertising and Information Activities," Nationwide

After extensive pretesting in 1957 and 1958, the Bell Systems made their first Systemwide Advertising–Public Information Study in the spring

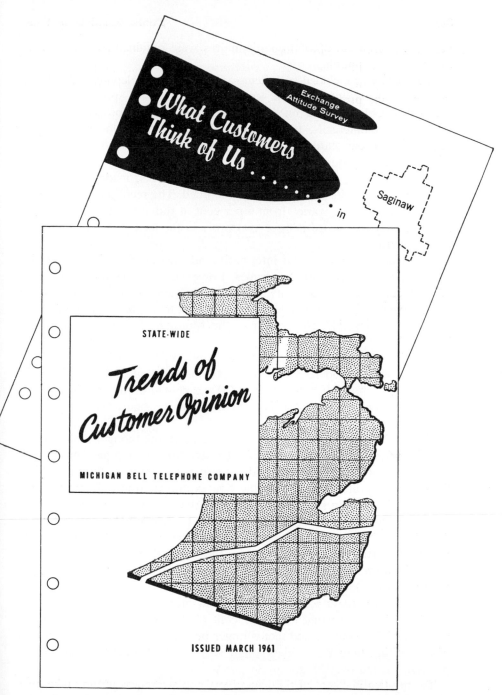

Figure 13-1. The Bell Telephone Companies keep a constant check upon the pulse of public opinion toward their service and standing by means of regular evaluations. These two from Michigan are duplicated by scores more from all over the United States.

of 1959. More than 30,000 questionnaires were obtained from customers throughout the nation.

Subject matter included such items as the recall of telephone advertising from newspapers, informational leaflets, magazines, TV spot commercials, the Bell Telephone Hour on TV, the science series of programs on TV, spot radio commercials, truck posters, booth cards, billboards, window displays, and car cards. All respondents were tabulated by age and economic-status groups.

The answers of those who heard lectures or talks, made central-office visits, or saw exhibits or displays were recorded. The recollection of lectures or talks, for example, varied from 6 per cent in Indiana (these respondents said that they had heard talks several times in the past year) to 1 per cent in Cincinnati.

Recall of promotional and informative advertising themes was likewise catalogued by systems and by themes. For example, a national average of 33 per cent recalled publicity about the advantages of the Telephone Company as a good place in which to work, but this percentage represented a variation from only 21 per cent in the Mountain States to 54 per cent in Canada.

Questions concerning sources of ideas and impressions about the Company met with varied responses. For example, in Southern New England Telephone Company territory almost 20 per cent said they got ideas from telephone speakers and open houses; in Ohio the figure was only about one-quarter as much.

Nationwide, about 70 per cent of the respondents thought that it was a good idea for the telephone companies to advertise; about 5 per cent thought that it was not; and 25 per cent did not express themselves. On this subject there was very little variation in the figures drawn from different regions.

A very interesting subject uncovered by the survey was the relationship of *awareness* of advertising in general to the favorable nature of responses. A series of five questions, such as "How much attention do you usually pay to advertising?" were asked, in the hope that the answers would establish an awareness record for individuals. This was then correlated with their responses to other questions asked in the survey.

Awareness surveys seem to indicate that men are somewhat less aware of advertising than women (33 per cent of the men are "low" versus 26 per cent of the women) and that younger people are somewhat more aware of advertising than their elders (high score in the under-35 group is 43 per cent; in the over-55 group, 35 per cent).

Twenty-two per cent of the low advertising-awareness group make over 30 local telephone calls a week, and 26 per cent make long-distance calls more than once a month. In the high-awareness group, 38 per cent make over 30 local calls weekly, and 46 per cent make long-distance calls more than once a month.

The effect of economic status or of location upon awareness is not clear and does not seem to vary much.

As might be expected, those who are aware of advertising recall advertising themes much more clearly than those who are not so alert. In newspaper advertising, for example, the variation ranges from 14 per cent recall among those of low awareness to 60 per cent among those of high awareness. In television advertising, the low-awareness group scores higher (19 per cent), but the high-awareness group scores lower (53 per cent). Magazines occupy an intermediate position.

"As trends of recall are obtained for this study," said the first report, "awareness could prove to be a useful analytical tool. For example, analyses could be made of the relative time it takes new themes to penetrate the three awareness groups. Similar work can be done in studying the relative standing of older themes for the three groups."

Summary

Evaluation of the effects of actions and communications is the wilderness of American public relations, but it is also the wilderness of the social sciences in general. While evaluation is not an exact science, some groups, such as A.T. & T., are doing much by its use to advance its standing and usefulness.

Three steps in evaluation are recommended for public relations practitioners:

1. At least an annual audit to review accomplishments, shortcomings, and goals. This should concern itself primarily not with effort expended, lest inches of clippings or numbers of mailings substitute for results, but rather with evidences of reception and response.

2. The use of empirical methods to check response.

3. The use of more scientific methods of opinion research as they have been explained earlier in Chapter 10. If a more thorough study is desirable, an outside research organization can be employed, and will bring to the work the considerable advantages of objectivity and experience.

The amount of money to be spent upon evaluation depends upon several factors, including the scope of the effort being evaluated, its duration, novelty, and importance to the organization. Internal considerations, for example, the need of support for public relations staffs and the need to present concrete evidence of the worth of their somewhat intangible work, are also important. In some organizations such as utilities, which are generally quite conscious of the importance of their public relations, matters of cost need not occupy more than a minor part of the public relations staff's total time; in others, such as trade associations, they may be almost a major consideration.

The Wider Development
of Public Relations

PART III

Worldwide Public Relations Developments

14

Americans today have become almost accustomed to revolutionary changes. A generation which has seen the fall of empires, two world wars and a depression, the development of automobiles and airplanes, and now atomic power, missiles, and interplanetary navigation can be excused for failing to notice some of the less obvious changes in its immediate surroundings.

Yet a quiet "communications revolution," which began on a worldwide basis in the late 1920s, today is racing on at an ever-accelerating pace and is perhaps more important than these more spectacular manifestations of human inventiveness and confusion because it brings new ideas to men's minds. How men think today will determine how they act, for good or ill, tomorrow.

The big change began with radio in the 1920s; was pushed along by fast air transport enabling travelers, mail, and printed matter to go all over the globe in a few days; was spurred further by great movements of troops and civilians during World Wars I and II; and faces a world-television phase which is just getting under way. In a short time, perhaps, human beings everywhere will be able to receive television broadcasts, in many different languages, sent from almost any spot on the surface of the earth or bounced off satellites.

Consider a village in India in 1914. The inhabitants lived and thought much as they had at the time of the Mogul emperors hundreds of years before, or even at the time of Alexander the Great, over two thousand years ago. There were no roads or automobiles. The railroad was probably miles away, and few, if any, of the inhabitants had ever seen a train, much less traveled on one. No one went anywhere; no one visited the village; no one (or almost no one) read, and there was little to read anyway. Life was hard and uncertain, but life had always been that way. And wasn't such an existence the common and necessary lot of mankind?

But now in thousands of such villages, the genie is out of the bottle! The day the first radio receiver came into the village or the first automobile arrived; the day when some people learned to read and began to receive newspapers or books, the whole mental atmosphere of the village began to change, never to be the same again. The coming of television will transform it still further. This revolution is happening all over the world. Changes which in the United States and Western Europe took hundreds of years, are being compressed elsewhere into decades. No wonder confusion, conflict, and great hopes are mingled with great frustration. Never before have so many people been exposed to so many new ideas in so short a time.

This is a particularly serious problem because it is so much easier to bring about a communications revolution which gives men new ideas than it is to develop the industrial revolution necessary to satisfy the hopes that a torrent of new concepts arouses in previously inarticulate and naïve people.

To put a radio set into a village, to ship in pamphlets or agitators, or to train a few people to read and debate is a much simpler task than to modernize farming, develop new mineral and other natural resources, build factories, and harmonize conflicting claims and beliefs based upon hundreds of years of experience. Communications revolutions inevitably outrun industrial revolutions, and unless men are wise enough to accept this inevitable time lag and to act accordingly, the result is likely to give power to those who are the most adept agitators. The problem of harmonizing these two revolutions must ultimately be dealt with through public relations. The problem would demand solution even if no such conflicting philosophies as democracy and communism existed in the world; with the complication of these two ideologies, it becomes doubly difficult to help industry to catch up with knowledge.

Government Public Relations Efforts Propaganda

Governments have been more or less alert to the effects of the communications revolution. First, they have needed to keep their own citizens happy through internal information, or propaganda. In nations where the impact of modern communications is just beginning to be felt, or where the government faces possible strong opposition, keeping the citizens happy is a major endeavor, enlisting all the mass media—newspapers, magazines, and broadcasting—as well as the arts of painting, dance, music, and writing. Knowing that communication is most effective among ill-informed people when it is one-sided, governments usually stress positive propaganda and accompany it with a strong negative censorship of incoming messages, including those by travelers, both native and foreign.

Second, governments wish to use communications to spread their influence abroad in order to acquire more trade and prestige, or to carry on a form of propaganda warfare. This is really what the so-called "cold war" is all about. Through communications, the Soviet Union and Red China seek to lead as many people as possible in other nations to accept the communist philosophy of life, to emulate their governmental institutions, and to look to Moscow or Peking for guidance. Such communications campaigns are reinforced by gifts, loans, military aid to rebellions, and even active Communist troop intervention when it is possible and safe.

In counteraction, other governments try to prevent such infiltration by promoting their own plans among their citizens and, in some cases, by reaching out to communicate behind the iron curtain which Russia and China throw about their own countries to prevent their citizens from hearing anything which might disturb approved communist ideology.

This global battle of words is not just the sideshow to a main event which centers in military weapons or money; it probably *is* the main event! In 1954, after the hydrogen bomb had demonstrated its awesome capacity to wipe out all life over hundreds of square miles, Sir Winston Churchill remarked that since wars could now destroy the leaders of all nations and their prized possessions, he expected "elaborate and cautious cross-cultural persuasion" to take the place of warfare as an instrument of national policy. It is no longer safe or profitable to use military power to force other people to do what you want them to do, and as the secret of the atom spreads to more and more small nations, hostile action will become increasingly unsafe. With a stalemate of military terror, nations now must attempt to spread their influence by persuasion and by other methods which fall short of total destruction for all concerned.

The "big three" in worldwide persuasion efforts are the Soviet Union, the United States, and Great Britain—in that order.

Figure 14-1. Communist propaganda. Purporting to picture a meeting of world press photographers in East Berlin, it is loaded with anti-Western themes, such as arousing fears of Nazism or colonialism.

Communist Propaganda

The Soviet Union, it is estimated, spends about 500 million dollars a year in its external propaganda efforts alone, but this is only an educated guess, since much low-cost labor, many embassy staffs, and the whole machinery of government are also working toward the goal of converting the whole world to communism. To these Russian programs the efforts of Communist China and of the European Communist satellite nations must be added. In one recent year, for example, the Soviet Union spent more money jamming "Voice of America" radio programs, so that they would be hard to receive in the Soviet Union, than the United States spent on sending them.

Much of this Communist propaganda material is of good production quality. The magazines are colorful and well illustrated, and the broadcasts are lively. Strong local agitation groups in the countries where it is received help to back up the propaganda.

In addition, the Communists have some natural advantages in appealing to the newly freed, little-developed countries of Africa and Asia and even to some in Latin America. Communists can capitalize upon hatreds directed toward former European colonial masters. The Communist industrial development has been more recent than ours and seems more attainable to poor people who are just beginning the climb. In many countries some form of state capitalism seems necessary, since so little private money is available for industry.

The weaknesses of Communist communication efforts are often caused by racial differences, by the strong feelings of nationalism evident in new countries, by the antipathy of Communist doctrine to religions, and by its insistence upon a materialistic philosophy which denies the basic human right of freedom of speech and other liberties to which many people, no matter how poor, still aspire. Communist propaganda efforts undoubtedly have had great influence upon the thought and governmental doctrines of many nations, but the result frequently seems to be not a polarization toward Moscow or Peking, but rather some form of national statism.

American Persuasion Efforts

The United States, through its U.S. Information Agency, spends about 124 million dollars annually in efforts to spread American prestige and ideals throughout the world. In concrete terms, the USIA employs about 11,000 people (4,000 Americans and 7,000 foreigners); spends 27 million dollars yearly upon broadcasts; maintains a news service, libraries, exhibitions, and cultural exchanges; produces films and publications of all sorts; and engages in book publishing in foreign languages.

Figure 14-2. The United States Information Agency sends out pictures and news like this one of Mrs. Kennedy speaking in Spanish to crowds in Venezuela on the occasion of the President's visit there in 1962.

Although USIA production quality has been good—occasionally too good for the standards of the people toward whom it has been aimed—the whole program has been under increasing fire for many years. Disregarding common Pecksniffian minor criticisms and the fact that lack of money, continuity of direction, and freedom are continual difficulties, we may profit-ably consider certain basic problems.

1. America doesn't know what it wants, and as a result, frequently wants the unobtainable. The height of unrealism after World War II was to imagine that the world could ever be put back into a snug Victorian mold, especially after the secrets of the atomic bomb had passed into Russian and other hands. Yet this is just what some Americans seemed to expect. It was equally foolish to think that American democratic government could be exported *in toto* to countries which lacked the literacy, unity, and tradi-tion to practice it unmodified. Much less could all American free enterprise business methods be copied by countries which at the moment had almost no enterprise of any sort. Insistence upon such unrealistic goals was ac-companied by excessive blame and despair when the USIA failed to help to attain them.

What America *really* wants is a friendly, orderly world, open to trade and travel, not organized against any one nation or polarized by strong economic and military ties to Peking or Moscow. This goal will be hard enough to attain, and it is a major task for all mankind; but it represents an ideal which most peoples outside the Communist bloc can accept. There is little chance of creating "little Americas" all over the globe. In the meantime Americans must uphold their own beliefs and keep alive the inspiring American legend as the embodiment of an ultimate goal for all peoples.

2. American communications shoot over people's heads. The standard rule of effective communication is that the communicator must start where the receiver is and must not get too far above him too quickly. If the receiver is accustomed to an oxcart, you don't tell him that in America most people drive automobiles costing several thousands of dollars each on roads whose construction costs millions of dollars. The hearer will disbelieve you or will be consumed with envy or will despair of ever making so big a step within his own land in his own lifetime. He may even dislike you intensely, accuse you of being a materialist, and say that he does not want automobiles. Too much United States overseas information emphasizes the incredible opulence of America, and too many of our tourists and businessmen and servicemen abroad have reinforced the impression.

3. American communications have relied too much on gifts and power. It is naïve to suppose that gifts automatically elicit gratitude from those who receive them. Gifts may be squandered, go to the wrong people, be used for the wrong things, and even if they are well used, leave a sense of frustration and indebtedness.

Power displays don't make friends at all, except among those who need a shield against some enemy. To those who do not perceive an immediate threat, such brandished power is simply cause for unease and fear; and usually men hate what they fear. Power should be masked and exposed only discreetly.

4. America engages in one-way conversations. Probably the chief weakness of USIA programs in the 1950s was that they were primarily output, telling others how good America was and not giving them much chance to tell us their problems and accomplishments, and to get in return our understanding and appreciation. This is particularly true among the newer, less-developed nations, who often want nothing more ardently than to be appreciated. Communication is a two-way process. If we expect others to listen to American ideas, we must first show that we listen to their ideas; and our attention must be demonstrated beyond the shadow of a doubt by our response to their words, their culture, their products, and their virtues.

American one-wayness manifests itself in seeking to turn others toward *our* goals. We should rather ascertain *their* desires and then identify American policies and information with such goals.

British Public Relations Efforts

The third big power in world persuasive communication is Great Britain, whose Central Office of Information spent about 67 million dollars in 1960 upon both its external and internal efforts.

This British government information organization is unique in that it consists of about 1,500 communications experts centered in London and serves the needs of almost all the departments of British government without itself setting policy. If the Commonwealth Office, for example, needs a poster, a member of the staff of that department decides upon its general nature, asks the Central Office of Information to get out such a poster, approves its production, and then pays the bill. The same system would apply to orders from the Foreign Office or other departments of the British government. In this way the praise or blame for the concept of an idea lies with the originating department, but centralization of technical skill and communications understanding in the Central Office of Information makes for greater efficiency at lower cost. The functions of the Central Office of Information may be compared to those of a public relations counseling firm or an advertising agency whose sole account is the British government and

Figure 14-3. The British Government Pavilion at the Brussels World's Fair in 1958 was part of the work of that nation's Central Office of Information which produces exhibits, films, booklets, and other public relations material.

Figure 14-4. Similar work is done inside the United Kingdom, as shown in this photo of Liverpool schoolgirls visiting a 1959 Commonwealth Exhibit designed to give the British public a comprehensive picture of the countries united in the Commonwealth.

whose relations with the departments of government are like those of a public relations firm with its clients.

As a result, British propaganda tends to be economically produced and very well conceived. It is low-key, reliable, and self-centered. Despite the smallness of the budget, it has undoubtedly been effective. British propaganda has the longest experience and the closest world contacts behind it and has exercised a pervasive influence that seems likely to far outshine the greatly diminished physical powers of the British Empire. On many points, of course, such as the rights of man and parliamentary freedoms, American and British political beliefs reinforce each other in the arena of world opinion.

Public Relations Representation of Foreign Governments

Although the Soviet Union, the United States, and Great Britain spend hundreds of millions of dollars annually in their public relations (or propaganda) programs over the world, their efforts by no means exhaust the field of worldwide government international public relations, much of which, among smaller nations, is handled by private public relations counseling firms.

Not only are the many new nations today in Africa and Asia engaged in communication, but many older nations in Latin America and elsewhere are also taking a new interest in the use of public relations to attain such goals as more tourists, increased trade, foreign loans and gifts, and greater political influence. These nations have representatives in Washington, London, and New York and also hire representation in many smaller European and other capitals. Much of this business has been, and still is, handled through national embassies or by special government information services; but more and more frequently local public relations firms are being offered foreign government accounts also. New small nations often do not have sufficiently trained foreign-service personnel for public relations needs, and even larger nations may find the special knowledge of local public relations men invaluable in presenting their case.

Some of this business is irreproachable. What can be wrong with promoting tourism to Ireland or to Western Germany? Some promotion efforts run into a conflict of interest in the United States; for example, Japanese textiles may compete with the products of North Carolina mills or Swiss watches with those made in Massachusetts. Here the anticipation of benefits to international trade may provide a justification for the propaganda. But some sponsorship of foreign interests poses ethical questions related to an individual's loyalty to the United States while representing other governments and their political and social beliefs.

The Union of South Africa, for example, has made a strong effort to get its accomplishments and views understood in the world. Before the Suez crisis, Nasser's Egypt was similarly active. At one time Hitler's Germany tried to present the best case it could before the bar of American opinion. The Dominican Republic's dictator went even further one time and spent a half million dollars to put hidden promotion on an American television network. What if an American firm was offered the public relations account of Israel or of the United Arab Republic in the United States? What if one of the Communist satellites, say Poland, sought representation for its tourism and trade promotion? How about Cuba? Perhaps even Red China?

The answers are not simple and cause much soul-searching among public relations men. These are dangerous accounts; a shift in the international political wind may turn innocent representation of the exotic tourist delights and interesting handcrafts of Bongo-Bongo into disloyalty to one's native land overnight, with accompanying ruin or great injury to the reputation of the public relations man or firm involved.

Foreign representation in local firms also reflects the communications revolution which has swept the world. Public opinion is now so important to many governments that they will inevitably try to influence it. Diplomacy itself often becomes a series of plays to the grandstand of world public opinion rather than a serious discussion. It is useless to deplore this development, which is probably no worse than the old-fashioned secret diplomacy, in which a few men gathered around a green baize table and carved up empires and people's lives without so much as mentioning the fact to those involved. Modern public diplomacy is noisier and more upsetting and forces us to listen and think whether we wish to or not. But discussion in the light of day, even when heated, partisan, and sometimes false, is probably preferable to quiet darkness; we shall have to live with this new dimension of international communications, set up ground rules, and adapt ourselves to it. Those who offer quiet darkness in diplomacy often have undemocratic objectives.

The Public Relations of International Groups

When the United Nations was organized in 1945 and the European Economic Community (the Common Market or The Six) came into being in 1958, a new type of public relations machine began to appear. International organizations, of which there are many, need to issue information and persuasion if they are to live and grow, and they cannot depend upon member governments for this purpose. Organizations which are entities in themselves need to explain what they are doing and to seek worldwide support for it. If their doings cannot be reported directly to the people in the various nations of which they are composed, they cannot expect support from the government alone, and they may well wither; governments of national states tend to regard jealously any popular enthusiasm for supranational organizations.

The strength of the United Natons, for example, lies to a large extent in the wide coverage of its activities by the news media, in the many people who visit it, and in the many publications and activities of organizations such as the United Nations Educational, Scientific, and Cultural Organization (UNESCO). If a "parliament of man" is really ever to develop, it must be founded upon a free flow of information which will guarantee *popular* support as well as the support of governments.

Developments in the European Economic Community, by which France, West Germany, Italy, Belgium, Holland, and Luxembourg, beginning in 1958, substantially united their economies, have followed much the same pattern. There is an obvious need within these various countries for citizen information about the doings of this supranational organization. EEC activities will affect jobs, purchases, travel, and culture. There is need for European citizen support for the work of the EEC because frictions are certain to arise in which local national interests may be opposed to broader European interests, and if the EEC cannot express its viewpoint directly to its publics, its growth will inevitably be limited. Most of this EEC public relations work has been volunteered by enthusiasts or by business or other interests which benefit from greater European unity, but in one form or another such information and support must be provided if the Community is to prosper.

The whole future of the world lies in ideas about world organization and their dissemination. There is no doubt that—with recent great advances in air transport and in missile weapons some form of world organization is the only alternative to ruinous war. The United States of America, the United Nations, the European Economic Community, and the British Commonwealth of Nations have all set up forms of voluntary free association for better living and self-protection. The Communist world has another idea for world organization—monolithic, restricted, allowing for little diversity or freedom. Both concepts today compete in their appeal to undecided people by means of mass communication and many other methods of information and persuasion.

The Private Development of Public Relations Practice Abroad

Figures on government propaganda, such as 500 million dollars spent by the U.S.S.R. or 124 million dollars spent by the United States, might create the impression that the private practice of public relations within a nation is very small by comparison, until we recall that the estimated expense for public relations salaries in private practice in the United States in 1957 was 500 million dollars and that this sum does not include the cost of preparing material by printers, film makers, broadcasters, and others, which was undoubtedly several times as large. When we discuss the development of private public relations practice abroad, we must realize that its apparently small scale does not indicate its importance and rapid growth.

America is still the world's most developed nation in public relations practice, but the same conditions that produced growth here are now prevalent in other countries also.

1. The rise of industry and a reasonable standard of living, popular education, and literacy. Without these there is nothing for private public relations men to communicate about.

2. The availability of mass communications media such as newspapers, magazines, radio, direct mail, and television. Without these, there is no way to reach people on a large scale.

3. Freedom to communicate. There is little private public relations practice in a police state because the government monopolizes all persuasion and information. If public opinion is to rule, men must be free to speak their minds to one another.

Whenever these three conditions prevail, the development of private public relations practice is ready to begin. As a public relations man in Holland once observed, "The seeds are always there. It just takes the right combination of weather to cause them to sprout." With a communications revolution under way in the world, the weather has been increasingly right in many places in the past twenty years.

The Public Relations of International Business

When an American company sells goods abroad or establishes a subsidiary company on foreign soil, or when foreign manufacturers such as the Swiss Watch Association, the Belgian lacemakers, or the British woolen manufacturers desire to promote their wares in the United States, a host of new public relations problems come into play. As world trade has increased, especially with the lowering of tariff barriers within organizations like the Common Market or the British Commonwealth of Nations, new scope and dimensions have been given to the public relations of international business. Questions are not only economic, such as those arising from the sale of goods, but are also political, social, and cultural as different values and ways of thinking meet.

When an American firm, for example, exports its capital to buy a European factory, it very sensibly establishes as good public relations as possible within the country where the new plant is located. Indeed, much of the impetus of postwar development of public relations in Western Europe, has come from the example of American firms there, especially in the operations which concern oil and aviation. Those who set out to do business in any foreign country face several problems that they might not encounter at home.

Foreigners are automatically suspect. People fear that foreigners may have too much power within their country; local employers may complain that wage rates offered by foreign-owned firms are too high and that they lure the local workers away from their home firms; and there is always the ultimate danger that popular clamor may lead to government seizure and nationalization of an outside-owned plant, sometimes with very little compensation. No longer is it readily possible, any place on the globe, to call in the United States Marines to set things right if confiscation does take place. Exporting capital without also exporting understanding is foolish.

Good public relations are essential abroad even in the normal course of doing business. There are often natural patriotic preferences for home-produced goods over foreign-owned makes, preferences which competitors will be sure to take advantage of. No two countries are alike, and the wisest course for an American business abroad is to heed certain good counsels.

1. Hire good local public relations men if possible. Without years of experience, few Americans can know all the things about a foreign situation that they ought to know, and in any case they are at a disadvantage in public relations compared with native-born communicators simply because they are foreigners. Americans show their origin in speech, looks, and ways of thinking. Finding

a good local public relations man is not always easy; in less-developed countries he may not even exist. An American firm may have to train him itself, or it may be able to use the services of an American public relations counseling firm with connections abroad. The firm will need to do a great deal of hunting and checking, because public relations is an elusive intangible. There are quacks, front men, lazy men, and disloyal or dishonest men in any field, and in a little-developed profession in some countries they are particularly hard to sort out.

2. Don't expect public relations in Brazil, Italy, Japan, or any other country to be just like public relations in the United States. Not only are there differences in the stage of industrial development, but there are also vast differences in social and cultural customs, in the media of communication, in the character-istics of leaders of opinion, and in the basic patterns of thought and influences upon thought. Some public relations ideas which work in the United States *may* work well in another country; but on the other hand, they may fail or even do harm. Before you take action in public relations, ask more questions and listen more attentively. Don't try to tell a foreign public relations man to do something without getting his viewpoint. Another land may have a different sense of the value of time; may have different ways of valuing money and position; and very often may have an ingrained suspicion of motives. A classic illustration concerns an American oil company which found it could not give away free university scholarships in a Latin-American country until it tacked on a require-ment that the recipients had to work for a stated period of years for the company after graduation. The suspicious inhabitants could see through this requirement and accept it; but doing good deeds for the sake of general good will was so unfamiliar a concept that no one could believe that it did not conceal some deeply buried plot such as brainwashing. In the United States a similar offer would have been accepted as a matter of course and applauded.

3. If you hire a good foreign public relations man, spend some time with him. Loyalty, interest, and enthusiasm are qualities which cannot be bought. Only personal contact and friendship can engender them, and this is particularly true in many foreign countries where people insist upon liking their employers as well as accepting their pay.

Knowledge of the business is another thing which cannot be bought, although it can be given. Large American companies doing business abroad make it a point not only to visit their foreign public relations men but also to bring them to this country to meet executives, to see processes, and to know the company as a group of people rather than just as a name.

Status of Private Public Relations Development Abroad

The United States is acknowledged to be the leader in world develop-ment of private public relations practice, but the conditions of educational, industrial, and communications media development and democratic free-doms which made the rise possible here are now being rapidly diffused around the globe.

Western Europe, of course, is the area most like the United States, and the growth of public relations there, although recent, is most similar to that in America. Leading Western European countries have professional public relations associations, and practitioners are often men of high ability with an exact understanding of their work and a keen concern about ethical practices.

Most professional public relations development in Western Europe dates back to about 1946, the end of World War II. The example of American military forces at that time, and of American firms later, lent powerful impetus to public relations ideas which would probably have come anyway with the booming business of the 1950s. Factors still being overcome, however, are paternalism and secrecy in industry, ingrained class and sectional frictions leading to suspicion, government controls, the weakness (or in some cases the purchasability) of the communications media, a strong lingering distrust of propaganda dating back to World War II and prior days in Nazi Germany and Fascist Italy, and an almost complete lack of university-level education in public relations or related communications fields.

Great Britain is the most highly developed country in public relations and is most like the United States. The size and stature of its professional organization provide a measure of the progress of the country. The British Institute of Public Relations, founded in 1948, grew to 770 members by 1955, and in 1962 had more than 1,400 members. (By comparison, the Public Relations Society of America, founded in 1946, now has about 4,500 members. The population of Great Britain is about 50 million and that of the United States about 180 million.)

In 1958 the British Institute of Public Relations issued the first guidebook to public relations in Great Britain and reprinted it in 1960. The Institute has been active in meetings and conferences and has sponsored educational courses. A system of examinations has been devised, and it is planned that eventually admission to the Institute will be open only to those who have passed these tests, although at present, membership is achieved through five years' comprehensive public relations experience, recommendation, and a vote. The headquarters of the Institute are in London, and provincial chapters have been formed.

As in the United States, most British public relations people come from newspaper backgrounds, and the press is the greatest means of communication, although tours, exhibits, films, and booklets are more extensively used in Great Britain than here. Government public relations work was developed earlier than industrial public relations in Britain, going back to about 1912, when Prime Minister Lloyd George hired a group of speakers to go about the country explaining the new National Insurance Act. Government information activity in World Wars I and II expanded the field, which is now centered in the Central Office of Information in London.

Industrial and other commercial or association public relations efforts began later and are still developing.

Like most things British, public relations in the United Kingdom is conducted in a quieter key than in the United States. It tends to be more informative and personal, and in spite of its avoidance of noise, is thoroughly modern and effective.

France. The Association Française des Relations Publiques, which was established in 1955, has about 280 members. Public relations practice began in France about 1949 and led to a club, La Maison de Verre (the Glass House), in 1950. The association issues a quarterly magazine, meets regularly, and has sponsored schools for practitioners.

Relatively slower development in France has been a reflection of the social and political problems of France's postwar years. For competitive or governmental reasons, French business has been conducted in a tradition of secrecy. Class and political divisions have been bitter, absorbing popular energies. The long opposition to the painful liquidation of the empire, especially in Indo-China and Algeria, divided the national mind. The press, lacking economic strength and a tradition of independence, often sells news space or allows advertising to be tied in with news stories. This practice has made it hard for public relations men to get proper news releases run (if someone else has already bought the newspaper), and has made the public suspicious of the truth of reports in many newspapers and magazines. Because of the lack of a large independent advertising base, French newspapers are smaller, with less news content, and because they represent various political loyalties, they are numerous, each one with a relatively small circulation. Radio and television are controlled by the government and are not generally available as media except under special circumstances of supervision.

Yet despite these handicaps, a small number of gifted, hardworking public relations men turn in an excellent performance. With a quickening economy, new social outlook, and greater unity within the nation, their opportunities may be expected to improve. French public relations material is often characterized by high artistic standards, dramatic ideas, a personal touch, and the extensive use of meetings, tours, and school contacts.

Italy. L'Associazione Italiana per le Relazioni Pubbliche is the second-largest professional public relations group in Europe. It has about 500 members, was founded in 1954, issues a large monthly magazine (with parts in English, French, and Spanish), holds numerous meetings and schools, and as an association, has the second-largest budget in the world. There are several reasons.

One reason, of course, is the natural enthusiasm of the Italian temperament, to which both the desire and ease of communication come naturally.

Another is the knowledge of the Italians that to make their way in the world as a nation, they have to depend on brains, alertness, and charm as much as on natural resources. But even more important is the effect of the special problems of Italy.

Ever since World War II Italy has had the largest Communist party in Europe. Most of the population of Italy lives in the beautiful but poor country south of Rome, and most of the wealth is north of Rome. Italy suffered considerable war damage, and fascism left an aftermath of bitterness and division. Industry had been inefficient, highly protected, and monopolistic. There is a tradition of citizen noncooperation with the policeman and tax collector. Illiteracy was high in the poverty-stricken south, and although many people ardently desired a free and responsible democratic system of government, the necessary conditions of economic growth, education, and citizen understanding and participation, particularly on the local level, were nonexistent.

These circumstances have affected the public relations activities in Italy. They have necessarily been much concerned (more so than in Great Britain or the United States) with aiding the very fundamentals of democracy through training for tax public relations, police public relations, and municipal official relations; through programs on citizen participation in government, school education in citizenship, international exchanges, and business-system understanding. Italian public relations has a strong civic and governmental emphasis.

At the same time, university contacts, especially in the fields of sociology and psychology, have been developing. Italian public relations is serious-minded with a sense of social mission. The greatest part of its business development is ahead.

West Germany. The long period of rebuilding after war damage, preoccupation with the partition of the country, soul-searching about war guilt and the former acceptance of Nazi propaganda lies, and a deep authoritarian habit (we-know-what-is-best-for-you) in both government and industry delayed the development of professional public relations in West Germany longer than in any other European country. It was not until 1958 that the Deutsche Public Relations Gesellschaft, centering in the lower Rhine industrial area, was formed. It now has about 80 members, and in 1959 the first book on public relations in Germany by Adalbert Schmidt, then of Bonn, was published.

The press is generally independent in West Germany, and other means of communication are well developed. Better public relations men look westward toward world trade and a place among the six Common Market nations union of which West Germany is a member; but there is also a strong pull toward Soviet and Eastern European trade. German labor and public opinion were generally quiescent in the years from 1945 to 1960, but may be expected to be more vocal as the nation advances in new directions. Public relations practice should develop more rapidly in the future.

The Low Countries. Before 1952 the idea of public relations was generally unknown in Belgium, but in the latter part of that year a number of practitioners formed the Centre Belgique des Relations Publiques, which now has an active program and about 70 members. In Holland the Nederlands Genootschap voor Public Relations was formed in 1954 and now has about 60 members. These two groups have joined in issuing a small bimonthly magazine on public relations, written in French, Dutch, and Flemish.

Located in a highly industrial area at the main sea entry into Europe, Dutch and Belgian public relations practitioners have worldwide connections and serve as a bridge between Britain, whose public relations practices theirs much resemble, and the Continent. Since many of the practitioners have university connections, they have occasionally been allowed to hold courses. As the seat of the headquarters of the European Economic Community (Common Market) is at Brussels, Belgians are much interested in European developments, and most public relations practitioners are advocates of greater unity.

Switzerland. Switzerland is a little country of only 5 million people, and its public relations is often close to "personal relations," although there are some excellent practitioners who work not only in Switzerland but in the Swiss headquarters of several international industries. Because of the smallness of the country, meetings, tours, exhibits, and booklets can easily be used in communication. Press relations have involved much effort to reach a common understanding of the proper roles of advertising and publicity.

Other European nations. Professional public relations groups are also to be found in Norway, Sweden, Finland, Greece, Spain, and Ireland. Denmark has no group but has active practitioners.

Elsewhere. The Canadian Public Relations Society has about five hundred members and an active program. Australia, New Zealand, South Africa, and India have groups. In Latin America, Brazil and Mexico are most developed. Japan, an industrialized nation, has a developing public relations practice. Interest is strong in the Philippines. Public relations groups are also listed for China (Taiwan) and were at one time listed in Cuba.

Practices naturally vary greatly, those in Canada, for example, being equivalent to those in the United States; but in less-developed countries public relations is often confused with handshaking and "partying." We must realize, however, that articulate and powerful publics are limited in less-industrialized, less-literate countries without a long tradition of popular participation in government and business. Hence the attempt to reach a smaller number of leaders may serve for the present as a substitute for widespread *public* relations. The danger is that the public may think that communication of information is confined to the rulers only. With coming advances in the dissemination of ideas, a broader popular basis of understanding may be both more possible and more valuable.

International Professional Activities

The International Public Relations Association, a worldwide group of public relations practitioners, doing business outside the borders of their member nations as well as within, was founded in 1955 and has headquarters in London. There are about 180 members. General meetings are held yearly in chief cities of members' countries. The main objectives are to exchange information, to improve practices and goals, and to establish contacts.

In 1958 the First World Congress of Public Relations was held in Brussels in connection with the World's Fair there. The Belgian Public Relations Association acted as host, and 237 delegates from 23 countries attended. The Second World Congress was held in Venice in 1961, with an attendance of about 300 from 28 countries. The Italian association acted as host. The Third World Congress is slated for Montreal in 1964, with the Canadian association as host.

In addition to the International Public Relations Association (IPRA), there is also the Centre Européen des Relations Publiques formed in 1959 and headquartered at Brussels. This regional group consists of members from the six nations of the Common Market and has among its objectives advancing public relations work within the Common Market countries and encouraging the acceptance of the Common Market idea. Much of this latter work is done voluntarily by members who believe in greater European unity and wish to popularize the concept within their own countries.

In 1960 the First Inter-American Public Relations Conference was held in Mexico City, attended by representatives of associations in Brazil, Colombia, Cuba, Chile, the United States, Panama, Puerto Rico, and Venezuela. Plans were set up to establish a federation of public relations associations in the Americas, improve education, and raise ethical standards.

In 1961 an International Center for the Study of Public Relations Education was established at the University of Louvain, Belgium, and has been busy collecting information upon public relations educational practices.

Many needs are yet to be met within the international public relations field, but the rapid growth of its practice and the awareness of practitioners of their problems lead to hopes that, in the free-speech part of the world at least, the standards of competence, honesty, fairness, and service in the public good will be constantly advanced.

ADDITIONAL READING

International Public Relations

La Maison de Verre, quarterly journal of the French Association of Public Relations, Paris.

"Proceedings of the Second World Congress of Public Relations in Venice, May, 1961," the Italian Public Relations Association, Rome, 1961.

Public Relations, quarterly journal of the Institute of Public Relations of Great Britain, London.

"Public Relations in the Service of Social Progress: Proceedings of the First World Congress of Public Relations," Belgian Center of Public Relations, Brussels.

Relazioni Pubbliche, monthly journal of the Italian Public Relations Association, Rome.

Barrett, Edward W.: *Truth Is Our Weapon,* Funk & Wagnalls Company, New York, 1953.

Scott, John: *Political Warfare,* The John Day Company, Inc., New York, 1955.

Stephens, Oren: *Facts to a Candid World: America's Overseas Information Program,* Stanford University Press, Stanford, Calif., 1955.

Positions, Preparation, and Professionalism

15

"The common service department [public relations]," a British government public relations chief said several years ago, "must never forget that, like the public relations officers of any organization, it is a servant and not the master. It has been said that the Queen of England has three functions: to advise her ministers, to warn them, and to encourage them. In the same way [the public relations head] can advise, warn, or encourage his clients . . . but finally he must *do* what they want and *not do* what they do not want, because they are taking the policy responsibility and will receive most of the blame . . . if anything goes wrong. . . ."

This accurate description of the nature of a staff service function outlines the circumstances under which public relations leadership within an organization usually works.

Organizational Rank

The public relations director of a company or other organization is almost always a staff functionary, usually responsible to the highest, or the next to the highest, line officer—ordinarily the president, vice-president, or general manager. He is on a par with the legal counsel, a financial adviser, or others whose expert services are offered to anyone in the company where they are most needed and will do the most good. Unlike line officers, who usually have an immediate superior and numbers of inferiors in a chain of command, the staff public relations man is really responsible to numbers of superiors (or at least peers) for whom he directly or indirectly does public relations work, and he has relatively few subordinates except the usually small numbers on his own staff, such as his assistants, specialists, and clerical workers.

The public relations head is a middleman dealing in ideas, who engages in informal communication both downward and upward. Some of his public relations ideas may perhaps come from his immediate superiors, the vice-presidents, for example, or the general manager. His problem is to analyze them, to agree or disagree, to work them into operating form, and then to gain the cooperation and good will of others in the organization whose approval and aid are needed if the ideas are to be carried out. The public relations head's ultimate trump card, seldom openly acknowledged and almost never played, is his support from, and his access to, higher power. But if he leans on his special access to power too much, though he may be respected he may also be feared and disliked because, unlike the line men of production or of sales, he touches all departments and knows something about everybody. His work circulates through the entire organization and crisscrosses boundaries of authority. His relationship to the top power may range from truly right-hand to purportedly right-hand, or may simply rest insecurely upon the high, but detached, spot he occupies on the organizational chart.

Many public relations plans originate within the active imagination of a good public relations man, who then faces the problem of selling them, perhaps first to top management, which will support them, perhaps first to special-interest areas of management, which will carry them to the top for final authorization. Public relations ideas may also originate down the line. If they are good, they can be carried to the top for approval, with proper credit to the source and perhaps with revisions; but if they are poor, they can be acknowledged with an explanation and thanks, but without action. (There is always the possibility that the originator will then take his ideas directly to headquarters himself—and, even worse, that headquarters may think them wonderful.)

Unlike the good soldier of the line ranks, who simply obeys his superiors, does his work well, and is a good officer to his inferiors, the public relations staff man sends his ideas coursing through the veins of the entire organization in a manner both exhilarating and dangerous, his work rendered doubly interesting by its constant traffic with intangibles. The production head can point to the volume, low cost, and high quality of his output as evidence of good work; the sales department can count its figures; and another fellow staff member, the company attorney, can lean for authority upon a ponderous knowledge of what one can or cannot do while staying safely within the law. But although effective public relations, like the air itself, exists, it is as difficult to measure as air, and the layman finds the measurements equally unsubstantial and unconvincing.

In addition, the good public relations man must be able to convey upward or sidewise communications as effectively as downward communications. He should know what people in the lower ranks think or what influential publics outside the organization feel, and be able to carry the information to the top. To do this, he must often be away from his desk and plant, spending his time at apparently useless meetings or talking idly, both of which occupations are natural irritants to cost-and-duty–conscious line officers. The public relations gadfly lives in several worlds; his connections are mysterious; and his output is difficult to assess.

Personal Qualities

It is not surprising, then, that several traps are connected with the lively and interesting post of public relations director of an organization.

Gossiping. It is hard to be a many-voiced communicator without carrying tales from contact to contact—a cardinal sin, of course, except to the head man to whom reports are due. The chief who supports you is entitled to know, and presumably he is a gentleman of honor in whom it is safe to confide. With others, however, a reputation for being an "old wife" quickly gets around and ruins all trust and friendship.

Butterflyism. The affliction of "butterflyism" is akin to a similar occupational disease of salesmen—an enthusiasm for motion, sensation, and sheer busyness as a substitute for thought. In a salesman hectic activity may look like work, but in a public relations man it is usually fatal, because it prevents the careful research and thought which are so fundamental to effective communication programs. Its only real merit, in fact, is that it impresses observers who do not know the subject very well.

Megalomania. Production or other line administrators are frequently accounted important because of the *number* of persons they have working for them. Public relations departments on the other hand are and should be usually small. Keeping down the number of workers is sound common sense, because a large department invites trimming. Peak loads can usually be handled by borrowing help or by hiring temporary outsiders.

Officiousness. The wide range within which the public relations head circulates gives him a broad acquaintance with the whole organization. If he is intelligent, he will see things that might be improved, and unless he is careful, he will forget his boundaries and imagine that he, rather than the president or the board of directors, is running the company. It is very unlikely that he could do a better job than they do, and if his vanity is discovered it will not be appreciated. To comprehend a function is far easier than to carry it out skillfully, and there is always danger that a flash of comprehension may blind one to the virtues of hard work, patience, and wisdom which are the real secrets of much successful administration.

These are some of the main traps. But what qualities of character are needed to avoid them and also to achieve success in the practice of public relations?

Integrity. Integrity means a quality of moral courage which will enable a public relations man to point out a danger when it would be more diplomatic to keep silent; to vote "no" in good spirit and with good reasons and yet, if overruled, to accept a higher verdict; and to see things as they really are, despite his or other people's desires to have them different.

Integrity follows a hard road, and those who are merely cantankerous or self-assertive should not think that they are showing integrity by throwing their weight around upon many small issues. Professional "no" men are almost as absurd in their way as professional "yes" men; but there are times when, after careful investigation and mature thought, a man feels that he should oppose a plan for which top management pushes hard or, even worse, feels impelled to advocate a program which is certain to meet with management hostility.

It must be recognized, however, that some employers prefer servants who always say "yes." If agreement is what they want, that is what they are paying for, and sometimes, if employers have sufficient ability, they may even succeed with "yes" men. It should not be forgotten that in the final decisions, the head of the organization makes the rules, orders them carried out, and takes the responsibility. At this point, line and staff men alike have no choice except to support or to resign.

But with all of these qualifying cautions, we must still maintain that integrity of mind and character is the only thing in a public relations man which can inspire an organization's confidence and give him any proper claim to leadership.

Personal communicative ability. Because public relations work is intangible, it may require a great deal of explaining within its own organization. One public relations head said wearily, "I spend half my time explaining to people what I'm doing, and the other half doing it!" A line production man can often be the strong, silent type, because his work speaks for itself. A public relations man, however, must talk, write, and promote his work constantly, because usually it does not speak for itself. He *must* practice at home what he preaches abroad or else be misunderstood.

Personal communicative ability means much more than readiness to make a good speech or to write a good letter. It springs from a sincere interest in people and pleasure in their presence and is not to be confused with the outgoing of the so-called extrovert personality which sometimes takes pleasure only in its own presence and which desires to dominate every situation, to the distress of others who would like some recognition. Sometimes the public relations man is expected to occupy the limelight; more often he prepares the stage for others to be seen and heard. But he constantly needs to keep his associates aware of what he is doing and thinking, to make their goals his goals, to respond to their enthusiasms, and to have the capacity to inspire enthusiasm in them for his plans. This cannot be done by an individual who simply does not like people and prefers to deal with things instead of humanity; such a man belongs in the laboratory or in the accounting office.

Real friendliness is unforced, although it can be cultivated. Often people may seem unfriendly because they are too self-conscious, a feeling often traceable to physical or social inferiority suffered in youth. A public relations man also needs empathy to place himself in other persons' shoes quickly and to see things in the light in which they see them. The chief hindrance to quick empathy, or understanding of others, is egocentrism. The man who is too busy seeing the world from his own viewpoint cannot appreciate the viewpoints of others and as a rule cannot get along with them. The phrase "to know all is to understand all" may well be extended by adding the additional words "and to like better."

Emotional stability. There is no denying that the chief problem of people is people; and since the public relations man works with people all the time, he has his full quota of emotional strains. He operates often as a middleman between those who are easily angered, slow, bullheaded, or irresponsible; and at times he may need every ounce of emotional stability that he can summon to avoid falling into absurd behavior himself. How is this steadiness to be achieved?

The cultivation of several qualities and the avoidance of others are important. *Egocentrism* is a hindrance to emotional stability because it prevents separating issues from personalities. "Love me, love my ideas!" A realistic, well-proportioned sense of one's personal worth and shortcomings is not easily achieved, and it is often taught only by age and experience, by hard knocks and success. "Let no man think more highly of himself than he ought," said St. Paul.

A *broad intellectual background* helps a man to place himself in the long perspectives of history and science. Travel and varied experiences are also an aid. A *sense of humor* is the priceless possession of a man who does not take either himself, or other people, too seriously.

And finally an adequate *personal religious philosophy* is a great aid to emotional stability. Different men arrive at an understanding of life by different roads, but all who maturely approach the riddle of human existence must eventually start thinking of ultimate meanings. The facts of life and death alone force the consideration of religion upon every man.

Intelligence. Public relations is not a life for the slow-witted. Besides a pleasing personality and a sound outlook, public relations practice demands mental quickness, creative thought, and sound judgment.

Some of these qualities are acquired through study and experience, but an intelligent man has also an inherent basic capacity. It is not entirely to a man's credit or discredit either to be blessed with, or to fall short of excellence in natural ability. Intelligent people generally know that they are intelligent, but the egos of slow people sometimes make them think that they, too, are quick-witted.

Measuring intelligence is as yet an inexact process; but those whose tests indicate a consistently low level will find it wiser to go into some other field than public relations.

Studiousness. More public relations money is wasted through doing the wrong things or failing to do the right things than through any other cause. The usual reason for the mistakes is lack of study of the situation in advance. An uninformed bright man is often no more capable than a stupid man and sometimes much more erratic.

Studiousness arises from sheer intellectual curiosity and from reasoned determination to master the facts of a situation. It is a habit which may be the most valuable by-product of an education, if indeed it should not be the main product.

Many failures in public relations spring from lack of understanding of the organization for which the public relations man is working and from ignorance of communications processes or target audiences; yet details of the history, organization, personalities, and processes of almost any institution are usually easily available to those who would like to know them before presuming to advise. Public relations depends upon facts as a basis for action, just as good journalism rests upon facts for significant communication.

Health. There are no particular occupational hazards in the practice of public relations, such as Madison Avenue ulcers or presidential coronaries, but the creative and emotional demands of the work, its long and uncertain hours, and the occasional hazards of banquet tables, cocktail parties, and travel circuits make a stable, if not a rugged, physical constitution desirable. Since for most public relations men their work is also their hobby in the conventional sense, outdoor sports are to be recommended. In a recent survey of the avocations of du Pont public relations men, swimming ranked first in popularity, with golf, tennis, and fishing following in that order. The forty men surveyed were also great readers; they liked music and news on the radio, and they watched sports and news on television.

Work abilities. After asking "What sort of person is he?" the prospective employer of a public relations man also wants to know "What can he do?" As seen earlier in this book, the scope of activities within public relations is so broad that the problem is to draw out of this multitude of abilities the absolute fundamentals upon which almost everyone is agreed. Surprisingly enough, they are rather few.

WRITING ABILITY was named as the most important ability in public relations by 70 per cent of those responding to a national Public Relations Society of America survey in 1956 [1] and by 87 per cent of those respond-

---

[1] Report of the National Research Committee of the Public Relations Society of America, New York, 1956.

ing to a similar New York City survey in 1961.[2] By "writing ability" is generally meant the power to express oneself in clear English prose suitable to the presentation of a good news story, a feature article, or a plan for a new public relations program.

Writing ability, of course, depends upon general intelligence and education; no one can possibly write better than he thinks. It is also the result of much reading, of practice in writing and rewriting, as well as of the critical study of good writing in many fields. Writing demands sufficient confidence on the part of the writer to feel that he has something worth saying and that he can say it, and sufficient humility to realize that he must make an effort to interest others and must be willing to repolish or even recast a piece of writing entirely in order to make it clearer and more coherent.

Many good writers (commercial writers, that is, such as journalists, advertising writers, or public relations writers) go through three stages:

First comes what might be termed "the high school sophomore stage," which is, perhaps, but one step above illiteracy. It is a state of simple unhappiness and fear of facing a great number of words. At this stage the assignment to write a 2,000-word essay seems like a prison sentence, and most individuals never progress beyond it.

Second comes an intoxication with words. Suddenly self-expression becomes delightful; often carried along on a tide of freely flowing language, a man would rather write than eat. If his writing happens to coincide with the interests of his readers, well and good; if not, it makes no difference to him; he will write anyway, even if he has no audience but himself. Many one-book fiction writers, including some of the best-sellers, belong in this category. Writing is simply a form of self-expression.

Finally comes acceptance of the discipline of writing for a purpose. The question is not "Will I like it?" but rather "Will the recipients like and understand it?" Such discipline develops a high standard of literary craftsmanship, unwillingness to be satisfied with anything but the best words or phrases, and a versatility which manifests itself in efforts as varied as business letters, addresses of welcome, and advertisements stating company positions in a labor dispute. A disciplined writer is like a big eight-cylinder car with a great reserve of power, running smoothly in any gear. Such writing is hard but rewarding, both in personal satisfaction and in material gains.

EXPERIENCE IN RELATED FIELDS can hardly be considered an "ability"; yet in the previously mentioned surveys, from the employer's viewpoint such experience ranked second in importance.

Historically, the field most nearly related to public relations has been journalism, and today about half of America's public relations men still

---

[2] "Career Opportunities in Public Relations," a survey by John E. Sattler, first vice president, New York Chapter of the Public Relations Society of America, 1961.

come from newspaper staffs, where their work has not only developed writing ability, but has also facilitated wide contacts and has assisted in developing many of the qualities of character previously mentioned in this chapter.

Such fields of communication as broadcasting, selling, advertising, teaching, and preaching can also be drawn upon for practitioners of public relations. The process of passing from one field to another will be discussed more completely in the section of "Education," which follows.

SPEAKING ABILITY was also mentioned by 30 per cent of the respondents in the PRSA survey. Some public relations men are semiprofessional speakers; all have to have the ability to speak adequately, clearly, and convincingly before various groups.

Education for Public Relations

Occupying a staff advisory position fairly high up the executive scale, the public relations man is hired not only for his personal qualities, skills, and experience, but also for his wisdom. As a counselor, he must have the background to inspire confidence in his counsels. How is wisdom to be gained?

Academic education. Everyone agrees that a college diploma is almost essential for entering public relations today, and the necessity is increasing. A survey of pre-1935 public relations practitioners, for example, showed that 35 per cent were college graduates; by 1953 the figure had risen to 57 per cent;[3] a 1960 Michigan survey found that 81 per cent of the public relations people in that state had college degrees and noted that "all recent employees have";[4] and a listing of several thousand names in the *1960 Public Relations Blue Book* revealed that 84 per cent of those appearing there were degree holders.[5]

On the general nature of college education needed, almost everyone agrees that a high percentage of liberal arts studies such as economics, psychology, sociology, history, languages, literature, and writing is desirable. In addition, courses in journalism and other forms of communications study—broadcasting, advertising, and related subjects—are thought to contribute valuable material and ideas. A recent humorous adding up of all the "good" subjects totaled, for the ideal, approximately *eight* years in college. Actually, the four-year A.B. degree is most common, although an increasing number of graduate-degree programs are being instituted.

The development of special public relations courses in colleges and uni-

[3] Benjamin B. Ringer, "The Changing Pattern of Recruitment in Public Relations," *Public Relations Journal,* December, 1953.

[4] Survey by Robert Johanson of the Michigan Chapter of the Public Relations Society of America, Detroit, September, 1960.

[5] *1960 Public Relations Blue Book,* Meriden, N.H.

versities has largely taken place since 1946. The survey taken by PRSA in 1956 referred to earlier, revealed that 21 per cent of 653 United States colleges responding taught courses in public relations, and that half of the major sequences available in public relations were to be found in connection with schools of journalism.

One point that should be made is that all accredited schools of journalism in the United States devote from 75 to 80 per cent of their students' four years to a broad liberal arts program and only the remainder of the time to the specific study of journalistic writing, public relations, advertising, and similar subjects. A person who wants to train for public relations does not have to choose between either a liberal arts curriculum or a communications curriculum; he can make a blend of the two.

A 1959 PRSA national survey found that one-third of the public relations practitioners responding had hired someone fresh from college who had taken public relations courses while in school, and almost all of these employers reported that such work seemed to be helpful.[6] In the 1961 survey of New York City public relations men referred to earlier, 94 per cent of those now practicing public relations, largely mature men whose formal education was undertaken some years ago, reported that they had not taken public relations courses in college, but 51 per cent said that if they were doing it over again now, they would remedy the deficiency.

Because of the increasing complexity of the world's political, economic, scientific, and international organization, a good education is a necessary foundation for successful public relations practice; and because of the new discoveries in opinion research and in the use of many complex communications media, study in these fields also is needed to give a young man or woman a good start. The very factors which have created public relations itself have also made higher education for public relations a necessity. The unlearned cannot expect to interpret to the learned.

Education by experience. Because public relations departments are usually small, there is less opportunity for on-the-job training in this field than in many others. Training an additional man in a department of only four or five people takes a high percentage of the available time of the working staff. A small department usually needs a newcomer who can pull his weight quickly; he is hired for his record of past performance and for his good judgment. Like the young lawyer or the young doctor, the young public relations man's most valuable possession is the confidence of his patients or clients, and this has to be deserved and not remain very long just a potential which may be realized sometime in the future.

For these reasons, to which we might add the lack of available college training in public relations in the past, the entry into public relations is

      [6] "Staffing for Public Relations," the National Educational Committee of the Public Relations Society of America, 1959.

frequently *by way of other professions.* At one time this oblique approach was often accidental, but today it is largely planned by those who have their own career goals.

In the Michigan survey referred to earlier, 7 persons said that they would not hire beginners without working experience, 5 said they would, and 2 said they might "occasionally." Among the New York practitioners, 18 advised a college graduate to start work in public relations at once, 15 suggested several years of business or general experience first, and 68 suggested experience in some creative field such as journalism, advertising, or promotion. These surveys of course reflect the experience of men who have been in the field for some years, and the percentage now going directly into public relations from college training is increasing as the availability and quality of college public relations courses increase. The 1959 PRSA educational survey also indicated, for example, that 59 per cent of the advertising agencies, 52 per cent of the industries, 46 per cent of the institutions, and 41 per cent of the service businesses which were planning to hire public relations people in the next five years said that they expected to get them directly from college.

The future efforts of the public relations profession to improve the university training of the young men and women who will succeed those now practicing may also contribute to this development.

But even considering these changes in attitude and procedure, the young person planning to enter the public relations field might well try to obtain the best academic training possible, including graduate work in public relations, and then make a planned succession of moves toward the place that he eventually wants to occupy. Some years of varied, related experience will enhance his value, and if he puts honest labor and interest into his work all along the line, he will give fair value for his pay and can part friends with his employers when he gets a better opportunity; and he can seek a position far more advantageously when working than when unemployed or in school. The survey of 4,200 men in *Who's Who in Public Relations in 1960* showed that 14 per cent had started their careers in public relations; 42 per cent in journalism or free-lance writing; 10 per cent in advertising, radio, or TV; 6 per cent in teaching (largely journalism, English, and speech); and 28 per cent in a variety of occupations including religious work, selling, and accountancy.

Both the risks and the rewards are somewhat higher in public relations careers than in more settled jobs; but in spite of difficulties the profession is popular. Of fourteen Michigan public relations men, all said they would like to see their sons in the same career, and nine said they would like to see their daughters enter the profession also.

A man's transfer from journalism to public relations, it should be noted, is not without its perils, and a good reporter does not necessarily make a good public relations man. One of the main problems lies in outlook. The good newsman is trained in *objectivity,* in telling facts just as they are without any attempt to affect the reader's reaction; but in practicing public relations he finds that he is a persuader, trying to get his readers to think and act in certain ways. Confusion follows if he is either ignorant of the principles of persuasion or is opposed to persuasion itself.

Writing in *The Quill,* the national magazine of Sigma Delta Chi, a journalism fraternity, in 1961, a young journalism school graduate explained why he went to work in public relations after two years of military service after graduation:

> I found that for those who love to write there are other professions which . . . still adhere to the high grade of principles taught in journalism schools. Why advertising and public relations? I found that many companies do not deal with as many half-truths as I had thought. Their objective is merely to present a true picture of their company and its product to the public. Secondly, in so doing, they encourage creative writing and thinking, and are willing to pay good salaries to achieve it. . . .

Characteristics of Different Public Relations Fields

Although, as mentioned in Chapter 5, the practice of public relations is a unity, work for different types of institutions tends to run somewhat in patterns. (There are, of course, many exceptions to any generalizations.)

Probably the most stable public relations employment is found among the utility companies. As service organizations resting solely upon public acceptance, the telephone and electric companies were pioneers in realizing the need of good public relations for their independent and profitable existence. Their public relations activities are characterized by long-range planning, foresight, great attention to the quality of their employees and their service, and frequently by a "political" cast in their thinking, since they are so dependent upon public rate regulatory bodies. Utilities tend to have fairly large public relations departments, to select their men carefully, and to promote their staffs from within.

Industries employ the largest number of public relations people, but the size of their departments and their work vary greatly. In small plants in small cities, the chief emphasis may be upon community and employee contacts, and perhaps upon product promotion and stockholder relationships. The public relations director in a small industry is likely to be a solo performer. In large or multiplant industries, more specialization within larger departments occurs. Wages vary also; a 1960 survey indicated that the public relations director of a small industry might expect from $12,000 to $15,000 a year and the public relations director of a larger industry from

$15,000 to $25,000. Salaries around $25,000 to $50,000 are found in many of the large industries, usually accompanied by titles such as vice-president, bonuses, and generous expense accounts.

There are about 9,000 associations in the United States. In all of them, both internal and external public relations fulfill an important function, whether the title of the association indicates the fact or not. The larger ones, especially those in which promotion is a major purpose, often have designated public relations directors with quite large staffs.

Welfare groups, such as United Funds and the health or youth agencies, all depend upon public relations and employ public relations people. Here the maximum pay is about $15,000 to $20,000 and is usually below that of men in comparable industrial situations. The greatest satisfactions in this kind of work, however, come from the opportunity to do good and to advance causes in which the public relations worker can take a genuine personal enthusiasm.

Education is now employing an increasing number of public relations people, because the need for their services is growing rapidly. However, educational public relations work is often intentionally disguised, and to further this camouflage, its practitioners are frequently drawn from teaching or administrative ranks and may be on part-time assignment. Only the stronger universities, colleges, and school systems bring in outside public relations personnel to any extent; and usually a director of publicity is an assistant to the president. Educational public relations thus tends to suffer from inbreeding and from talking to itself. It would benefit by more interchange with the outside world. If the public had a more enlightened and less suspicious attitude toward educational public relations, instead of assuming that "virtue speaks for itself," the work could be more openly and effectively accomplished. As it is, educational public relations offers great satisfaction; but it must frequently be combined with other administrative duties or with teaching in areas of related subject matter such as journalism.

Government public relations, in general, shares the same problems, but it is usually more secure because of civil service requirements. Most government organizations prefer "information bureaus" for the dissemination of news to the public relations organizations used in the business world. The strictly promotional is avoided; four-fifths of government public relations people are former newspapermen.

Independent public relations counseling is (or should be) the capstone of a public relations career. Having had various clients and possessing long experience and wide knowledge, the counselor is hired to advise, to perform special tasks, to set up a corporate public relations organization, and sometimes, in a period of emergency, to handle the entire program of a company. Some small companies also hire public relations firms to do all their public relations work for them because their own volume of business does not justify full-time staffing.

Most counseling work is centered in the nation's largest cities, where both the clients and major communications facilities—national magazines, publishers, broadcasting networks, and film producers—may be found.

A comparison of outside public relations counselors with inside public relations staffs shows advantages on both sides. The outside counselor often has wider experience, a detached viewpoint, and greater knowledge of the media. On the other hand, he may be superficial in his knowledge of his client and hasty in his actions. An outsider has the courage and freedom of enterprise but not the caution engendered by having to live with his mistakes. The inside-staff public relations man knows his organization and has the confidence and cooperation of his management and his fellow workers, but on the other hand, he may tend to say "yes" too often and to be unable to remain objective. Increasingly, a combination of the two is being used by large organizations.

The counselor's work demands experience. It is usually not an occupation for beginners, except in a subordinate capacity.

Women in Public Relations

The 1961 "Occupational Guide" issued by PRSA notes:

> Public relations affords considerable opportunity for women. Many women are attracted to it, and they frequently bring talents and interests to their work which are not easily duplicated by men. Women's "intuitive" faculties in dealing with people may prove highly useful. In many areas of publicity connected with personality exploitation, such as the entertainment arts and the restaurant, hotel, and transportation industries, which call for the use of imagination and friendly contacts, women frequently demonstrate superior skills. In special commodity areas, such as food, fashion, cosmetics, home furnishings, and in retail merchandising, women often find excellent opportunities open to them. Women also find public relations opportunity in the nonprofit field. There are some high-salaried women who have risen to top managerial positions.

How to Get a Job in Public Relations

The sound advice of the PRSA "Occupational Guide" is:

> . . . there is probably no clear-cut formula for getting a job in most lines of work, and this seems to be especially true of public relations. . . . It is necessary that you undertake an energetic, well-directed search.
>
> If you have not already developed some familiarity with the field through school training or other means, you should take immediate steps to do so. Two ways to do this are by reading publications about the field and by talking with people engaged in public relations work. The knowl-

edge you acquire will help you seek out the right kind of job. It will also add evidence of your alertness and maturity.

It is also important that you prepare a written résumé. This should contain a convincing, but not lengthy, account of yourself, particularly as it might bear upon your potential usefulness in a job. It should include your name, address, telephone number, age, a statement of job objectives, training, and work experience, chronologically reported, or in terms of the types of skills demonstrated or work accomplished. No matter how brief your résumé is, the chances are that it will not always be read word-for-word. Therefore the most important data should be laid out so that they can be quickly assimilated. You should also be attentive to the impression that your résumé makes by its layout, language used, and crisp graphic production. Duplicated processing is acceptable, and you will probably find it useful to have your résumé run off in quantity.

You may learn about possible job openings in advance of contacting employers, or you may canvass organizations where there is some possibility that staff needs may occur. Perhaps the best source for job news is by personal contacts, to which may be joined the advantage of a personal referral. Placement agencies, associations, firms which service other organizations, and advertisements also are sources of information about specific openings. Business directories may be consulted when making a direct canvass by letter and résumé. When possible you should address by name the person immediately responsible for the department in which you might be employed. For junior-level positions it is a decided advantage to be located within the area and within easy reach by telephone.

More important than the résumé is the interview, whose pattern cannot be predetermined. To prepare for this you should learn independently as much as possible about the organization, even, if possible, about the public relations position for which you will be considered. Showing a portfolio of examples of your work may prove useful. But bear in mind that the interviewer has many other concerns besides hiring, and may have a busy schedule. So do not prolong the meeting. Nevertheless, take adequate time for him to become acquainted with you, if he provides you with the opportunity. Be prepared to take the initiative in describing your qualifications and what you believe you can accomplish upon the job, if he does not choose to lead the discussion.

And bear in mind, also, that the ratio of persons hired for any particular opening to the number interviewed is small. Employers tend to look for a specific combination of qualifications to fit a specific need. Rejection is no cause to suppose that you would not qualify elsewhere. Among other things, consider your job hunt as a learning experience. Through perseverance you will win the opportunity to begin your public relations career.

Is There a "Profession" of Public Relations?

Writing in *Public Relations Journal* late in 1958, Charles P. Rockwood, public relations director of the American Institute of Certified Public Accountants (which has done a good job of establishing its own occupation as a "profession"), said:

> We are witnessing a scramble among new professions for recognition. The pace is quickening and public relations is in the midst of it. Time was when the professions were thought to consist of law, medicine, the ministry, teaching, and military arms. Now there are others like accounting, architecture, and engineering, and there are many semi- or quasi-professions: insurance, advertising, banking, journalism, the fine arts, and pharmacy come readily to mind.
>
> Professionalism is also claimed by morticians, beauticians, watchmakers, florists, photographers, plumbers, and also by egg graders, dog trainers, well diggers, and yacht salesmen!
>
> This is not necessarily bad. All things considered, it is probably good. Modern society has fostered specialization to the general betterment of the more advanced economies. More people are better educated than they used to be, and there is more training to be had in a wider variety of vocations. It has been noted by Professor Walter Gellhorn that nurses and other "semi-professionals" today must master a larger and more useful body of knowledge for the care of the sick than the *entire medical knowledge of a century ago.* People like to distinguish their work from mere "jobs." The public relations problem posed by the trend is this: the more vocations that strive for professional status and take on themselves professional trappings, the harder it becomes to distinguish them from other jobs. The image of professionalism gets blurred.
>
> Running through all the reasons for this movement is the desire for public *recognition* as a profession. In the end, it is *public opinion* which bestows the coveted mantle. When it is assumed otherwise, it is ill-fitting and the wearer looks comical. . . . What is the public's image of professionalism? . . .

But before considering standards of professionalism, we should note that *self-consciousness* is the first prerequisite to the development of a profession. The members of the craft, or art, or skill, must first feel a bond of union within their common work; and in the case of public relations this unity has been realized only recently. The 1953 survey by Ringer referred to earlier in this chapter revealed that before 1935 only 17 per cent of those entering public relations had done so intentionally. Sixty-seven per cent had entered the work by force of circumstances and 17 per cent for a combination of reasons. Of those entering after 1935, however, 61 per cent had planned to go into public relations, 30 per cent had wandered in by accident, and only 9 per cent had a number of reasons. A survey today among similarly successful practitioners would doubtless show a much higher percentage of planned entry.

But beyond the consciousness of a common field of work and a desire to gain public prestige, what *are* the hallmarks of a profession? How does the practice of public relations measure up to them?

Education. Mastery of an organized body of knowledge involving considerable time, both in formal schooling and perhaps in internship and experience, is certainly one of the distinguishing characteristics of a true profession. Anything which can be learned adequately in six weeks, useful though it may be, can hardly qualify as professional knowledge. "An organized body of knowledge" implies a literature of the profession including books, magazines, articles, films, and other records of experience and theory. It implies teachers, students, and standards of attainment before the student may be called a professional. In medicine, as in law, these requirements are quite apparent and well known.

Formal entry into the field. People have to trust a professional man because they do not have the personal training to appraise the merit of his work. The layman, for instance, cannot tell immediately whether a doctor of medicine is a competent man or a quack. The initials "M.D." after a name assure the laymen that at least the doctor has attended a recognized medical school and has completed an internship. "D.D.S." after a dentist's name implies that the practitioner is able to fill or extract a tooth, and "John Doe, Attorney," indicates a certain knowledge of the law.

A profession may be entered in several ways. Law or medicine, for instance, requires *licensing,* which means that no one may claim a title or legally engage in a practice without having passed certain government requirements such as schooling, examination, and experience.

Another form of entry into some professions is by *certification,* which means that the persons so qualified have completed certain studies and examinations. Others not certified, however, may also practice the profession, although they may not claim certification. Examples of people with this qualification would be CPAs (Certified Public Accountants) or members of the AIA (American Institute of Architects). These initials are, in effect, brand names giving assurance to the users of the services of these persons. Such brand names are worth only as much as can be implied by the integrity, depth, and record of the professional association which does the certification. Sometimes the prestige conferred is considerable, sometimes almost negligible.

A third way in which professions are entered is by generally accepted informal standards of entry, usually educational. The initials "Ph.D." after the name of a teacher tell the reader that the holder has attended a university (or universities) usually for seven years, has obtained graduate grades generally above "B," and has probably written a thesis upon something or engaged in equivalent research. Or the letters "B.D." after the name of a minister tell one that he has graduated from a seminary. Since there are colleges, universities, and seminaries of many kinds, the problem of knowing what the holder of the degree actually professes a knowledge about must be carefully considered by the inquirer.

Education of future practitioners. Truly professional people characteristically want to provide that their successors shall be at least as well trained as they have been, so that the standards of the profession will rise rather than decline. This means that truly professional people give their time, money, and experience to establish and aid schools of higher education in their fields. If they fail to do so, a new generation of shallow, ignorant practitioners will arise to destroy the reputation for skill and honesty which an older generation has laboriously acquired.

Independence of action. The doctor's or lawyer's or CPA's real assets are in his head. He may work for himself in independent practice, or he may have his entire time and knowledge hired in the service of someone else; but his value lies in what he knows and can do. He is expected to tell the truth in his professional capacity. A good lawyer cannot be a "yes" man just to please some corporate mogul; he must declare the facts of the law, pleasant or unpleasant. "Yes" men are not worth much to those who seek to act upon realities rather than flattery.

Exchange of information. Professional learning never stops. In anything complex enough to be called a profession, there are always new developments and continuing education. This means that a true professional shares his knowledge with his colleagues, usually through his professional association, instead of keeping new discoveries secret. By his generosity all are benefited, including the clients.

Limited self-promotion. Because of the need for professional men to wear the same trademark, many professional groups place an ethical ban upon the use of conventional advertising by members of the profession. Prospective users of professional services are expected to learn about the merits of professional people through the fact of their belonging to the profession, through personal contact, and through making inquiries to others who have used their services. Professional men are not supposed to talk about each other to clients, as a rule, except in a purely informational manner.

This reticence does not mean, of course, that many professional men are not alert to opportunities for self-promotion. But though the young lawyer who runs for political office without much expectation of winning, or the physician who undertakes the leadership of a welfare drive, may be acting from mixed motives of both altruism and personal publicity, at least the altruism, or its shadow, is there.

Discipline. In strong professional societies, incompetence or unethical practices may be punished by expulsion from the profession. In the case of licensed professions expulsion means deprivation of a legal means of livelihood; in the certified professions perhaps a loss of practice and prestige; and in the professions which have merely a general public-acceptance standard of entry, usually not much loss at all. In fact, in the latter professions, expulsion usually cannot be proposed or enforced.

Discipline depends upon the willingness and ability of the members of a professional association to develop and enforce a clear moral code. A weak association has great difficulty in showing this strength because its standards are unclear, its members are not sure of their own professional competence, and (since there is little public prestige or profit attached to membership in such a professional organization) delinquents will not be concerned whether they are thrown out or retained.

Service in the public welfare. The ultimate test of a professional man is that he measures the worth of his special abilities not entirely in money, but rather in the good that he can do for his fellow human beings. The money-mad doctor, the architect who erects hideous buildings for the whims of rich but stupid clients, and the attorney who subverts the law and justice for fat fees are all properly objects of public scorn because professional people are not supposed to act this way: we expect more of them! The doctor is not supposed to be poor—in fact, we do not mind if he makes a rather good living, considering his long years of schooling and internship— but we expect him to do his best for each patient, regardless of whether the fee is $100 or $1,000 or even nothing at all. The architect is supposed to help make his city more beautiful; he is more than a bricklayer. And the attorney is supposed to aid justice, not to obstruct it.

More than this, professional people are expected to be the leaders in America's community, educational, and intellectual life. It is as if the citizens said to them, "By your training, work, and ethical standards we expect you to be more public-spirited than other men who are either more ignorant or more interested in affairs of the moment than you are."

As the nation grows and becomes more complex, the types of possible "professional" people become more numerous. Their codes, sense of direction, and willingness to serve may well play a very great part in giving greater coherence and strength to this nation in a period of rapid change.

Is Public Relations Becoming a Profession?

In the strictest sense the answer to the above question would have to be "Not yet." However, compared with only a few decades ago, the movement toward professionalism has been considerable. Measuring public relations against the criteria previously mentioned, we might estimate the results as follows:

> *Self-consciousness.* Strong. Good national association.
> *Education.* Widespread, adequate in some respects.
> *Formal entry.* Licensing not to be expected, certification possible. The

British Institute of Public Relations leads in this field, planning that all
new entry into this national association after 1965 will be by five years'
executive experience in public relations and successfully passing several
comprehensive examinations.

Independence. Good.

Exchange of information. Through *Public Relations Journal* of PRSA,
Public Relations News, Public Relations Reporter, and other privately
operated newsletters. Through meetings of the Public Relations Society
of America and its many chapters. The annual summer institutes of
PRSA have also helped greatly in continuing the education of practitioners.

Limited self-promotion. Despite lack of formal rules upon this subject, the
pattern has been similar to that of other well-developed professions.

Discipline. Weak.

Service in the public welfare. The record has been good (too good for a
profitable living, some public relations practitioners will mutter) because
public relations people are naturally outgoing and adopt causes as
hobbies, and also because they are often called upon by management,
as part of their general line of work, to help put over drives for trade
expansion, building new hospitals, or raising money for colleges. These
calls hit public relations counselors often for too large a portion of their
time, which, as Abraham Lincoln once said of lawyers, is all they have
to sell.

But in another sense, the record is not so good as it might be, because
government and churches, for example, and many other organizations,
have not availed themselves of public relations advice or considered as
carefully as they might matters which are largely dependent upon good
public relations for their success. Much more could be done in these
fields for the benefit of all concerned if public relations people were
consulted more often.

General ethics. Much above the public image (not much of a compliment,
to be sure) and on a par with law or business in general. Comparisons
with other professions are best avoided lest they seem invidious or too
ambitious, but it would be fair to say that the ethics of United States
public relations men are often considerably better than those of others
in the surroundings in which they live and work.

ADDITIONAL READING

On Public Relations Work and Professionalism

Bateman, J. Carroll: "The Path to Professionalism," *Public Relations Journal,*
March, 1957.

Bernays, Edward L.: *Your Future in Public Relations,* Richards Rosen Press,
Inc., New York, 1961.

Cain, Paul: "Public Relations Is Ready for Professionalism," *PR: The Quarterly Review of Public Relations,* July, 1959.

Public Relations Society of America: "Let's Consider Public Relations: An Occupational Guide," New York, 1963.

Rockwood, Charles P.: "The Image of Professionalism," *Public Relations Journal,* October, 1958.

Schapper, Henry: "Six Steps to Get That Job," *Public Relations Journal,* July, 1958.

"You Want to Be in Public Relations?" *Public Relations Journal,* July, 1956.

Right and Wrong
in Public Relations

16

Persuasive communication is a very ancient art. In modern times it has many forms of expression. Public relations persuasion is only one member of a large, diverse family that includes fields ranging all the way from politics and law to teaching, selling, editing, and the religious ministry. In all these occupations communicators try to persuade.

A political speaker tries to gain support for a cause or to get himself elected to public office; a lawyer tries to convince a jury of his client's innocence; a teacher is enthusiastic about his subject and would like to make his students enthusiastic also; a salesman tries to get others to buy; an editor urges viewpoints in his editorials; and a minister of religion is "persuaded of his beliefs" and feels it his duty to convert others also.

Persuasion Is Honorable

There is nothing wrong with persuasion. We may be skeptical or even amused as we watch the enthusiasm of persuaders now and then, but we do not regard them as dishonorable citizens. We do not question the fact that persuaders are engaged in a recognized activity. Instead, we ask, "What means do they use to persuade?" and "For what purpose do they persuade?"

It is perfectly natural that men living together should try to persuade each other. Humans work in groups, and they form their voluntary groups largely by means of the communication of ideas. The power of speech distinguishes man from the beasts.

There are, of course, other ways of getting people to work together. In Chapter 2 we discussed *power,* which simply says, "Do this or you will suffer," and *purchase*, which promises rewards in money, goods, leisure, or honors. In actual situations power and purchase are almost always inter-mingled with persuasion.

Persuasion is the method used along with others in democratic societies.

346

The very nature of democracy involves the opportunity to try to persuade people by reason or emotion (or both) and then to abide by their group decisions. By means of the influence of communication, society changes, progressing steadily and peacefully, without recourse to the brutalities of raw power or the corruption of generous feelings so often associated with widespread purchase. Persuasive communications are therefore privileged in a democracy. A citizen is free to change men's opinions, if he can, because only in this way can society adapt itself to new times and needs. If freedom of persuasion were to cease, democracy would also cease because men could then no longer be exposed to the newly discovered facts and different viewpoints which would help them to make up their minds.

Moreover, in a democracy *all* communication shares this freedom to persuade. The editor is privileged to urge his views upon his readers. They do not have to read, or believe, or even buy his publication. The lawyer is privileged to urge the merits of his client's case before a jury to the best of his ability. The political office seeker may speak to those who can hear him and will listen. The advertising writer may sell his wares, and the public relations man present the facts and arguments which are at his disposal.

A Privilege and a Responsibility

Privilege cannot be separated from responsibility; the freedom to speak, write, broadcast, and print means power and therefore must be controlled. Some responsibility for communications can be enforced by law, principally by the laws of libel. If a man is falsely accused of a crime, he may sue and recover damages. Those who falsely present material leading to a criminal act, such as marching upon the state capitol and burning it down, may find themselves charged with criminal libel, an offense against the peace and security of the state. But the larger part of a citizen's true responsibility in the exercise of persuasion cannot be determined by law because it rests on the moral sense of the persuader. Responsibility cannot be written out and hedged about in advance, nor can tribunals sit upon it without seriously undermining the necessary democratic right of freedom of speech. A man's liberty to speak is what makes the ethical problems of every persuader so important and interesting.

Right now there is a great deal of public unease about persuasion, and many people would like to believe that it does not exist, or else they wish that it would go away. They would like to think that in some way they simply receive into their minds all the facts of a case and then operate only as reasonable thinking machines to arrive at true conclusions; yet no one who considers the matter carefully can really believe that anyone is so unbiased. We know that we receive our ideas and information from many sources and that we have firm beliefs about many things of which we really have little knowledge. This covert suspicion of our own integrity bothers us, and we sometimes react by wishing that some all-wise source could decide things for us, or by desiring to silence the contending persuaders so that we shall have to listen only to the "right" one, or by dreaming that, like hermits, we need not consider contentions at all.

These reactions are not new. Over two thousand years ago in ancient Athens, the great teacher Socrates sought to warn his students about listening to the speeches of the Sophists, persuaders who were hired to appear at public meetings and elsewhere to urge various causes, or who taught others how to do so. The Sophists made their livings and great reputations by being effective in oratory, skilled in debate, and strong in their appeals to emotion. Socrates warned his students of the devious tricks of the Sophists, pointed out that they got paid for their performances and that therefore a listener might expect them to be more interested in winning an argument than in finding ultimate truth. All men who do business in the world of affairs, Socrates said, work for personal gain, and their own interests influence their opinions.

But Socrates did *not* say that the Sophists should be silenced so that the perplexing problem of deciding which one was right could be eliminated, nor did he suggest that his students should cease to listen to them or retire from the world. Instead, he urged his students to sharpen their critical faculties so that they would be able to recognize faulty reasoning and specious arguments wherever they found them. His counsel was not to seek refuge but to seek wisdom.

Perhaps some of the unease about persuasion among many people in the world today arises from the very factors which have entered into the development of public relations itself—huge mass communications which reach large groups of people primarily living in large urban centers; our own rootlessness and tendency to move about; changes in jobs, society, government, and world conditions; and a very rapid expansion in the number of matters of debate upon which we need to be persuaded. There are so many important issues—all the way from Red China and race relations to education and automation—upon which we are expected to have intelligent opinions, and so many people are so busy urging their viewpoints upon us! No wonder receivers are at times confused!

CODES OF THE HIRED PROFESSIONAL

The Soldier

At first glance, professional soldiers, lawyers, journalists, and public relations men may not seem to have much in common; yet they all try to influence (or sometimes force) other people to do things, albeit by different means.

Hired free-lance soldiers disappeared from the scene years ago, the last important ones in American memory being the German Hessians whom the British hired to help coerce the rebelling American colonists into sub- mission in 1776. Soldiers today may be paid, but they usually work for a national state, such as France or the United States, of which they are usually citizens, and in whose army they serve. But until comparatively recent times many soldiers were hired, and they had various codes of conduct.

Probably the most fundamental thing about the conduct of a hired soldier, from his employer's point of view at least, was that he should stay hired at the wages agreed upon in advance. Employers naturally take a dim view of vacillating conduct, such as that of the Swiss mercenaries of the Duke of Milan in the late Middle Ages, who met a better offer from the King of France, just before the battle was to begin, and changed sides at once. The Duke spent the last eight years of his life in a cage in Paris, the victim of his foreign, paid troops. Loyalty to one's employer was the most funda- mental and lowest level of the code of the professional soldier, even if it was, at times, rather uncertain.

Beyond loyalty, the next question in the code of the professional soldier might be "How does he fight?" This was of particular interest to the pro- fessional soldiers themselves, who after all were of the same brotherhood and were more interested in drawing their wages, taking it easy, and plundering than in killing each other. The little armies of *condottieri* who fought for Italian city-states and principalities in the Renaissance period were more interested in winning than in slaying, and evolved elaborate codes of fighting which allowed a battle to go on all day with very few casualties. As in a gigantic chess game, the victory came when one side worked the soldiers of the other side into a corner, where by the rules they were allowed to surrender and thus live to fight another day—or perhaps even to join the opposition.

But all these mercenary arrangements disappeared at the time of the French Revolution, when the determined citizen-soldier appeared upon the scene. Now the question was not "How does he fight?" but only "For whom does he fight?" The Marseillaise-singing hordes of revolutionary France knew: They fought for France and liberty!

The citizen soldier still exists, of course, as our armed services testify. But now *why* a man fights has become the primary question. No longer does anyone trust an army that fights only for money.

The Lawyer

The lawyer, according to the Anglo-Saxon concept, is also a hired per- suader in the argument between the state or a person who has suffered a wrong and someone who is asserted to have done the wrong. It is a contest, and the lawyer operates within the framework of a court in which facts and viewpoints from both sides are presented to the end that justice may be achieved through the decision of the judge and jury.

When a lawyer takes a case, he may do so knowing that his client is innocent, partly guilty, or entirely guilty of the offense with which he is charged. He takes the case in the belief that all persons have certain rights which must be represented and protected. The lawyer's code calls for loyalty to his client in giving his utmost persuasive efforts in his behalf. If he believes that his client is half guilty, he will not give only half a plea. Half-persuasion would mean that he is judging his client, which is a function left to the court, in the knowledge that lawyers on both sides will present their cases as well as they can. Nor is the lawyer required to volunteer the *whole* truth about his client. He cannot lie, but he is not required to bring forth matters which would argue against his client.

In his presentation the lawyer is guided by the rules of the court, which constitute the framework of a contest whose end is a decision between two contending points of view—a decision which takes into account their relationship to the law. The lawyer, whether for the defense or for the prosecution, works as part of a court procedure whose goal is justice and the public welfare, and his freedom of persuasion is permitted, within limits, to this end. The system, admittedly, is not perfect: A capable lawyer with a weak case can sometimes overcome a poor lawyer with a good case. But it is not easy to find a better system without perhaps entrusting too much power to fallible human beings.

The Journalist

Consider also the code of the journalist. In a daily newspaper of any size, for example, he presents a view of the world. Yet his view can never be entirely objective because by selecting what to run and how big to play it, he is presenting an estimate of what he, or someone else, considers important. Moreover, he frequently finds himself presenting persuasions which are also in themselves facts, as when he reports arguments made in political speeches or in labor issues. In addition, most newspapers have their own editorial points of view, which they urge upon readers as the right way to see facts. The journalist is not as a rule a propagandist hired by someone else, but his communications are at least partly persuasion as well as information, entertainment, and self-expression; and his code must answer the question of "why" he persuades, as it does in the famous Journalist's Creed written by Dean Walter Williams, founder of the University of Missouri School of Journalism, in 1908:

> I believe that the public journal is a public trust; that all connected with it are, to the full measure of their responsibilities, trustees for the public. . . .

Here the touchstone is not loyalty to an employer or the nature and tone of the presentation, but instead the primacy of the public good.

The Public Relations Man

What should be the code of the public relations man?

Since he is a hired persuader, loyalty to his employer is fundamental. This requirement is specifically covered in three of the sixteen points of the Public Relations Society of America's 1960 Code of Professional Standards for the Practice of Public Relations.[1]

> 4) A member shall not represent conflicting or competing interests without the express consent of those concerned. . . .
> 5) A member shall safeguard the confidences of . . . clients or employers. . . .
> 11) In performing services for a client or employer a member shall not accept fees, commissions or any other valuable consideration in connection with those services from anyone other than his client or employer without . . . express consent. . . .

Three other points refer to conduct of public relations men toward each other:

> 9) A member shall not intentionally injure the professional reputation or practice of another member. . . .
> 10) A member shall not employ methods tending to be derogatory of another member's client or employer or of the products, business or services of such client or employer.
> 12) A member shall not propose . . . that his fee . . . be contingent on the achievement of certain results. . . .

Five other points refer to the responsibility of public relations men to promote the public welfare. Of these, numbers 1 and 2 simply refer to the duty of fair dealing and of conduct in accord with the public welfare. But numbers 6, 7, and 8 say:

> 6) A member shall not engage in any practice which tends to corrupt the integrity of channels of public communication.
> 7) A member shall not intentionally disseminate false or misleading information. . . .
> 8) A member shall not make use of any organization purporting to serve some announced cause but actually serving an undisclosed special or private interest of a member or his client or his employer.

The remaining three items of the code deal with enforcement. Codes are generally a collection of "thou shalt nots." They suggest need for restraint rather than positive goals, and their enforcement is often little activated;

[1] See PRSA Code at the end of this chapter.

but this does not mean that they are not important. They are like the standard that George Washington once referred to as one to which "the wise and honest can repair."

The power of communication in modern America is so great that while some can abuse it some of the time, it cannot be *generally* abused without demands arising that freedom of communication be curbed because of fears of "poisoning the wellsprings of public opinion." Without self-regulation, other regulation may ensue, perhaps disastrously for freedom itself. Codes set minimum standards to which wise and honest men can adhere, but the real achievement of high ethical practices in persuasive communication depends mainly upon the personal qualities of honor and dedication to the public good of those who practice persuasion—and of those who hire them to do so.

Problems of "Real Life" Practice

It is not always easy to be honest and public-spirited, because the rewards of being otherwise often seem tempting. David Finn, president of Ruder & Finn, New York, one of the nation's largest public relations firms, discussed this subject in an article in the *Harvard Business Review* in 1959. In it he asked:

> How honest a picture of its product should a company present to the public?
> What part should the artificial "build-up" play in public relations?
> How far should a company go in exploiting its contacts with influential people?
> Is a company obligated to be truthful about labor, pricing, and other touchy problems?
> What role, if any, should ulterior motives play in framing public relations policies?

(Most of these questions could also be asked of an individual in his personal relations with other people.) To be specific upon these points, Finn gave a number of simple examples of cases which illustrated the temptations, conflicts, and agonizing appraisals that can develop.

> Company A decided to build an image of one of its major products as being purer than its competitors. This was actually so. However, advertising claims of purity had been used and abused so heavily in the past by other companies that it decided to undertake a public relations program to get the story across. Accordingly a complicated scheme was invented involving the development of an "independent" research report that was to provide the basis for newspaper and magazine articles.
> The trouble was that the research was engineered; in fact it was not

even to be paid for unless the publicity appeared in print. To ensure the success of the project, the man who arranged all this had some editors on his payroll as consultants for the research, thus almost guaranteeing eventual publication. It was a neat scheme—effective for the company and profitable for researcher, editor, and middleman.

The question was: Is this a responsible method of communicating the image of purity to the public?

Arguments in favor of the action maintained that the product was pure, that the public was not being deceived thereby, that no one was being bribed, and that the research was done by qualified scientists. Against the scheme was the argument that the research was not truly "independent" as represented, and that, because of their special payments, the editors were not free from bias.

After much consideration the idea was dropped. The risk was too great. Exposure would have not only ruined this particular program, but also severely damaged the reputation of the company that engaged in it. The plan was somewhat dishonest as well as dangerous. Instead, research on a truly independent basis was recommended; it would probably be just as effective. In this case, ethical considerations and practical fears coincided.

Finn prefaced his next example with a question.

To what extent should a company build up its growth on deserved recognition and earned prestige, and eschew the fanfare of artificially stimulated applause?

The accusation that public relations involves an artificial build-up is one of the most serious ever leveled at it. . . .

Company B was seeking special recognition for a new variation of a standard product. To highlight the innovation, a new package had been created. The design was particularly striking, and the suggestion was made that somehow a design award should be arranged. Publicizing this award would help impress both salesmen and customers with the company's concern for high quality and, by association, would bring recognition to the new product's features.

The question was: Should public relations exploit only means of gaining recognition which would be above influence and partisanship?

The design was of high quality and could earn an award on its own merits. However, in order that it might be known by the judges, the package would have to be widely publicized; for instance, samples would have to be sent to experts for examination.

What is an "artificial" build-up? Do not many good things lie neglected because no one tries to make their virtues known? Is it perhaps not true that silence or letting publicity drift with the winds of chance may play down meritorious subjects as surely as undue promotion may build up poor ones? And in today's world of mass communications and few face-to-face contacts, at what point does a build-up using the mass media necessarily become "artificial"? These were some of the questions that lay behind the case of company B. Eventually it was decided that publicizing and sending out samples of the package in the hope that it would win an award were not at all wrong when no undue influence was exerted upon those who chose to make an award.

Influence peddling is another matter, observed Finn, who cited the case of company C:

> Company C was extremely anxious to gain attention at an annual trade show. One way to accomplish this was through the local newspaper in the city where the show was being held. The competition for publicity in that newspaper was fierce, with every manufacturer at the trade show vying for it.
>
> A public relations representative of Company C knew a photographer on the newspaper and spoke to him about the problem. The photographer developed a cute idea for a specially contrived photograph which might succeed in getting the company mentioned in the newspaper. He said he would set up and take the photograph for a small fee, with the understanding that if the picture was published in the paper, he would get considerably more money.
>
> The question was: Should the company exploit this special "in" with the newspaper to solve an important problem?

The conclusion was that it should not, because the payment to the photographer contingent upon publication amounted to a bribe; it was an action taken behind the editor's back; and the company could not defend it if questioned about it later. "Honesty is the best policy" may sound more like expediency than the highest level of ethics, but the aphorism voices a practical, working philosophy.

Public relations activities are closely bound to the honesty of the business practices of a company or organization as a whole. There is not much use in trying to gloss over or whitewash basically bad practices. When something is wrong, public relations questions are frequently the first to bring it to light because in the practice of publicity the actions of the company must be examined in the pitiless light of "what will other people think?"

> Company D sold its high-quality product to a few scattered discount houses but claimed it did not sell to any. This was common enough policy. But if the truth were told, the company's regular customers would be very angry. And yet the few discount houses it did sell to brought in a great deal of business.
>
> The question was: Was dissimulation a justified business practice?

The practice could be defended on the basis that *generally* the company did not sell to discount houses, but this subterfuge led to an untruth when company salesmen were talking to regular customers or when the company was stating its position publicly. It was decided that the sales to discount houses should be dropped. The practice could not always be hidden from the trade; questions would have to be met with lies; and the whole marketing position of the firm would be jeopardized. The test might be: "Never do anything you would not want to see published in tomorrow morning's newspaper."

The Pennsylvania Truckers v. Railroads Case

Most ethical questions in public relations are questions of personal and organization morals rather than of law, because the relatively simple laws of libel do not extend very far into the areas of freedom of speech and its ethics. But in recent times, in two important instances, courts and proposed legislation have begun to codify ethics into law. One was the 1957 decision by Judge Clary of the United States District Court of the Eastern District of Pennsylvania in the suit brought by the Pennsylvania Truckers against the Eastern Railroad Presidents' Conference. The other was legislation proposed in the Eighty-fourth United States Congress (1956) following hearings before the Special Committee, headed by Senator McClellan, to investigate political activities, lobbying, and campaign contributions.

In the Pennsylvania Truckers versus Eastern Railroads case the railroads and their public relations firm, the Carl Byoir organization of New York, were charged by the truckers with having entered into a conspiracy to destroy the business of the truckers by unethical means.

The suit was brought under the Sherman and Clayton Antitrust Acts, alleging that the railroads were seeking to gain a monopoly of long-distance freight hauling in Pennsylvania by creating public and legislative ill will against trucking to the point where truck-hauling activities were likely to be so severely limited by law as to be no longer competitive.

Methods of injury complained of by the truckers included half-truths, the use of third-party organizations to propagandize with their sources of support carefully concealed, and hidden-source feeding of partly true news and feature stories to newspapers and magazines.

For example, in New Jersey an organization known as "New Jersey Automobile Owners, Inc.," which was supported by the railroads, sent out speakers before civic clubs attacking trucking, and when its support was questioned, completely denied all railroad connections. Mats of photographs were distributed free to smaller newspapers from a railroad-supported "Central States News View Company" in Chicago. Along with sex and sports pictures, the company frequently offered photos of road or bridge damage caused by trucks. In a campaign engineered by the Byoir Company, magazine articles exposing the damage supposedly done to highways by trucks were sent by free-lance writers to leading American national magazines. There were many other instances, all handled by the Byoir Company, but all paid for and approved by the railroads.

In awarding damages against the railroads, Judge Clary made several points:

1. The case was considered because it came within the purview of antitrust legislation in that an attempt was made to injure a competitor so as to create a monopoly.

2. There was no objection to positive public relations which sought to obtain benefits by building up an organization's own merits or by informing the public or legislative bodies of facts and views upon a situation.

3. The use of persuasive techniques to injure a competitor was questionable, especially if done by means of half-truths, hidden third-party fronts, and concealment of origins of material from editors and others. If a public relations firm engaged in this sort of activity, it could not escape responsibility by pleading the orders of its employer.

Judge Clary assessed 20 per cent of the cost of a large fine against the Byoir Company and stipulated that the railroads could not reimburse it.

In February of 1961 the United States Supreme Court reversed the award of $852,074 against the railroads made by Judge Clary and upheld by an appeals court. Justice Hugo Black, writing the opinion, said that a campaign aimed at public and political opinion, no matter how nasty, did not come within the realm of the antitrust acts. "Such deception," he said, "reprehensible as it is, has nothing to do with the Sherman Antitrust Act."

This does not mean, of course, that responsible persons think that the tactics used in the truckers–railroad case were good or that they did not do considerable harm by the abuse of public confidence. Probably the suit by the truckers served its main purpose of exposing the opposition, and Judge Clary's opinion, although not upheld in regard to the Sherman Act, is also a landmark which will be well worth watching.

Oil and Gas Lobby Hearings

The hearings before the Special Committee of the United States Senate in 1956 investigating political activities, lobbying, and campaign contributions in connection with the oil and gas lobby investigation also brought forth a number of interesting points.

The word "lobbying" has acquired a sinister connotation because of its occasional connection with corruption and bribery; yet an individual or an organization does nothing wrong in presenting a case before legislators. The citizen has a constitutional right of petition. Those who fail to plead their causes as well as they can before legislators and legislative bodies have only themselves to thank if their negligence results in the passage of adverse or unjust laws.

To enable the members of Congress to know better who is speaking for whom, however, Congress has enacted laws requiring the registration of lobbyists and identification of their clients. In recent years, also, some congressmen have become concerned about "indirect lobbying," or attempts to influence their legislative attitudes without direct contact. The pressure may be exerted by political campaign contributions from those who hope that their support will be repaid in favors, or by building a fire in a congressman's own home constituency. At one time an oil company paid for hundreds of telegrams to be sent to a certain congressman protesting a bill which would have affected the oil company adversely. Many wires were sent without the knowledge or approval of the persons whose names were signed. The action was clearly unethical and illegal.

But writing a law to prevent indirect lobbying in general is another matter. Consider campaign contributions, for example: In these days of expensive mass communications by means of newspapers, radio, television, and billboards which reach millions of voters, large sums of money are needed to finance any important political campaign. How can this amassing of funds be prevented? Should corporations and unions be forbidden to give money? Can a private citizen, no matter how wealthy, be barred from buying an advertisement to express his views? It does not seem likely. At what point does freedom of speech end, if end it does?

In deciding upon the rights of "building a fire" under congressmen in their home areas, the decision is equally difficult. False telegrams are obviously unethical. But what about company representatives going about stimulating letters to the congressman, giving speeches, or seeking newspaper editorials in support of their views? Should they or anyone else be prevented from such actions? The area of freedom of speech is soon invaded. Do congressmen have a right to try to protect themselves from these "spurs to prick the sides of their intent"? Or do they just have to use their own judgment upon the motives and sources of petitions?

These questions have not been decided, and in our democracy it is doubtful whether they ever will be fully answered, their consideration brings to light some of the ethical questions in public relations practice.

Rules of the Game and Personal Honor

As long as men have interests to achieve or things to sell, they will urge them upon buyers. Persuasive communications exist for all sorts of ends— to get Congress to enact a bill which its unselfish sponsors sincerely believe will lead to world peace; to achieve safety on the highways; to prohibit the sale of alcoholic beverages; to raise minimum wages; to establish free universal medical care; to sell life insurance, automobiles, education, or concrete. Each group believes that its goals are legitimate and good.

Here another ethical problem confronts persuasion. A good end cannot be held to justify a bad means. To use a fantastic example, the hope of enacting a world peace bill would not justify bribery, lies, and deception to obtain its passage (although some of its sponsors might feel that it did). Public relations, like democracy itself, is a *way* of achieving agreement through understanding and persuasion. The way is just as important as the ends sought at any particular moment by fallible human beings; and indeed it may be more important, because democracy lives by the road it travels.

Lies, half-truths, concealed support, personal attacks, false appeals to unworthy emotions, smears upon personal or group integrity are all *bad* means—bad, because their employment destroys the confidence between men, which is the basis of our freedom. Their use is selfish and irresponsible and injures the public welfare, which sustains our very form of government. They have within them seeds of hatred, internal warfare, and suppression.

The power of free communication is great, and with great power goes great responsibility. Public relations men must not only persuade fairly, but they must also guide themselves by what they feel is best for the public welfare as any honest, intelligent, well-informed person may see it.

The Integrity of Us All

We cannot say that, like a stream, public relations practice can rise no higher than its source; occasionally it does. Many public relations men have a keener sense than their employers have of right and wrong and of what conduces to the public welfare; but it is hard to rise much above the source, because this is where the money and orders come from. Like the Queen of England, the public relations man can advise, warn, and encourage— but then he must eventually either do as requested or resign the account or his job. This is a hard choice which, happily, not many men have to face often. Fortunate indeed is the public relations man who can be in wholehearted agreement with his cause all the time!

Public relations persuasion is a weapon in modern society. Even when used loyally and fairly, its effects will still depend upon the purposes of those who wield it and upon the morals of the businessmen, public officials, educators, churchmen, and others who hire men skilled in persuasive communication in order to help argue their cases before the bar of public opinion.

But, in another way, public relations is a guardian of the social conscience. Light is always better than darkness, and public relations activities focus light upon organizations. The organization that claims to be good assumes obligations to live up to its claims or to suffer double outcries if it fails. There is no doubt that social consciousness in the United States today is much higher than it was a generation or two ago, and public relations is both an effect and cause of this improvement. Organizations are better, and extol their own virtues; they wish to be better thought of, and therefore make claims which they have to live up to. Public sensitivity toward failures of performance to match claims is at a high peak. A commercial conscience, perhaps—but public relations is still a conscience about which cynicism is a luxury, because light should be encouraged rather than extinguished.

ADDITIONAL READING

The Pennsylvania Truckers v. Railroads Case

Opinion in the United States District Court for the Eastern District of Pennsylvania. Civil Action. *Noerr Motor Freight, Inc., et al. v. Eastern Railroads Presidents' Conference, et al.*, No. 14715. May be obtained from American Trucking Associations Inc., Washington, D.C.

Kepler, Edwin C.: "Notes on Judge Clary's Opinion," *PR, The Quarterly Review of Public Relations*, July, 1958.

"Truck Case Upset by Supreme Court," *New York Times*, Feb. 21, 1961.

Oil and Gas Lobby Investigation

Hearings before the Special Committee to Investigate Political Activities, Lobbying, and Campaign Contributions. United States Senate, 84th Cong., 2d Sess. pursuant to S. Res. 219.1956. Available in larger libraries.

Ethics in Public Relations

Finn, David: "Struggle for Ethics in Public Relations," *Harvard Business Review*, January–February, 1959.

Fitzgerald, Stephen E.: "Ethics," *Public Relations Journal*, October, 1951.

Flynn, Lawrence J.: "The Aristotelian Basis for the Ethics of Speaking," *The Speech Teacher*, September, 1957.

Heilbroner, R. L.: "Public Relations, the Invisible Sell," *Harper's Magazine*, June, 1957.

Kelley, Stanley, Jr.: *Professional Public Relations and Political Power*, The Johns Hopkins Press, Baltimore, 1956.

Samstag, Nicholas: *Persuasion for Profit*, University of Oklahoma Press, Norman, Okla., 1957.

Selekman, Benjamin M.: *A Moral Philosophy for Management*, McGraw-Hill Book Company, Inc., New York, 1959.

CHAPTER APPENDIX

PUBLIC RELATIONS SOCIETY OF AMERICA

Code adopted in November 1959 by the 1959 PRSA Board of Directors and ratified by the 1960 PRSA Assembly. Replaces and strengthens a similar Code of Professional Standards for the Practice of Public Relations previously in force since 1954.

DECLARATION OF PRINCIPLES

Members of the Public Relations Society of America acknowledge and publicly declare that the public relations profession in serving the legitimate interests of clients or employers is dedicated fundamentally to the goals of better mutual understanding and cooperation among the diverse individuals, groups, institutions and elements of our modern society.

In the performance of this mission, we pledge ourselves:

1. To conduct ourselves both privately and professionally in accord with the public welfare.

2. To be guided in all our activities by the generally accepted standards of truth, accuracy, fair dealing and good taste.

3. To support efforts designed to increase the proficiency of the profession by encouraging the continuous development of sound training and resourceful education in the practice of public relations.

4. To adhere faithfully to provisions of the duly adopted Code of Professional Standards for the Practice of Public Relations, a copy of which is in the possession of every member.

CODE OF PROFESSIONAL STANDARDS
FOR THE PRACTICE OF PUBLIC RELATIONS

This Code of Professional Standards for the Practice of Public Relations is adopted by the Public Relations Society of America to promote and maintain high standards of public service and conduct among its members in order that membership in the Society may be deemed a badge of ethical conduct; that Public Relations justly may be regarded as a profession; that the public may have increasing confidence in its integrity; and that the practice of Public Relations may best serve the public interest.

1) A member has a general duty of fair dealing towards his clients or employers, past and present, his fellow members and the general public.

2) A member shall conduct his professional life in accord with the public welfare.

3) A member has the affirmative duty of adhering to generally accepted standards of accuracy, truth and good taste.

4) A member shall not represent conflicting or competing interests without the express consent of those concerned, given after a full disclosure of the facts.

5) A member shall safeguard the confidences of both present and former clients or employers and shall not accept retainers or employment which may involve the disclosure or use of these confidences to the disadvantage or prejudice of such clients or employers.

6) A member shall not engage in any practice which tends to corrupt the integrity of channels of public communication.

7) A member shall not intentionally disseminate false or misleading information and is obligated to use ordinary care to avoid dissemination of false or misleading information.

8) A member shall not make use of any organization purporting to serve some announced cause but actually serving an undisclosed special or private interest of a member or his client or his employer.

9) A member shall not intentionally injure the professional reputation or practice of another member. However, if a member has evidence that another member has been guilty of unethical, illegal or unfair practices, including practices in violation of this Code, he should present the information to the proper authorities of the Society for action in accordance with the procedure set forth in Article XIII of the Bylaws.

10) A member shall not employ methods tending to be derogatory of another member's client or employer or of the products, business or services of such client or employer.

11) In performing services for a client or employer a member shall not accept fees, commissions or any other valuable consideration in connection with those services from anyone other than his client or employer without the express consent of his client or employer, given after a full disclosure of the facts.

12) A member shall not propose to a prospective client or employer that his fee or other compensation be contingent on the achievement of certain results; nor shall he enter into any fee agreement to the same effect.

13) A member shall not encroach upon the professional employment of another member unless both are assured that there is no conflict between the two engagements and are kept advised of the negotiations.

14) A member shall, as soon as possible, sever his relations with any organization when he believes his continued employment would require him to conduct himself contrary to the principles of this Code.

15) A member called as a witness in a proceeding for the enforcement of this Code shall be bound to appear unless, for sufficient reason, he shall be excused by the panel hearing the same.

16) A member shall co-operate with fellow members in upholding and enforcing this Code.

The Future of Public Relations

17

"Public relations," or the activity of planned, persuasive communication in behalf of widely assorted causes (by whatever name it may be called), is certain to continue to expand rapidly in the years ahead.

Immediate economic conditions may bring ups and downs in its use, and feelings within particular areas may swing from favorable to unfavorable regard, but all the conditions which called public relations into being earlier in this century not only are continuing but are being constantly intensified. Populations are greater, communications are more widespread, and issues in dispute have increased in number. The only way that the growth in the practice of public relations could be halted would be by the disruption of a major war, a steady decline in the conditions of economic life to a subsistence level, or the imposition of the dead hand of state control in the form of censorship or a state monopoly of communications such as exists within the Iron Curtain countries or existed in Nazi Germany or Fascist Italy.

Otherwise, as the size of the units of human organization continues to expand, as the interactions of groups of people become more important to all, and as the communications media multiply, change is ever-present, creating a need for the services of interpreters and a market for advocates of these new viewpoints. Since the constant alterations in modern ways of life are sparked by a worldwide revolution in scientific technology, it is not likely that changes will soon cease or that anybody in this world will ever again return to a primitive mental Garden of Eden. Too many people have tasted of the apple of the tree of knowledge, and there are no more Shangri-Las concealed behind unscaled mountains. No unexplored areas are left on the physical face of the globe, and few isolated mental areas exist undisturbed anywhere. To be sure, barriers to the transmission of ideas are forcefully maintained in some places; but even such Chinese Walls against thought are being constantly undermined all the time both from without and from within. Ideas are—and should be—hard to confine.

Public relations is but another manifestation of the new day in communication of thought in which this small planet begins its period of turmoil in drawing up a grand new design for a workable world order and in reaching for the stars. Like the times in which we live, the practice of public relations is still confused, its needs perforce rushing ahead of its knowledge. Some tasks have been accomplished, and others have hardly been begun.

Tasks Largely Accomplished

Consciousness of identity. In order that a discipline may progress, its practitioners must know who they are, what role they play in society, and what they seek. In the past several decades, men and women in American public relations have become increasingly conscious of their common identity and community of interest. They know who they are and more and more tend to agree upon what they do. They have formed themselves into organizations, exchanged ideas, encouraged each other (even in the midst of sharp competition), improved their knowledge, and raised their standards. Sometimes they have been almost embarrassingly vocal about their newly acquired self-knowledge; often they have claimed too much; but since it is their business to be vocal, all this talk has had great value in working out identity and has been beneficial when it has not degenerated into self-delusion or self-worship. Public relations is much more important in the plans of almost all organizations than it was twenty or thirty years ago.

Literature. Since public relations men are in the business of communication, they have written many books and articles about their work. Some aspects of public relations have been discussed over and over again to the point of satiety, while other areas have been barely or not at all touched. Public relations literature is profuse, but not yet so complete or well organized as it might be; more needs to be done in this field by professional organizations and others.

Public awareness. Although many people misunderstand the nature and purpose of public relations, almost all educated people in the United States are aware of its existence, whether they like it or not. This was not so forty years ago.

Tasks Underway

Broader employer understanding. A great many thousands of employers of all sorts, from businessmen to school boards, have in the past few years realized the need of skilled communication and have supported at least some of the essentials of good public relations practice. That they have been willing to put out enough money to enter the field is a tribute to the alertness and education of American businessmen and their counterparts in welfare, education, government, and other fields.

The problem now is not so much that of getting employers to use public relations as of creating a better understanding of its true potential and its limitations. Too many businesses, for example, still fail at the vital point of customer relations; too many still expect a flood of last-minute communications to do a speedy job of righting situations in which an intended audience has already decided and stopped listening; too many fail to realize that if an organization has become famous through publicity, the public will expect much more of it than of an obscure group or business.

Education and habits of thought can best be given, usually, to future executives while they are still in colleges or in training programs. Widely distributed articles, talks, books, and films are also helpful, but broader understanding of public relations principles remains a major need for employers—as for every leader in a democratic society.

Greater cooperation with the social sciences. Neither scholars nor public relations men of affairs yet know as much as they should about the reactions of human beings to situations and communications. Although by its very nature public relations is concerned with social psychology, it has been deficient in the support of research in this area and in the use of what has been done. Much has been accomplished in universities and in private organizations supplied with funds from business and government sources, but the big break-throughs in understanding human responses still seem to be ahead. Perhaps they are primarily dependent upon the development of new measuring devices to detect human responses. Today we remain still largely ignorant about how people obtain the ideas they have and why they select some ideas in preference to others; yet there is no more important subject to be studied.

Education for public relations. Hundreds of American universities and colleges teach one or more courses labeled "public relations," and many offer sequences of courses leading to an undergraduate major, or even a degree, usually undergraduate, but occasionally a Master of Arts. As the idea of public relations has widened from the concept of a set of skills, such as those in newswriting or broadcasting, to these skills plus a broad understanding of people, of organizations, and of the changing world, the scope of public relations education has also grown. Today the increasing tendency is to make it possible for those who expect to go into its practice to specialize in the subject at the graduate level, and to offer a number of "principles" courses for the many students in other major fields of interest. Students of business or political science, for example, may want to know at least something about public relations for use in their own areas.

Better education will lead to better users and practitioners of public relations, but there are still many problems to be solved in adequate public relations education. Provision of systematized case material for teachers, better education of teachers, greater cooperation between practitioners and teachers in student enlightenment, and more opportunities for students to obtain practical experience at a decision-making level are among the most needed developments.

Better international contacts. As public relations develops rapidly in many nations of the world, a great need arises for closer fellowship between the practitioners in many places. The stimulation and encouragement obtained by studying similar problems under highly varying conditions are extremely valuable. In addition, the shared interests of public relations people of various nations are a strong force for international cooperation, because public relations people of all nations realize that their art may be developed only under conditions of peace and freedom.

In addition to active national public relations associations in various well-developed countries, there is an International Public Relations Association. There have been two World Congresses, one in Brussels in 1958 and the other in Venice in 1961, and a third is planned for Montreal in 1964. Wealthy public relations men and those belonging to international corporations are able to travel much and to meet their counterparts elsewhere, but much still remains to be done in organizing other well-planned visits, student exchanges, foreign internships, worldwide publications, and conferences.

The development of ethical practices. The problems of "right and wrong" in public relations, which were discussed in the preceding chapter, are not peculiar to this activity alone; they reflect the moral standards of those who employ advocates and the standards of society as a whole. Nevertheless, the moral problems of public relations seem to be pushed into prominence because the activity makes claims for products or projects, and public relations men are forced to be the keepers, not only of their own consciences, but also of the consciences of the organizations for which they work.

The fact that many public relations people struggle and suffer with their own moral problems as advocates, and also with the problems of their clients is all to the good. There should be more of such wrestling with conscience! If a public relations man does not act as the public's spokesman in the councils of his employers, who else will? (The idea of a corporation chaplain has never been tried, so far as is known. Probably he would be ignored as were most of the chaplains of the nobility in the past!) If no one speaks for the public, if the consciences of those in power do not prompt them to speech, then the public will surely find its own defenders elsewhere—in government or perhaps in labor. A good public relations man should have a tender conscience, and those who hire him should be willing to listen.

Tasks Hardly Begun

Professional development. Since public relations offers a service which its buyers find hard to evaluate, the establishment of high professional standards for its practitioners becomes of urgent importance to the development of the activity. Professional standing involves the adoption of basic standards of education and of some form of certification testifying to the competence and trustworthiness of the practitioners. The attainment of these standards constitutes the strength of the professions of both law and medicine. Because of its intangible nature and relative newness, public relations has a much longer road to travel; probably the goal of state licensing is neither possible nor desirable.

The development of professionalism by the British Institute of Public Relations, exemplified by its pending requirement that admission to that body may be only by examination, is interesting for Americans to watch. The need and search for better standards for evaluation of public relations competence will continue in this country for many years.

Broader public understanding of public relations. The practice of public relations rests upon the right of freedom of speech which is given to all citizens—including journalists, authors, advertisers, and broadcasters—and the public's right to hear all sides of issues may not be denied. Yet many people are unaware that freedom of speech is for the benefit of the hearers as well as of the speakers. The public is uneasy about possible manipulation of its views and the hidden sources of its ideas, and the wild claims of some communications experts have fostered this fear. As a result, there is always the danger of popular support for censorship or intimidation.

The more the nature of public relations is understood and its practice is accepted as an inevitable corollary of the democratic freedoms of speech and listening, the better it will be for society all over the world. Very little has been done thus far to assist public understanding of the role of public relations practice within a democracy.

Clarification of public relations' role in government. The practice of public relations within a democratic government may be a means of informing citizens and of obtaining their cooperation in government. The noisy feuds between Congress and the executive, investigations, and heckling need to be replaced with a more sober consideration of the uses of government public relations efforts to obtain citizen cooperation in such matters as civil defense, conservation of natural resources, national security, and the development of our national economy. The position that the successful conduct of a huge democratic government does not need some form of public relations aid is increasingly absurd at a time when international closeness makes the cohesiveness of the American people and their speed of intelligent reaction more important than ever before. If this nation is to be governed by its people, then the people must be informed and encouraged, or they will not be able to govern.

The development of public relations in America's world role. Although the last and greatest task of public relations has been discussed in detail before, the explanation of America's position in the world cannot be over emphasized. It is the biggest communications problem that this nation has ever faced. A generation or more ago, the world's image of the United States was unimportant; today it seems vital. Skilled as Americans are at home in the arts of communication, they still do badly in their attempts to influence onlookers abroad.

Our national record must be better, not because of vanity or a simple desire to be liked, but because freedom and open discussion are the only basis upon which a workable, lasting world order can be hammered out. And there can be no mistake; such an order must be created soon. Men cannot remain on this small planet, much less explore the stars and the universe, unless they "forsake their foolish ways" that earth may be one.

There is no place in the world's future for studied deprivation of access to information or for planned deceit, which are truly crimes against humanity. Freedom of speech and hearing and the means of speech must be open to all. In such an emerging new world, public relations as the planned advocacy of causes before the bar of public opinion has a unique freedom and a unique responsibility. How well it fulfills its promise depends in large part upon the courage, energy, wisdom, and honor of the men and women who work in this exciting new field.

APPENDIX A. Some Additional Examples of Public Relations in Action

1. A Company Moves into a Community: Allis-Chalmers at York, Pennsylvania[1]

A national organization entering a community by the purchase of a local company which has had for years the confidence, loyalty, and pride of its own neighbors, buys certain benefits which can soon be dissipated by poor handling. Community goodwill toward a company can quickly change to dislike of its purchaser, especially if the newcomer is both powerful and distant.

This was the situation that might have been encountered by the Allis-Chalmers Manufacturing Company of Milwaukee, Wisconsin, upon its purchase in 1958 of the S. Morgan Smith Company of York, Pennsylvania.

S. Morgan Smith made hydraulic turbines and valves, of which Allis-Chalmers was also a large manufacturer. Expansion in the field seemed desirable to Allis-Chalmers, and it was best accomplished by the purchase of a going concern with excellent manufacturing facilities and competent people. The company which was purchased had had eighty-one years of experience in its field, was one of the leading businesses in York, and until 1952 had been family-owned. Its community relationships were excellent, and the Smith family was highly respected.

The problem confronting Allis-Chalmers management was to effect a smooth take-over of the Smith plant and to get the newly organized company's policies and practices accepted by its employees and the community.

The steps actually followed by Allis-Chalmers management were carefully planned.

1. After negotiations between the officers of both companies had been completed, but before stockholders had voted on the transaction, the president of Allis-Chalmers and several of the officers of the company traveled to York to attend a luncheon meeting with twenty-five leading citizens of the community and the officers of the S. Morgan Smith Company. The purpose of this meeting was to allow local people to become acquainted with Allis-Chalmers' top executives and to understand the company better.

2. On the day of the actual take-over, a letter from the president of Allis-Chalmers was sent to all S. Morgan Smith employees. The letter welcomed them to the Allis-Chalmers family, named the new general manager who would be in charge of all Allis-Chalmers Hydraulic Division activities, and looked forward to future benefits.

On the same day a national news release was issued explaining the basis upon which stock was exchanged in the purchase, and mentioning that the chief members of the former management of S. Morgan Smith Company would

[1] Kenneth Haagenson, director of public relations, Allis-Chalmers Company, Milwaukee, Wis.

remain in key posts with the concern in York. Also on that day an advertisement in the local York newspapers announced the purchase.

3. The following day a letter was sent to some four hundred community leaders in York from B. E. Smith, president of the S. Morgan Smith Company and now general manager of the newly created Hydraulic Division of Allis-Chalmers. Descriptive material was enclosed about Allis-Chalmers, including an annual report and a copy of the company magazine.

4. Two days later the local company newspaper reached the homes of York employees with complete news of the change.

5. After this initial-announcement program, the communication continued.

Shortly after the purchase, a booklet and a set of charts, "The Story of Power Generation," were made available to the York schools for use in science classes. Later in the year "The Story of Man and Food" was also made available for social studies. In the fall of 1959, York Works people were informed that their children were now eligible to compete in the "Scholarship Program for Sons and Daughters of Allis-Chalmers Employees."

6. Almost an exact year after the take-over, a regular Allis-Chalmers board of directors meeting, followed by a community luncheon, was held in York. Immediately after the meeting the directors toured the York plant. Several hundred people were invited to the luncheon. At each table of eight an Allis-Chalmers person acted as host. At each place there was a special edition of the local plant newspaper with news of the event, and a special program showed the seating of persons at each table.

Evaluation. This is not a spectacular program, but it succeeded in giving the employees and citizens of York assurance that they were joining a progressive, interested organization and that their special background and skills were appreciated. The attitude of city and school leaders continued good, press relations were excellent, and York Works employees continued to have pride in their company and confidence in the future. Without a well-planned, thoughtful public relations program, many of these valuable assets could well have been lost in the natural upheaval of the purchase.

2. A Less Happy Circumstance—Two Companies Move Out of Town: International Harvester Leaves Rock Falls, Illinois[2]

A combination of circumstances forced International Harvester Company to close its fifty-six-year-old Rock Falls, Illinois, plant in 1961. The plant made smaller items of farm machinery. The number of United States farms was diminishing, while the surviving farms were getting larger. Three-fifths of the buildings at the Rock Falls plant were from fifty to eighty-six years old, and 27 per cent were more than forty-five years old. Most of them were multistory buildings, with low floor loads and high materials-handling costs. Production policy for some years had been to concentrate in more efficient plants. In 1939 plans to close the plant had been announced, but World War II needs had given it a new lease on life until 1961.

[2] John W. Vance, director of public relations, International Harvester Company, Chicago, Ill.

The problem was complicated by the fact that as other I-H plants had more than their full quota of employees, the chance of transfers was small.

What was done?

1. A complete news release covering all the facts about the obsolescence of the plant and other information was sent out on November 22, 1960, the day after the I-H board of directors decided to close. A letter went to all employees of the plant on the same date, and also a letter to other employees of the farm-implement division who would know of the change and would wonder how it affected them.

2. A letter was sent to Rock Falls employees four weeks later, detailing work schedules for several months ahead during the closing out of production. Subsequent letters covered pensions, retirement, severance pay, insurance, and other matters of employee concern.

3. An advertisement in the *Wall Street Journal* promoted the sale of the plant buildings. This was reprinted as a page ad in the local daily newspaper nearest to Rock Falls.

3. Atlas Powder Company Closes Its White Haven, Pennsylvania, Plant[3]

The closing of an Atlas Powder Company's plant entailed another series of hard problems. In 1932 Atlas had acquired a dynamite plant at White Haven, Pennsylvania, only 30 miles from another company plant at Reynolds. About 40 per cent of the output of the two plants was used in anthracite coal mining, a percentage that declined to only 10 per cent within the past decade because of the drop in total coal production. At the same time, ammonium nitrate, which was increasingly coming into use as an explosive, was a product which the White Haven plant was not equipped to make, although the Reynolds plant was.

By 1958 the existence of two plants only 30 miles apart had become uneconomical, and it was decided to concentrate all production at Reynolds. About 184 White Haven employees were affected, 70 of whom had been laid off for some time because of lack of work. Closure was announced September 5, to be completed by December 1.

The publics involved included:

Employees (particularly at White Haven and Reynolds but also throughout the company)
Unions at White Haven and Reynolds
Local, state, and national government representatives
Community leaders in White Haven
Explosives customers, including the trade press
Shareowners
Local, state, and general public press
Security analysts
Financial and business publications
Suppliers in the White Haven area

[3] Sidney K. Steele, director, Public Relations Department, Atlas Powder Company, Wilmington, Del.

To coordinate contact with these groups, the Atlas public relations staff prepared a management guide containing reasons for the shutdown; questions and answers; plans for employee aid; a timetable for the shutdown; a letter to explosives-plant managers; telegrams to congressmen and members of the state legislature from the White Haven–Reynolds area; a letter to White Haven community leaders; a more detailed letter from the company president to legislators; a complete press release for local newspapers; briefer stories for the nearby metropolitan newspapers; stories for the wire services, explosives-trade press, chemicals and business press (copies with a covering letter were sent to Atlas major management); a letter to White Haven employees, to be given out after an employee meeting; and a bulletin for general office employees at company headquarters.

Discussion. As in the International Harvester case, there was no way in which the misfortune could be turned into a blessing. The important thing was to make known the facts and the reasons for the closings and to do as much as possible to cushion the blow. Good will could not be gained, but extremes of ill will could at least be avoided by early, complete information, and magnified rumors reflecting upon the whole company in widely distant areas could be prevented. Full disclosure is better than a policy of secrecy or minimization.

4. A Company Centralizes Its Purchasing System[4]

Falstaff Brewing Corporation, St. Louis, Missouri, in early 1961 decided to centralize its purchasing system. The company operated several plants throughout the United States, and until that time had made purchases of supplies for each plant locally. Each plant had its own purchasing agent.

Considering both the economical use of manpower and the possibility of buying in larger volume, this system was less efficient than centralized purchasing, but it was obvious that any change might cause ill feeling on the part of local suppliers. It was *not* proposed to cease dealing with local suppliers. If the company was buying light bulbs, for example, they could be purchased in quantity on one order from central headquarters, but the number destined for each plant could still be handled by the local dealer for the firm from which they were purchased.

The following steps were taken by the St. Louis headquarters public relations staff of Falstaff Brewing Corporation to meet this problem:

1. An internal announcement of the pending purchasing-department reorganization, describing the need for the change, was sent to employees. This included a "welcome aboard" to the plant purchasing agents who were being transferred to St. Louis and a new departmental organization chart.

2. A letter was sent to suppliers apprising them of the change, saying that the intention was to buy from local sources whenever possible and giving the St. Louis address to which future correspondence should be addressed.

3. At the same time, local plant managers sent a similar letter to their suppliers.

[4] Robert N. Hutchingson, director of public relations, Falstaff Brewing Corporation, St. Louis, Mo.

4. A supply of informational bulletins was kept on hand at each plant reception desk to give to callers who were not aware of the new purchasing policy.

5. Plans were made to have the director of purchases or his representatives visit local plant suppliers from time to time to keep up contacts.

6. It was suggested that a small printed booklet be prepared as a permanent guide to purchasing-department policies and practices.

5. Press Plans for One of the Biggest News Stories in Decades[5]

The launching of the United States Navy's first atomic-powered submarine, the *Nautilus,* by the Electric Boat Division of General Dynamics Corporation at Groton, Connecticut, in 1954, was easily one of the biggest news stories, with the exception of national political conventions, since the end of World War II.

More than 300 members of the working press attended. The launching was front-page news throughout the nation, and more than 40,000 words were moved by Western Union from the General Dynamics press room, with follow-up stories and pictures continuing for several days. Three major radio and three major TV networks covered the story along with five newsreel services. The three national photo services wired 54 pictures; representatives of all major news and photo magazines and many trade magazines were present at the launching; and "Radio Free Europe," "Voice of America," and USIA films sent coverage to all the world.

Since news events of this magnitude seldom happen, the study of how the General Dynamics public relations staff handled all details of this "biggest" is instructive.

Ten major phases of the launching coverage suggested themselves for consideration.

1. Advance publicity
2. Press invitations
3. Briefing and security clearance
4. Assistance for the working press
5. Working-press facilities
6. Photo coverage
7. Freedom of movement
8. Potential trouble spots
9. Direct relationship with the public
10. Follow-up

Advance publicity. Little could be said about the operational aspects of the *Nautilus* since they were primarily within the sphere of Navy responsibility. It was felt that competitive press associations would like individual feature stories, and they were given the opportunity to publish them. Out of fourteen advance stories beginning about a month ahead of the launching, seven were "exclusives." Syndicates and feature-article writers were given personal attention.

[5] Patrick J. Sullivan, public relations director, General Dynamics Corporation, New York City.

Press invitations. A detailed list was prepared of all media likely to have any interest in sending staff to cover the event, and editors received a memorandum-invitation including background facts and maps of approaches to reach the site. In addition, invitations were sent to several hundred friends and contacts in all media who might wish to attend even if they did not cover the event.

Briefing and security clearance. In accordance with United States Navy contract requirements, every member of the press had to supply information certifying to his own trustworthiness. Data regarding the launching and the ship had to be given in a special briefing session. Since newsmen normally arrive at the last minute, it was evident that this handling of security and briefing for more than 300 men on the morning of the event would be impossible. Several approaches were taken to the problem.

1. More than a week in advance, TV and press-association photographers were invited to a conference in General Dynamics' New York office, where they were acquainted with the problem and a drawing was held for photo locations. All agreed that they would come to Groton the day preceding the launching, and security checks and briefings were set for that time.

2. All radio outlets which had indicated that they planned to attend were similarly called on the telephone; and they, too, promised to attend the day before the launching.

3. On the evening preceding the launching, a press center was established at the Mohican Hotel, where briefings and security clearances were handled.

4. A press car was attached to the "Nautilus Special" train leaving New York City on the morning of the launching. Public relations staffers handled problems and security clearance en route. By these means more than 200 press members were checked in on the day preceding the event. The fulfillment of the other demands proceeded smoothly.

Assistance for the working press. With such large anticipated coverage, it was realized that Electric Boat's public relations staff of four, with the addition of two men from the New York office, would be inadequate. Twenty-four competent young men were therefore enlisted from various departments in the Groton plant as press aides, messengers, escorts, doorkeepers, or general assistants. All were briefed and given identification badges, press packets, and other material.

Working-press facilities. A large press room, installed in the building nearest the launching area, included three darkrooms, Western Union transmitters, phone booths, photo transmitters, thirty-eight typewriters, desk supplies, and refreshments—coffee, soft drinks, and doughnuts. A room manager, two girls, and four press aides assisted. Two guards manned the door.

A press reception center was set up near one of the plant gates to sign in working-press people for security clearance. Parking space was located directly across the street, and a pickup truck was at hand to move heavy TV equipment.

Elevated platforms were built at the launching site for the use of photographers and broadcasters. Seating space for 200 reporters was provided on bleachers.

A hot buffet luncheon was served to press personnel; complete press kits were distributed; the *Nautilus* skipper and some of the officers and enlisted men were available for interviews, as were also President Eisenhower's press secretary and Mrs. Eisenhower's personal secretary.

Photo coverage. Picture interest, it was realized, would center in the bottle breaking and in the ship going down the ways.

To cover the bottle breaking, a five-level photo platform was erected along the bow of the *Nautilus*. The words "General Dynamics Corporation" appeared on the christening platform in a direct line with the camera angles; the chairman of the GD board, who participated in the event, would of necessity be identified. Four platforms were erected to make it possible for photographers to shoot the ship going down the ways. A sign with the name of the company was placed so that it would appear in these photos also. As additional coverage, General Dynamics photographers made these and many other pictures, processed them, and made them available to all newsmen. One GD photographer, placed high in an overhead crane, made 100-odd prints available to all concerned.

Freedom of movement. Because of the large crowds, press facilities were clearly marked, special walkways constructed, aides posted with directions, and maps provided. Each press representative had a large and distinctive badge.

Buses and private cars were available to furnish transportation outside the plant and to meet the special train from New York City. To speed reporters on their way after the ceremony, a special ferryboat went from the shipyard across the Thames River to a pier near the railroad station, its trips connecting with scheduled trains to New York and Boston.

Potential trouble spots. All attention was centered upon the main event; speech texts were checked to see that they agreed; and a dry-run rehearsal of press aides and others was held two days in advance. To avoid confusion among radio, TV, and sound-newsreel people, arrangements were made to supply a special mixer equipped with thirty outlets.

To protect security, the Office of the Secretary of Defense assigned a qualified officer to the press room, and representatives of the Navy Office of Information were also present.

Direct relationship with the public. Besides press people, some 1,500 guests were fed at various luncheons, transported, seated, and cared for. A common art theme was used in all invitations, programs, and other printed matter. This "launching symbol" consisted of a sketch of the sea creature nautilus (for which the *Nautilus* was named) superimposed over a sketch of the submarine. The souvenir program was well printed in a style appropriate to the important event.

Follow-up. The day following the launching, a round-up news release and photos were sent to more than 100 trade magazines, news syndicates, and others who were not present. Photos went to all state newspapers. Press representatives were sent a letter asking for any suggestions on handling similar events in the future, and all who helped received letters of thanks.

APPENDIX B. Fourteen Do-it-yourself
Public Relations Problems

The following cases cited were all actual occurrences, though occasionally names have been changed. Consider that you are the public relations man for the organization concerned and decide what you would do to solve each of the problems posed.

Problem Case 1. The Burned-out Plant

What would you do if a sudden fire destroyed 80 per cent of your plant plus all sales records? That was the problem faced by A-to-Z Electric Batteries, Inc., of Bridgeville, New Jersey, on Sunday morning, December 1, 1955.

Not only did the main plant burn completely in the overnight fire, but in addition, the laboratory, office, and all sales records, orders, and correspondence were destroyed. A-to-Z, Inc., had no way of knowing what orders were on its books or what had been shipped.

The management decided to stay in business. Besides the problems of replacing equipment and leasing new quarters, there were two main public relations problems:

1. Preventing cancellation of orders by assuring customers that their orders would be filled promptly, and thus discouraging them from turning to other sources of supply

2. Informing employees that they would be needed back at work as soon as possible, thus maintaining a valuable skilled labor force without which work could not have been resumed

The problem was intensified by the fact that the fire had been spectacular, had been witnessed by thousands, and had received superb coverage in words and pictures on all the news media of the entire metropolitan area. Rumors that A-to-Z, Inc., would never resume business were perhaps started by competitors. Management estimated that it would take about three days to salvage some batteries which had escaped the blaze and which could be utilized to fill the most immediate orders, and several months of slower-than-normal production before the plant could be restored fully.

Questions

What would you do to solve the immediate public relations problems?
What about the longer-range problems?
Is there any way in which this disaster can be turned into an asset?

Problem Case 2. The Struck Steamship Line

The summer of 1960 was particularly difficult for Trans-Oceanic Steamship Company. During this peak tourist period, when almost every ship on the North Atlantic run was booked to capacity, a series of wildcat seamen's strikes caused the cancellation of about every other trip from British ports. Sailings were completely uncertain. In many cases passengers were aboard when the men walked off; in others so few crew members reported for duty that the ship could not sail.

Early in the summer season, when westbound space was still easy to get, the company managed to take care of stranded passengers by shifting them to later sailings and chartering planes for mass airlifts, allowing passengers to board on the ship until they were cared for. News of these efforts was well covered in the British and American press.

By late August, however, when the S.S. *Umbria* was scheduled to sail from a western British port, the company found it very difficult to charter planes (which by then all had a full complement of passengers) or to shift to other steamships; in addition great financial losses had been suffered. On the day before sailing, the 1,000 passengers planning to depart on the S.S. *Umbria* were informed that the ship would not sail and that their money would be refunded. No other aid was offered, and when an army of passengers descended upon the company offices, the clerks at the front desk had nothing more to tell them.

To many passengers the news was shocking. They had exhausted their funds at the end of their summer travels in the expectation that the ship was awaiting them. They had assumed that the company would be able to make alternate plans as it had been doing all summer. They were stranded in a strange land, not knowing how they were to get back home to their jobs and families or even what to do next, and their bad feeling was intense. Many resolved to fly in the future, to sail on ships of other nationalities, or never to return to Great Britain again.

The company had had several months to foresee this situation.

Question

What should have been done? Keep in mind that money is limited, but that a large supply of trained help is available in the company headquarters.

Problem Case 3. The Summer the Waterworks Broke Down

The Riverton Suburban Water Company served scores of thousands of people in a rapidly growing area surrounding a large city which had its own municipal water plant. There was no shortage of water, since the company's main pumping plant was on one of the largest rivers in the United States; but in the drought year of 1954 its service broke down badly.

There were several reasons. New houses were being built at a dizzy pace in the area served. Automatic washers, air coolers, swimming pools, and many other household uses boosted water consumption inordinately, and the drought forced much lawn and garden watering. A conservative management had been unwilling to face the costs involved in expansion and had tried to make inadequate mains, booster stations, and reservoirs do more than they could.

The results were disastrous. From 4 P.M. until 9 P.M. daily, all during the late summer, many homes in higher sections of the area had no water at all; others suffered from low pressure. Fire chiefs issued warnings of dire consequences. The company was forced to plead for cooperation, asking citizens not to wash cars or water parched lawns. When water pressure was increased, old mains broke and caused miniature floods. The catastrophe was particularly maddening to customers, since water rates had always been higher than in the neighboring big city (which had an actual surplus of water all through the drought) and since the river, the source of Riverton Suburban Water Company's supply, was at a normal summer level. An outcry arose that the company should be taken over and put into public hands.

The management of the company was changed. With fall rains in September the situation eased, and the management said to its newly hired public relations counseling firm, "Now what should we do?"

Question

What are the immediate steps to be taken?

Much physical work must be done on the company facilities before next summer. By then good service should be restored, but improved supply for every householder is not absolutely certain, since home building is very rapid. How do you face this problem?

Be sure to think of *all* the publics involved.

Problem Case 4. Closing Down a Plant

Shutting down a plant which employs several hundred people and has been an important source of payroll income for a medium-sized city for many years is never easy—especially when employment levels in the area are not generally good; when, because of reduction of forces through seniority, most of the plant employees are more than forty-five years old and have been long-time residents of the city; and when the causes of the uneconomical nature of the plant are complex and not easily apparent.

In one particular case, examination of the termination programs of other companies was of little help, and only a limited amount of money could be spent on the project. In fact, the main asset that the company public relations director had was time; he learned about the move in January and the closing date was not until August. He decided to use all the energy and ingenuity he could muster to meet the following objectives:

1. To meet the real human needs of people whose lives would be disrupted
2. To develop a program that would put as small a burden as possible upon the community and its taxpayers
3. To convince employees and the community that the company was interested and doing its best to help
4. To develop a communications program which would explain the reasons for the closing and enable the company to leave the city without serious damage to the company reputation or to that of the American business system

Question

How would you prepare for the termination of work? In this instance you have rather wide latitude in considering such items as termination pay, insurance continuance, intercompany job movements, and moving allowances.

Problem Case 5. Moving a Railroad Headquarters

The offices of the Great Southwestern Railroad for many years had been located in a large city in the Midwest in rented quarters in a large downtown office building. At the same time the company had maintained a smaller regional office in a much smaller Texas city.

The railroad's business was highly competitive, since the same area was served by several other lines as well as by truck and air competition; the management therefore decided that it would be more efficient to centralize headquarters in the smaller Texas city, where a much smaller passenger and freight staff could do all that was needed, and to avoid the rental of large metropolitan offices. In fact, a new building, much roomier and better planned, could be built in the smaller city at a considerable saving.

The problems were:

1. Moving the 150 central-office employees, most of whom had lived all their lives in the Midwestern big city, owned their homes, and could hardly imagine living in a "hick town"

2. Keeping the good will of other people in the big city, which was the main eastern terminus of the railroad and a major source of freight and passengers

Question

As the line's public relations director, with about six months to act, what would you do?

Problem Case 6. Low-status Public Servants

Westcity, U.S.A., a huge metropolis, has one of the nation's largest city-government public welfare assistance agencies. Its annual expenditures of more than 10 million dollars are exceeded by those of only a few *states*. But a few years ago its 1,000 college-trained social workers were paid low salaries, only a little better than area high school students could get on their first jobs; public regard for their work was low and sometimes even hostile. As a result there was a high turnover of personnel and very poor morale.

Several hundred of these social workers formed an association to seek better public understanding, support, and higher pay. Officers were elected and research was completed to show the need of higher pay and to point out that less-skilled city employees were going ahead more rapidly. A statement of facts made to the city supervisors resulted in a small increase.

At the same time the supervisors said privately that they had no more money and that further raises could come only from higher taxes made possible through better public support.

Facing the problems squarely, the members of the association decided they had neither the time nor the public relations skill to organize the effort themselves, and therefore, after an assessment, they hired a public relations counsel to plan a program and start them to work.

They had almost no money to work with and would have to depend on possible donations.

The social workers could count on the good will of the news media after they explained what was going on. Public feelings were mixed. More liberal elements and the recipients of aid were favorable; conservatives and the well-to-do were in opposition, often protesting on moral grounds rather than on reasonable considerations.

Questions

What steps would the public relations counselor suggest?
What appeals would be made to the public, and in what manner?

Problem Case 7. A School–Newspaper Feud

Centerville, a town of 2,000, is located on a Federal highway in the southern part of a large northern state. Its high school has some 600 students and 40 teachers and other staff members.

In the United States, school systems and the local press usually get along well enough. In Centerville they didn't. The local weekly paper leveled a constant barrage of criticism against the school administration, the curriculum, the quality of the teaching, and the cost of operations. School people felt that the paper's editor had personal motives in making the attack and was profiting from increased sale of papers because of the controversy. Individually the teachers often expressed the view that the school and the paper should get together to resolve the differences, but apparently no serious venture had been made in this direction, the school administration simply assuming that nothing much could be done.

The surrender, though unwise, was not surprising in view of the biased attitude of the newspaper, which charged that teachers were interested only in their pay, that the university education of teachers had been a waste, that only inferior persons would go into teaching and that others would work where they could make more money, that superior children were not challenged enough by the school's program, that the board of education was concealing information by holding closed meetings, that teacher tenure should be abolished, and that most school students could neither read, write, spell, nor speak upon graduation from high school.

No one could feel that the program of the high school or the quality of all its teachers was perfect, but the violence of the attacks was unwarranted; it intensified confusion and inability to get good staff or raise more money, and thus made the situation even worse.

Question

What should the school administration do under these circumstances? Plan a program of action and communication.

Problem Case 8. Making a New Building Memorable

Cases thus far in this series have dealt largely with unhappy situations; those to follow generally center upon opportunities to be seized.

Janesville, Wisconsin, a town of 35,000 about 70 miles from Chicago, is the home of the internationally famous Parker Pen Company. A number of years ago Parker built a new factory and office headquarters there at a cost of several million dollars. While the white brick building was still in the blueprint stages, public relations plans were under way to get everyone in the town to understand and appreciate the building and to spread its fame abroad as far as possible.

Beyond the usual steps of dedication, some highly interesting theme was needed to lift it out of the ordinary.

Questions

What would you suggest? How would you translate the theme into action?

Problem Case 9. The Defunct Department Store

In New York City at one time a large department store, a branch of another large store in another eastern city, fell behind the times because of poor location and changing trade patterns; it ran downhill and eventually was closed.

When it died, a famous firm of public auctioneers was called in to sell its stock in liquidation at the best prices possible. When the auction staff began to tramp through the acres of vacant corridors, they were amazed. The estimated book value of the goods was several million, but in addition they turned up such items as an old Mack truck, forty-five tapestries of great age, ancient royal banners, clothing dummies of the early 1900s, and a family of stuffed polar bears donated by an Arctic explorer in 1928.

The auctioneer quickly decided that public interest would determine the success of this venture; he hired the services of a public relations firm to create interest in the short time before the auctions were scheduled.

Question

As the head of that public relations counseling firm, what would you do?

Problem Case 10. The Fearful Atom

Several years ago a number of private electric power companies in the United States pooled their funds to build an atomic energy plant to produce electricity commercially. Their objectives were to study costs of production and to show that private enterprise was able and ready to enter this new field, which otherwise might be handled eventually by the government by default. If in the future most of the electricity in this country was to be produced by atomic power, it was important that they should enter the field, even at considerable cost.

They decided to locate the plant in a rural area about 50 miles away from a large Midwestern city; the electric company in that city and area was to construct it and operate it. Immediately several problems arose:

1. Atoms are associated with bomb explosions. Would the people who lived near the plant be afraid of it?
2. Would people in the large city also become worried?
3. What should the press be told?
4. What about employees and stockholders?
5. Are there political implications?

The purchase of land for the plant was announced, and at once rumblings began, sparked in some cases by economic and political groups which saw a chance to capitalize upon popular fears.

Question

As public relations director of the local power company building and planning to operate the plant, what would you do?

Problem Case 11. Persuading Local People to Invest

The United Electric Company generates and sells power in a large Midwestern state. Some years ago it was part of a large national holding company which was dissolved and split up into smaller state organizations, with the original stockholders each getting shares of the successor organizations. Now it wishes to increase the number of its stockholders in the state area which it serves. There are several reasons:

1. To organize influential local groups who have a financial stake in the company and who therefore will be sympathetic to its problems
2. To raise funds locally from people who can best see the company's needs and opportunities
3. To establish a better two-way channel of communication between the company and its public by being home-owned as well as home-operated

The immediate goal of the company is to get 50 per cent of its stock held within the state in which it operates.

Question

How would you suggest organizing this campaign?

Problem Case 12. Publicizing a New Cooking-utensil Material

The main business of the Thor Company of Ohio is making high-quality ceramic insulators for electric equipment, industrial chinaware, and plastics. This work led it into a government contract to make high-heat-resistant ceramic parts for missiles, and this project in turn resulted in the discovery of a white ceramic-like material of great strength and almost complete resistance to either great heat or sudden changes of temperatures.

Someone in the company saw that this new product would make a cooking-utensil material of superior quality. However, there were several drawbacks:

1. The company was not widely known in the consumer field, since it sold most of its products to industry.
2. The material was more expensive than the aluminum, steel, or glass cooking vessels it might replace.
3. The material was in short supply. The company could introduce enough gradually to supply one portion of the nation at a time, but did not dare to launch a general sales effort throughout the nation, because it would be impossible to satisfy a rapidly developing demand.
4. Management did not feel like appropriating very much money to sell what was essentially a by-product. If it could be moved on a limited appropri-

ation of a few thousand dollars per each region of the country, well and good. If not, the gamble was regarded as not worthwhile.

You are in charge of a three-man public relations staff assigned to the introduction and publicizing of this new product under these conditions.

Question

What are you going to do? Draw up a plan to present to your management.

Problem Case 13. The Floor-covering Battle

Manufacturers often find themselves not only in competition with other people making the same line of product, but even more with other possible uses of the consumer's dollar. One such group is the carpet manufacturers of America. Several years ago they found that their sales were not keeping pace with the volume of demand expected from new homes being built and from necessary replacements. Evidently consumers were buying increasing amounts of linoleum, plastics, or asphalt tile (all well supported by advertising), or were leaving wooden floors bare except for scattered throw rugs.

Here was obviously a situation in which group effort made sense. In the highly competitive carpet-manufacturing field (both at home and abroad), no single manufacturer could spend large amounts of his own advertising budget to sell carpeting in general; yet this was what needed to be done.

An association of carpet manufacturers was formed and a public relations counseling firm hired to popularize the use of carpeting in American homes. A modest amount of money was available for advertising purposes and the selection of an advertising theme. The choice of media and all other devices for reaching the public was left to the decision of the public relations firm (although the actual preparation and placing of the ads was handled through an advertising agency).

Problem

Set up a one-year plan to present to the board of directors of the association with suggestions for further steps if the year's program is successful.

Problem Case 14. Selling Ownership of a Stake in American Business

Many thoughtful persons have felt that support of the American free enterprise system would be strengthened if more people had a share in the ownership and profits of the system instead of being merely wage earners. Several years ago the New York Stock Exchange surveyed stockownership among American people and found that only 6½ million persons owned shares as compared with an expected 20 million; but the survey also showed that 19 million Americans were interested in stock purchases and would like to know more.

Not only were small investors politically and economically important; they were also needed to supply the large sums of money which must be available to finance the vast expansion of United States firms over the next decade. If private money could not be found in any field, government money obtained through taxes was likely to be the answer.

For all these reasons the New York Stock Exchange began a vigorous program to inform the American public about investing in stocks. Several dangers were recognized: Stocks do not always increase in value or pay good dividends; some become worthless; they are sometimes hard to dispose of except at a loss; the average small investor needs a nest egg of cash in safe form before he should invest in stocks.

A program keyed to "Own Your Share of American Business" was set up.

Problem

Outline what you would do in putting this program to work. Remember that there are many aspects and many publics to be considered. An adequate amount of money can be counted on, and the facilities of stockbrokers are available in all major cities.

Index